PostgreSQL

PostgreSQL 9.0
Official Documentation

Volume V

Internals and Appendixes

❖

Fultus™ Books

PostgreSQL

PostgreSQL 9.0 Official Documentation

Volume V

Internals and Appendixes

ISBN-10: 1-59682-250-3
ISBN-13: 978-1-59682-250-4

Cover design and book layout by Fultus Corporation

Published by Fultus Corporation

Publisher Web: *www.fultus.com*
Linbrary - Linux Library: *www.linbrary.com*
Online Bookstore: *store.fultus.com*
email: *production@fultus.com*

Table of Contents

List of Tables

License

Abstract

Welcome to the *PostgreSQL 9.0 Official Documentation*! After many years of development, PostgreSQL has become feature-complete in many areas. This release shows a targeted approach to adding features (e.g., authentication, monitoring, space reuse), and adds capabilities defined in the later SQL standards.

Part VII. Internals

This part contains assorted information that might be of use to PostgreSQL developers.

Chapter 44. Overview of PostgreSQL Internals

Author: This chapter originated as part of *Enhancement of the ANSI SQL Implementation of PostgreSQL* (see page 466), Stefan Simkovics' Master's Thesis prepared at Vienna University of Technology under the direction of O.Univ.Prof.Dr. Georg Gottlob and Univ.Ass. Mag. Katrin Seyr.

This chapter gives an overview of the internal structure of the backend of PostgreSQL. After having read the following sections you should have an idea of how a query is processed. This chapter does not aim to provide a detailed description of the internal operation of PostgreSQL, as such a document would be very extensive. Rather, this chapter is intended to help the reader understand the general sequence of operations that occur within the backend from the point at which a query is received, to the point at which the results are returned to the client.

44.1. The Path of a Query

Here we give a short overview of the stages a query has to pass in order to obtain a result.

1. A connection from an application program to the PostgreSQL server has to be established. The application program transmits a query to the server and waits to receive the results sent back by the server.
2. The *parser stage* checks the query transmitted by the application program for correct syntax and creates a *query tree*.
3. The *rewrite system* takes the query tree created by the parser stage and looks for any *rules* (stored in the *system catalogs*) to apply to the query tree. It performs the transformations given in the *rule bodies*.

   One application of the rewrite system is in the realization of *views*. Whenever a query against a view (i.e., a *virtual table*) is made, the rewrite system rewrites the user's query to a query that accesses the *base tables* given in the *view definition* instead.
4. The *planner/optimizer* takes the (rewritten) query tree and creates a *query plan* that will be the input to the *executor*.

It does so by first creating all possible *paths* leading to the same result. For example if there is an index on a relation to be scanned, there are two paths for the scan. One possibility is a simple sequential scan and the other possibility is to use the index. Next the cost for the execution of each path is estimated and the cheapest path is chosen. The cheapest path is expanded into a complete plan that the executor can use.

5. The executor recursively steps through the *plan tree* and retrieves rows in the way represented by the plan. The executor makes use of the *storage system* while scanning relations, performs *sorts* and *joins*, evaluates *qualifications* and finally hands back the rows derived.

In the following sections we will cover each of the above listed items in more detail to give a better understanding of PostgreSQL's internal control and data structures.

44.2. How Connections are Established

PostgreSQL is implemented using a simple "process per user" client/server model. In this model there is one *client process* connected to exactly one *server process*. As we do not know ahead of time how many connections will be made, we have to use a *master process* that spawns a new server process every time a connection is requested. This master process is called `postgres` and listens at a specified TCP/IP port for incoming connections. Whenever a request for a connection is detected the `postgres` process spawns a new server process. The server tasks communicate with each other using *semaphores* and *shared memory* to ensure data integrity throughout concurrent data access.

The client process can be any program that understands the PostgreSQL protocol described in *Chapter 46* (page 79). Many clients are based on the C-language library libpq, but several independent implementations of the protocol exist, such as the Java JDBC driver.

Once a connection is established the client process can send a query to the *backend* (server). The query is transmitted using plain text, i.e., there is no parsing done in the *frontend* (client). The server parses the query, creates an *execution plan*, executes the plan and returns the retrieved rows to the client by transmitting them over the established connection.

44.3. The Parser Stage

The *parser stage* consists of two parts:

- The *parser* defined in `gram.y` and `scan.l` is built using the Unix tools bison and flex.
- The *transformation process* does modifications and augmentations to the data structures returned by the parser.

44.3.1. Parser

The parser has to check the query string (which arrives as plain ASCII text) for valid syntax. If the syntax is correct a *parse tree* is built up and handed back; otherwise an error is returned. The parser and lexer are implemented using the well-known Unix tools bison and flex.

The *lexer* is defined in the file `scan.l` and is responsible for recognizing *identifiers*, the *SQL key words* etc. For every key word or identifier that is found, a *token* is generated and handed to the parser.

The parser is defined in the file `gram.y` and consists of a set of *grammar rules* and *actions* that are executed whenever a rule is fired. The code of the actions (which is actually C code) is used to build up the parse tree.

The file `scan.l` is transformed to the C source file `scan.c` using the program flex and `gram.y` is transformed to `gram.c` using bison. After these transformations have taken place a normal C compiler can be used to create the parser. Never make any changes to the generated C files as they will be overwritten the next time flex or bison is called.

Note

The mentioned transformations and compilations are normally done automatically using the *makefiles* shipped with the PostgreSQL source distribution.

A detailed description of bison or the grammar rules given in `gram.y` would be beyond the scope of this paper. There are many books and documents dealing with flex and bison. You should be familiar with bison before you start to study the grammar given in `gram.y` otherwise you won't understand what happens there.

44.3.2. Transformation Process

The parser stage creates a parse tree using only fixed rules about the syntactic structure of SQL. It does not make any lookups in the system catalogs, so there is no possibility to understand the detailed semantics of the requested operations. After the parser completes, the *transformation process* takes the tree handed back by the parser as input and does the semantic interpretation needed to understand which tables, functions, and operators are referenced by the query. The data structure that is built to represent this information is called the *query tree*.

The reason for separating raw parsing from semantic analysis is that system catalog lookups can only be done within a transaction, and we do not wish to start a transaction immediately upon receiving a query string. The raw parsing stage is sufficient to identify the transaction control commands (`BEGIN`, `ROLLBACK`, etc), and these can then be correctly executed without any further analysis. Once we know that we are dealing with an actual query (such as `SELECT` or `UPDATE`), it is okay to start a transaction if we're not already in one. Only then can the transformation process be invoked.

The query tree created by the transformation process is structurally similar to the raw parse tree in most places, but it has many differences in detail. For example, a `FuncCall` node in the parse tree represents something that looks syntactically like a function call. This might be transformed to either a `FuncExpr` or `Aggref` node depending on whether the referenced name turns out to be an ordinary function or an aggregate function. Also, information about the actual data types of columns and expression results is added to the query tree.

44.4. The PostgreSQL Rule System

PostgreSQL supports a powerful *rule system* for the specification of *views* and ambiguous *view updates*. Originally the PostgreSQL rule system consisted of two implementations:

- The first one worked using *row level* processing and was implemented deep in the *executor*. The rule system was called whenever an individual row had been accessed. This implementation was removed in 1995 when the last official release of the Berkeley Postgres project was transformed into Postgres95.
- The second implementation of the rule system is a technique called *query rewriting*. The *rewrite system* is a module that exists between the *parser stage* and the *planner/optimizer*. This technique is still implemented.

The query rewriter is discussed in some detail in *Chapter 37* (Vol.III), so there is no need to cover it here. We will only point out that both the input and the output of the rewriter are query trees, that is, there is no change in the representation or level of semantic detail in the trees. Rewriting can be thought of as a form of macro expansion.

44.5. Planner/Optimizer

The task of the *planner/optimizer* is to create an optimal execution plan. A given SQL query (and hence, a query tree) can be actually executed in a wide variety of different ways, each of which will produce the same set of results. If it is computationally feasible, the query optimizer will examine each of these possible execution plans, ultimately selecting the execution plan that is expected to run the fastest.

Note

In some situations, examining each possible way in which a query can be executed would take an excessive amount of time and memory space. In particular, this occurs when executing queries involving large numbers of join operations. In order to determine a reasonable (not necessarily optimal) query plan in a reasonable amount of time, PostgreSQL uses a Genetic Query Optimizer (see *Chapter 50* - page 137) when the number of joins exceeds a threshold (see `geqo_threshold` - Vol.II).

The planner's search procedure actually works with data structures called *paths*, which are simply cut-down representations of plans containing only as much information as the planner needs to make its decisions. After the cheapest path is determined, a full-fledged *plan tree* is built to pass to the executor. This represents the desired execution plan in sufficient detail for the executor to run it. In the rest of this section we'll ignore the distinction between paths and plans.

44.5.1. Generating Possible Plans

The planner/optimizer starts by generating plans for scanning each individual relation (table) used in the query. The possible plans are determined by the available indexes on each relation. There is always the possibility of performing a sequential scan on a relation, so a sequential scan plan is always created. Assume an index is defined on a relation (for example a B-tree index) and a query contains the restriction `relation.attribute OPR constant`. If `relation.attribute` happens to match the key of the B-tree index and `OPR` is one of the operators listed in the index's *operator class* , another plan is created using the B-tree index to scan the relation. If there are further indexes present and the restrictions in the query happen to match a key of an index, further plans will be considered. Index scan plans are also generated for indexes that have a sort ordering that can match the query's `ORDER BY` clause (if any), or a sort ordering that might be useful for merge joining (see below).

If the query requires joining two or more relations, plans for joining relations are considered after all feasible plans have been found for scanning single relations. The three available join strategies are:

- *nested loop join*: The right relation is scanned once for every row found in the left relation. This strategy is easy to implement but can be very time consuming. (However, if the right relation can be scanned with an index scan, this can be a good strategy. It is possible to use values from the current row of the left relation as keys for the index scan of the right.)
- *merge join*: Each relation is sorted on the join attributes before the join starts. Then the two relations are scanned in parallel, and matching rows are combined to form join rows. This kind of join is more attractive because each relation has to be scanned only once. The required sorting might be achieved either by an explicit sort step, or by scanning the relation in the proper order using an index on the join key.
- *hash join*: the right relation is first scanned and loaded into a hash table, using its join attributes as hash keys. Next the left relation is scanned and the appropriate values of every row found are used as hash keys to locate the matching rows in the table.

When the query involves more than two relations, the final result must be built up by a tree of join steps, each with two inputs. The planner examines different possible join sequences to find the cheapest one.

If the query uses fewer than `geqo_threshold` (Vol.II) relations, a near-exhaustive search is conducted to find the best join sequence. The planner preferentially considers joins between any two relations for which there exist a corresponding join clause in the `WHERE` qualification (i.e., for which a restriction like `where rel1.attr1=rel2.attr2` exists). Join pairs with no join clause are considered only when there is no other choice, that is, a particular relation has no available join clauses to any other relation. All possible plans are generated for every join pair considered by the planner, and the one that is (estimated to be) the cheapest is chosen.

When `geqo_threshold` is exceeded, the join sequences considered are determined by heuristics, as described in *Chapter 50* (page 137). Otherwise the process is the same.

The finished plan tree consists of sequential or index scans of the base relations, plus nested-loop, merge, or hash join nodes as needed, plus any auxiliary steps needed, such as sort nodes or aggregate-function calculation nodes. Most of these plan node types have the additional ability to do *selection* (discarding rows that do not meet a specified Boolean condition) and *projection* (computation of a derived column set based on given column values, that is, evaluation of scalar expressions where needed). One of the responsibilities of the planner is to attach selection conditions from the `WHERE` clause and computation of required output expressions to the most appropriate nodes of the plan tree.

44.6. Executor

The *executor* takes the plan created by the planner/optimizer and recursively processes it to extract the required set of rows. This is essentially a demand-pull pipeline mechanism. Each time a plan node is called, it must deliver one more row, or report that it is done delivering rows.

To provide a concrete example, assume that the top node is a `MergeJoin` node. Before any merge can be done two rows have to be fetched (one from each subplan). So the executor recursively calls itself to process the subplans (it starts with the subplan attached to `lefttree`). The new top node (the top node of the left subplan) is, let's say, a `Sort` node and again recursion is needed to obtain an input row. The child node of the `Sort` might be a `SeqScan` node, representing actual reading of a table. Execution of this node causes the executor to fetch a row from the table and return it up to the calling node. The `Sort` node will repeatedly call its child to obtain all the rows to be sorted. When the input is exhausted (as indicated by the child node returning a NULL instead of a row), the `Sort` code performs the sort, and finally is able to return its first output row, namely the first one in sorted order. It keeps the remaining rows stored so that it can deliver them in sorted order in response to later demands.

The `MergeJoin` node similarly demands the first row from its right subplan. Then it compares the two rows to see if they can be joined; if so, it returns a join row to its caller. On the next call, or immediately if it cannot join the current pair of inputs, it advances to the next row of one table or the other (depending on how the comparison came out), and again checks for a match. Eventually, one subplan or the other is exhausted, and the `MergeJoin` node returns NULL to indicate that no more join rows can be formed.

Complex queries can involve many levels of plan nodes, but the general approach is the same: each node computes and returns its next output row each time it is called. Each node is also responsible for applying any selection or projection expressions that were assigned to it by the planner.

The executor mechanism is used to evaluate all four basic SQL query types: `SELECT`, `INSERT`, `UPDATE`, and `DELETE`. For `SELECT`, the top-level executor code only needs to send each row returned by the query plan tree off to the client. For `INSERT`, each returned row is inserted into the target table specified for the `INSERT`. This is done in a special top-level plan node called `ModifyTable`. (A simple `INSERT ... VALUES` command creates a trivial plan tree consisting of a single `Result` node, which computes just one result row, and `ModifyTable` above it to perform the insertion. But `INSERT ... SELECT` can demand the full power of the executor mechanism.) For `UPDATE`, the planner arranges that each computed row includes all the updated column values, plus the *TID* (tuple ID, or row ID) of the original target row; this data is fed into a `ModifyTable` node, which uses the information to create a new updated row and mark the old row deleted. For `DELETE`, the only column that is actually returned by the plan is the TID, and the `ModifyTable` node simply uses the TID to visit each target row and mark it deleted.

Chapter 45. System Catalogs

The system catalogs are the place where a relational database management system stores schema metadata, such as information about tables and columns, and internal bookkeeping information. PostgreSQL's system catalogs are regular tables. You can drop and recreate the tables, add columns, insert and update values, and severely mess up your system that way. Normally, one should not change the system catalogs by hand, there are always SQL commands to do that. (For example, `CREATE DATABASE` inserts a row into the `pg_database` catalog - and actually creates the database on disk.) There are some exceptions for particularly esoteric operations, such as adding index access methods.

45.1. Overview

Table 45-1 (see below) lists the system catalogs. More detailed documentation of each catalog follows below.

Most system catalogs are copied from the template database during database creation and are thereafter database-specific. A few catalogs are physically shared across all databases in a cluster; these are noted in the descriptions of the individual catalogs.

Catalog Name	Purpose
`pg_aggregate`	aggregate functions
`pg_am`	index access methods
`pg_amop`	access method operators
`pg_amproc`	access method support procedures
`pg_attrdef`	column default values
`pg_attribute`	table columns ("attributes")
`pg_authid`	authorization identifiers (roles)
`pg_auth_members`	authorization identifier membership relationships
`pg_cast`	casts (data type conversions)
`pg_class`	tables, indexes, sequences, views ("relations")
`pg_constraint`	check constraints,unique constraints,primary key constraints,foreign key constraints
`pg_conversion`	encoding conversion information

Catalog Name	Purpose
pg_database	databases within this database cluster
pg_db_role_setting	per-role and per-database settings
pg_default_acl	default privileges for object types
pg_depend	dependencies between database objects
pg_description	descriptions or comments on database objects
pg_enum	enum label and value definitions
pg_foreign_data_wrapper	foreign-data wrapper definitions
pg_foreign_server	foreign server definitions
pg_index	additional index information
pg_inherits	table inheritance hierarchy
pg_language	languages for writing functions
pg_largeobject	data pages for large objects
pg_largeobject_metadata	metadata for large objects
pg_namespace	schemas
pg_opclass	access method operator classes
pg_operator	operators
pg_opfamily	access method operator families
pg_pltemplate	template data for procedural languages
pg_proc	functions and procedures
pg_rewrite	query rewrite rules
pg_shdepend	dependencies on shared objects
pg_shdescription	comments on shared objects
pg_statistic	planner statistics
pg_tablespace	tablespaces within this database cluster
pg_trigger	triggers
pg_ts_config	text search configurations
pg_ts_config_map	text search configurations' token mappings
pg_ts_dict	text search dictionaries
pg_ts_parser	text search parsers
pg_ts_template	text search templates
pg_type	data types
pg_user_mapping	mappings of users to foreign servers

Table 45-1. System Catalogs

45.2. pg_aggregate

The catalog `pg_aggregate` stores information about aggregate functions. An aggregate function is a function that operates on a set of values (typically one column from each row that matches a query condition) and returns a single value computed from all these values. Typical aggregate functions are `sum`, `count`, and `max`. Each entry in `pg_aggregate` is an extension of an entry in `pg_proc`. The `pg_proc` entry carries the aggregate's name, input and output data types, and other information that is similar to ordinary functions.

Name	Type	References	Description
aggfnoid	regproc	pg_proc.oid	`pg_proc` OID of the aggregate function
aggtransfn	regproc	pg_proc.oid	Transition function
aggfinalfn	regproc	pg_proc.oid	Final function (zero if none)
aggsortop	oid	pg_operator.oid	Associated sort operator (zero if none)
aggtranstype	oid	pg_type.oid	Data type of the aggregate function's internal transition (state) data
agginitval	text		The initial value of the transition state. This is a text field containing the initial value in its external string representation. If this field is null, the transition state value starts out null

Table 45-2. `pg_aggregate` Columns

New aggregate functions are registered with the CREATE AGGREGATE command. See *Section 35.10* (Vol.III) for more information about writing aggregate functions and the meaning of the transition functions, etc.

45.3. pg_am

The catalog `pg_am` stores information about index access methods. There is one row for each index access method supported by the system. The contents of this catalog are discussed in detail in *Chapter 51* (page 141).

Name	Type	References	Description
amname	name		Name of the access method
amstrategies	int2		Number of operator strategies for this access method, or zero if access method does not have a fixed set of operator strategies
amsupport	int2		Number of support routines for this access method
amcanorder	bool		Does the access method support ordered scans?
amcanbackward	bool		Does the access method support backward scanning?

Name	Type	References	Description
amcanunique	bool		Does the access method support unique indexes?
amcanmulticol	bool		Does the access method support multicolumn indexes?
amoptionalkey	bool		Does the access method support a scan without any constraint for the first index column?
amindexnulls	bool		Does the access method support null index entries?
amsearchnulls	bool		Does the access method support IS NULL/NOT NULL searches?
amstorage	bool		Can index storage data type differ from column data type?
amclusterable	bool		Can an index of this type be clustered on?
amkeytype	oid	pg_type.oid	Type of data stored in index, or zero if not a fixed type
aminsert	regproc	pg_proc.oid	"Insert this tuple" function
ambeginscan	regproc	pg_proc.oid	"Start new scan" function
amgettuple	regproc	pg_proc.oid	"Next valid tuple" function, or zero if none
amgetbitmap	regproc	pg_proc.oid	"Fetch all valid tuples" function, or zero if none
amrescan	regproc	pg_proc.oid	"Restart this scan" function
amendscan	regproc	pg_proc.oid	"End this scan" function
ammarkpos	regproc	pg_proc.oid	"Mark current scan position" function
amrestrpos	regproc	pg_proc.oid	"Restore marked scan position" function
ambuild	regproc	pg_proc.oid	"Build new index" function
ambulkdelete	regproc	pg_proc.oid	Bulk-delete function
amvacuumcleanup	regproc	pg_proc.oid	Post- VACUUM cleanup function
amcostestimate	regproc	pg_proc.oid	Function to estimate cost of an index scan
amoptions	regproc	pg_proc.oid	Function to parse and validate reloptions for an index

Table 45-3. pg_am Columns

45.4. pg_amop

The catalog pg_amop stores information about operators associated with access method operator families. There is one row for each operator that is a member of an operator family. An operator can appear in more than one family, but cannot appear in more than one position within a family.

Name	Type	References	Description
amopfamily	oid	pg_opfamily.oid	The operator family this entry is for

Name	Type	References	Description
amoplefttype	oid	pg_type.oid	Left-hand input data type of operator
amoprighttype	oid	pg_type.oid	Right-hand input data type of operator
amopstrategy	int2		Operator strategy number
amopopr	oid	pg_operator.oid	OID of the operator
amopmethod	oid	pg_am.oid	Index access method operator family is for

Table 45-4. pg_amop Columns

An entry's amopmethod must match the opfmethod of its containing operator family (including amopmethod here is an intentional denormalization of the catalog structure for performance reasons). Also, amoplefttype and amoprighttype must match the oprleft and oprright fields of the referenced pg_operator entry.

45.5. pg_amproc

The catalog pg_amproc stores information about support procedures associated with access method operator families. There is one row for each support procedure belonging to an operator family.

Name	Type	References	Description
amprocfamily	oid	pg_opfamily.oid	The operator family this entry is for
amproclefttype	oid	pg_type.oid	Left-hand input data type of associated operator
amprocrighttype	oid	pg_type.oid	Right-hand input data type of associated operator
amprocnum	int2		Support procedure number
amproc	regproc	pg_proc.oid	OID of the procedure

Table 45-5. pg_amproc Columns

The usual interpretation of the amproclefttype and amprocrighttype fields is that they identify the left and right input types of the operator(s) that a particular support procedure supports. For some access methods these match the input data type(s) of the support procedure itself, for others not. There is a notion of "default" support procedures for an index, which are those with amproclefttype and amprocrighttype both equal to the index opclass's opcintype .

45.6. pg_attrdef

The catalog pg_attrdef stores column default values. The main information about columns is stored in pg_attribute (see below). Only columns that explicitly specify a default value (when the table is created or the column is added) will have an entry here.

Name	Type	References	Description
adrelid	oid	pg_class.oid	The table this column belongs to
adnum	int2	pg_attribute.attnum	The number of the column
adbin	text		The internal representation of the column default value
adsrc	text		A human-readable representation of the default value

Table 45-6. pg_attrdef Columns

The adsrc field is historical, and is best not used, because it does not track outside changes that might affect the representation of the default value. Reverse-compiling the adbin field (with pg_get_expr for example) is a better way to display the default value.

45.7. pg_attribute

The catalog pg_attribute stores information about table columns. There will be exactly one pg_attribute row for every column in every table in the database. (There will also be attribute entries for indexes, and indeed all objects that have pg_class entries.)

The term attribute is equivalent to column and is used for historical reasons.

Name	Type	References	Description
attrelid	oid	pg_class.oid	The table this column belongs to
attname	name		The column name
atttypid	oid	pg_type.oid	The data type of this column
attstattarget	int4		attstattarget controls the level of detail of statistics accumulated for this column by ANALYZE. A zero value indicates that no statistics should be collected. A negative value says to use the system default statistics target. The exact meaning of positive values is data type-dependent. For scalar data types, attstattarget is both the target number of "most common values" to collect, and the target number of histogram bins to create.
attlen	int2		A copy of pg_type.typlen of this column's type
attnum	int2		The number of the column. Ordinary columns are numbered from 1 up. System columns, such as oid, have (arbitrary) negative numbers.
attndims	int4		Number of dimensions, if the column is an array type; otherwise 0. (Presently, the number of dimensions of an array is not enforced, so any nonzero value effectively means "it's an array").
attcacheoff	int4		Always -1 in storage, but when loaded into a row descriptor in memory this might be updated to cache the offset of the attribute within the row

Name	Type	References	Description
atttypmod	int4		atttypmod records type-specific data supplied at table creation time (for example, the maximum length of a varchar column). It is passed to type-specific input functions and length coercion functions. The value will generally be -1 for types that do not need atttypmod.
attbyval	bool		A copy of pg_type.typbyval of this column's type
attstorage	char		Normally a copy of pg_type.typstorage of this column's type. For TOAST-able data types, this can be altered after column creation to control storage policy.
attalign	char		A copy of pg_type.typalign of this column's type
attnotnull	bool		This represents a not-null constraint. It is possible to change this column to enable or disable the constraint.
atthasdef	bool		This column has a default value, in which case there will be a corresponding entry in the pg_attrdef catalog that actually defines the value.
attisdropped	bool		This column has been dropped and is no longer valid. A dropped column is still physically present in the table, but is ignored by the parser and so cannot be accessed via SQL.
attislocal	bool		This column is defined locally in the relation. Note that a column can be locally defined and inherited simultaneously.
attinhcount	int4		The number of direct ancestors this column has. A column with a nonzero number of ancestors cannot be dropped nor renamed.
attacl	aclitem[]		Column-level access privileges, if any have been granted specifically on this column.
attoptions	text[]		Attribute-level options, as "keyword=value" strings

Table 45-7. pg_attribute Columns

In a dropped column's pg_attribute entry, atttypid is reset to zero, but attlen and the other fields copied from pg_type are still valid. This arrangement is needed to cope with the situation where the dropped column's data type was later dropped, and so there is no pg_type row anymore. attlen and the other fields can be used to interpret the contents of a row of the table.

45.8. pg_authid

The catalog pg_authid contains information about database authorization identifiers (roles). A role subsumes the concepts of "users" and "groups". A user is essentially just a role with the `rolcanlogin` flag set. Any role (with or without `rolcanlogin`) can have other roles as members; see `pg_auth_members` (page 35).

Since this catalog contains passwords, it must not be publicly readable. `pg_roles` (page 72) is a publicly readable view on `pg_authid` that blanks out the password field.

Chapter 20 (Vol.II) contains detailed information about user and privilege management.

Because user identities are cluster-wide, `pg_authid` is shared across all databases of a cluster: there is only one copy of `pg_authid` per cluster, not one per database.

Name	Type	Description
rolname	name	Role name
rolsuper	bool	Role has superuser privileges
rolinherit	bool	Role automatically inherits privileges of roles it is a member of
rolcreaterole	bool	Role can create more roles
rolcreatedb	bool	Role can create databases
rolcatupdate	bool	Role can update system catalogs directly. (Even a superuser cannot do this unless this column is true)
rolcanlogin	bool	Role can log in. That is, this role can be given as the initial session authorization identifier.
rolconnlimit	int4	For roles that can log in, this sets maximum number of concurrent connections this role can make. -1 means no limit.
rolpassword	text	Password (possibly encrypted); null if none. If the password is encrypted, this column will contain the string md5 followed by a 32-character hexadecimal MD5 hash. The MD5 hash will be of the user's password concatenated to their username (for example, if user joe has password xyzzy, PostgreSQL will store the md5 hash of xyzzyjoe).
rolvaliduntil	timestamptz	Password expiry time (only used for password authentication); null if no expiration

Table 45-8. `pg_authid` Columns

45.9. `pg_auth_members`

The catalog `pg_auth_members` shows the membership relations between roles. Any non-circular set of relationships is allowed.

Because user identities are cluster-wide, `pg_auth_members` is shared across all databases of a cluster: there is only one copy of `pg_auth_members` per cluster, not one per database.

Name	Type	References	Description
roleid	oid	pg_authid.oid	ID of a role that has a member

Name	Type	References	Description
member	oid	pg_authid.oid	ID of a role that is a member of roleid
grantor	oid	pg_authid.oid	ID of the role that granted this membership
admin_option	bool		True if member can grant membership in roleid to others

Table 45-9. pg_auth_members Columns

45.10. pg_cast

The catalog pg_cast stores data type conversion paths, both built-in paths and those defined with CREATE CAST.

It should be noted that pg_cast does not represent every type conversion that the system knows how to perform; only those that cannot be deduced from some generic rule. For example, casting between a domain and its base type is not explicitly represented in pg_cast. Another important exception is that "automatic I/O conversion casts", those performed using a data type's own I/O functions to convert to or from text or other string types, are not explicitly represented in pg_cast.

Name	Type	References	Description
castsource	oid	pg_type.oid	OID of the source data type
casttarget	oid	pg_type.oid	OID of the target data type
castfunc	oid	pg_proc.oid	The OID of the function to use to perform this cast. Zero is stored if the cast method doesn't require a function.
castcontext	char		Indicates what contexts the cast can be invoked in. e means only as an explicit cast (using CAST or :: syntax). a means implicitly in assignment to a target column, as well as explicitly. i means implicitly in expressions, as well as the other cases.
castmethod	char		Indicates how the cast is performed. f means that the function specified in the castfunc field is used. i means that the input/output functions are used. b means that the types are binary-coercible, thus no conversion is required.

Table 45-10. pg_cast Columns

The cast functions listed in pg_cast must always take the cast source type as their first argument type, and return the cast destination type as their result type. A cast function can have up to three arguments. The second argument, if present, must be type integer; it receives the type modifier associated with the destination type, or -1 if there is none. The third argument, if present, must be type boolean; it receives true if the cast is an explicit cast, false otherwise.

It is legitimate to create a pg_cast entry in which the source and target types are the same, if the associated function takes more than one argument. Such entries represent "length coercion functions" that coerce values of the type to be legal for a particular type modifier value.

When a pg_cast entry has different source and target types and a function that takes more than one argument, it represents converting from one type to another and applying a length coercion in a single step. When no such entry is available, coercion to a type that uses a type modifier involves two steps, one to convert between data types and a second to apply the modifier.

45.11. pg_class

The catalog pg_class catalogs tables and most everything else that has columns or is otherwise similar to a table. This includes indexes (but see also pg_index), sequences, views, composite types, and TOAST tables; see relkind. Below, when we mean all of these kinds of objects we speak of "relations". Not all columns are meaningful for all relation types.

Name	Type	References	Description
relname	name		Name of the table, index, view, etc.
relnamespace	oid	pg_namespace.oid	The OID of the namespace that contains this relation
reltype	oid	pg_type.oid	The OID of the data type that corresponds to this table's row type, if any (zero for indexes, which have no pg_type entry)
reloftype	oid	pg_type.oid	For typed tables, the OID of the underlying composite type, zero for all other relations
relowner	oid	pg_authid.oid	Owner of the relation
relam	oid	pg_am.oid	If this is an index, the access method used (B-tree, hash, etc.)
relfilenode	oid		Name of the on-disk file of this relation; zero means this is a "mapped" relation whose disk file name is determined by low-level state
reltablespace	oid	pg_tablespace.oid	The tablespace in which this relation is stored. If zero, the database's default tablespace is implied. (Not meaningful if the relation has no on-disk file.)
relpages	int4		Size of the on-disk representation of this table in pages (of size BLCKSZ). This is only an estimate used by the planner. It is updated by VACUUM, ANALYZE, and a few DDL commands such as CREATE INDEX.
reltuples	float4		Number of rows in the table. This is only an estimate used by the planner. It is updated by VACUUM, ANALYZE, and a few DDL commands such as CREATE INDEX.

Name	Type	References	Description
reltoastrelid	oid	pg_class.oid	OID of the TOAST table associated with this table, 0 if none. The TOAST table stores large attributes "out of line" in a secondary table.
reltoastidxid	oid	pg_class.oid	For a TOAST table, the OID of its index. 0 if not a TOAST table.
relhasindex	bool		True if this is a table and it has (or recently had) any indexes. This is set by CREATE INDEX, but not cleared immediately by DROP INDEX. VACUUM clears relhasindex if it finds the table has no indexes.
relisshared	bool		True if this table is shared across all databases in the cluster. Only certain system catalogs (such as pg_database) are shared.
relistemp	bool		True if this table is a temporary relation. If so, only the creating session can safely access its contents.
relkind	char		r = ordinary table, i = index, S = sequence, v = view, c = composite type, t = TOAST table
relnatts	int2		Number of user columns in the relation (system columns not counted). There must be this many corresponding entries in pg_attribute. See also pg_attribute.attnum.
relchecks	int2		Number of CHECK constraints on the table; see pg_constraint catalog
relhasoids	bool		True if we generate an OID for each row of the relation
relhaspkey	bool		True if the table has (or once had) a primary key
relhasexclusion	bool		For a table, true if the table has (or once had) any exclusion constraints; for an index, true if the index supports an exclusion constraint
relhasrules	bool		True if table has (or once had) rules; see pg_rewrite catalog
relhastriggers	bool		True if table has (or once had) triggers; see pg_trigger catalog
relhassubclass	bool		True if table has (or once had) any inheritance children
relfrozenxid	xid		All transaction IDs before this one have been replaced with a permanent ("frozen") transaction ID in this table. This is used to track whether the table needs to be vacuumed in order to prevent transaction ID wraparound or to allow pg_clog to be shrunk. Zero (InvalidTransactionId) if the relation is not a table.
relacl	aclitem[]		Access privileges; see GRANT and REVOKE for details
reloptions	text[]		Access-method-specific options, as "keyword=value" strings

Table 45-11. pg_class Columns

Several of the Boolean flags in pg_class are maintained lazily: they are guaranteed to be true if that's the correct state, but may not be reset to false immediately when the condition is no longer true. For example, relhasindex is set by CREATE INDEX, but it is never cleared by DROP INDEX. Instead, VACUUM clears relhasindex if it finds the table has no indexes. This arrangement avoids race conditions and improves concurrency.

45.12. pg_constraint

The catalog pg_constraint stores check, primary key, unique, foreign key, and exclusion constraints on tables. (Column constraints are not treated specially. Every column constraint is equivalent to some table constraint.) Not-null constraints are represented in the pg_attribute catalog, not here.

User-defined constraint triggers (created with CREATE CONSTRAINT TRIGGER) also give rise to an entry in this table.

Check constraints on domains are stored here, too.

Name	Type	References	Description
conname	name		Constraint name (not necessarily unique!)
connamespace	oid	pg_namespace.oid	The OID of the namespace that contains this constraint
contype	char		c = check constraint, f = foreign key constraint, p = primary key constraint, u = unique constraint, t = constraint trigger, x = exclusion constraint
condeferrable	bool		Is the constraint deferrable?
condeferred	bool		Is the constraint deferred by default?
conrelid	oid	pg_class.oid	The table this constraint is on; 0 if not a table constraint
contypid	oid	pg_type.oid	The domain this constraint is on; 0 if not a domain constraint
conindid	oid	pg_class.oid	The index supporting this constraint, if it's a unique, primary key, foreign key, or exclusion constraint; else 0
confrelid	oid	pg_class.oid	If a foreign key, the referenced table; else 0
confupdtype	char		Foreign key update action code: a = no action, r = restrict, c = cascade, n = set null, d = set default
confdeltype	char		Foreign key deletion action code: a = no action, r = restrict, c = cascade, n = set null, d = set default
confmatchtype	char		Foreign key match type: f = full, p = partial, u = simple (unspecified)
conislocal	bool		This constraint is defined locally for the relation. Note that a constraint can be locally defined and inherited simultaneously.

Name	Type	References	Description
coninhcount	int4		The number of direct inheritance ancestors this constraint has. A constraint with a nonzero number of ancestors cannot be dropped nor renamed.
conkey	int2[]	pg_attribute.attnum	If a table constraint (including foreign keys, but not constraint triggers), list of the constrained columns
confkey	int2[]	pg_attribute.attnum	If a foreign key, list of the referenced columns
conpfeqop	oid[]	pg_operator.oid	If a foreign key, list of the equality operators for PK = FK comparisons
conppeqop	oid[]	pg_operator.oid	If a foreign key, list of the equality operators for PK = PK comparisons
conffeqop	oid[]	pg_operator.oid	If a foreign key, list of the equality operators for FK = FK comparisons
conexclop	oid[]	pg_operator.oid	If an exclusion constraint, list of the per-column exclusion operators
conbin	text		If a check constraint, an internal representation of the expression
consrc	text		If a check constraint, a human-readable representation of the expression

Table 45-12. `pg_constraint` Columns

In the case of an exclusion constraint, `conkey` is only useful for constraint elements that are simple column references. For other cases, a zero appears in `conkey` and the associated index must be consulted to discover the expression that is constrained. (`conkey` thus has the same contents as `pg_index.indkey` for the index.)

Note: `consrc` is not updated when referenced objects change; for example, it won't track renaming of columns. Rather than relying on this field, it's best to use `pg_get_constraintdef()` to extract the definition of a check constraint.

Note: `pg_class.relchecks` needs to agree with the number of check-constraint entries found in this table for each relation. Also, `pg_class.relhasexclusion` must be true if there are any exclusion-constraint entries for the relation.

45.13. `pg_conversion`

The catalog `pg_conversion` describes the available encoding conversion procedures. See CREATE CONVERSION for more information.

Name	Type	References	Description
conname	name		Conversion name (unique within a namespace)
connamespace	oid	pg_namespace.oid	The OID of the namespace that contains this conversion

Name	Type	References	Description
conowner	oid	pg_authid.oid	Owner of the conversion
conforencoding	int4		Source encoding ID
contoencoding	int4		Destination encoding ID
conproc	regproc	pg_proc.oid	Conversion procedure
condefault	bool		True if this is the default conversion

Table 45-13. pg_conversion Columns

45.14. pg_database

The catalog pg_database stores information about the available databases. Databases are created with the CREATE DATABASE command. Consult *Chapter 21* (Vol.II) for details about the meaning of some of the parameters.

Unlike most system catalogs, pg_database is shared across all databases of a cluster: there is only one copy of pg_database per cluster, not one per database.

Name	Type	References	Description
datname	name		Database name
datdba	oid	pg_authid.oid	Owner of the database, usually the user who created it
encoding	int4		Character encoding for this database (pg_encoding_to_char() can translate this number to the encoding name)
datcollate	name		LC_COLLATE for this database
datctype	name		LC_CTYPE for this database
datistemplate	bool		If true then this database can be used in the TEMPLATE clause of CREATE DATABASE to create a new database as a clone of this one
datallowconn	bool		If false then no one can connect to this database. This is used to protect the template0 database from being altered.
datconnlimit	int4		Sets maximum number of concurrent connections that can be made to this database. -1 means no limit.
datlastsysoid	oid		Last system OID in the database; useful particularly to pg_dump
datfrozenxid	xid		All transaction IDs before this one have been replaced with a permanent ("frozen") transaction ID in this database. This is used to track whether the database needs to be vacuumed in order to prevent transaction ID wraparound or to allow pg_clog to be shrunk. It is the minimum of the per-table pg_class .relfrozenxid values.

Name	Type	References	Description
dattablespace	oid	pg_tablespace.oid	The default tablespace for the database. Within this database, all tables for which pg_class.reltablespace is zero will be stored in this tablespace; in particular, all the non-shared system catalogs will be there.
datacl	aclitem[]		Access privileges; see GRANT and REVOKE for details

Table 45-14. pg_database Columns

45.15. pg_db_role_setting

The catalog pg_db_role_setting records the default values that have been set for run-time configuration variables, for each role and database combination.

Unlike most system catalogs, pg_db_role_setting is shared across all databases of a cluster: there is only one copy of pg_db_role_setting per cluster, not one per database.

Name	Type	References	Description
setdatabase	oid	pg_database.oid	The OID of the database the setting is applicable to, or zero if not database-specific
setrole	oid	pg_authid.oid	The OID of the role the setting is applicable to, or zero if not role-specific
setconfig	text[]		Defaults for run-time configuration variables

Table 45-15. pg_db_role_setting Columns

45.16. pg_default_acl

The catalog pg_default_acl stores initial privileges to be assigned to newly created objects.

Name	Type	References	Description
defaclrole	oid	pg_authid.oid	The OID of the role associated with this entry
defaclnamespace	oid	pg_namespace.oid	The OID of the namespace associated with this entry, or 0 if none
defaclobjtype	char		Type of object this entry is for: r = relation (table, view), S = sequence, f = function
defaclacl	aclitem[]		Access privileges that this type of object should have on creation

Table 45-16. pg_default_acl Columns

A pg_default_acl entry shows the initial privileges to be assigned to an object belonging to the indicated user. There are currently two types of entry: "global" entries with defaclnamespace = 0, and "per-schema" entries that reference a particular schema. If a global entry is present then it *overrides* the normal hard-wired default privileges for the object type. A per-schema entry, if present, represents privileges to be *added to* the global or hard-wired default privileges.

Note that when an ACL entry in another catalog is null, it is taken to represent the hard-wired default privileges for its object, *not* whatever might be in pg_default_acl at the moment. pg_default_acl is only consulted during object creation.

45.17. pg_depend

The catalog pg_depend records the dependency relationships between database objects. This information allows DROP commands to find which other objects must be dropped by DROP CASCADE or prevent dropping in the DROP RESTRICT case.

See also pg_shdepend (page 55), which performs a similar function for dependencies involving objects that are shared across a database cluster.

Name	Type	References	Description
classid	oid	pg_class.oid	The OID of the system catalog the dependent object is in
objid	oid	any OID column	The OID of the specific dependent object
objsubid	int4		For a table column, this is the column number (the objid and classid refer to the table itself). For all other object types, this column is zero.
refclassid	oid	pg_class.oid	The OID of the system catalog the referenced object is in
refobjid	oid	any OID column	The OID of the specific referenced object
refobjsubid	int4		For a table column, this is the column number (the refobjid and refclassid refer to the table itself). For all other object types, this column is zero.
deptype	char		A code defining the specific semantics of this dependency relationship; see text

Table 45-17. pg_depend Columns

In all cases, a pg_depend entry indicates that the referenced object cannot be dropped without also dropping the dependent object. However, there are several subflavors identified by deptype:

DEPENDENCY_NORMAL (n)

> A normal relationship between separately-created objects. The dependent object can be dropped without affecting the referenced object. The referenced object can only be dropped by specifying CASCADE, in which case the dependent object is dropped, too. Example: a table column has a normal dependency on its data type.

DEPENDENCY_AUTO (a)

The dependent object can be dropped separately from the referenced object, and should be automatically dropped (regardless of RESTRICT or CASCADE mode) if the referenced object is dropped. Example: a named constraint on a table is made autodependent on the table, so that it will go away if the table is dropped.

DEPENDENCY_INTERNAL (i)

The dependent object was created as part of creation of the referenced object, and is really just a part of its internal implementation. A DROP of the dependent object will be disallowed outright (we'll tell the user to issue a DROP against the referenced object, instead). A DROP of the referenced object will be propagated through to drop the dependent object whether CASCADE is specified or not. Example: a trigger that's created to enforce a foreign-key constraint is made internally dependent on the constraint's pg_constraint entry.

DEPENDENCY_PIN (p)

There is no dependent object; this type of entry is a signal that the system itself depends on the referenced object, and so that object must never be deleted. Entries of this type are created only by initdb. The columns for the dependent object contain zeroes.

Other dependency flavors might be needed in future.

45.18. pg_description

The catalog pg_description stores optional descriptions (comments) for each database object. Descriptions can be manipulated with the COMMENT command and viewed with psql's \d commands. Descriptions of many built-in system objects are provided in the initial contents of pg_description.

See also pg_shdescription (page 56), which performs a similar function for descriptions involving objects that are shared across a database cluster.

Name	Type	References	Description
objoid	oid	any OID column	The OID of the object this description pertains to
classoid	oid	pg_class.oid	The OID of the system catalog this object appears in
objsubid	int4		For a comment on a table column, this is the column number (the objoid and classoid refer to the table itself). For all other object types, this column is zero.
description	text		Arbitrary text that serves as the description of this object

Table 45-18. pg_description Columns

45.19. pg_enum

The pg_enum catalog contains entries matching enum types to their associated values and labels. The internal representation of a given enum value is actually the OID of its associated row in pg_enum. The OIDs for a particular enum type are guaranteed to be ordered in the way the type should sort, but there is no guarantee about the ordering of OIDs of unrelated enum types.

Name	Type	References	Description
enumtypid	oid	pg_type.oid	The OID of the pg_type entry owning this enum value
enumlabel	name		The textual label for this enum value

Table 45-19. pg_enum Columns

45.20. pg_foreign_data_wrapper

The catalog pg_foreign_data_wrapper stores foreign-data wrapper definitions. A foreign-data wrapper is the mechanism by which external data, residing on foreign servers, is accessed.

Name	Type	References	Description
fdwname	name		Name of the foreign-data wrapper
fdwowner	oid	pg_authid.oid	Owner of the foreign-data wrapper
fdwvalidator	oid	pg_proc.oid	References a validator function that is responsible for checking the validity of the generic options given to the foreign-data wrapper, as well as to foreign servers and user mappings using the foreign-data wrapper. Zero if no validator is provided.
fdwacl	aclitem[]		Access privileges; see GRANT and REVOKE for details
fdwoptions	text[]		Foreign-data wrapper specific options, as "keyword=value" strings

Table 45-20. pg_foreign_data_wrapper Columns

45.21. pg_foreign_server

The catalog pg_foreign_server stores foreign server definitions. A foreign server describes the connection to a remote server, managing external data. Foreign servers are accessed via foreign-data wrappers.

Name	Type	References	Description
srvname	name		Name of the foreign server
srvowner	oid	pg_authid.oid	Owner of the foreign server

Name	Type	References	Description
srvfdw	oid	pg_foreign_data_wrapper.oid	The OID of the foreign-data wrapper of this foreign server
srvtype	text		Type of the server (optional)
srvversion	text		Version of the server (optional)
srvacl	aclitem[]		Access privileges; see GRANT and REVOKE for details
srvoptions	text[]		Foreign server specific options, as "keyword=value" strings

Table 45-21. `pg_foreign_server` Columns

45.22. `pg_index`

The catalog `pg_index` contains part of the information about indexes. The rest is mostly in `pg_class`.

Name	Type	References	Description
indexrelid	oid	pg_class.oid	The OID of the `pg_class` entry for this index
indrelid	oid	pg_class.oid	The OID of the `pg_class` entry for the table this index is for
indnatts	int2		The number of columns in the index (duplicates `pg_class.relnatts`)
indisunique	bool		If true, this is a unique index
indisprimary	bool		If true, this index represents the primary key of the table (`indisunique` should always be true when this is true)
indimmediate	bool		If true, the uniqueness check is enforced immediately on insertion (indisunique should always be true when this is true)
indisclustered	bool		If true, the table was last clustered on this index
indisvalid	bool		If true, the index is currently valid for queries. False means the index is possibly incomplete: it must still be modified by `INSERT`/`UPDATE` operations, but it cannot safely be used for queries. If it is unique, the uniqueness property is not true either.
indcheckxmin	bool		If true, queries must not use the index until the `xmin` of this `pg_index` row is below their TransactionXmin event horizon, because the table may contain broken HOT chains with incompatible rows that they can see
indisready	bool		If true, the index is currently ready for inserts. False means the index must be ignored by `INSERT`/`UPDATE` operations.

Name	Type	References	Description
indkey	int2vector	pg_attribute.attnum	This is an array of indnatts values that indicate which table columns this index indexes. For example a value of 1 3 would mean that the first and the third table columns make up the index key. A zero in this array indicates that the corresponding index attribute is an expression over the table columns, rather than a simple column reference.
indclass	oidvector	pg_opclass.oid	For each column in the index key, this contains the OID of the operator class to use. See pg_opclass (page 49) for details.
indoption	int2vector		This is an array of indnatts values that store per-column flag bits. The meaning of the bits is defined by the index's access method.
indexprs	text		Expression trees (in nodeToString() representation) for index attributes that are not simple column references. This is a list with one element for each zero entry in indkey. Null if all index attributes are simple references.
indpred	text		Expression tree (in nodeToString() representation) for partial index predicate. Null if not a partial index.

Table 45-22. `pg_index` Columns

45.23. `pg_inherits`

The catalog `pg_inherits` records information about table inheritance hierarchies. There is one entry for each direct child table in the database. (Indirect inheritance can be determined by following chains of entries.)

Name	Type	References	Description
inhrelid	oid	pg_class.oid	The OID of the child table
inhparent	oid	pg_class.oid	The OID of the parent table
inhseqno	int4		If there is more than one direct parent for a child table (multiple inheritance), this number tells the order in which the inherited columns are to be arranged. The count starts at 1.

Table 45-23. `pg_inherits` Columns

45.24. `pg_language`

The catalog `pg_language` registers languages in which you can write functions or stored procedures. See CREATE LANGUAGE and *Chapter 38* (Vol.III) for more information about language handlers.

Name	Type	References	Description
lanname	name		Name of the language
lanowner	oid	pg_authid.oid	Owner of the language
lanispl	bool		This is false for internal languages (such as SQL) and true for user-defined languages. Currently, pg_dump still uses this to determine which languages need to be dumped, but this might be replaced by a different mechanism in the future.
lanpltrusted	bool		True if this is a trusted language, which means that it is believed not to grant access to anything outside the normal SQL execution environment. Only superusers can create functions in untrusted languages.
lanplcallfoid	oid	pg_proc.oid	For noninternal languages this references the language handler, which is a special function that is responsible for executing all functions that are written in the particular language
laninline	oid	pg_proc.oid	This references a function that is responsible for executing "inline" anonymous code blocks (DO blocks). Zero if inline blocks are not supported.
lanvalidator	oid	pg_proc.oid	This references a language validator function that is responsible for checking the syntax and validity of new functions when they are created. Zero if no validator is provided.
lanacl	aclitem[]		Access privileges; see GRANT and REVOKE for details

Table 45-24. `pg_language` Columns

45.25. `pg_largeobject`

The catalog `pg_largeobject` holds the data making up "large objects". A large object is identified by an OID assigned when it is created. Each large object is broken into segments or "pages" small enough to be conveniently stored as rows in `pg_largeobject`. The amount of data per page is defined to be `LOBLKSIZE` (which is currently `BLCKSZ/4`, or typically 2 kB).

Prior to PostgreSQL 9.0, there was no permission structure associated with large objects. As a result, `pg_largeobject` was publicly readable and could be used to obtain the OIDs (and contents) of all large objects in the system. This is no longer the case; use `pg_largeobject_metadata` to obtain a list of large object OIDs.

Name	Type		Description
loid	oid	pg_largeobject_metadata.oid	Identifier of the large object that includes this page
pageno	int4		Page number of this page within its large object (counting from zero)

Name	Type		Description
data	bytea		Actual data stored in the large object. This will never be more than LOBLKSIZE bytes and might be less

Table 45-25. pg_largeobject Columns

Each row of pg_largeobject holds data for one page of a large object, beginning at byte offset (pageno * LOBLKSIZE) within the object. The implementation allows sparse storage: pages might be missing, and might be shorter than LOBLKSIZE bytes even if they are not the last page of the object. Missing regions within a large object read as zeroes.

45.26. pg_largeobject_metadata

The catalog pg_largeobject_metadata holds metadata associated with large objects. The actual large object data is stored in pg_largeobject.

Name	Type	References	Description
lomowner	oid	pg_authid.oid	Owner of the large object
lomacl	aclitem[]		Access privileges; see GRANT and REVOKE for details

Table 45-26. pg_largeobject_metadata Columns

45.27. pg_namespace

The catalog pg_namespace stores namespaces. A namespace is the structure underlying SQL schemas: each namespace can have a separate collection of relations, types, etc. without name conflicts.

Name	Type	References	Description
nspname	name		Name of the namespace
nspowner	oid	pg_authid.oid	Owner of the namespace
nspacl	aclitem[]		Access privileges; see GRANT and REVOKE for details

Table 45-27. pg_namespace Columns

45.28. pg_opclass

The catalog pg_opclass defines index access method operator classes. Each operator class defines semantics for index columns of a particular data type and a particular index access method. An operator class essentially specifies that a particular operator family is applicable to a particular indexable column data type. The set of operators from the family that are actually usable with the indexed column are whichever ones accept the column's data type as their lefthand input.

Operator classes are described at length in *Section 35.14* (Vol.III).

Name	Type	References	Description
opcmethod	oid	pg_am.oid	Index access method operator class is for
opcname	name		Name of this operator class
opcnamespace	oid	pg_namespace.oid	Namespace of this operator class
opcowner	oid	pg_authid.oid	Owner of the operator class
opcfamily	oid	pg_opfamily.oid	Operator family containing the operator class
opcintype	oid	pg_type.oid	Data type that the operator class indexes
opcdefault	bool		True if this operator class is the default for opcintype
opckeytype	oid	pg_type.oid	Type of data stored in index, or zero if same as opcintype

Table 45-28. `pg_opclass` Columns

An operator class's `opcmethod` must match the `opfmethod` of its containing operator family. Also, there must be no more than one `pg_opclass` row having `opcdefault` true for any given combination of `opcmethod` and `opcintype`.

45.29. `pg_operator`

The catalog `pg_operator` stores information about operators. See CREATE OPERATOR and *Section 35.12* (Vol.III) for more information.

Name	Type	References	Description
oprname	name		Name of the operator
oprnamespace	oid	pg_namespace.oid	The OID of the namespace that contains this operator
oprowner	oid	pg_authid.oid	Owner of the operator
oprkind	char		b = infix ("both"), l = prefix ("left"), r = postfix ("right")
oprcanmerge	bool		This operator supports merge joins
oprcanhash	bool		This operator supports hash joins
oprleft	oid	pg_type.oid	Type of the left operand
oprright	oid	pg_type.oid	Type of the right operand
oprresult	oid	pg_type.oid	Type of the result
oprcom	oid	pg_operator.oid	Commutator of this operator, if any
oprnegate	oid	pg_operator.oid	Negator of this operator, if any

Name	Type	References	Description
oprcode	regproc	pg_proc.oid	Function that implements this operator
oprrest	regproc	pg_proc.oid	Restriction selectivity estimation function for this operator
oprjoin	regproc	pg_proc.oid	Join selectivity estimation function for this operator

Table 45-29. pg_operator Columns

Unused column contain zeroes. For example, `oprleft` is zero for a prefix operator.

45.30. pg_opfamily

The catalog `pg_opfamily` defines operator families. Each operator family is a collection of operators and associated support routines that implement the semantics specified for a particular index access method. Furthermore, the operators in a family are all "compatible", in a way that is specified by the access method. The operator family concept allows cross-data-type operators to be used with indexes and to be reasoned about using knowledge of access method semantics.

Operator families are described at length in *Section 35.14* (Vol.III).

Name	Type	References	Description
opfmethod	oid	pg_am.oid	Index access method operator family is for
opfname	name		Name of this operator family
opfnamespace	oid	pg_namespace.oid	Namespace of this operator family
opfowner	oid	pg_authid.oid	Owner of the operator family

Table 45-30. pg_opfamily Columns

The majority of the information defining an operator family is not in its `pg_opfamily` row, but in the associated rows in `pg_amop` (page 31), `pg_amproc` (page 32), and `pg_opclass` (page 49).

45.31. pg_pltemplate

The catalog `pg_pltemplate` stores "template" information for procedural languages. A template for a language allows the language to be created in a particular database by a simple `CREATE LANGUAGE` command, with no need to specify implementation details.

Unlike most system catalogs, `pg_pltemplate` is shared across all databases of a cluster: there is only one copy of `pg_pltemplate` per cluster, not one per database. This allows the information to be accessible in each database as it is needed.

Name	Type	Description
tmplname	name	Name of the language this template is for
tmpltrusted	boolean	True if language is considered trusted
tmpldbacreate	boolean	True if language may be created by a database owner
tmplhandler	text	Name of call handler function
tmplinline	text	Name of anonymous-block handler function, or null if none
tmplvalidator	text	Name of validator function, or null if none
tmpllibrary	text	Path of shared library that implements language
tmplacl	aclitem[]	Access privileges for template (not yet used)

Table 45-31. `pg_pltemplate` Columns

There are not currently any commands that manipulate procedural language templates; to change the built-in information, a superuser must modify the table using ordinary `INSERT`, `DELETE`, or `UPDATE` commands. It is likely that a future release of PostgreSQL will offer commands to change the entries in a cleaner fashion.

When implemented, the `tmplacl` field will provide access control for the template itself (i.e., the right to create a language using it), not for the languages created from the template.

45.32. `pg_proc`

The catalog `pg_proc` stores information about functions (or procedures). See CREATE FUNCTION and *Section 34.3* (Vol.III) for more information.

The table contains data for aggregate functions as well as plain functions. If `proisagg` is true, there should be a matching row in `pg_aggregate`.

Name	Type	References	Description
proname	name		Name of the function
pronamespace	oid	pg_namespace.oid	The OID of the namespace that contains this function
proowner	oid	pg_authid.oid	Owner of the function
prolang	oid	pg_language.oid	Implementation language or call interface of this function
procost	float4		Estimated execution cost (in units of cpu_operator_cost - Vol.II); if `proretset`, this is cost per row returned
prorows	float4		Estimated number of result rows (zero if not `proretset`)
provariadic	oid	pg_type.oid	Data type of the variadic array parameter's elements, or zero if the function does not have a variadic parameter
proisagg	bool		Function is an aggregate function
proiswindow	bool		Function is a window function
prosecdef	bool		Function is a security definer (i.e., a "setuid" function)

Name	Type	References	Description
proisstrict	bool		Function returns null if any call argument is null. In that case the function won't actually be called at all. Functions that are not "strict" must be prepared to handle null inputs.
proretset	bool		Function returns a set (i.e., multiple values of the specified data type)
provolatile	char		provolatile tells whether the function's result depends only on its input arguments, or is affected by outside factors. It is i for "immutable" functions, which always deliver the same result for the same inputs. It is s for "stable" functions, whose results (for fixed inputs) do not change within a scan. It is v for "volatile" functions, whose results might change at any time. (Use v also for functions with side-effects, so that calls to them cannot get optimized away.)
pronargs	int2		Number of input arguments
pronargdefaults	int2		Number of arguments that have defaults
prorettype	oid	pg_type.oid	Data type of the return value
proargtypes	oidvector	pg_type.oid	An array with the data types of the function arguments. This includes only input arguments (including INOUT and VARIADIC arguments), and thus represents the call signature of the function.
proallargtypes	oid[]	pg_type.oid	An array with the data types of the function arguments. This includes all arguments (including OUT and INOUT arguments); however, if all the arguments are IN arguments, this field will be null. Note that subscripting is 1-based, whereas for historical reasons proargtypes is subscripted from 0.
proargmodes	char[]		An array with the modes of the function arguments, encoded as i for IN arguments, o for OUT arguments, b for INOUT arguments, v for VARIADIC arguments, t for TABLE arguments. If all the arguments are IN arguments, this field will be null. Note that subscripts correspond to positions of proallargtypes not proargtypes.
proargnames	text[]		An array with the names of the function arguments. Arguments without a name are set to empty strings in the array. If none of the arguments have a name, this field will be null. Note that subscripts correspond to positions of proallargtypes not proargtypes.
proargdefaults	text		Expression trees (in nodeToString() representation) for default values. This is a list with pronargdefaults elements, corresponding to the last *N input* arguments (i.e., the last *N* proargtypes positions). If none of the arguments have defaults, this field will be null.

Name	Type	References	Description
prosrc	text		This tells the function handler how to invoke the function. It might be the actual source code of the function for interpreted languages, a link symbol, a file name, or just about anything else, depending on the implementation language/call convention.
probin	text		Additional information about how to invoke the function. Again, the interpretation is language-specific.
proconfig	text[]		Function's local settings for run-time configuration variables
proacl	aclitem[]		Access privileges; see GRANT and REVOKE for details

Table 45-32. `pg_proc` Columns

For compiled functions, both built-in and dynamically loaded, `prosrc` contains the function's C-language name (link symbol). For all other currently-known language types, `prosrc` contains the function's source text. `probin` is unused except for dynamically-loaded C functions, for which it gives the name of the shared library file containing the function.

45.33. `pg_rewrite`

The catalog `pg_rewrite` stores rewrite rules for tables and views.

Name	Type	References	Description
rulename	name		Rule name
ev_class	oid	pg_class.oid	The table this rule is for
ev_attr	int2		The column this rule is for (currently, always zero to indicate the whole table)
ev_type	char		Event type that the rule is for: 1 = `SELECT`, 2 = `UPDATE`, 3 = `INSERT`, 4 = `DELETE`
ev_enabled	char		Controls in which `session_replication_role` (Vol.II) modes the rule fires. `O` = rule fires in "origin" and "local" modes, `D` = rule is disabled, `R` = rule fires in "replica" mode, `A` = rule fires always.
is_instead	bool		True if the rule is an `INSTEAD` rule
ev_qual	text		Expression tree (in the form of a `nodeToString()` representation) for the rule's qualifying condition
ev_action	text		Query tree (in the form of a `nodeToString()` representation) for the rule's action

Table 45-33. `pg_rewrite` Columns

Note: `pg_class.relhasrules` must be true if a table has any rules in this catalog.

45.34. pg_shdepend

The catalog pg_shdepend records the dependency relationships between database objects and shared objects, such as roles. This information allows PostgreSQL to ensure that those objects are unreferenced before attempting to delete them.

See also pg_depend (page 42), which performs a similar function for dependencies involving objects within a single database.

Unlike most system catalogs, pg_shdepend is shared across all databases of a cluster: there is only one copy of pg_shdepend per cluster, not one per database.

Name	Type	References	Description
dbid	oid	pg_database.oid	The OID of the database the dependent object is in, or zero for a shared object
classid	oid	pg_class.oid	The OID of the system catalog the dependent object is in
objid	oid	any OID column	The OID of the specific dependent object
objsubid	int4		For a table column, this is the column number (the objid and classid refer to the table itself). For all other object types, this column is zero.
refclassid	oid	pg_class.oid	The OID of the system catalog the referenced object is in (must be a shared catalog)
refobjid	oid	any OID column	The OID of the specific referenced object
deptype	char		A code defining the specific semantics of this dependency relationship; see text

Table 45-34. pg_shdepend Columns

In all cases, a pg_shdepend entry indicates that the referenced object cannot be dropped without also dropping the dependent object. However, there are several subflavors identified by deptype:

SHARED_DEPENDENCY_OWNER (o)

The referenced object (which must be a role) is the owner of the dependent object.

SHARED_DEPENDENCY_ACL (a)

The referenced object (which must be a role) is mentioned in the ACL (access control list, i.e., privileges list) of the dependent object. (A SHARED_DEPENDENCY_ACL entry is not made for the owner of the object, since the owner will have a SHARED_DEPENDENCY_OWNER entry anyway.)

`SHARED_DEPENDENCY_PIN` (`p`)

There is no dependent object; this type of entry is a signal that the system itself depends on the referenced object, and so that object must never be deleted. Entries of this type are created only by `initdb`. The columns for the dependent object contain zeroes.

Other dependency flavors might be needed in future. Note in particular that the current definition only supports roles as referenced objects.

45.35. pg_shdescription

The catalog `pg_shdescription` stores optional descriptions (comments) for shared database objects. Descriptions can be manipulated with the COMMENT command and viewed with psql's `\d` commands.

See also `pg_description` (page 44), which performs a similar function for descriptions involving objects within a single database.

Unlike most system catalogs, `pg_shdescription` is shared across all databases of a cluster: there is only one copy of `pg_shdescription` per cluster, not one per database.

Name	Type	References	Description
objoid	oid	any OID column	The OID of the object this description pertains to
classoid	oid	pg_class.oid	The OID of the system catalog this object appears in
description	text		Arbitrary text that serves as the description of this object

Table 45-35. pg_shdescription Columns

45.36. pg_statistic

The catalog `pg_statistic` stores statistical data about the contents of the database. Entries are created by ANALYZE and subsequently used by the query planner. Note that all the statistical data is inherently approximate, even assuming that it is up-to-date.

Normally there is one entry, with `stainherit = false`, for each table column that has been analyzed. If the table has inheritance children, a second entry with `stainherit = true` is also created. This row represents the column's statistics over the inheritance tree, i.e., statistics for the data you'd see with `SELECT` *`column`* `FROM` *`table*`*, whereas the `stainherit = false` row represents the results of `SELECT` *`column`* `FROM ONLY` *`table`*.

`pg_statistic` also stores statistical data about the values of index expressions. These are described as if they were actual data columns; in particular, `starelid` references the index.

No entry is made for an ordinary non-expression index column, however, since it would be redundant with the entry for the underlying table column. Currently, entries for index expressions always have `stainherit = false`.

Since different kinds of statistics might be appropriate for different kinds of data, `pg_statistic` is designed not to assume very much about what sort of statistics it stores. Only extremely general statistics (such as nullness) are given dedicated columns in `pg_statistic`. Everything else is stored in "slots", which are groups of associated columns whose content is identified by a code number in one of the slot's columns. For more information see `src/include/catalog/pg_statistic.h`.

`pg_statistic` should not be readable by the public, since even statistical information about a table's contents might be considered sensitive. (Example: minimum and maximum values of a salary column might be quite interesting.) `pg_stats` (page 75) is a publicly readable view on `pg_statistic` that only exposes information about those tables that are readable by the current user.

Name	Type	References	Description
`starelid`	`oid`	`pg_class.oid`	The table or index that the described column belongs to
`staattnum`	`int2`	`pg_attribute.attnum`	The number of the described column
`stainherit`	`bool`		If true, the stats include inheritance child columns, not just the values in the specified relation
`stanullfrac`	`float4`		The fraction of the column's entries that are null
`stawidth`	`int4`		The average stored width, in bytes, of nonnull entries
`stadistinct`	`float4`		The number of distinct nonnull data values in the column. A value greater than zero is the actual number of distinct values. A value less than zero is the negative of a multiplier for the number of rows in the table; for example, a column in which values appear about twice on the average could be represented by `stadistinct` = -0.5. A zero value means the number of distinct values is unknown.
`stakind`*N*	`int2`		A code number indicating the kind of statistics stored in the *N*th "slot" of the `pg_statistic` row.
`staop`*N*	`oid`	`pg_operator.oid`	An operator used to derive the statistics stored in the *N*th "slot". For example, a histogram slot would show the `<` operator that defines the sort order of the data.
`stanumbers`*N*	`float4[]`		Numerical statistics of the appropriate kind for the *N*th "slot", or null if the slot kind does not involve numerical values.

Name	Type	References	Description
stavaluesN	anyarray		Column data values of the appropriate kind for the Nth "slot", or null if the slot kind does not store any data values. Each array's element values are actually of the specific column's data type, so there is no way to define these columns' type more specifically than anyarray.

Table 45-36. **pg_statistic** Columns

45.37. pg_tablespace

The catalog pg_tablespace stores information about the available tablespaces. Tables can be placed in particular tablespaces to aid administration of disk layout.

Unlike most system catalogs, pg_tablespace is shared across all databases of a cluster: there is only one copy of pg_tablespace per cluster, not one per database.

Name	Type	References	Description
spcname	name		Tablespace name
spcowner	oid	pg_authid.oid	Owner of the tablespace, usually the user who created it
spclocation	text		Location (directory path) of the tablespace
spcacl	aclitem[]		Access privileges; see GRANT and REVOKE for details
spcoptions	text[]		Tablespace-level options, as "keyword=value" strings

Table 45-37. **pg_tablespace** Columns

45.38. pg_trigger

The catalog pg_trigger stores triggers on tables. See CREATE TRIGGER for more information.

Name	Type	References	Description
tgrelid	oid	pg_class.oid	The table this trigger is on
tgname	name		Trigger name (must be unique among triggers of same table)
tgfoid	oid	pg_proc.oid	The function to be called
tgtype	int2		Bit mask identifying trigger conditions
tgenabled	char		Controls in which session_replication_role (Vol.II) modes the trigger fires. O = trigger fires in "origin" and "local" modes, D = trigger is disabled, R = trigger fires in "replica" mode, A = trigger fires always.

Name	Type	References	Description
tgisinternal	bool		True if trigger is internally generated (usually, to enforce the constraint identified by tgconstraint)
tgconstrrelid	oid	pg_class.oid	The table referenced by a referential integrity constraint
tgconstrindid	oid	pg_class.oid	The index supporting a unique, primary key, or referential integrity constraint
tgconstraint	oid	pg_constraint.oid	The pg_constraint entry associated with the trigger, if any
tgdeferrable	bool		True if constraint trigger is deferrable
tginitdeferred	bool		True if constraint trigger is initially deferred
tgnargs	int2		Number of argument strings passed to trigger function
tgattr	int2vector	pg_attribute.attnum	Column numbers, if trigger is column-specific; otherwise an empty array
tgargs	bytea		Argument strings to pass to trigger, each NULL-terminated
tgqual	text		Expression tree (in nodeToString() representation) for the trigger's WHEN condition, or null if none

Table 45-38. `pg_trigger` Columns

Currently, column-specific triggering is supported only for `UPDATE` events, and so `tgattr` is relevant only for that event type. `tgtype` might contain bits for other event types as well, but those are presumed to be table-wide regardless of what is in `tgattr`.

Note: When `tgconstraint` is nonzero, `tgconstrrelid`, `tgconstrindid`, `tgdeferrable`, and `tginitdeferred` are largely redundant with the referenced `pg_constraint` entry. However, it is possible for a non-deferrable trigger to be associated with a deferrable constraint: foreign key constraints can have some deferrable and some non-deferrable triggers.

Note: `pg_class.relhastriggers` must be true if a table has any triggers in this catalog.

45.39. `pg_ts_config`

The `pg_ts_config` catalog contains entries representing text search configurations. A configuration specifies a particular text search parser and a list of dictionaries to use for each of the parser's output token types. The parser is shown in the `pg_ts_config` entry, but the token-to-dictionary mapping is defined by subsidiary entries in `pg_ts_config_map` (page 60).

PostgreSQL's text search features are described at length in *Chapter 12* (Vol.I).

Name	Type	References	Description
cfgname	name		Text search configuration name
cfgnamespace	oid	pg_namespace.oid	The OID of the namespace that contains this configuration
cfgowner	oid	pg_authid.oid	Owner of the configuration
cfgparser	oid	pg_ts_parser.oid	The OID of the text search parser for this configuration

Table 45-39. `pg_ts_config` Columns

45.40. `pg_ts_config_map`

The `pg_ts_config_map` catalog contains entries showing which text search dictionaries should be consulted, and in what order, for each output token type of each text search configuration's parser.

PostgreSQL's text search features are described at length in *Chapter 12* (Vol.I).

Name	Type	References	Description
mapcfg	oid	pg_ts_config.oid	The OID of the `pg_ts_config` entry owning this map entry
maptokentype	integer		A token type emitted by the configuration's parser
mapseqno	integer		Order in which to consult this entry (lower `mapseqno`s first)
mapdict	oid	pg_ts_dict.oid	The OID of the text search dictionary to consult

Table 45-40. `pg_ts_config_map` Columns

45.41. `pg_ts_dict`

The `pg_ts_dict` catalog contains entries defining text search dictionaries. A dictionary depends on a text search template, which specifies all the implementation functions needed; the dictionary itself provides values for the user-settable parameters supported by the template. This division of labor allows dictionaries to be created by unprivileged users. The parameters are specified by a text string `dictinitoption`, whose format and meaning vary depending on the template.

PostgreSQL's text search features are described at length in *Chapter 12* (Vol.I).

Name	Type	References	Description
dictname	name		Text search dictionary name
dictnamespace	oid	pg_namespace.oid	The OID of the namespace that contains this dictionary
dictowner	oid	pg_authid.oid	Owner of the dictionary

Name	Type	References	Description
dicttemplate	oid	pg_ts_template.oid	The OID of the text search template for this dictionary
dictinitoption	text		Initialization option string for the template

Table 45-41. pg_ts_dict Columns

45.42. pg_ts_parser

The pg_ts_parser catalog contains entries defining text search parsers. A parser is responsible for splitting input text into lexemes and assigning a token type to each lexeme. Since a parser must be implemented by C-language-level functions, creation of new parsers is restricted to database superusers.

PostgreSQL's text search features are described at length in *Chapter 12* (Vol.I).

Name	Type	References	Description
prsname	name		Text search parser name
prsnamespace	oid	pg_namespace.oid	The OID of the namespace that contains this parser
prsstart	regproc	pg_proc.oid	OID of the parser's startup function
prstoken	regproc	pg_proc.oid	OID of the parser's next-token function
prsend	regproc	pg_proc.oid	OID of the parser's shutdown function
prsheadline	regproc	pg_proc.oid	OID of the parser's headline function
prslextype	regproc	pg_proc.oid	OID of the parser's lextype function

Table 45-42. pg_ts_parser Columns

45.43. pg_ts_template

The pg_ts_template catalog contains entries defining text search templates. A template is the implementation skeleton for a class of text search dictionaries. Since a template must be implemented by C-language-level functions, creation of new templates is restricted to database superusers.

PostgreSQL's text search features are described at length in *Chapter 12* (Vol.I).

Name	Type	References	Description
tmplname	name		Text search template name
tmplnamespace	oid	pg_namespace.oid	The OID of the namespace that contains this template
tmplinit	regproc	pg_proc.oid	OID of the template's initialization function
tmpllexize	regproc	pg_proc.oid	OID of the template's lexize function

Table 45-43. pg_ts_template Columns

45.44. pg_type

The catalog `pg_type` stores information about data types. Base types and enum types (scalar types) are created with CREATE TYPE, and domains with CREATE DOMAIN. A composite type is automatically created for each table in the database, to represent the row structure of the table. It is also possible to create composite types with `CREATE TYPE AS`.

Name	Type	References	Description
typname	name		Data type name
typnamespace	oid	pg_namespace.oid	The OID of the namespace that contains this type
typowner	oid	pg_authid.oid	Owner of the type
typlen	int2		For a fixed-size type, `typlen` is the number of bytes in the internal representation of the type. But for a variable-length type, `typlen` is negative. -1 indicates a "varlena" type (one that has a length word), -2 indicates a null-terminated C string.
typbyval	bool		`typbyval` determines whether internal routines pass a value of this type by value or by reference. `typbyval` had better be false if `typlen` is not 1, 2, or 4 (or 8 on machines where Datum is 8 bytes). Variable-length types are always passed by reference. Note that `typbyval` can be false even if the length would allow pass-by-value.
typtype	char		`typtype` is `b` for a base type, `c` for a composite type (e.g., a table's row type), `d` for a domain, `e` for an enum type, or `p` for a pseudo-type. See also `typrelid` and `typbasetype`.
typcategory	char		`typcategory` is an arbitrary classification of data types that is used by the parser to determine which implicit casts should be "preferred". See *Table 45-45* (page 65).
typispreferred	bool		True if the type is a preferred cast target within its `typcategory`.
typisdefined	bool		True if the type is defined, false if this is a placeholder entry for a not-yet-defined type. When `typisdefined` is false, nothing except the type name, namespace, and OID can be relied on.
typdelim	char		Character that separates two values of this type when parsing array input. Note that the delimiter is associated with the array element data type, not the array data type.
typrelid	oid	pg_class.oid	If this is a composite type (see `typtype`), then this column points to the `pg_class` entry that defines the corresponding table. (For a free-standing composite

Name	Type	References	Description
			type, the pg_class entry doesn't really represent a table, but it is needed anyway for the type's pg_attribute entries to link to.) Zero for non-composite types.
typelem	oid	pg_type.oid	If typelem is not 0 then it identifies another row in pg_type. The current type can then be subscripted like an array yielding values of type typelem. A "true" array type is variable length (typlen = -1), but some fixed-length (typlen > 0) types also have nonzero typelem, for example name and point. If a fixed-length type has a typelem then its internal representation must be some number of values of the typelem data type with no other data. Variable-length array types have a header defined by the array subroutines.
typarray	oid	pg_type.oid	If typarray is not 0 then it identifies another row in pg_type, which is the "true" array type having this type as element
typinput	regproc	pg_proc.oid	Input conversion function (text format)
typoutput	regproc	pg_proc.oid	Output conversion function (text format)
typreceive	regproc	pg_proc.oid	Input conversion function (binary format), or 0 if none
typsend	regproc	pg_proc.oid	Output conversion function (binary format), or 0 if none
typmodin	regproc	pg_proc.oid	Type modifier input function, or 0 if type does not support modifiers
typmodout	regproc	pg_proc.oid	Type modifier output function, or 0 to use the standard format
typanalyze	regproc	pg_proc.oid	Custom ANALYZE function, or 0 to use the standard function
typalign	char		typalign is the alignment required when storing a value of this type. It applies to storage on disk as well as most representations of the value inside PostgreSQL. When multiple values are stored consecutively, such as in the representation of a complete row on disk, padding is inserted before a datum of this type so that it begins on the specified boundary. The alignment reference is the beginning of the first datum in the sequence. Possible values are: c = char alignment, i.e., no alignment needed. s = short alignment (2 bytes on most machines). i = int alignment (4 bytes on most machines). d = double alignment (8 bytes on many machines, but by no means all).

Name	Type	References	Description
			Note: For types used in system tables, it is critical that the size and alignment defined in `pg_type` agree with the way that the compiler will lay out the column in a structure representing a table row.
`typstorage`	`char`		`typstorage` tells for varlena types (those with `typlen` = -1) if the type is prepared for toasting and what the default strategy for attributes of this type should be. Possible values are `p`: Value must always be stored plain. `e`: Value can be stored in a "secondary" relation (if relation has one, see `pg_class.reltoastrelid`). `m`: Value can be stored compressed inline. `x`: Value can be stored compressed inline or stored in "secondary" storage. Note that `m` columns can also be moved out to secondary storage, but only as a last resort (`e` and `x` columns are moved first).
`typnotnull`	`bool`		`typnotnull` represents a not-null constraint on a type. Used for domains only.
`typbasetype`	`oid`	`pg_type.oid`	If this is a domain (see `typtype`), then `typbasetype` identifies the type that this one is based on. Zero if this type is not a domain.
`typtypmod`	`int4`		Domains use `typtypmod` to record the `typmod` to be applied to their base type (-1 if base type does not use a `typmod`). -1 if this type is not a domain.
`typndims`	`int4`		`typndims` is the number of array dimensions for a domain that is an array (that is, `typbasetype` is an array type; the domain's `typelem` will match the base type's `typelem`). Zero for types other than domains over array types.
`typdefaultbin`	`text`		If `typdefaultbin` is not null, it is the `nodeToString()` representation of a default expression for the type. This is only used for domains.
`typdefault`	`text`		`typdefault` is null if the type has no associated default value. If `typdefaultbin` is not null, `typdefault` must contain a human-readable version of the default expression represented by `typdefaultbin`. If `typdefaultbin` is null and `typdefault` is not, then `typdefault` is the external representation of the type's default value, which might be fed to the type's input converter to produce a constant.

Table 45-44. `pg_type` Columns

Table 45-45 (see below) lists the system-defined values of `typcategory`. Any future additions to this list will also be upper-case ASCII letters. All other ASCII characters are reserved for user-defined categories.

Code	Category
A	Array types
B	Boolean types
C	Composite types
D	Date/time types
E	Enum types
G	Geometric types
I	Network address types
N	Numeric types
P	Pseudo-types
S	String types
T	Timespan types
U	User-defined types
V	Bit-string types
X	`unknown` type

Table 45-45. `typcategory` Codes

45.45. `pg_user_mapping`

The catalog `pg_user_mapping` stores the mappings from local user to remote. Access to this catalog is restricted from normal users, use the view `pg_user_mappings` (page 78) instead.

Name	Type	References	Description
umuser	oid	pg_authid.oid	OID of the local role being mapped, 0 if the user mapping is public
umserver	oid	pg_foreign_server.oid	The OID of the foreign server that contains this mapping
umoptions	text[]		User mapping specific options, as "keyword=value" strings

Table 45-46. `pg_user_mapping` Columns

45.46. System Views

In addition to the system catalogs, PostgreSQL provides a number of built-in views. Some system views provide convenient access to some commonly used queries on the system catalogs. Other views provide access to internal server state.

The information schema (*Chapter 34* - Vol.II) provides an alternative set of views which overlap the functionality of the system views. Since the information schema is SQL-standard whereas the views described here are PostgreSQL-specific, it's usually better to use the information schema if it provides all the information you need.

Table 45-47 (see below) lists the system views described here. More detailed documentation of each view follows below. There are some additional views that provide access to the results of the statistics collector; they are described in *Table 27-1* (Vol.II).

Except where noted, all the views described here are read-only.

View Name	Purpose
pg_cursors	open cursors
pg_group	groups of database users
pg_indexes	indexes
pg_locks	currently held locks
pg_prepared_statements	prepared statements
pg_prepared_xacts	prepared transactions
pg_roles	database roles
pg_rules	rules
pg_settings	parameter settings
pg_shadow	database users
pg_stats	planner statistics
pg_tables	tables
pg_timezone_abbrevs	time zone abbreviations
pg_timezone_names	time zone names
pg_user	database users
pg_user_mappings	user mappings
pg_views	views

Table 45-47. System Views

45.47. `pg_cursors`

The `pg_cursors` view lists the cursors that are currently available. Cursors can be defined in several ways:

- via the DECLARE statement in SQL
- via the Bind message in the frontend/backend protocol, as described in *Section 46.2.3* (page 86)
- via the Server Programming Interface (SPI), as described in *Section 43.1* (Vol.II)

The `pg_cursors` view displays cursors created by any of these means. Cursors only exist for the duration of the transaction that defines them, unless they have been declared `WITH HOLD`. Therefore non-holdable cursors are only present in the view until the end of their creating transaction.

Note

Cursors are used internally to implement some of the components of PostgreSQL, such as procedural languages. Therefore, the `pg_cursors` view might include cursors that have not been explicitly created by the user.

Name	Type	Description
`name`	`text`	The name of the cursor
`statement`	`text`	The verbatim query string submitted to declare this cursor
`is_holdable`	`boolean`	`true` if the cursor is holdable (that is, it can be accessed after the transaction that declared the cursor has committed); `false` otherwise
`is_binary`	`boolean`	`true` if the cursor was declared `BINARY`; `false` otherwise
`is_scrollable`	`boolean`	`true` if the cursor is scrollable (that is, it allows rows to be retrieved in a nonsequential manner); `false` otherwise
`creation_time`	`timestamptz`	The time at which the cursor was declared

Table 45-48. `pg_cursors` Columns

The `pg_cursors` view is read only.

45.48. `pg_group`

The view `pg_group` exists for backwards compatibility: it emulates a catalog that existed in PostgreSQL before version 8.1. It shows the names and members of all roles that are marked as not `rolcanlogin`, which is an approximation to the set of roles that are being used as groups.

Name	Type	References	Description
groname	name	pg_authid.rolname	Name of the group
grosysid	oid	pg_authid.oid	ID of this group
grolist	oid[]	pg_authid.oid	An array containing the IDs of the roles in this group

Table 45-49. pg_group Columns

45.49. pg_indexes

The view `pg_indexes` provides access to useful information about each index in the database.

Name	Type	References	Description
schemaname	name	pg_namespace.nspname	Name of schema containing table and index
tablename	name	pg_class.relname	Name of table the index is for
indexname	name	pg_class.relname	Name of index
tablespace	name	pg_tablespace.spcname	Name of tablespace containing index (null if default for database)
indexdef	text		Index definition (a reconstructed `CREATE INDEX` command)

Table 45-50. pg_indexes Columns

45.50. pg_locks

The view `pg_locks` provides access to information about the locks held by open transactions within the database server. See *Chapter 13* (Vol.I) for more discussion of locking.

`pg_locks` contains one row per active lockable object, requested lock mode, and relevant transaction. Thus, the same lockable object might appear many times, if multiple transactions are holding or waiting for locks on it. However, an object that currently has no locks on it will not appear at all.

There are several distinct types of lockable objects: whole relations (e.g., tables), individual pages of relations, individual tuples of relations, transaction IDs (both virtual and permanent IDs), and general database objects (identified by class OID and object OID, in the same way as in `pg_description` or `pg_depend`). Also, the right to extend a relation is represented as a separate lockable object.

Name	Type	References	Description
locktype	text		type of the lockable object: `relation`, `extend`, `page`, `tuple`, `transactionid`, `virtualxid`, `object`, `userlock`, or `advisory`

Name	Type	References	Description
database	oid	pg_database.oid	OID of the database in which the object exists, or zero if the object is a shared object, or null if the object is a transaction ID
relation	oid	pg_class.oid	OID of the relation, or null if the object is not a relation or part of a relation
page	integer		Page number within the relation, or null if the object is not a tuple or relation page
tuple	smallint		Tuple number within the page, or null if the object is not a tuple
virtualxid	text		Virtual ID of a transaction, or null if the object is not a virtual transaction ID
transactionid	xid		ID of a transaction, or null if the object is not a transaction ID
classid	oid	pg_class.oid	OID of the system catalog containing the object, or null if the object is not a general database object
objid	oid	any OID column	OID of the object within its system catalog, or null if the object is not a general database object. For advisory locks it is used to distinguish the two key spaces (1 for an int8 key, 2 for two int4 keys).
objsubid	smallint		For a table column, this is the column number (the classid and objid refer to the table itself). For all other object types, this column is zero. Null if the object is not a general database object
virtualtransaction	text		Virtual ID of the transaction that is holding or awaiting this lock
pid	integer		Process ID of the server process holding or awaiting this lock. Null if the lock is held by a prepared transaction.
mode	text		Name of the lock mode held or desired by this process (see *Section 13.3.1* - Vol.I)
granted	boolean		True if lock is held, false if lock is awaited

Table 45-51. `pg_locks` Columns

`granted` is true in a row representing a lock held by the indicated transaction. False indicates that this transaction is currently waiting to acquire this lock, which implies that some other transaction is holding a conflicting lock mode on the same lockable object. The waiting transaction will sleep until the other lock is released (or a deadlock situation is detected). A single transaction can be waiting to acquire at most one lock at a time.

Every transaction holds an exclusive lock on its virtual transaction ID for its entire duration. If a permanent ID is assigned to the transaction (which normally happens only if the transaction changes the state of the database), it also holds an exclusive lock on its permanent transaction ID until it ends. When one transaction finds it necessary to wait specifically for another transaction, it does so by attempting to acquire share lock on the other transaction ID (either virtual or permanent ID depending on the situation). That will succeed only when the other transaction terminates and releases its locks.

Although tuples are a lockable type of object, information about row-level locks is stored on disk, not in memory, and therefore row-level locks normally do not appear in this view. If a transaction is waiting for a row-level lock, it will usually appear in the view as waiting for the permanent transaction ID of the current holder of that row lock.

Advisory locks can be acquired on keys consisting of either a single `bigint` value or two integer values. A `bigint` key is displayed with its high-order half in the `classid` column, its low-order half in the `objid` column, and `objsubid` equal to 1. Integer keys are displayed with the first key in the `classid` column, the second key in the `objid` column, and `objsubid` equal to 2. The actual meaning of the keys is up to the user. Advisory locks are local to each database, so the `database` column is meaningful for an advisory lock.

When the `pg_locks` view is accessed, the internal lock manager data structures are momentarily locked, and a copy is made for the view to display. This ensures that the view produces a consistent set of results, while not blocking normal lock manager operations longer than necessary. Nonetheless there could be some impact on database performance if this view is frequently accessed.

`pg_locks` provides a global view of all locks in the database cluster, not only those relevant to the current database. Although its `relation` column can be joined against `pg_class.oid` to identify locked relations, this will only work correctly for relations in the current database (those for which the `database` column is either the current database's OID or zero).

The `pid` column can be joined to the `procpid` column of the `pg_stat_activity` view to get more information on the session holding or waiting to hold each lock. Also, if you are using prepared transactions, the `transaction` column can be joined to the `transaction` column of the `pg_prepared_xacts` view to get more information on prepared transactions that hold locks. (A prepared transaction can never be waiting for a lock, but it continues to hold the locks it acquired while running.)

45.51. pg_prepared_statements

The `pg_prepared_statements` view displays all the prepared statements that are available in the current session. See PREPARE for more information about prepared statements.

pg_prepared_statements contains one row for each prepared statement. Rows are added to the view when a new prepared statement is created and removed when a prepared statement is released (for example, via the DEALLOCATE command).

Name	Type	Description
name	text	The identifier of the prepared statement
statement	text	The query string submitted by the client to create this prepared statement. For prepared statements created via SQL, this is the PREPARE statement submitted by the client. For prepared statements created via the frontend/backend protocol, this is the text of the prepared statement itself.
prepare_time	timestamptz	The time at which the prepared statement was created
parameter_types	regtype[]	The expected parameter types for the prepared statement in the form of an array of regtype. The OID corresponding to an element of this array can be obtained by casting the regtype value to oid.
from_sql	boolean	true if the prepared statement was created via the PREPARE SQL statement; false if the statement was prepared via the frontend/backend protocol

Table 45-52. pg_prepared_statements Columns

The pg_prepared_statements view is read only.

45.52. pg_prepared_xacts

The view pg_prepared_xacts displays information about transactions that are currently prepared for two-phase commit (see PREPARE TRANSACTION for details).

pg_prepared_xacts contains one row per prepared transaction. An entry is removed when the transaction is committed or rolled back.

Name	Type	References	Description
transaction	xid		Numeric transaction identifier of the prepared transaction
gid	text		Global transaction identifier that was assigned to the transaction
prepared	timestamp with time zone		Time at which the transaction was prepared for commit
owner	name	pg_authid.rolname	Name of the user that executed the transaction
database	name	pg_database.datname	Name of the database in which the transaction was executed

Table 45-53. pg_prepared_xacts Columns

When the pg_prepared_xacts view is accessed, the internal transaction manager data structures are momentarily locked, and a copy is made for the view to display. This ensures that the view produces a consistent set of results, while not blocking normal operations longer than necessary. Nonetheless there could be some impact on database performance if this view is frequently accessed.

45.53. pg_roles

The view pg_roles provides access to information about database roles. This is simply a publicly readable view of pg_authid (page 34) that blanks out the password field.

This view explicitly exposes the OID column of the underlying table, since that is needed to do joins to other catalogs.

Name	Type	References	Description
rolname	name		Role name
rolsuper	bool		Role has superuser privileges
rolinherit	bool		Role automatically inherits privileges of roles it is a member of
rolcreaterole	bool		Role can create more roles
rolcreatedb	bool		Role can create databases
rolcatupdate	bool		Role can update system catalogs directly. (Even a superuser cannot do this unless this column is true.)
rolcanlogin	bool		Role can log in. That is, this role can be given as the initial session authorization identifier
rolconnlimit	int4		For roles that can log in, this sets maximum number of concurrent connections this role can make. -1 means no limit.
rolpassword	text		Not the password (always reads as ********)
rolvaliduntil	timestamptz		Password expiry time (only used for password authentication); null if no expiration
oid	oid	pg_authid.oid	ID of role

Table 45-54. pg_roles Columns

45.54. pg_rules

The view pg_rules provides access to useful information about query rewrite rules.

Name	Type	References	Description
schemaname	name	pg_namespace.nspname	Name of schema containing table
tablename	name	pg_class.relname	Name of table the rule is for

Name	Type	References	Description
rulename	name	pg_rewrite.rulename	Name of rule
definition	text		Rule definition (a reconstructed creation command)

Table 45-55. pg_rules Columns

The pg_rules view excludes the ON SELECT rules of views; those can be seen in pg_views.

45.55. pg_settings

The view pg_settings provides access to run-time parameters of the server. It is essentially an alternative interface to the SHOW and SET commands. It also provides access to some facts about each parameter that are not directly available from SHOW, such as minimum and maximum values.

Name	Type	Description
name	text	Run-time configuration parameter name
setting	text	Current value of the parameter
unit	text	Implicit unit of the parameter
category	text	Logical group of the parameter
short_desc	text	A brief description of the parameter
extra_desc	text	Additional, more detailed, description of the parameter
context	text	Context required to set the parameter's value
vartype	text	Parameter type (bool, enum, integer, real , or string)
source	text	Source of the current parameter value
min_val	text	Minimum allowed value of the parameter (null for non-numeric values)
max_val	text	Maximum allowed value of the parameter (null for non-numeric values)
enumvals	text[]	Allowed values of an enum parameter (null for non-enum values)
boot_val	text	Parameter value assumed at server startup if the parameter is not otherwise set
reset_val	text	Value that RESET would reset the parameter to in the current session
sourcefile	text	Configuration file the current value was set in (null for values set from sources other than configuration files, or when examined by a non-superuser); helpful when using include directives in configuration files
sourceline	integer	Line number within the configuration file the current value was set at (null for values set from sources other than configuration files, or when examined by a non-superuser)

Table 45-56. pg_settings Columns

The pg_settings view cannot be inserted into or deleted from, but it can be updated. An UPDATE applied to a row of pg_settings is equivalent to executing the SET command on that named parameter. The change only affects the value used by the current session. If an UPDATE is issued within a transaction that is later aborted, the effects of the UPDATE command disappear when the transaction is rolled back. Once the surrounding transaction is committed, the effects will persist until the end of the session, unless overridden by another UPDATE or SET.

45.56. pg_shadow

The view pg_shadow exists for backwards compatibility: it emulates a catalog that existed in PostgreSQL before version 8.1. It shows properties of all roles that are marked as rolcanlogin.

The view pg_shadow exists for backwards compatibility: it emulates a catalog that existed in PostgreSQL before version 8.1. It shows properties of all roles that are marked as rolcanlogin in pg_authid.

The name stems from the fact that this table should not be readable by the public since it contains passwords. pg_user (page 77) is a publicly readable view on pg_shadow that blanks out the password field.

Name	Type	References	Description
usename	name	pg_authid.rolname	User name
usesysid	oid	pg_authid.oid	ID of this user
usecreatedb	bool		User can create databases
usesuper	bool		User is a superuser
usecatupd	bool		User can update system catalogs. (Even a superuser cannot do this unless this column is true.)
passwd	text		Password (possibly encrypted); null if none. See pg_authid for details of how encrypted passwords are stored.
valuntil	abstime		Password expiry time (only used for password authentication)
useconfig	text[]		Session defaults for run-time configuration variables

Table 45-57. pg_shadow Columns

45.57. pg_stats

The view pg_stats provides access to the information stored in the pg_statistic (page 56) catalog. This view allows access only to rows of pg_statistic that correspond to tables the user has permission to read, and therefore it is safe to allow public read access to this view.

`pg_stats` is also designed to present the information in a more readable format than the underlying catalog - at the cost that its schema must be extended whenever new slot types are defined for `pg_statistic`.

Name	Type	References	Description
schemaname	name	pg_namespace.nspname	Name of schema containing table
tablename	name	pg_class.relname	Name of table
attname	name	pg_attribute.attname	Name of the column described by this row
inherited	bool		If true, this row includes inheritance child columns, not just the values in the specified table
null_frac	real		Fraction of column entries that are null
avg_width	integer		Average width in bytes of column's entries
n_distinct	real		If greater than zero, the estimated number of distinct values in the column. If less than zero, the negative of the number of distinct values divided by the number of rows. (The negated form is used when ANALYZE believes that the number of distinct values is likely to increase as the table grows; the positive form is used when the column seems to have a fixed number of possible values.) For example, -1 indicates a unique column in which the number of distinct values is the same as the number of rows.
most_common_vals	anyarray		A list of the most common values in the column. (Null if no values seem to be more common than any others.) For some datatypes such as `tsvector`, this is a list of the most common element values rather than values of the type itself.
most_common_freqs	real[]		A list of the frequencies of the most common values or elements, i.e., number of occurrences of each divided by total number of rows. (Null when `most_common_vals` is.) For some datatypes such as `tsvector`, it can also store some additional information, making it longer than the `most_common_vals` array.
histogram_bounds	anyarray		A list of values that divide the column's values into groups of approximately equal population. The values in `most_common_vals`, if present, are omitted from this histogram calculation. (This column is Null if the column data type

Name	Type	References	Description
			does not have a < operator or if the `most_common_vals` list accounts for the entire population.)
`correlation`	`real`		Statistical correlation between physical row ordering and logical ordering of the column values. This ranges from -1 to +1. When the value is near -1 or +1, an index scan on the column will be estimated to be cheaper than when it is near zero, due to reduction of random access to the disk. (This column is Null if the column data type does not have a < operator.)

Table 45-58. `pg_stats` Columns

The maximum number of entries in the `most_common_vals` and `histogram_bounds` arrays can be set on a column-by-column basis using the `ALTER TABLE SET STATISTICS` command, or globally by setting the `default_statistics_target` (Vol.II) run-time parameter.

45.58. `pg_tables`

The view `pg_tables` provides access to useful information about each table in the database.

Name	Type	References	Description
`schemaname`	`name`	`pg_namespace.nspname`	Name of schema containing table
`tablename`	`name`	`pg_class.relname`	Name of table
`tableowner`	`name`	`pg_authid.rolname`	Name of table's owner
`tablespace`	`name`	`pg_tablespace.spcname`	Name of tablespace containing table (Null if default for database)
`hasindexes`	`boolean`	`pg_class.relhasindex`	True if table has (or recently had) any indexes
`hasrules`	`boolean`	`pg_class.relhasrules`	True if table has (or once had) rules
`hastriggers`	`boolean`	`pg_class.relhastriggers`	True if table has (or once had) triggers

Table 45-59. `pg_tables` Columns

45.59. `pg_timezone_abbrevs`

The view `pg_timezone_abbrevs` provides a list of time zone abbreviations that are currently recognized by the datetime input routines. The contents of this view change when the `timezone_abbreviations` (Vol.II) run-time parameter is modified.

Name	Type	Description
abbrev	text	Time zone abbreviation
utc_offset	interval	Offset from UTC (positive means east of Greenwich)
is_dst	boolean	True if this is a daylight-savings abbreviation

Table 45-60. pg_timezone_abbrevs Columns

45.60. pg_timezone_names

The view pg_timezone_names provides a list of time zone names that are recognized by SET TIMEZONE, along with their associated abbreviations, UTC offsets, and daylight-savings status. Unlike the abbreviations shown in pg_timezone_abbrevs (page 77) , many of these names imply a set of daylight-savings transition date rules. Therefore, the associated information changes across local DST boundaries. The displayed information is computed based on the current value of CURRENT_TIMESTAMP.

Name	Type	Description
name	text	Time zone name
abbrev	text	Time zone abbreviation
utc_offset	interval	Offset from UTC (positive means east of Greenwich)
is_dst	boolean	True if currently observing daylight savings

Table 45-61. pg_timezone_names Columns

45.61. pg_user

The view pg_user provides access to information about database users. This is simply a publicly readable view of pg_shadow (page 74) that blanks out the password field.

Name	Type	Description
usename	name	User name
usesysid	int4	User ID (arbitrary number used to reference this user)
usecreatedb	bool	User can create databases
usesuper	bool	User is a superuser
usecatupd	bool	User can update system catalogs. (Even a superuser cannot do this unless this column is true.)
passwd	text	Not the password (always reads as ********)
valuntil	abstime	Password expiry time (only used for password authentication)
useconfig	text[]	Session defaults for run-time configuration variables

Table 45-62. pg_user Columns

45.62. pg_user_mappings

The view pg_user_mappings provides access to information about user mappings. This is essentially a publicly readable view of pg_user_mapping (page 65) that leaves out the options field if the user has no rights to use it.

Table 44-61. pg_user_mappings Columns

Name	Type	References	Description
umid	oid	pg_user_mapping.oid	OID of the user mapping
srvid	oid	pg_foreign_server.oid	The OID of the foreign server that contains this mapping
srvname	text		Name of the foreign server
umuser	oid	pg_authid.oid	OID of the local role being mapped, 0 if the user mapping is public
usename	name		Name of the local user to be mapped
umoptions	text[]		User mapping specific options, as "keyword=value" strings, if the current user is the owner of the foreign server, else null

45.63. pg_views

The view pg_views provides access to useful information about each view in the database.

Table 44-62. pg_views Columns

Name	Type	References	Description
schemaname	name	pg_namespace.nspname	Name of schema containing view
viewname	name	pg_class.relname	Name of view
viewowner	name	pg_authid.rolname	Name of view's owner
definition	text		View definition (a reconstructed SELECT query)

Chapter 46.
Frontend/Backend Protocol

PostgreSQL uses a message-based protocol for communication between frontends and backends (clients and servers). The protocol is supported over TCP/IP and also over Unix-domain sockets. Port number 5432 has been registered with IANA as the customary TCP port number for servers supporting this protocol, but in practice any non-privileged port number can be used.

This document describes version 3.0 of the protocol, implemented in PostgreSQL 7.4 and later. For descriptions of the earlier protocol versions, see previous releases of the PostgreSQL documentation. A single server can support multiple protocol versions. The initial startup-request message tells the server which protocol version the client is attempting to use, and then the server follows that protocol if it is able.

In order to serve multiple clients efficiently, the server launches a new "backend" process for each client. In the current implementation, a new child process is created immediately after an incoming connection is detected. This is transparent to the protocol, however. For purposes of the protocol, the terms "backend" and "server" are interchangeable; likewise "frontend" and "client" are interchangeable.

46.1. Overview

The protocol has separate phases for startup and normal operation. In the startup phase, the frontend opens a connection to the server and authenticates itself to the satisfaction of the server. (This might involve a single message, or multiple messages depending on the authentication method being used.) If all goes well, the server then sends status information to the frontend, and finally enters normal operation. Except for the initial startup-request message, this part of the protocol is driven by the server.

During normal operation, the frontend sends queries and other commands to the backend, and the backend sends back query results and other responses. There are a few cases (such as `NOTIFY`) wherein the backend will send unsolicited messages, but for the most part this portion of a session is driven by frontend requests.

Termination of the session is normally by frontend choice, but can be forced by the backend in certain cases. In any case, when the backend closes the connection, it will roll back any open (incomplete) transaction before exiting.

Within normal operation, SQL commands can be executed through either of two sub-protocols. In the "simple query" protocol, the frontend just sends a textual query string, which is parsed and immediately executed by the backend. In the "extended query" protocol, processing of queries is separated into multiple steps: parsing, binding of parameter values, and execution. This offers flexibility and performance benefits, at the cost of extra complexity.

Normal operation has additional sub-protocols for special operations such as `COPY`.

46.1.1. Messaging Overview

All communication is through a stream of messages. The first byte of a message identifies the message type, and the next four bytes specify the length of the rest of the message (this length count includes itself, but not the message-type byte). The remaining contents of the message are determined by the message type. For historical reasons, the very first message sent by the client (the startup message) has no initial message-type byte.

To avoid losing synchronization with the message stream, both servers and clients typically read an entire message into a buffer (using the byte count) before attempting to process its contents. This allows easy recovery if an error is detected while processing the contents. In extreme situations (such as not having enough memory to buffer the message), the receiver can use the byte count to determine how much input to skip before it resumes reading messages.

Conversely, both servers and clients must take care never to send an incomplete message. This is commonly done by marshaling the entire message in a buffer before beginning to send it. If a communications failure occurs partway through sending or receiving a message, the only sensible response is to abandon the connection, since there is little hope of recovering message-boundary synchronization.

46.1.2. Extended Query Overview

In the extended-query protocol, execution of SQL commands is divided into multiple steps. The state retained between steps is represented by two types of objects: *prepared statements* and *portals*. A prepared statement represents the result of parsing, semantic analysis, and (optionally) planning of a textual query string. A prepared statement is not necessarily ready to execute, because it might lack specific values for *parameters*. A portal represents a ready-to-execute or already-partially-executed statement, with any missing parameter values filled in. (For `SELECT` statements, a portal is equivalent to an open cursor, but we choose to use a different term since cursors don't handle non-`SELECT` statements.)

The overall execution cycle consists of a *parse* step, which creates a prepared statement from a textual query string; a *bind* step, which creates a portal given a prepared statement and values for any needed parameters; and an *execute* step that runs a portal's query. In the case of a query that returns rows (`SELECT`, `SHOW`, etc), the execute step can be told to fetch only a limited number of rows, so that multiple execute steps might be needed to complete the operation.

The backend can keep track of multiple prepared statements and portals (but note that these exist only within a session, and are never shared across sessions). Existing prepared statements and portals are referenced by names assigned when they were created. In addition, an "unnamed" prepared statement and portal exist. Although these behave largely the same as named objects, operations on them are optimized for the case of executing a query only once and then discarding it, whereas operations on named objects are optimized on the expectation of multiple uses.

46.1.3. Formats and Format Codes

Data of a particular data type might be transmitted in any of several different *formats*. As of PostgreSQL 7.4 the only supported formats are "text" and "binary", but the protocol makes provision for future extensions. The desired format for any value is specified by a *format code*. Clients can specify a format code for each transmitted parameter value and for each column of a query result. Text has format code zero, binary has format code one, and all other format codes are reserved for future definition.

The text representation of values is whatever strings are produced and accepted by the input/output conversion functions for the particular data type. In the transmitted representation, there is no trailing null character; the frontend must add one to received values if it wants to process them as C strings. (The text format does not allow embedded nulls, by the way.)

Binary representations for integers use network byte order (most significant byte first). For other data types consult the documentation or source code to learn about the binary representation. Keep in mind that binary representations for complex data types might change across server versions; the text format is usually the more portable choice.

46.2. Message Flow

This section describes the message flow and the semantics of each message type. (Details of the exact representation of each message appear in *Section 46.5* - page 97.) There are several different sub-protocols depending on the state of the connection: start-up, query, function call, `COPY`, and termination. There are also special provisions for asynchronous operations (including notification responses and command cancellation), which can occur at any time after the start-up phase.

46.2.1. Start-Up

To begin a session, a frontend opens a connection to the server and sends a startup message. This message includes the names of the user and of the database the user wants to connect to; it also identifies the particular protocol version to be used. (Optionally, the startup message can include additional settings for run-time parameters.) The server then uses this information and the contents of its configuration files (such as `pg_hba.conf`) to determine whether the connection is provisionally acceptable, and what additional authentication is required (if any).

The server then sends an appropriate authentication request message, to which the frontend must reply with an appropriate authentication response message (such as a password). For all authentication methods except GSSAPI and SSPI, there is at most one request and one response. In some methods, no response at all is needed from the frontend, and so no authentication request occurs. For GSSAPI and SSPI, multiple exchanges of packets may be needed to complete the authentication.

The authentication cycle ends with the server either rejecting the connection attempt (ErrorResponse), or sending AuthenticationOk.

The possible messages from the server in this phase are:

ErrorResponse

> The connection attempt has been rejected. The server then immediately closes the connection.

AuthenticationOk

> The authentication exchange is successfully completed.

AuthenticationKerberosV5

> The frontend must now take part in a Kerberos V5 authentication dialog (not described here, part of the Kerberos specification) with the server. If this is successful, the server responds with an AuthenticationOk, otherwise it responds with an ErrorResponse.

AuthenticationCleartextPassword

> The frontend must now send a PasswordMessage containing the password in clear-text form. If this is the correct password, the server responds with an AuthenticationOk, otherwise it responds with an ErrorResponse.

AuthenticationMD5Password

> The frontend must now send a PasswordMessage containing the password encrypted via MD5, using the 4-character salt specified in the

AuthenticationMD5Password message. If this is the correct password, the server responds with an AuthenticationOk, otherwise it responds with an ErrorResponse.

AuthenticationSCMCredential

This response is only possible for local Unix-domain connections on platforms that support SCM credential messages. The frontend must issue an SCM credential message and then send a single data byte. (The contents of the data byte are uninteresting; it's only used to ensure that the server waits long enough to receive the credential message.) If the credential is acceptable, the server responds with an AuthenticationOk, otherwise it responds with an ErrorResponse.

AuthenticationGSS

The frontend must now initiate a GSSAPI negotiation. The frontend will send a PasswordMessage with the first part of the GSSAPI data stream in response to this. If further messages are needed, the server will respond with AuthenticationGSSContinue.

AuthenticationSSPI

The frontend must now initiate a SSPI negotiation. The frontend will send a PasswordMessage with the first part of the SSPI data stream in response to this. If further messages are needed, the server will respond with AuthenticationGSSContinue.

AuthenticationGSSContinue

This message contains the response data from the previous step of GSSAPI or SSPI negotiation (AuthenticationGSS, AuthenticationSSPI or a previous AuthenticationGSSContinue). If the GSSAPI or SSPI data in this message indicates more data is needed to complete the authentication, the frontend must send that data as another PasswordMessage. If GSSAPI or SSPI authentication is completed by this message, the server will next send AuthenticationOk to indicate successful authentication or ErrorResponse to indicate failure.

If the frontend does not support the authentication method requested by the server, then it should immediately close the connection.

After having received AuthenticationOk, the frontend must wait for further messages from the server. In this phase a backend process is being started, and the frontend is just an interested bystander. It is still possible for the startup attempt to fail (ErrorResponse), but in the normal case the backend will send some ParameterStatus messages, BackendKeyData, and finally ReadyForQuery.

During this phase the backend will attempt to apply any additional run-time parameter settings that were given in the startup message. If successful, these values become session defaults. An error causes ErrorResponse and exit.

The possible messages from the backend in this phase are:

BackendKeyData

> This message provides secret-key data that the frontend must save if it wants to be able to issue cancel requests later. The frontend should not respond to this message, but should continue listening for a ReadyForQuery message.

ParameterStatus

> This message informs the frontend about the current (initial) setting of backend parameters, such as `client_encoding` (Vol.II) or `DateStyle` (Vol.II). The frontend can ignore this message, or record the settings for its future use; see *Section 46.2.6* (page 92) for more details. The frontend should not respond to this message, but should continue listening for a ReadyForQuery message.

ReadyForQuery

> Start-up is completed. The frontend can now issue commands.

ErrorResponse

> Start-up failed. The connection is closed after sending this message.

NoticeResponse

> A warning message has been issued. The frontend should display the message but continue listening for ReadyForQuery or ErrorResponse.

The ReadyForQuery message is the same one that the backend will issue after each command cycle. Depending on the coding needs of the frontend, it is reasonable to consider ReadyForQuery as starting a command cycle, or to consider ReadyForQuery as ending the start-up phase and each subsequent command cycle.

46.2.2. Simple Query

A simple query cycle is initiated by the frontend sending a Query message to the backend. The message includes an SQL command (or commands) expressed as a text string. The backend then sends one or more response messages depending on the contents of the query command string, and finally a ReadyForQuery response message. ReadyForQuery informs the frontend that it can safely send a new command. (It is not actually necessary for the frontend to wait for ReadyForQuery before issuing another command, but the frontend must then take responsibility for figuring out what happens if the earlier command fails and already-issued later commands succeed.)

The possible response messages from the backend are:

CommandComplete

An SQL command completed normally.

CopyInResponse

The backend is ready to copy data from the frontend to a table; see *Section 46.2.5* (page 91).

CopyOutResponse

The backend is ready to copy data from a table to the frontend; see *Section 46.2.5* (page 91).

RowDescription

Indicates that rows are about to be returned in response to a `SELECT`, `FETCH`, etc query. The contents of this message describe the column layout of the rows. This will be followed by a DataRow message for each row being returned to the frontend.

DataRow

One of the set of rows returned by a `SELECT` , `FETCH`, etc query.

EmptyQueryResponse

An empty query string was recognized.

ErrorResponse

An error has occurred.

ReadyForQuery

Processing of the query string is complete. A separate message is sent to indicate this because the query string might contain multiple SQL commands. (CommandComplete marks the end of processing one SQL command, not the whole string.) ReadyForQuery will always be sent, whether processing terminates successfully or with an error.

NoticeResponse

A warning message has been issued in relation to the query. Notices are in addition to other responses, i.e., the backend will continue processing the command.

The response to a `SELECT` query (or other queries that return row sets, such as `EXPLAIN` or `SHOW`) normally consists of RowDescription, zero or more DataRow messages, and then CommandComplete. `COPY` to or from the frontend invokes special protocol as described in *Section 46.2.5* (page 91). All other query types normally produce only a CommandComplete message.

Since a query string could contain several queries (separated by semicolons), there might be several such response sequences before the backend finishes processing the query string. ReadyForQuery is issued when the entire string has been processed and the backend is ready to accept a new query string.

If a completely empty (no contents other than whitespace) query string is received, the response is EmptyQueryResponse followed by ReadyForQuery.

In the event of an error, ErrorResponse is issued followed by ReadyForQuery. All further processing of the query string is aborted by ErrorResponse (even if more queries remained in it). Note that this might occur partway through the sequence of messages generated by an individual query.

In simple Query mode, the format of retrieved values is always text, except when the given command is a `FETCH` from a cursor declared with the `BINARY` option. In that case, the retrieved values are in binary format. The format codes given in the RowDescription message tell which format is being used.

A frontend must be prepared to accept ErrorResponse and NoticeResponse messages whenever it is expecting any other type of message. See also *Section 46.2.6* (page 92) concerning messages that the backend might generate due to outside events.

Recommended practice is to code frontends in a state-machine style that will accept any message type at any time that it could make sense, rather than wiring in assumptions about the exact sequence of messages.

46.2.3. Extended Query

The extended query protocol breaks down the above-described simple query protocol into multiple steps. The results of preparatory steps can be re-used multiple times for improved efficiency. Furthermore, additional features are available, such as the possibility of supplying data values as separate parameters instead of having to insert them directly into a query string.

In the extended protocol, the frontend first sends a Parse message, which contains a textual query string, optionally some information about data types of parameter placeholders, and the name of a destination prepared-statement object (an empty string selects the unnamed prepared statement). The response is either ParseComplete or ErrorResponse. Parameter data types can be specified by OID; if not given, the parser attempts to infer the data types in the same way as it would do for untyped literal string constants.

Note

A parameter data type can be left unspecified by setting it to zero, or by making the array of parameter type OIDs shorter than the number of parameter symbols (`$` *n*) used in the query string. Another special case is that a parameter's type can be specified as `void` (that is, the OID of the `void` pseudotype). This is meant to allow parameter symbols to be used for function parameters that are actually OUT parameters. Ordinarily there is no context in which a `void` parameter could be used, but if such a parameter symbol appears in a function's parameter list, it is effectively ignored. For example, a function call such as `foo($1,$2,$3,$4)` could match a function with two IN and two OUT arguments, if `$3` and `$4` are specified as having type `void`.

Note

The query string contained in a Parse message cannot include more than one SQL statement; else a syntax error is reported. This restriction does not exist in the simple-query protocol, but it does exist in the extended protocol, because allowing prepared statements or portals to contain multiple commands would complicate the protocol unduly.

If successfully created, a named prepared-statement object lasts till the end of the current session, unless explicitly destroyed. An unnamed prepared statement lasts only until the next Parse statement specifying the unnamed statement as destination is issued. (Note that a simple Query message also destroys the unnamed statement.) Named prepared statements must be explicitly closed before they can be redefined by a Parse message, but this is not required for the unnamed statement. Named prepared statements can also be created and accessed at the SQL command level, using `PREPARE` and `EXECUTE`.

Once a prepared statement exists, it can be readied for execution using a Bind message. The Bind message gives the name of the source prepared statement (empty string denotes the unnamed prepared statement), the name of the destination portal (empty string denotes the unnamed portal), and the values to use for any parameter placeholders present in the prepared statement. The supplied parameter set must match those needed by the prepared statement. (If you declared any `void` parameters in the Parse message, pass NULL values for them in the Bind message.) Bind also specifies the format to use for any data returned by the query; the format can be specified overall, or per-column. The response is either BindComplete or ErrorResponse.

Note

The choice between text and binary output is determined by the format codes given in Bind, regardless of the SQL command involved. The `BINARY` attribute in cursor declarations is irrelevant when using extended query protocol.

Query planning for named prepared-statement objects occurs when the Parse message is processed. If a query will be repeatedly executed with different parameters, it might be beneficial to send a single Parse message containing a parameterized query, followed by multiple Bind and Execute messages. This will avoid replanning the query on each execution.

The unnamed prepared statement is likewise planned during Parse processing if the Parse message defines no parameters. But if there are parameters, query planning occurs every time Bind parameters are supplied. This allows the planner to make use of the actual values of the parameters provided by each Bind message, rather than use generic estimates.

Note

Query plans generated from a parameterized query might be less efficient than query plans generated from an equivalent query with actual parameter values substituted. The query planner cannot make decisions based on actual parameter values (for example, index selectivity) when planning a parameterized query assigned to a named prepared-statement object. This possible penalty is avoided when using the unnamed statement, since it is not planned until actual parameter values are available. The cost is that planning must occur afresh for each Bind, even if the query stays the same.

If successfully created, a named portal object lasts till the end of the current transaction, unless explicitly destroyed. An unnamed portal is destroyed at the end of the transaction, or as soon as the next Bind statement specifying the unnamed portal as destination is issued. (Note that a simple Query message also destroys the unnamed portal.) Named portals must be explicitly closed before they can be redefined by a Bind message, but this is not required for the unnamed portal. Named portals can also be created and accessed at the SQL command level, using `DECLARE CURSOR` and `FETCH`.

Once a portal exists, it can be executed using an Execute message. The Execute message specifies the portal name (empty string denotes the unnamed portal) and a maximum result-row count (zero meaning "fetch all rows"). The result-row count is only meaningful for portals containing commands that return row sets; in other cases the command is always executed to completion, and the row count is ignored. The possible responses to Execute are the same as those described above for queries issued via simple query protocol, except that Execute doesn't cause ReadyForQuery or RowDescription to be issued.

If Execute terminates before completing the execution of a portal (due to reaching a nonzero result-row count), it will send a PortalSuspended message; the appearance of this message tells the frontend that another Execute should be issued against the same portal to complete the operation. The CommandComplete message indicating completion of the source SQL command is not sent until the portal's execution is completed. Therefore, an Execute phase is always terminated by the appearance of exactly one of these messages: CommandComplete, EmptyQueryResponse (if the portal was created from an empty query string), ErrorResponse, or PortalSuspended.

At completion of each series of extended-query messages, the frontend should issue a Sync message. This parameterless message causes the backend to close the current transaction if it's not inside a `BEGIN`/`COMMIT` transaction block ("close" meaning to commit if no error, or roll back if error). Then a ReadyForQuery response is issued. The purpose of Sync is to provide a resynchronization point for error recovery. When an error is detected while processing any extended-query message, the backend issues ErrorResponse, then reads and discards messages until a Sync is reached, then issues ReadyForQuery and returns to normal message processing. (But note that no skipping occurs if an error is detected *while* processing Sync - this ensures that there is one and only one ReadyForQuery sent for each Sync.)

Note

Sync does not cause a transaction block opened with `BEGIN` to be closed. It is possible to detect this situation since the ReadyForQuery message includes transaction status information.

In addition to these fundamental, required operations, there are several optional operations that can be used with extended-query protocol.

The Describe message (portal variant) specifies the name of an existing portal (or an empty string for the unnamed portal). The response is a RowDescription message describing the rows that will be returned by executing the portal; or a NoData message if the portal does not contain a query that will return rows; or ErrorResponse if there is no such portal.

The Describe message (statement variant) specifies the name of an existing prepared statement (or an empty string for the unnamed prepared statement). The response is a ParameterDescription message describing the parameters needed by the statement, followed by a RowDescription message describing the rows that will be returned when the statement is eventually executed (or a NoData message if the statement will not return rows). ErrorResponse is issued if there is no such prepared statement. Note that since Bind has not yet been issued, the formats to be used for returned columns are not yet known to the backend; the format code fields in the RowDescription message will be zeroes in this case.

Tip

In most scenarios the frontend should issue one or the other variant of Describe before issuing Execute, to ensure that it knows how to interpret the results it will get back.

The Close message closes an existing prepared statement or portal and releases resources. It is not an error to issue Close against a nonexistent statement or portal name. The response is normally CloseComplete, but could be ErrorResponse if some difficulty is encountered while releasing resources. Note that closing a prepared statement implicitly closes any open portals that were constructed from that statement.

The Flush message does not cause any specific output to be generated, but forces the backend to deliver any data pending in its output buffers. A Flush must be sent after any extended-query command except Sync, if the frontend wishes to examine the results of that command before issuing more commands. Without Flush, messages returned by the backend will be combined into the minimum possible number of packets to minimize network overhead.

Note

The simple Query message is approximately equivalent to the series Parse, Bind, portal Describe, Execute, Close, Sync, using the unnamed prepared statement and portal objects and no parameters. One difference is that it will accept multiple SQL statements in the query string, automatically performing the bind/describe/execute sequence for each one in succession. Another difference is that it will not return ParseComplete, BindComplete, CloseComplete, or NoData messages.

46.2.4. Function Call

The Function Call sub-protocol allows the client to request a direct call of any function that exists in the database's `pg_proc` system catalog. The client must have execute permission for the function.

Note

The Function Call sub-protocol is a legacy feature that is probably best avoided in new code. Similar results can be accomplished by setting up a prepared statement that does `SELECT function($1, ...)`. The Function Call cycle can then be replaced with Bind/Execute.

A Function Call cycle is initiated by the frontend sending a FunctionCall message to the backend. The backend then sends one or more response messages depending on the results of the function call, and finally a ReadyForQuery response message. ReadyForQuery informs the frontend that it can safely send a new query or function call.

The possible response messages from the backend are:

ErrorResponse

An error has occurred.

FunctionCallResponse

The function call was completed and returned the result given in the message. (Note that the Function Call protocol can only handle a single scalar result, not a row type or set of results.)

ReadyForQuery

Processing of the function call is complete. ReadyForQuery will always be sent, whether processing terminates successfully or with an error.

NoticeResponse

A warning message has been issued in relation to the function call. Notices are in addition to other responses, i.e., the backend will continue processing the command.

46.2.5. COPY Operations

The `COPY` command allows high-speed bulk data transfer to or from the server. Copy-in and copy-out operations each switch the connection into a distinct sub-protocol, which lasts until the operation is completed.

Copy-in mode (data transfer to the server) is initiated when the backend executes a `COPY FROM STDIN` SQL statement. The backend sends a CopyInResponse message to the frontend. The frontend should then send zero or more CopyData messages, forming a stream of input data. (The message boundaries are not required to have anything to do with row boundaries, although that is often a reasonable choice.) The frontend can terminate the copy-in mode by sending either a CopyDone message (allowing successful termination) or a CopyFail message (which will cause the `COPY` SQL statement to fail with an error). The backend then reverts to the command-processing mode it was in before the `COPY` started, which will be either simple or extended query protocol. It will next send either CommandComplete (if successful) or ErrorResponse (if not).

In the event of a backend-detected error during copy-in mode (including receipt of a CopyFail message), the backend will issue an ErrorResponse message. If the `COPY` command was issued via an extended-query message, the backend will now discard frontend messages until a Sync message is received, then it will issue ReadyForQuery and return to normal processing. If the `COPY` command was issued in a simple Query message, the rest of that message is discarded and ReadyForQuery is issued. In either case, any subsequent CopyData, CopyDone, or CopyFail messages issued by the frontend will simply be dropped.

The backend will ignore Flush and Sync messages received during copy-in mode. Receipt of any other non-copy message type constitutes an error that will abort the copy-in state as described above. (The exception for Flush and Sync is for the convenience of client libraries that always send Flush or Sync after an Execute message, without checking whether the command to be executed is a `COPY FROM STDIN`.)

Copy-out mode (data transfer from the server) is initiated when the backend executes a `COPY TO STDOUT` SQL statement. The backend sends a CopyOutResponse message to the frontend, followed by zero or more CopyData messages (always one per row), followed by

CopyDone. The backend then reverts to the command-processing mode it was in before the `COPY` started, and sends CommandComplete. The frontend cannot abort the transfer (except by closing the connection or issuing a Cancel request), but it can discard unwanted CopyData and CopyDone messages.

In the event of a backend-detected error during copy-out mode, the backend will issue an ErrorResponse message and revert to normal processing. The frontend should treat receipt of ErrorResponse as terminating the copy-out mode.

It is possible for NoticeResponse and ParameterStatus messages to be interspersed between CopyData messages; frontends must handle these cases, and should be prepared for other asynchronous message types as well (see *Section 46.2.6* - page 92). Otherwise, any message type other than CopyData or CopyDone may be treated as terminating copy-out mode.

The CopyInResponse and CopyOutResponse messages include fields that inform the frontend of the number of columns per row and the format codes being used for each column. (As of the present implementation, all columns in a given `COPY` operation will use the same format, but the message design does not assume this.)

46.2.6. Asynchronous Operations

There are several cases in which the backend will send messages that are not specifically prompted by the frontend's command stream. Frontends must be prepared to deal with these messages at any time, even when not engaged in a query. At minimum, one should check for these cases before beginning to read a query response.

It is possible for NoticeResponse messages to be generated due to outside activity; for example, if the database administrator commands a "fast" database shutdown, the backend will send a NoticeResponse indicating this fact before closing the connection. Accordingly, frontends should always be prepared to accept and display NoticeResponse messages, even when the connection is nominally idle.

ParameterStatus messages will be generated whenever the active value changes for any of the parameters the backend believes the frontend should know about. Most commonly this occurs in response to a `SET` SQL command executed by the frontend, and this case is effectively synchronous - but it is also possible for parameter status changes to occur because the administrator changed a configuration file and then sent the SIGHUP signal to the server. Also, if a `SET` command is rolled back, an appropriate ParameterStatus message will be generated to report the current effective value.

At present there is a hard-wired set of parameters for which ParameterStatus will be generated: they are server_version, server_encoding, client_encoding, application_name, is_superuser, session_authorization, DateStyle, IntervalStyle, TimeZone, integer_datetimes, and standard_conforming_strings. (server_encoding, TimeZone, and integer_datetimes were not reported by releases before 8.0; standard_conforming_strings was not reported by releases before 8.1; IntervalStyle was not reported by releases before 8.4; application_name was not reported by releases before 9.0.) Note that server_version, server_encoding and integer_datetimes are pseudo-parameters that cannot change after startup. This set might change in the future, or even become configurable. Accordingly, a frontend should simply ignore ParameterStatus for parameters that it does not understand or care about.

If a frontend issues a `LISTEN` command, then the backend will send a NotificationResponse message (not to be confused with NoticeResponse!) whenever a `NOTIFY` command is executed for the same channel name.

Note

At present, NotificationResponse can only be sent outside a transaction, and thus it will not occur in the middle of a command-response series, though it might occur just before ReadyForQuery. It is unwise to design frontend logic that assumes that, however. Good practice is to be able to accept NotificationResponse at any point in the protocol.

46.2.7. Cancelling Requests in Progress

During the processing of a query, the frontend might request cancellation of the query. The cancel request is not sent directly on the open connection to the backend for reasons of implementation efficiency: we don't want to have the backend constantly checking for new input from the frontend during query processing. Cancel requests should be relatively inferquent, so we make them slightly cumbersome in order to avoid a penalty in the normal case.

To issue a cancel request, the frontend opens a new connection to the server and sends a CancelRequest message, rather than the StartupMessage message that would ordinarily be sent across a new connection. The server will process this request and then close the connection. For security reasons, no direct reply is made to the cancel request message.

A CancelRequest message will be ignored unless it contains the same key data (PID and secret key) passed to the frontend during connection start-up. If the request matches the PID and secret key for a currently executing backend, the processing of the current query is aborted. (In the existing implementation, this is done by sending a special signal to the backend process that is processing the query.)

The cancellation signal might or might not have any effect - for example, if it arrives after the backend has finished processing the query, then it will have no effect. If the cancellation is effective, it results in the current command being terminated early with an error message.

The upshot of all this is that for reasons of both security and efficiency, the frontend has no direct way to tell whether a cancel request has succeeded. It must continue to wait for the backend to respond to the query. Issuing a cancel simply improves the odds that the current query will finish soon, and improves the odds that it will fail with an error message instead of succeeding.

Since the cancel request is sent across a new connection to the server and not across the regular frontend/backend communication link, it is possible for the cancel request to be issued by any process, not just the frontend whose query is to be canceled. This might provide additional flexibility when building multiple-process applications. It also introduces a security risk, in that unauthorized persons might try to cancel queries. The security risk is addressed by requiring a dynamically generated secret key to be supplied in cancel requests.

46.2.8. Termination

The normal, graceful termination procedure is that the frontend sends a Terminate message and immediately closes the connection. On receipt of this message, the backend closes the connection and terminates.

In rare cases (such as an administrator-commanded database shutdown) the backend might disconnect without any frontend request to do so. In such cases the backend will attempt to send an error or notice message giving the reason for the disconnection before it closes the connection.

Other termination scenarios arise from various failure cases, such as core dump at one end or the other, loss of the communications link, loss of message-boundary synchronization, etc. If either frontend or backend sees an unexpected closure of the connection, it should clean up and terminate. The frontend has the option of launching a new backend by recontacting the server if it doesn't want to terminate itself. Closing the connection is also advisable if an unrecognizable message type is received, since this probably indicates loss of message-boundary sync.

For either normal or abnormal termination, any open transaction is rolled back, not committed. One should note however that if a frontend disconnects while a non-`SELECT` query is being processed, the backend will probably finish the query before noticing the disconnection. If the query is outside any transaction block (`BEGIN` ... `COMMIT` sequence) then its results might be committed before the disconnection is recognized.

46.2.9. SSL Session Encryption

If PostgreSQL was built with SSL support, frontend/backend communications can be encrypted using SSL. This provides communication security in environments where attackers might be able to capture the session traffic. For more information on encrypting PostgreSQL sessions with SSL, see *Section 17.8* (Vol.II).

To initiate an SSL-encrypted connection, the frontend initially sends an SSLRequest message rather than a StartupMessage. The server then responds with a single byte containing `S` or `N`, indicating that it is willing or unwilling to perform SSL, respectively. The frontend might close the connection at this point if it is dissatisfied with the response. To continue after `S`, perform an SSL startup handshake (not described here, part of the SSL specification) with the server. If this is successful, continue with sending the usual StartupMessage. In this case the StartupMessage and all subsequent data will be SSL-encrypted. To continue after `N`, send the usual StartupMessage and proceed without encryption.

The frontend should also be prepared to handle an ErrorMessage response to SSLRequest from the server. This would only occur if the server predates the addition of SSL support to PostgreSQL. In this case the connection must be closed, but the frontend might choose to open a fresh connection and proceed without requesting SSL.

An initial SSLRequest can also be used in a connection that is being opened to send a CancelRequest message.

While the protocol itself does not provide a way for the server to force SSL encryption, the administrator can configure the server to reject unencrypted sessions as a byproduct of authentication checking.

46.3. Streaming Replication Protocol

To initiate streaming replication, the frontend sends the `replication` parameter in the startup message. This tells the backend to go into walsender mode, wherein a small set of replication commands can be issued instead of SQL statements. Only the simple query protocol can be used in walsender mode. The commands accepted in walsender mode are:

IDENTIFY_SYSTEM

Requests the server to identify itself. Server replies with a result set of a single row, containing two fields:

systemid

The unique system identifier identifying the cluster. This can be used to check that the base backup used to initialize the standby came from the same cluster.

timeline

Current TimelineID. Also useful to check that the standby is consistent with the master.

START_REPLICATION *XXX*/*XXX*

Instructs server to start streaming WAL, starting at WAL position *XXX*/*XXX*. The server can reply with an error, e.g. if the requested section of WAL has already been recycled. On success, server responds with a CopyOutResponse message, and then starts to stream WAL to the frontend. WAL will continue to be streamed until the connection is broken; no further commands will be accepted.

WAL data is sent as a series of CopyData messages. (This allows other information to be intermixed; in particular the server can send an ErrorResponse message if it encounters a failure after beginning to stream.) The payload in each CopyData message follows this format:

XLogData (B)

Byte1('w')

Identifies the message as WAL data.

Byte8

The starting point of the WAL data in this message, given in XLogRecPtr format.

Byte8

The current end of WAL on the server, given in XLogRecPtr format.

Byte8

The server's system clock at the time of transmission, given in TimestampTz format.

Byte*n*

A section of the WAL data stream.

A single WAL record is never split across two CopyData messages. When a WAL record crosses a WAL page boundary, and is therefore already split using continuation records, it can be split at the page boundary. In other words, the first main WAL record and its continuation records can be sent in different CopyData messages.

Note that all fields within the WAL data and the above-described header will be in the sending server's native format. Endianness, and the format for the timestamp, are unpredictable unless the receiver has verified that the sender's system identifier matches its own `pg_control` contents.

If the WAL sender process is terminated normally (during postmaster shutdown), it will send a CommandComplete message before exiting. This might not happen during an abnormal shutdown, of course.

46.4. Message Data Types

This section describes the base data types used in messages.

Int*n*(*i*)

An *n*-bit integer in network byte order (most significant byte first). If *i* is specified it is the exact value that will appear,otherwise the value is variable.Eg.Int16,Int32(42).

Int*n*[*k*]

An array of *k* *n*-bit integers, each in network byte order. The array length *k* is always determined by an earlier field in the message. Eg. Int16[M].

String(*s*)

A null-terminated string (C-style string). There is no specific length limitation on strings. If *s* is specified it is the exact value that will appear, otherwise the value is variable. Eg. String, String("user").

Note

There is no predefined limit on the length of a string that can be returned by the backend. Good coding strategy for a frontend is to use an expandable buffer so that anything that fits in memory can be accepted. If that's not feasible, read the full string and discard trailing characters that don't fit into your fixed-size buffer.

Byte*n*(*c*)

Exactly *n* bytes. If the field width *n* is not a constant, it is always determinable from an earlier field in the message. If *c* is specified it is the exact value. Eg. Byte2, Byte1('\n').

46.5. Message Formats

This section describes the detailed format of each message. Each is marked to indicate that it can be sent by a frontend (F), a backend (B), or both (F & B). Notice that although each message includes a byte count at the beginning, the message format is defined so that the message end can be found without reference to the byte count. This aids validity checking. (The CopyData message is an exception, because it forms part of a data stream; the contents of any individual CopyData message cannot be interpretable on their own.)

AuthenticationOk (B)

Byte1('R')

Identifies the message as an authentication request.

Int32(8)

Length of message contents in bytes, including self.

Int32(0)

Specifies that the authentication was successful.

AuthenticationKerberosV5 (B)

Byte1('R')

Identifies the message as an authentication request.

Int32(8)

Length of message contents in bytes, including self.

Int32(2)

Specifies that Kerberos V5 authentication is required.

AuthenticationCleartextPassword (B)

Byte1('R')

Identifies the message as an authentication request.

Int32(8)

Length of message contents in bytes, including self.

Int32(3)

Specifies that a clear-text password is required.

AuthenticationMD5Password (B)

Byte1('R')

Identifies the message as an authentication request.

Int32(12)

Length of message contents in bytes, including self.

Int32(5)

Specifies that an MD5-encrypted password is required.

Byte4

The salt to use when encrypting the password.

AuthenticationSCMCredential (B)

Byte1('R')

Identifies the message as an authentication request.

Int32(8)

Length of message contents in bytes, including self.

Int32(6)

Specifies that an SCM credentials message is required.

AuthenticationGSS (B)

Byte1('R')

Identifies the message as an authentication request.

Int32(8)

Length of message contents in bytes, including self.

Int32(7)

Specifies that GSSAPI authentication is required.

AuthenticationSSPI (B)

Byte1('R')

Identifies the message as an authentication request.

Int32(8)

Length of message contents in bytes, including self.

Int32(9)

Specifies that SSPI authentication is required.

AuthenticationGSSContinue (B)

Byte1('R')

Identifies the message as an authentication request.

Int32

Length of message contents in bytes, including self.

Int32(8)

Specifies that this message contains GSSAPI or SSPI data.

Byte*n*

GSSAPI or SSPI authentication data.

BackendKeyData (B)

Byte1('K')

Identifies the message as cancellation key data. The frontend must save these values if it wishes to be able to issue CancelRequest messages later.

Int32(12)

Length of message contents in bytes, including self.

Int32

The process ID of this backend.

Int32

The secret key of this backend.

Bind (F)

Byte1('B')

Identifies the message as a Bind command.

Int32

Length of message contents in bytes, including self.

String

The name of the destination portal (an empty string selects the unnamed portal).

String

The name of the source prepared statement (an empty string selects the unnamed prepared statement).

Int16

The number of parameter format codes that follow (denoted *C* below). This can be zero to indicate that there are no parameters or that the parameters all use the default format (text); or one, in which case the specified format code is applied to all parameters; or it can equal the actual number of parameters.

Int16[*C*]

The parameter format codes. Each must presently be zero (text) or one (binary).

Int16

The number of parameter values that follow (possibly zero). This must match the number of parameters needed by the query.

Next, the following pair of fields appear for each parameter:

Int32

The length of the parameter value, in bytes (this count does not include itself). Can be zero. As a special case, -1 indicates a NULL parameter value. No value bytes follow in the NULL case.

Byte*n*

The value of the parameter, in the format indicated by the associated format code. *n* is the above length.

After the last parameter, the following fields appear:

Int16

The number of result-column format codes that follow (denoted `R` below). This can be zero to indicate that there are no result columns or that the result columns should all use the default format (text); or one, in which case the specified format code is applied to all result columns (if any); or it can equal the actual number of result columns of the query.

Int16[*R*]

The result-column format codes. Each must presently be zero (text) or one (binary).

BindComplete (B)

Byte1('2')

Identifies the message as a Bind-complete indicator.

Int32(4)

Length of message contents in bytes, including self.

CancelRequest (F)

Int32(16)

Length of message contents in bytes, including self.

Int32(80877102)

The cancel request code. The value is chosen to contain `1234` in the most significant 16 bits, and `5678` in the least 16 significant bits. (To avoid confusion, this code must not be the same as any protocol version number.)

Int32

The process ID of the target backend.

Int32

The secret key for the target backend.

Close (F)

Byte1('C')

Identifies the message as a Close command.

Int32

Length of message contents in bytes, including self.

Byte1

`'S'` to close a prepared statement; or `'P'` to close a portal.

String

The name of the prepared statement or portal to close (an empty string selects the unnamed prepared statement or portal).

CloseComplete (B)

Byte1('3')

Identifies the message as a Close-complete indicator.

Int32(4)

Length of message contents in bytes, including self.

CommandComplete (B)

Byte1('C')

Identifies the message as a command-completed response.

Int32

Length of message contents in bytes, including self.

String

The command tag. This is usually a single word that identifies which SQL command was completed.

For an `INSERT` command, the tag is `INSERT` *`oid rows`*, where *`rows`* is the number of rows inserted. *`oid`* is the object ID of the inserted row if *`rows`* is 1 and the target table has OIDs; otherwise *`oid`* is 0.

For a `DELETE` command, the tag is `DELETE` *`rows`* where *`rows`* is the number of rows deleted.

For an `UPDATE` command, the tag is `UPDATE` *`rows`* where *`rows`* is the number of rows updated.

For a `SELECT` or `CREATE TABLE AS` command, the tag is `SELECT rows` where *rows* is the number of rows retrieved.

For a `MOVE` command, the tag is `MOVE rows` where *rows* is the number of rows the cursor's position has been changed by.

For a `FETCH` command, the tag is `FETCH rows` where *rows* is the number of rows that have been retrieved from the cursor.

For a `COPY` command, the tag is `COPY rows` where *rows* is the number of rows copied. (Note: the row count appears only in PostgreSQL 8.2 and later.)

CopyData (F & B)

Byte1('d')

Identifies the message as `COPY` data.

Int32

Length of message contents in bytes, including self.

Byte*n*

Data that forms part of a `COPY` data stream. Messages sent from the backend will always correspond to single data rows, but messages sent by frontends might divide the data stream arbitrarily.

CopyDone (F & B)

Byte1('c')

Identifies the message as a `COPY`-complete indicator.

Int32(4)

Length of message contents in bytes, including self.

CopyFail (F)

Byte1('f')

Identifies the message as a `COPY`-failure indicator.

Int32

Length of message contents in bytes, including self.

String

An error message to report as the cause of failure.

CopyInResponse (B)

Byte1('G')

Identifies the message as a Start Copy In response. The frontend must now send copy-in data (if not prepared to do so, send a CopyFail message).

Int32

Length of message contents in bytes, including self.

Int8

0 indicates the overall `COPY` format is textual (rows separated by newlines, columns separated by separator characters, etc). 1 indicates the overall copy format is binary (similar to DataRow format). See COPY for more information.

Int16

The number of columns in the data to be copied (denoted *N* below).

Int16[*N*]

The format codes to be used for each column. Each must presently be zero (text) or one (binary). All must be zero if the overall copy format is textual.

CopyOutResponse (B)

Byte1('H')

Identifies the message as a Start Copy Out response. This message will be followed by copy-out data.

Int32

Length of message contents in bytes, including self.

Int8

0 indicates the overall `COPY` format is textual (rows separated by newlines, columns separated by separator characters, etc). 1 indicates the overall copy format is binary (similar to DataRow format). See COPY for more information.

Int16

The number of columns in the data to be copied (denoted *N* below).

Int16[*N*]

The format codes to be used for each column. Each must presently be zero (text) or one (binary). All must be zero if the overall copy format is textual.

DataRow (B)

Byte1('D')

Identifies the message as a data row.

Int32

Length of message contents in bytes, including self.

Int16

The number of column values that follow (possibly zero).

Next, the following pair of fields appear for each column:

Int32

The length of the column value, in bytes (this count does not include itself). Can be zero. As a special case, -1 indicates a NULL column value. No value bytes follow in the NULL case.

Byte*n*

The value of the column, in the format indicated by the associated format code. *n* is the above length.

Describe (F)

Byte1('D')

Identifies the message as a Describe command.

Int32

Length of message contents in bytes, including self.

Byte1

`'S'` to describe a prepared statement; or `'P'` to describe a portal.

String

The name of the prepared statement or portal to describe (an empty string selects the unnamed prepared statement or portal).

EmptyQueryResponse (B)

Byte1('I')

Identifies the message as a response to an empty query string. (This substitutes for CommandComplete.)

Int32(4)

Length of message contents in bytes, including self.

ErrorResponse (B)

Byte1('E')

Identifies the message as an error.

Int32

Length of message contents in bytes, including self.

The message body consists of one or more identified fields, followed by a zero byte as a terminator. Fields can appear in any order. For each field there is the following:

Byte1

A code identifying the field type; if zero, this is the message terminator and no string follows. The presently defined field types are listed in *Section 46.6* (page 114). Since more field types might be added in future, frontends should silently ignore fields of unrecognized type.

String

The field value.

Execute (F)

Byte1('E')

Identifies the message as an Execute command.

Int32

Length of message contents in bytes, including self.

String

The name of the portal to execute (an empty string selects the unnamed portal).

Int32

Maximum number of rows to return, if portal contains a query that returns rows (ignored otherwise). Zero denotes "no limit".

Flush (F)

Byte1('H')

Identifies the message as a Flush command.

Int32(4)

Length of message contents in bytes, including self.

FunctionCall (F)

Byte1('F')

Identifies the message as a function call.

Int32

Length of message contents in bytes, including self.

Int32

Specifies the object ID of the function to call.

Int16

The number of argument format codes that follow (denoted *c* below). This can be zero to indicate that there are no arguments or that the arguments all use the default format (text); or one, in which case the specified format code is applied to all arguments; or it can equal the actual number of arguments.

Int16[*c*]

The argument format codes. Each must presently be zero (text) or one (binary).

Int16

Specifies the number of arguments being supplied to the function.

Next, the following pair of fields appear for each argument:

Int32

The length of the argument value, in bytes (this count does not include itself). Can be zero. As a special case, -1 indicates a NULL argument value. No value bytes follow in the NULL case.

Byte*n*

The value of the argument, in the format indicated by the associated format code. *n* is the above length.

After the last argument, the following field appears:

Int16

The format code for the function result. Must presently be zero (text) or one (binary).

FunctionCallResponse (B)

Byte1('V')

Identifies the message as a function call result.

Int32

Length of message contents in bytes, including self.

Int32

The length of the function result value, in bytes (this count does not include itself). Can be zero. As a special case, -1 indicates a NULL function result. No value bytes follow in the NULL case.

Byte*n*

The value of the function result, in the format indicated by the associated format code. *n* is the above length.

NoData (B)

Byte1('n')

Identifies the message as a no-data indicator.

Int32(4)

Length of message contents in bytes, including self.

NoticeResponse (B)

Byte1('N')

Identifies the message as a notice.

Int32

Length of message contents in bytes, including self.

The message body consists of one or more identified fields, followed by a zero byte as a terminator. Fields can appear in any order. For each field there is the following:

Byte1

A code identifying the field type; if zero, this is the message terminator and no string follows. The presently defined field types are listed in *Section 46.6* (page 114). Since more field types might be added in future, frontends should silently ignore fields of unrecognized type.

String

The field value.

NotificationResponse (B)

Byte1('A')

Identifies the message as a notification response.

Int32

Length of message contents in bytes, including self.

Int32

The process ID of the notifying backend process.

String

The name of the channel that the notify has been raised on.

String

The "payload" string passed from the notifying process.

ParameterDescription (B)

Byte1('t')

Identifies the message as a parameter description.

Int32

Length of message contents in bytes, including self.

Int16

The number of parameters used by the statement (can be zero).

Then, for each parameter, there is the following:

Int32

Specifies the object ID of the parameter data type.

ParameterStatus (B)

Byte1('S')

Identifies the message as a run-time parameter status report.

Int32

Length of message contents in bytes, including self.

String

The name of the run-time parameter being reported.

String

The current value of the parameter.

Parse (F)

Byte1('P')

Identifies the message as a Parse command.

Int32

Length of message contents in bytes, including self.

String

The name of the destination prepared statement (an empty string selects the unnamed prepared statement).

String

The query string to be parsed.

Int16

The number of parameter data types specified (can be zero). Note that this is not an indication of the number of parameters that might appear in the query string, only the number that the frontend wants to prespecify types for.

Then, for each parameter, there is the following:

Int32

Specifies the object ID of the parameter data type. Placing a zero here is equivalent to leaving the type unspecified.

ParseComplete (B)

Byte1('1')

Identifies the message as a Parse-complete indicator.

Int32(4)

Length of message contents in bytes, including self.

PasswordMessage (F)

Byte1('p')

Identifies the message as a password response. Note that this is also used for GSSAPI and SSPI response messages (which is really a design error, since the contained data is not a null-terminated string in that case, but can be arbitrary binary data).

Int32

Length of message contents in bytes, including self.

String

The password (encrypted, if requested).

PortalSuspended (B)

Byte1('s')

Identifies the message as a portal-suspended indicator. Note this only appears if an Execute message's row-count limit was reached.

Int32(4)

Length of message contents in bytes, including self.

Query (F)

Byte1('Q')

Identifies the message as a simple query.

Int32

Length of message contents in bytes, including self.

String

The query string itself.

ReadyForQuery (B)

Byte1('Z')

Identifies the message type. ReadyForQuery is sent whenever the backend is ready for a new query cycle.

Int32(5)

Length of message contents in bytes, including self.

Byte1

Current backend transaction status indicator. Possible values are 'I' if idle (not in a transaction block); 'T' if in a transaction block; or 'E' if in a failed transaction block (queries will be rejected until block is ended).

RowDescription (B)

Byte1('T')

Identifies the message as a row description.

Int32

Length of message contents in bytes, including self.

Int16

Specifies the number of fields in a row (can be zero).

Then, for each field, there is the following:

String

The field name.

Int32

If the field can be identified as a column of a specific table, the object ID of the table; otherwise zero.

Int16

If the field can be identified as a column of a specific table, the attribute number of the column; otherwise zero.

Int32

The object ID of the field's data type.

Int16

The data type size (see `pg_type.typlen`). Note that negative values denote variable-width types.

Int32

The type modifier (see `pg_attribute.atttypmod`). The meaning of the modifier is type-specific.

Int16

The format code being used for the field. Currently will be zero (text) or one (binary). In a RowDescription returned from the statement variant of Describe, the format code is not yet known and will always be zero.

SSLRequest (F)

Int32(8)

Length of message contents in bytes, including self.

Int32(80877103)

The SSL request code. The value is chosen to contain `1234` in the most significant 16 bits, and `5679` in the least 16 significant bits. (To avoid confusion, this code must not be the same as any protocol version number.)

StartupMessage (F)

Int32

Length of message contents in bytes, including self.

Int32(196608)

The protocol version number. The most significant 16 bits are the major version number (3 for the protocol described here). The least significant 16 bits are the minor version number (0 for the protocol described here).

The protocol version number is followed by one or more pairs of parameter name and value strings. A zero byte is required as a terminator after the last name/value pair. Parameters can appear in any order. `user` is required, others are optional. Each parameter is specified as:

String

The parameter name. Currently recognized names are:

`user`

The database user name to connect as. Required; there is no default.

`database`

The database to connect to. Defaults to the user name.

`options`

Command-line arguments for the backend. (This is deprecated in favor of setting individual run-time parameters.)

In addition to the above, any run-time parameter that can be set at backend start time might be listed. Such settings will be applied during backend start (after parsing the command-line options if any). The values will act as session defaults.

String

The parameter value.

Sync (F)

Byte1('S')

Identifies the message as a Sync command.

Int32(4)

Length of message contents in bytes, including self.

Terminate (F)

Byte1('X')

Identifies the message as a termination.

Int32(4)

Length of message contents in bytes, including self.

46.6. Error and Notice Message Fields

This section describes the fields that can appear in ErrorResponse and NoticeResponse messages. Each field type has a single-byte identification token. Note that any given field type should appear at most once per message.

S

Severity: the field contents are `ERROR`, `FATAL`, or `PANIC` (in an error message), or `WARNING`, `NOTICE`, `DEBUG`, `INFO`, or `LOG` (in a notice message), or a localized translation of one of these. Always present.

C

Code: the SQLSTATE code for the error (see *Appendix A* - page 192). Not localizable. Always present.

M

Message: the primary human-readable error message. This should be accurate but terse (typically one line). Always present.

D

Detail: an optional secondary error message carrying more detail about the problem. Might run to multiple lines.

H

Hint: an optional suggestion what to do about the problem. This is intended to differ from Detail in that it offers advice (potentially inappropriate) rather than hard facts. Might run to multiple lines.

P

Position: the field value is a decimal ASCII integer, indicating an error cursor position as an index into the original query string. The first character has index 1, and positions are measured in characters not bytes.

p

Internal position: this is defined the same as the `P` field, but it is used when the cursor position refers to an internally generated command rather than the one submitted by the client. The `q` field will always appear when this field appears.

q

Internal query: the text of a failed internally-generated command. This could be, for example, a SQL query issued by a PL/pgSQL function.

W

Where: an indication of the context in which the error occurred. Presently this includes a call stack traceback of active procedural language functions and internally-generated queries. The trace is one entry per line, most recent first.

F

File: the file name of the source-code location where the error was reported.

L

Line: the line number of the source-code location where the error was reported.

R

Routine: the name of the source-code routine reporting the error.

The client is responsible for formatting displayed information to meet its needs; in particular it should break long lines as needed. Newline characters appearing in the error message fields should be treated as paragraph breaks, not line breaks.

46.7. Summary of Changes since Protocol 2.0

This section provides a quick checklist of changes, for the benefit of developers trying to update existing client libraries to protocol 3.0.

The initial startup packet uses a flexible list-of-strings format instead of a fixed format. Notice that session default values for run-time parameters can now be specified directly in the startup packet. (Actually, you could do that before using the `options` field, but given the limited width of `options` and the lack of any way to quote whitespace in the values, it wasn't a very safe technique.)

All messages now have a length count immediately following the message type byte (except for startup packets, which have no type byte). Also note that PasswordMessage now has a type byte.

ErrorResponse and NoticeResponse ('E' and 'N') messages now contain multiple fields, from which the client code can assemble an error message of the desired level of verbosity. Note that individual fields will typically not end with a newline, whereas the single string sent in the older protocol always did.

The ReadyForQuery ('Z') message includes a transaction status indicator.

The distinction between BinaryRow and DataRow message types is gone; the single DataRow message type serves for returning data in all formats. Note that the layout of DataRow has changed to make it easier to parse. Also, the representation of binary values has changed: it is no longer directly tied to the server's internal representation.

There is a new "extended query" sub-protocol, which adds the frontend message types Parse, Bind, Execute, Describe, Close, Flush, and Sync, and the backend message types ParseComplete, BindComplete, PortalSuspended, ParameterDescription, NoData, and CloseComplete. Existing clients do not have to concern themselves with this sub-protocol, but making use of it might allow improvements in performance or functionality.

`COPY` data is now encapsulated into CopyData and CopyDone messages. There is a well-defined way to recover from errors during `COPY`. The special "`\.`" last line is not needed anymore, and is not sent during `COPY OUT`. (It is still recognized as a terminator during `COPY IN`, but its use is deprecated and will eventually be removed.) Binary `COPY` is supported. The CopyInResponse and CopyOutResponse messages include fields indicating the number of columns and the format of each column.

The layout of FunctionCall and FunctionCallResponse messages has changed. FunctionCall can now support passing NULL arguments to functions. It also can handle passing parameters and retrieving results in either text or binary format. There is no longer any reason to consider FunctionCall a potential security hole, since it does not offer direct access to internal server data representations.

The backend sends ParameterStatus ('S') messages during connection startup for all parameters it considers interesting to the client library. Subsequently, a ParameterStatus message is sent whenever the active value changes for any of these parameters.

The RowDescription ('T') message carries new table OID and column number fields for each column of the described row. It also shows the format code for each column.

The CursorResponse ('P') message is no longer generated by the backend.

The NotificationResponse ('A') message has an additional string field, which can carry a "payload" string passed from the `NOTIFY` event sender.

The EmptyQueryResponse ('I') message used to include an empty string parameter; this has been removed.

Chapter 47. PostgreSQL Coding Conventions

47.1. Formatting

Source code formatting uses 4 column tab spacing, with tabs preserved (i.e., tabs are not expanded to spaces). Each logical indentation level is one additional tab stop.

Layout rules (brace positioning, etc) follow BSD conventions. In particular, curly braces for the controlled blocks of `if`, `while`, `switch` , etc go on their own lines.

Do not use C++ style comments (`//` comments). Strict ANSI C compilers do not accept them. For the same reason, do not use C++ extensions such as declaring new variables mid-block.

The preferred style for multi-line comment blocks is

```
/*
 * comment text begins here
 * and continues here
 */
```

Note that comment blocks that begin in column 1 will be preserved as-is by pgindent, but it will re-flow indented comment blocks as though they were plain text. If you want to preserve the line breaks in an indented block, add dashes like this:

```
    /*----------
     * comment text begins here
     * and continues here
     *----------
     */
```

While submitted patches do not absolutely have to follow these formatting rules, it's a good idea to do so. Your code will get run through pgindent before the next release, so there's no point in making it look nice under some other set of formatting conventions.

The `src/tools` directory contains sample settings files that can be used with the emacs, xemacs or vim editors to help ensure that they format code according to these conventions.

The text browsing tools more and less can be invoked as:

```
more -x4
less -x4
```

to make them show tabs appropriately.

47.2. Reporting Errors Within the Server

Error, warning, and log messages generated within the server code should be created using `ereport`, or its older cousin `elog`. The use of this function is complex enough to require some explanation.

There are two required elements for every message: a severity level (ranging from `DEBUG` to `PANIC`) and a primary message text. In addition there are optional elements, the most common of which is an error identifier code that follows the SQL spec's SQLSTATE conventions. `ereport` itself is just a shell function, that exists mainly for the syntactic convenience of making message generation look like a function call in the C source code. The only parameter accepted directly by `ereport` is the severity level. The primary message text and any optional message elements are generated by calling auxiliary functions, such as `errmsg`, within the `ereport` call.

A typical call to `ereport` might look like this:

```
ereport(ERROR,
        (errcode(ERRCODE_DIVISION_BY_ZERO),
         errmsg("division by zero")));
```

This specifies error severity level `ERROR` (a run-of-the-mill error). The `errcode` call specifies the SQLSTATE error code using a macro defined in `src/include/utils/errcodes.h`. The `errmsg` call provides the primary message text. Notice the extra set of parentheses surrounding the auxiliary function calls - these are annoying but syntactically necessary.

Here is a more complex example:

```
ereport(ERROR,
        (errcode(ERRCODE_AMBIGUOUS_FUNCTION),
         errmsg("function %s is not unique",
                func_signature_string(funcname, nargs,
                                      NIL, actual_arg_types)),
         errhint("Unable to choose a best candidate function. "
                 "You might need to add explicit typecasts.")));
```

This illustrates the use of format codes to embed run-time values into a message text. Also, an optional "hint" message is provided.

The available auxiliary routines for `ereport` are:

- `errcode(sqlerrcode)` specifies the SQLSTATE error identifier code for the condition. If this routine is not called, the error identifier defaults to `ERRCODE_INTERNAL_ERROR` when the error severity level is `ERROR` or higher, `ERRCODE_WARNING` when the error level is `WARNING`, otherwise (for `NOTICE` and below) `ERRCODE_SUCCESSFUL_COMPLETION` . While these defaults are often convenient, always think whether they are appropriate before omitting the `errcode()` call.

- `errmsg(const char *msg, ...)` specifies the primary error message text, and possibly run-time values to insert into it. Insertions are specified by `sprintf` -style format codes. In addition to the standard format codes accepted by `sprintf`, the format code `%m` can be used to insert the error message returned by `strerror` for the current value of `errno`.[1] `%m` does not require any corresponding entry in the parameter list for `errmsg`. Note that the message string will be run through `gettext` for possible localization before format codes are processed.
- `errmsg_internal(const char *msg, ...)` is the same as `errmsg`, except that the message string will not be translated nor included in the internationalization message dictionary. This should be used for "cannot happen" cases that are probably not worth expending translation effort on.
- `errmsg_plural(const char *fmt_singular, const char *fmt_plural, unsigned long n, ...)` is like `errmsg`, but with support for various plural forms of the message. *`fmt_singular`* is the English singular format, *`fmt_plural`* is the English plural format, *`n`* is the integer value that determines which plural form is needed, and the remaining arguments are formatted according to the selected format string. For more information see *Section 48.2.2* (page 131).
- `errdetail(const char *msg, ...)` supplies an optional "detail" message; this is to be used when there is additional information that seems inappropriate to put in the primary message. The message string is processed in just the same way as for `errmsg`.
- `errdetail_log(const char *msg, ...)` is the same as `errdetail` except that this string goes only to the server log, never to the client. If both `errdetail` and `errdetail_log` are used then one string goes to the client and the other to the log. This is useful for error details that are too security-sensitive or too bulky to include in the report sent to the client.
- `errdetail_plural(const char *fmt_singular, const char *fmt_plural, unsigned long n, ...)` is like `errdetail`, but with support for various plural forms of the message. For more information see *Section 48.2.2* (page 131).
- `errhint(const char *msg, ...)` supplies an optional "hint" message; this is to be used when offering suggestions about how to fix the problem, as opposed to factual details about what went wrong. The message string is processed in just the same way as for `errmsg`.

---

[1] That is, the value that was current when the `ereport` call was reached; changes of `errno` within the auxiliary reporting routines will not affect it. That would not be true if you were to write `strerror(errno)` explicitly in `errmsg`'s parameter list; accordingly, do not do so.

- `errcontext(const char *msg, ...)` is not normally called directly from an `ereport` message site; rather it is used in `error_context_stack` callback functions to provide information about the context in which an error occurred, such as the current location in a PL function. The message string is processed in just the same way as for `errmsg`. Unlike the other auxiliary functions, this can be called more than once per `ereport` call; the successive strings thus supplied are concatenated with separating newlines.
- `errposition(int cursorpos)` specifies the textual location of an error within a query string. Currently it is only useful for errors detected in the lexical and syntactic analysis phases of query processing.
- `errcode_for_file_access()` is a convenience function that selects an appropriate SQLSTATE error identifier for a failure in a file-access-related system call. It uses the saved `errno` to determine which error code to generate. Usually this should be used in combination with `%m` in the primary error message text.
- `errcode_for_socket_access()` is a convenience function that selects an appropriate SQLSTATE error identifier for a failure in a socket-related system call.
- `errhidestmt(bool hide_stmt)` can be called to specify suppression of the `STATEMENT:` portion of a message in the postmaster log. Generally this is appropriate if the message text includes the current statement already.

There is an older function `elog` that is still heavily used. An `elog` call:

```
elog(level, "format string", ...);
```

is exactly equivalent to:

```
ereport(level, (errmsg_internal("format string", ...)));
```

Notice that the SQLSTATE error code is always defaulted, and the message string is not subject to translation. Therefore, `elog` should be used only for internal errors and low-level debug logging. Any message that is likely to be of interest to ordinary users should go through `ereport`. Nonetheless, there are enough internal "cannot happen" error checks in the system that `elog` is still widely used; it is preferred for those messages for its notational simplicity.

Advice about writing good error messages can be found in *Section 47.3* (page 120).

47.3. Error Message Style Guide

This style guide is offered in the hope of maintaining a consistent, user-friendly style throughout all the messages generated by PostgreSQL.

47.3.1. What goes where

The primary message should be short, factual, and avoid reference to implementation details such as specific function names. "Short" means "should fit on one line under normal conditions". Use a detail message if needed to keep the primary message short, or if you feel a need to mention implementation details such as the particular system call that failed. Both primary and detail messages should be factual. Use a hint message for suggestions about what to do to fix the problem, especially if the suggestion might not always be applicable.

For example, instead of:

```
IpcMemoryCreate: shmget(key=%d, size=%u, 0%o) failed: %m
(plus a long addendum that is basically a hint)
```

write:

```
Primary:    could not create shared memory segment: %m
Detail:     Failed syscall was shmget(key=%d, size=%u, 0%o).
Hint:       the addendum
```

Rationale: keeping the primary message short helps keep it to the point, and lets clients lay out screen space on the assumption that one line is enough for error messages. Detail and hint messages can be relegated to a verbose mode, or perhaps a pop-up error-details window. Also, details and hints would normally be suppressed from the server log to save space. Reference to implementation details is best avoided since users don't know the details anyway.

47.3.2. Formatting

Don't put any specific assumptions about formatting into the message texts. Expect clients and the server log to wrap lines to fit their own needs. In long messages, newline characters (\n) can be used to indicate suggested paragraph breaks. Don't end a message with a newline. Don't use tabs or other formatting characters. (In error context displays, newlines are automatically added to separate levels of context such as function calls.)

Rationale: Messages are not necessarily displayed on terminal-type displays. In GUI displays or browsers these formatting instructions are at best ignored.

47.3.3. Quotation marks

English text should use double quotes when quoting is appropriate. Text in other languages should consistently use one kind of quotes that is consistent with publishing customs and computer output of other programs.

Rationale: The choice of double quotes over single quotes is somewhat arbitrary, but tends to be the preferred use. Some have suggested choosing the kind of quotes depending on the type of object according to SQL conventions (namely, strings single quoted, identifiers double quoted). But this is a language-internal technical issue that many users aren't even familiar with, it won't scale to other kinds of quoted terms, it doesn't translate to other languages, and it's pretty pointless, too.

47.3.4. Use of quotes

Use quotes always to delimit file names, user-supplied identifiers, and other variables that might contain words. Do not use them to mark up variables that will not contain words (for example, operator names).

There are functions in the backend that will double-quote their own output at need (for example, `format_type_be` ()). Do not put additional quotes around the output of such functions.

Rationale: Objects can have names that create ambiguity when embedded in a message. Be consistent about denoting where a plugged-in name starts and ends. But don't clutter messages with unnecessary or duplicate quote marks.

47.3.5. Grammar and punctuation

The rules are different for primary error messages and for detail/hint messages:

Primary error messages: Do not capitalize the first letter. Do not end a message with a period. Do not even think about ending a message with an exclamation point.

Detail and hint messages: Use complete sentences, and end each with a period. Capitalize the first word of sentences. Put two spaces after the period if another sentence follows (for English text; might be inappropriate in other languages).

Error context strings: Do not capitalize the first letter and do not end the string with a period. Context strings should normally not be complete sentences.

Rationale: Avoiding punctuation makes it easier for client applications to embed the message into a variety of grammatical contexts. Often, primary messages are not grammatically complete sentences anyway. (And if they're long enough to be more than one sentence, they should be split into primary and detail parts.) However, detail and hint messages are longer and might need to include multiple sentences. For consistency, they should follow complete-sentence style even when there's only one sentence.

47.3.6. Upper case vs. lower case

Use lower case for message wording, including the first letter of a primary error message. Use upper case for SQL commands and key words if they appear in the message.

Rationale: It's easier to make everything look more consistent this way, since some messages are complete sentences and some not.

47.3.7. Avoid passive voice

Use the active voice. Use complete sentences when there is an acting subject ("A could not do B"). Use telegram style without subject if the subject would be the program itself; do not use "I" for the program.

Rationale: The program is not human. Don't pretend otherwise.

47.3.8. Present vs past tense

Use past tense if an attempt to do something failed, but could perhaps succeed next time (perhaps after fixing some problem). Use present tense if the failure is certainly permanent.

There is a nontrivial semantic difference between sentences of the form:

```
could not open file "%s": %m
```

and:

```
cannot open file "%s"
```

The first one means that the attempt to open the file failed. The message should give a reason, such as "disk full" or "file doesn't exist". The past tense is appropriate because next time the disk might not be full anymore or the file in question might exist.

The second form indicates that the functionality of opening the named file does not exist at all in the program, or that it's conceptually impossible. The present tense is appropriate because the condition will persist indefinitely.

Rationale: Granted, the average user will not be able to draw great conclusions merely from the tense of the message, but since the language provides us with a grammar we should use it correctly.

47.3.9. Type of the object

When citing the name of an object, state what kind of object it is.

Rationale: Otherwise no one will know what "foo.bar.baz" refers to.

47.3.10. Brackets

Square brackets are only to be used (1) in command synopses to denote optional arguments, or (2) to denote an array subscript.

Rationale: Anything else does not correspond to widely-known customary usage and will confuse people.

47.3.11. Assembling error messages

When a message includes text that is generated elsewhere, embed it in this style:

```
could not open file %s: %m
```

Rationale: It would be difficult to account for all possible error codes to paste this into a single smooth sentence, so some sort of punctuation is needed. Putting the embedded text in parentheses has also been suggested, but it's unnatural if the embedded text is likely to be the most important part of the message, as is often the case.

47.3.12. Reasons for errors

Messages should always state the reason why an error occurred. For example:

```
BAD:    could not open file %s
BETTER: could not open file %s (I/O failure)
```

If no reason is known you better fix the code.

47.3.13. Function names

Don't include the name of the reporting routine in the error text. We have other mechanisms for finding that out when needed, and for most users it's not helpful information. If the error text doesn't make as much sense without the function name, reword it.

```
BAD:    pg_atoi: error in "z": cannot parse "z"
BETTER: invalid input syntax for integer: "z"
```

Avoid mentioning called function names, either; instead say what the code was trying to do:

```
BAD:    open() failed: %m
BETTER: could not open file %s: %m
```

If it really seems necessary, mention the system call in the detail message. (In some cases, providing the actual values passed to the system call might be appropriate information for the detail message.)

Rationale: Users don't know what all those functions do.

47.3.14. Tricky words to avoid

Unable. "Unable" is nearly the passive voice. Better use "cannot" or "could not", as appropriate.

Bad. Error messages like "bad result" are really hard to interpret intelligently. It's better to write why the result is "bad", e.g., "invalid format".

Illegal. "Illegal" stands for a violation of the law, the rest is "invalid". Better yet, say why it's invalid.

Unknown. Try to avoid "unknown". Consider "error: unknown response". If you don't know what the response is, how do you know it's erroneous? "Unrecognized" is often a better choice. Also, be sure to include the value being complained of.

```
BAD:    unknown node type
BETTER: unrecognized node type: 42
```

Find vs. Exists. If the program uses a nontrivial algorithm to locate a resource (e.g., a path search) and that algorithm fails, it is fair to say that the program couldn't "find" the resource. If, on the other hand, the expected location of the resource is known but the program cannot access it there then say that the resource doesn't "exist". Using "find" in this case sounds weak and confuses the issue.

May vs. Can vs. Might. "May" suggests permission (e.g., "You may borrow my rake."), and has little use in documentation or error messages. "Can" suggests ability (e.g., "I can lift that log."), and "might" suggests possibility (e.g., "It might rain today."). Using the proper word clarifies meaning and assists translation.

Contractions. Avoid contractions, like "can't"; use "cannot" instead.

47.3.15. Proper spelling

Spell out words in full. For instance, avoid:

- spec
- stats
- parens
- auth
- xact

Rationale: This will improve consistency.

47.3.16. Localization

Keep in mind that error message texts need to be translated into other languages. Follow the guidelines in *Section 48.2.2* (page 131) to avoid making life difficult for translators.

Chapter 48. Native Language Support

48.1. For the Translator

PostgreSQL programs (server and client) can issue their messages in your favorite language - if the messages have been translated. Creating and maintaining translated message sets needs the help of people who speak their own language well and want to contribute to the PostgreSQL effort. You do not have to be a programmer at all to do this. This section explains how to help.

48.1.1. Requirements

We won't judge your language skills - this section is about software tools. Theoretically, you only need a text editor. But this is only in the unlikely event that you do not want to try out your translated messages. When you configure your source tree, be sure to use the `--enable-nls` option. This will also check for the libintl library and the `msgfmt` program, which all end users will need anyway. To try out your work, follow the applicable portions of the installation instructions.

If you want to start a new translation effort or want to do a message catalog merge (described later), you will need the programs `xgettext` and `msgmerge`, respectively, in a GNU-compatible implementation. Later, we will try to arrange it so that if you use a packaged source distribution, you won't need `xgettext`. (If working from Git, you will still need it.) GNU Gettext 0.10.36 or later is currently recommended.

Your local gettext implementation should come with its own documentation. Some of that is probably duplicated in what follows, but for additional details you should look there.

48.1.2. Concepts

The pairs of original (English) messages and their (possibly) translated equivalents are kept in *message catalogs*, one for each program (although related programs can share a message catalog) and for each target language. There are two file formats for message catalogs: The first is the "PO" file (for Portable Object), which is a plain text file with special syntax that translators edit. The second is the "MO" file (for Machine Object), which is a binary file generated from the respective PO file and is used while the internationalized program is run. Translators do not deal with MO files; in fact hardly anyone does.

The extension of the message catalog file is to no surprise either `.po` or `.mo`. The base name is either the name of the program it accompanies, or the language the file is for, depending on the situation. This is a bit confusing. Examples are `psql.po` (PO file for psql) or `fr.mo` (MO file in French).

The file format of the PO files is illustrated here:

```
# comment

msgid "original string"
msgstr "translated string"

msgid "more original"
msgstr "another translated"
"string can be broken up like this"

...
```

The msgid's are extracted from the program source. (They need not be, but this is the most common way.) The msgstr lines are initially empty and are filled in with useful strings by the translator. The strings can contain C-style escape characters and can be continued across lines as illustrated. (The next line must start at the beginning of the line.)

The # character introduces a comment. If whitespace immediately follows the # character, then this is a comment maintained by the translator. There can also be automatic comments, which have a non-whitespace character immediately following the #. These are maintained by the various tools that operate on the PO files and are intended to aid the translator.

```
#. automatic comment
#: filename.c:1023
#, flags, flags
```

The #. style comments are extracted from the source file where the message is used. Possibly the programmer has inserted information for the translator, such as about expected alignment. The #: comment indicates the exact location(s) where the message is used in the source. The translator need not look at the program source, but he can if there is doubt about the correct translation. The #, comments contain flags that describe the message in some way. There are currently two flags: `fuzzy` is set if the message has possibly been outdated because of changes in the program source. The translator can then verify this and possibly remove the fuzzy flag. Note that fuzzy messages are not made available to the end user. The other flag is `c-format`, which indicates that the message is a `printf` -style format template. This means that the translation should also be a format string with the same number and type of placeholders. There are tools that can verify this, which key off the c-format flag.

48.1.3. Creating and maintaining message catalogs

OK, so how does one create a "blank" message catalog? First, go into the directory that contains the program whose messages you want to translate. If there is a file `nls.mk`, then this program has been prepared for translation.

If there are already some `.po` files, then someone has already done some translation work. The files are named *`language`*`.po`, where *`language`* is the *ISO 639-1 two-letter language code (in lower case)*[1], e.g., `fr.po` for French. If there is really a need for more than one translation effort per language then the files can also be named *`language_region`*`.po` where *`region`* is the *ISO 3166-1 two-letter country code (in upper case)*[2], e.g., `pt_BR.po` for Portuguese in Brazil. If you find the language you wanted you can just start working on that file.

If you need to start a new translation effort, then first run the command:

```
gmake init-po
```

This will create a file *`progname`*`.pot`. (`.pot` to distinguish it from PO files that are "in production". The `T` stands for "template".) Copy this file to *`language`*`.po` and edit it. To make it known that the new language is available, also edit the file `nls.mk` and add the language (or language and country) code to the line that looks like:

```
AVAIL_LANGUAGES := de fr
```

(Other languages can appear, of course.)

As the underlying program or library changes, messages might be changed or added by the programmers. In this case you do not need to start from scratch. Instead, run the command:

```
gmake update-po
```

which will create a new blank message catalog file (the pot file you started with) and will merge it with the existing PO files. If the merge algorithm is not sure about a particular message it marks it "fuzzy" as explained above. The new PO file is saved with a `.po.new` extension.

48.1.4. Editing the PO files

The PO files can be edited with a regular text editor. The translator should only change the area between the quotes after the msgstr directive, add comments, and alter the fuzzy flag. There is (unsurprisingly) a PO mode for Emacs, which I find quite useful.

The PO files need not be completely filled in. The software will automatically fall back to the original string if no translation (or an empty translation) is available. It is no problem to

---

[1] *http://lcweb.loc.gov/standards/iso639-2/englangn.html*

[2] *http://www.din.de/gremien/nas/nabd/iso3166ma/codlstp1/en_listp1.html*

submit incomplete translations for inclusions in the source tree; that gives room for other people to pick up your work. However, you are encouraged to give priority to removing fuzzy entries after doing a merge. Remember that fuzzy entries will not be installed; they only serve as reference for what might be the right translation.

Here are some things to keep in mind while editing the translations:

- Make sure that if the original ends with a newline, the translation does, too. Similarly for tabs, etc.
- If the original is a `printf` format string, the translation also needs to be. The translation also needs to have the same format specifiers in the same order. Sometimes the natural rules of the language make this impossible or at least awkward. In that case you can modify the format specifiers like this:

  ```
  msgstr "Die Datei %2$s hat %1$u Zeichen."
  ```

  Then the first placeholder will actually use the second argument from the list. The *`digits$`* needs to follow the % immediately, before any other format manipulators. (This feature really exists in the `printf` family of functions. You might not have heard of it before because there is little use for it outside of message internationalization.)
- If the original string contains a linguistic mistake, report that (or fix it yourself in the program source) and translate normally. The corrected string can be merged in when the program sources have been updated. If the original string contains a factual mistake, report that (or fix it yourself) and do not translate it. Instead, you can mark the string with a comment in the PO file.
- Maintain the style and tone of the original string. Specifically, messages that are not sentences (`cannot open file %s`) should probably not start with a capital letter (if your language distinguishes letter case) or end with a period (if your language uses punctuation marks). It might help to read *Section 47.3* (page 120).
- If you don't know what a message means, or if it is ambiguous, ask on the developers' mailing list. Chances are that English speaking end users might also not understand it or find it ambiguous, so it's best to improve the message.

48.2. For the Programmer

48.2.1. Mechanics

This section describes how to implement native language support in a program or library that is part of the PostgreSQL distribution. Currently, it only applies to C programs.

Adding NLS support to a program

1. Insert this code into the start-up sequence of the program:

   ```
   #ifdef ENABLE_NLS
   #include <locale.h>
   #endif

   ...

   #ifdef ENABLE_NLS
   setlocale(LC_ALL, "");
   bindtextdomain("progname", LOCALEDIR);
   textdomain("progname");
   #endif
   ```

   (The *progname* can actually be chosen freely.)

2. Wherever a message that is a candidate for translation is found, a call to `gettext()` needs to be inserted. E.g.:

   ```
   fprintf(stderr, "panic level %d\n", lvl);
   ```

   would be changed to:

   ```
   fprintf(stderr, gettext("panic level %d\n"), lvl);
   ```

   (`gettext` is defined as a no-op if NLS support is not configured.)

   This tends to add a lot of clutter. One common shortcut is to use:

   ```
   #define _(x) gettext(x)
   ```

   Another solution is feasible if the program does much of its communication through one or a few functions, such as `ereport()` in the backend. Then you make this function call `gettext` internally on all input strings.

3. Add a file nls.mk in the directory with the program sources. This file will be read as a makefile. The following variable assignments need to be made here:

   `CATALOG_NAME`

   The program name, as provided in the `textdomain()` call.

   `AVAIL_LANGUAGES`

   List of provided translations - initially empty.

   `GETTEXT_FILES`

   List of files that contain translatable strings, i.e., those marked with `gettext` or an alternative solution. Eventually, this will include nearly all source files of the program. If this list gets too long you can make the first "file" be a `+` and the second word be a file that contains one file name per line.

`GETTEXT_TRIGGERS`

The tools that generate message catalogs for the translators to work on need to know what function calls contain translatable strings. By default, only `gettext()` calls are known. If you used `_` or other identifiers you need to list them here. If the translatable string is not the first argument, the item needs to be of the form `func:2` (for the second argument). If you have a function that supports pluralized messages, the item should look like `func:1,2` (identifying the singular and plural message arguments).

The build system will automatically take care of building and installing the message catalogs.

48.2.2. Message-writing guidelines

Here are some guidelines for writing messages that are easily translatable.

- Do not construct sentences at run-time, like:

  ```
  printf("Files were %s.\n", flag ? "copied" : "removed");
  ```

  The word order within the sentence might be different in other languages. Also, even if you remember to call `gettext()` on each fragment, the fragments might not translate well separately. It's better to duplicate a little code so that each message to be translated is a coherent whole. Only numbers, file names, and such-like run-time variables should be inserted at run time into a message text.

- For similar reasons, this won't work:

  ```
  printf("copied %d file%s", n, n!=1 ? "s" : "");
  ```

  because it assumes how the plural is formed. If you figured you could solve it like this:

  ```
  if (n==1)
      printf("copied 1 file");
  else
      printf("copied %d files", n):
  ```

  then be disappointed. Some languages have more than two forms, with some peculiar rules. It's often best to design the message to avoid the issue altogether, for instance like this:

  ```
  printf("number of copied files: %d", n);
  ```

  If you really want to construct a properly pluralized message, there is support for this, but it's a bit awkward. When generating a primary or detail error message in `ereport()`, you can write something like this:

  ```
  errmsg_plural("copied %d file",
                "copied %d files",
                n,
                n)
  ```

The first argument is the format string appropriate for English singular form, the second is the format string appropriate for English plural form, and the third is the integer control value that determines which plural form to use. Subsequent arguments are formatted per the format string as usual. (Normally, the pluralization control value will also be one of the values to be formatted, so it has to be written twice.) In English it only matters whether `n` is 1 or not 1, but in other languages there can be many different plural forms. The translator sees the two English forms as a group and has the opportunity to supply multiple substitute strings, with the appropriate one being selected based on the run-time value of `n`.

If you need to pluralize a message that isn't going directly to an `errmsg` or `errdetail` report, you have to use the underlying function `ngettext`. See the gettext documentation.

- If you want to communicate something to the translator, such as about how a message is intended to line up with other output, precede the occurrence of the string with a comment that starts with `translator`, e.g.:

  ```
  /* translator: This message is not what it seems to be. */
  ```

  These comments are copied to the message catalog files so that the translators can see them.

Chapter 49. Writing A Procedural Language Handler

All calls to functions that are written in a language other than the current "version 1" interface for compiled languages (this includes functions in user-defined procedural languages, functions written in SQL, and functions using the version 0 compiled language interface), go through a *call handler* function for the specific language. It is the responsibility of the call handler to execute the function in a meaningful way, such as by interpreting the supplied source text. This chapter outlines how a new procedural language's call handler can be written.

The call handler for a procedural language is a "normal" function that must be written in a compiled language such as C, using the version-1 interface, and registered with PostgreSQL as taking no arguments and returning the type `language_handler`. This special pseudotype identifies the function as a call handler and prevents it from being called directly in SQL commands. For more details on C language calling conventions and dynamic loading, see *Section 35.9* (Vol.III).

The call handler is called in the same way as any other function: It receives a pointer to a `FunctionCallInfoData struct` containing argument values and information about the called function, and it is expected to return a `Datum` result (and possibly set the `isnull` field of the `FunctionCallInfoData` structure, if it wishes to return an SQL null result). The difference between a call handler and an ordinary callee function is that the `flinfo->fn_oid` field of the `FunctionCallInfoData` structure will contain the OID of the actual function to be called, not of the call handler itself. The call handler must use this field to determine which function to execute. Also, the passed argument list has been set up according to the declaration of the target function, not of the call handler.

It's up to the call handler to fetch the entry of the function from the `pg_proc` system catalog and to analyze the argument and return types of the called function. The `AS` clause from the `CREATE FUNCTION` command for the function will be found in the `prosrc` column of the `pg_proc` row. This is commonly source text in the procedural language, but in theory it could be something else, such as a path name to a file, or anything else that tells the call handler what to do in detail.

Often, the same function is called many times per SQL statement. A call handler can avoid repeated lookups of information about the called function by using the `flinfo->fn_extra` field. This will initially be `NULL`, but can be set by the call handler to point at information about the called function. On subsequent calls, if `flinfo->fn_extra` is already non-`NULL` then it can be used and the information lookup step skipped. The call handler must make sure that `flinfo->fn_extra` is made to point at memory that will live at least until the end of the current query, since an `FmgrInfo` data structure could be kept that long. One way to do this is to allocate the extra data in the memory context specified by `flinfo->fn_mcxt`; such data will normally have the same lifespan as the `FmgrInfo` itself. But the handler could also choose to use a longer-lived memory context so that it can cache function definition information across queries.

When a procedural-language function is invoked as a trigger, no arguments are passed in the usual way, but the `FunctionCallInfoData`'s `context` field points at a `TriggerData` structure, rather than being `NULL` as it is in a plain function call. A language handler should provide mechanisms for procedural-language functions to get at the trigger information.

This is a template for a procedural-language handler written in C:

```
#include "postgres.h"
#include "executor/spi.h"
#include "commands/trigger.h"
#include "fmgr.h"
#include "access/heapam.h"
#include "utils/syscache.h"
#include "catalog/pg_proc.h"
#include "catalog/pg_type.h"

#ifdef PG_MODULE_MAGIC
PG_MODULE_MAGIC;
#endif

PG_FUNCTION_INFO_V1(plsample_call_handler);

Datum
plsample_call_handler(PG_FUNCTION_ARGS)
{
    Datum          retval;

    if (CALLED_AS_TRIGGER(fcinfo))
    {
        /*
         * Called as a trigger procedure
         */
        TriggerData    *trigdata = (TriggerData *) fcinfo->context;

        retval = ...
    }
    else
```

```
    {
        /*
         * Called as a function
         */

        retval = ...
    }

    return retval;
}
```

Only a few thousand lines of code have to be added instead of the dots to complete the call handler.

After having compiled the handler function into a loadable module (see *Section 35.9.6* - Vol.III), the following commands then register the sample procedural language:

```
CREATE FUNCTION plsample_call_handler() RETURNS language_handler
    AS 'filename'
    LANGUAGE C;
CREATE LANGUAGE plsample
    HANDLER plsample_call_handler;
```

Although providing a call handler is sufficient to create a minimal procedural language, there are two other functions that can optionally be provided to make the language more convenient to use. These are a *validator* and an *inline handler*. A validator can be provided to allow language-specific checking to be done during CREATE FUNCTION. An inline handler can be provided to allow the language to support anonymous code blocks executed via the DO command.

If a validator is provided by a procedural language, it must be declared as a function taking a single parameter of type `oid`. The validator's result is ignored, so it is customarily declared to return `void`. The validator will be called at the end of a `CREATE FUNCTION` command that has created or updated a function written in the procedural language. The passed-in OID is the OID of the function's `pg_proc` row. The validator must fetch this row in the usual way, and do whatever checking is appropriate. Typical checks include verifying that the function's argument and result types are supported by the language, and that the function's body is syntactically correct in the language. If the validator finds the function to be okay, it should just return. If it finds an error, it should report that via the normal `ereport()` error reporting mechanism. Throwing an error will force a transaction rollback and thus prevent the incorrect function definition from being committed.

Validator functions should typically honor the *check_function_bodies* parameter: if it is turned off then any expensive or context-sensitive checking should be skipped. In particular, this parameter is turned off by pg_dump so that it can load procedural language functions without worrying about possible dependencies of the function bodies on other database objects. (Because of this requirement, the call handler should avoid assuming that the validator has fully checked the function. The point of having a validator is not to let the call handler omit checks, but to notify the user immediately if there are obvious errors in a `CREATE FUNCTION` command.)

If an inline handler is provided by a procedural language, it must be declared as a function taking a single parameter of type `internal`. The inline handler's result is ignored, so it is customarily declared to return `void`. The inline handler will be called when a `DO` statement is executed specifying the procedural language. The parameter actually passed is a pointer to an `InlineCodeBlock` struct, which contains information about the `DO` statement's parameters, in particular the text of the anonymous code block to be executed. The inline handler should execute this code and return.

The procedural languages included in the standard distribution are good references when trying to write your own language handler. Look into the `src/pl` subdirectory of the source tree. The CREATE LANGUAGE reference page also has some useful details.

Chapter 50. Genetic Query Optimizer

Author: Written by Martin Utesch (<`utesch@aut.tu-freiberg.de`>) for the Institute of Automatic Control at the University of Mining and Technology in Freiberg, Germany.

50.1. Query Handling as a Complex Optimization Problem

Among all relational operators the most difficult one to process and optimize is the *join*. The number of possible query plans grows exponentially with the number of joins in the query. Further optimization effort is caused by the support of a variety of *join methods* (e.g., nested loop, hash join, merge join in PostgreSQL) to process individual joins and a diversity of *indexes* (e.g., B-tree, hash, GiST and GIN in PostgreSQL) as access paths for relations.

The normal PostgreSQL query optimizer performs a *near-exhaustive search* over the space of alternative strategies. This algorithm, first introduced in IBM's System R database, produces a near-optimal join order, but can take an enormous amount of time and memory space when the number of joins in the query grows large. This makes the ordinary PostgreSQL query optimizer inappropriate for queries that join a large number of tables.

The Institute of Automatic Control at the University of Mining and Technology, in Freiberg, Germany, encountered some problems when it wanted to use PostgreSQL as the backend for a decision support knowledge based system for the maintenance of an electrical power grid. The DBMS needed to handle large join queries for the inference machine of the knowledge based system. The number of joins in these queries made using the normal query optimizer infeasible.

In the following we describe the implementation of a *genetic algorithm* to solve the join ordering problem in a manner that is efficient for queries involving large numbers of joins.

50.2. Genetic Algorithms

The genetic algorithm (GA) is a heuristic optimization method which operates through randomized search. The set of possible solutions for the optimization problem is considered as a *population* of *individuals*. The degree of adaptation of an individual to its environment is specified by its *fitness*.

The coordinates of an individual in the search space are represented by *chromosomes*, in essence a set of character strings. A *gene* is a subsection of a chromosome which encodes the value of a single parameter being optimized. Typical encodings for a gene could be *binary* or *integer*.

Through simulation of the evolutionary operations *recombination, mutation,* and *selection* new generations of search points are found that show a higher average fitness than their ancestors.

According to the comp.ai.genetic FAQ it cannot be stressed too strongly that a GA is not a pure random search for a solution to a problem. A GA uses stochastic processes, but the result is distinctly non-random (better than random).

P(t) generation of ancestors at a time t

P''(t) generation of descendants at a time t

```
+=========================================+
|>>>>>>>>>>>  Algorithm GA  <<<<<<<<<<<<<<|
+=========================================+
| INITIALIZE t := 0                       |
+=========================================+
| INITIALIZE P(t)                         |
+=========================================+
| evaluate FITNESS of P(t)                |
+=========================================+
| while not STOPPING CRITERION do         |
|   +-------------------------------------+
|   | P'(t)  := RECOMBINATION{P(t)}       |
|   +-------------------------------------+
|   | P''(t) := MUTATION{P'(t)}           |
|   +-------------------------------------+
|   | P(t+1) := SELECTION{P''(t) + P(t)}  |
|   +-------------------------------------+
|   | evaluate FITNESS of P''(t)          |
|   +-------------------------------------+
|   | t := t + 1                          |
+===+=====================================+
```

Figure 50-1. Structured Diagram of a Genetic Algorithm

50.3. Genetic Query Optimization (GEQO) in PostgreSQL

The GEQO module approaches the query optimization problem as though it were the well-known traveling salesman problem (TSP). Possible query plans are encoded as integer strings. Each string represents the join order from one relation of the query to the next. For example, the join tree

```
    /\
   /\ 2
  /\ 3
4  1
```

is encoded by the integer string '4-1-3-2', which means, first join relation '4' and '1', then '3', and then '2', where 1, 2, 3, 4 are relation IDs within the PostgreSQL optimizer.

Specific characteristics of the GEQO implementation in PostgreSQL are:

- Usage of a *steady state* GA (replacement of the least fit individuals in a population, not whole-generational replacement) allows fast convergence towards improved query plans. This is essential for query handling with reasonable time;
- Usage of *edge recombination crossover* which is especially suited to keep edge losses low for the solution of the TSP by means of a GA ;
- Mutation as genetic operator is deprecated so that no repair mechanisms are needed to generate legal TSP tours.

Parts of the GEQO module are adapted from D. Whitley's Genitor algorithm.

The GEQO module allows the PostgreSQL query optimizer to support large join queries effectively through non-exhaustive search.

50.3.1. Generating Possible Plans with GEQO

The GEQO planning process uses the standard planner code to generate plans for scans of individual relations. Then join plans are developed using the genetic approach. As shown above, each candidate join plan is represented by a sequence in which to join the base relations. In the initial stage, the GEQO code simply generates some possible join sequences at random. For each join sequence considered, the standard planner code is invoked to estimate the cost of performing the query using that join sequence. (For each step of the join sequence, all three possible join strategies are considered; and all the initially-determined relation scan plans are available. The estimated cost is the cheapest of these possibilities.) Join sequences with lower estimated cost are considered "more fit" than those with higher cost. The genetic algorithm discards the least fit candidates. Then new candidates are generated by combining genes of more-fit candidates - that is, by using randomly-chosen portions of known low-cost join sequences to create new sequences for consideration. This process is repeated until a preset number of join sequences have been considered; then the best one found at any time during the search is used to generate the finished plan.

This process is inherently nondeterministic, because of the randomized choices made during both the initial population selection and subsequent "mutation" of the best candidates. To avoid surprising changes of the selected plan, each run of the GEQO algorithm restarts its random number generator with the current *geqo_seed* parameter setting. As long as `geqo_seed` and the other GEQO parameters are kept fixed, the same plan will be generated for a given query (and other planner inputs such as statistics). To experiment with different search paths, try changing `geqo_seed`.

50.3.2. Future Implementation Tasks for PostgreSQL GEQO

Work is still needed to improve the genetic algorithm parameter settings. In file `src/backend/optimizer/geqo/geqo_main.c`, routines `gimme_pool_size` and `gimme_number_generations`, we have to find a compromise for the parameter settings to satisfy two competing demands:

- Optimality of the query plan
- Computing time

In the current implementation, the fitness of each candidate join sequence is estimated by running the standard planner's join selection and cost estimation code from scratch. To the extent that different candidates use similar sub-sequences of joins, a great deal of work will be repeated. This could be made significantly faster by retaining cost estimates for sub-joins. The problem is to avoid expending unreasonable amounts of memory on retaining that state.

At a more basic level, it is not clear that solving query optimization with a GA algorithm designed for TSP is appropriate. In the TSP case, the cost associated with any substring (partial tour) is independent of the rest of the tour, but this is certainly not true for query optimization. Thus it is questionable whether edge recombination crossover is the most effective mutation procedure.

50.4. Further Reading

The following resources contain additional information about genetic algorithms:

- The Hitch-Hiker's Guide to Evolutionary Computation[1], (FAQ for *news://comp.ai.genetic*)
- Evolutionary Computation and its application to art and design[2], by Craig Reynolds
- Fundamentals of Database Systems[3]
- The design and implementation of the POSTGRES query optimizer[4]

---

1 *http://www.cs.bham.ac.uk/Mirrors/ftp.de.uu.net/EC/clife/www/location.htm*
2 *http://www.red3d.com/cwr/evolve.html*
3 *http://www.postgresql.org/docs/9.0/static/biblio.html#ELMA04*
4 *http://s2k-ftp.cs.berkeley.edu:8000/postgres/papers/UCB-MS-zfong.pdf*

Chapter 51. Index Access Method Interface Definition

This chapter defines the interface between the core PostgreSQL system and *index access methods*, which manage individual index types. The core system knows nothing about indexes beyond what is specified here, so it is possible to develop entirely new index types by writing add-on code.

All indexes in PostgreSQL are what are known technically as *secondary indexes*; that is, the index is physically separate from the table file that it describes. Each index is stored as its own physical *relation* and so is described by an entry in the `pg_class` catalog. The contents of an index are entirely under the control of its index access method. In practice, all index access methods divide indexes into standard-size pages so that they can use the regular storage manager and buffer manager to access the index contents. (All the existing index access methods furthermore use the standard page layout described in *Section 54.5* (page 176), and they all use the same format for index tuple headers; but these decisions are not forced on an access method.)

An index is effectively a mapping from some data key values to *tuple identifiers*, or TIDs, of row versions (tuples) in the index's parent table. A TID consists of a block number and an item number within that block (see *Section 54.5* - page 176). This is sufficient information to fetch a particular row version from the table. Indexes are not directly aware that under MVCC, there might be multiple extant versions of the same logical row; to an index, each tuple is an independent object that needs its own index entry. Thus, an update of a row always creates all-new index entries for the row, even if the key values did not change. (HOT tuples are an exception to this statement; but indexes do not deal with those, either.) Index entries for dead tuples are reclaimed (by vacuuming) when the dead tuples themselves are reclaimed.

51.1. Catalog Entries for Indexes

Each index access method is described by a row in the `pg_am` system catalog (see *Section 45.3* - page 30). The principal contents of a `pg_am` row are references to `pg_proc` (page 52) entries that identify the index access functions supplied by the access method. The APIs for these functions are defined later in this chapter. In addition, the `pg_am` row specifies a few fixed properties of the access method, such as whether it can support multicolumn indexes. There is not currently any special support for creating or deleting `pg_am` entries; anyone able to write a new access method is expected to be competent to insert an appropriate row for themselves.

To be useful, an index access method must also have one or more *operator families* and *operator classes* defined in `pg_opfamily` (page 51), `pg_opclass` (page 49), `pg_amop` (page 31), and `pg_amproc` (page 32). These entries allow the planner to determine what kinds of query qualifications can be used with indexes of this access method. Operator families and classes are described in *Section 35.14* (Vol.II), which is prerequisite material for reading this chapter.

An individual index is defined by a `pg_class` (page 37) entry that describes it as a physical relation, plus a `pg_index` (page 46) entry that shows the logical content of the index - that is, the set of index columns it has and the semantics of those columns, as captured by the associated operator classes. The index columns (key values) can be either simple columns of the underlying table or expressions over the table rows. The index access method normally has no interest in where the index key values come from (it is always handed precomputed key values) but it will be very interested in the operator class information in `pg_index`. Both of these catalog entries can be accessed as part of the `Relation` data structure that is passed to all operations on the index.

Some of the flag columns of `pg_am` have nonobvious implications. The requirements of `amcanunique` are discussed in *Section 51.5* (page 150). The `amcanmulticol` flag asserts that the access method supports multicolumn indexes, while `amoptionalkey` asserts that it allows scans where no indexable restriction clause is given for the first index column. When `amcanmulticol` is false, `amoptionalkey` essentially says whether the access method allows full-index scans without any restriction clause. Access methods that support multiple index columns *must* support scans that omit restrictions on any or all of the columns after the first; however they are permitted to require some restriction to appear for the first index column, and this is signaled by setting `amoptionalkey` false. `amindexnulls` asserts that index entries are created for NULL key values. Since most indexable operators are strict and hence cannot return TRUE for NULL inputs, it is at first sight attractive to not store index entries for null values: they could never be returned by an index scan anyway. However, this argument fails when an index scan has no restriction clause for a given index column. In practice this means that indexes that have `amoptionalkey` true must index nulls, since the planner might decide to use such an index with no scan keys at all. A related restriction is that an index access method that supports multiple index columns *must* support indexing null values in columns after the first, because the planner will assume the index can be used for queries that do not restrict these columns. For example, consider an index on (a,b) and a query with `WHERE a = 4` . The system will assume the index can be used to scan for rows with `a = 4`, which is wrong if the index omits rows where `b` is null. It is, however, OK to omit rows where the first indexed column is null. Thus, `amindexnulls` should be set true only if the index access method indexes all rows, including arbitrary combinations of null values. An index access method that sets `amindexnulls` may also set `amsearchnulls`, indicating that it supports `IS NULL` and `IS NOT NULL` clauses as search conditions.

51.2. Index Access Method Functions

The index construction and maintenance functions that an index access method must provide are:

```
IndexBuildResult *
ambuild (Relation heapRelation,
         Relation indexRelation,
         IndexInfo *indexInfo);
```

Build a new index. The index relation has been physically created, but is empty. It must be filled in with whatever fixed data the access method requires, plus entries for all tuples already existing in the table. Ordinarily the `ambuild` function will call `IndexBuildHeapScan()` to scan the table for existing tuples and compute the keys that need to be inserted into the index. The function must return a palloc'd struct containing statistics about the new index.

```
bool
aminsert (Relation indexRelation,
          Datum *values,
          bool *isnull,
          ItemPointer heap_tid,
          Relation heapRelation,
          IndexUniqueCheck checkUnique);
```

Insert a new tuple into an existing index. The `values` and `isnull` arrays give the key values to be indexed, and `heap_tid` is the TID to be indexed. If the access method supports unique indexes (its `pg_am.amcanunique` flag is true) then `checkUnique` indicates the type of uniqueness check to perform. This varies depending on whether the unique constraint is deferrable; see *Section 51.5* (page 150) for details. Normally the access method only needs the `heapRelation` parameter when performing uniqueness checking (since then it will have to look into the heap to verify tuple liveness).

The function's Boolean result value is significant only when `checkUnique` is `UNIQUE_CHECK_PARTIAL`. In this case a TRUE result means the new entry is known unique, whereas FALSE means it might be non-unique (and a deferred uniqueness check must be scheduled). For other cases a constant FALSE result is recommended.

Some indexes might not index all tuples. If the tuple is not to be indexed, `aminsert` should just return without doing anything.

```
IndexBulkDeleteResult *
ambulkdelete (IndexVacuumInfo *info,
              IndexBulkDeleteResult *stats,
              IndexBulkDeleteCallback callback,
              void *callback_state);
```

Delete tuple(s) from the index. This is a "bulk delete" operation that is intended to be implemented by scanning the whole index and checking each entry to see if it should be deleted. The passed-in `callback` function must be called, in the style `callback(TID, callback_state) returns bool`, to determine whether any particular index entry, as identified by its referenced TID, is to be deleted. Must return either NULL or a palloc'd struct containing statistics about the effects of the deletion operation. It is OK to return NULL if no information needs to be passed on to `amvacuumcleanup`.

Because of limited `maintenance_work_mem`, `ambulkdelete` might need to be called more than once when many tuples are to be deleted. The `stats` argument is the result of the previous call for this index (it is NULL for the first call within a `VACUUM` operation). This allows the AM to accumulate statistics across the whole operation. Typically, `ambulkdelete` will modify and return the same struct if the passed `stats` is not null.

```
IndexBulkDeleteResult *
amvacuumcleanup (IndexVacuumInfo *info,
                 IndexBulkDeleteResult *stats);
```

Clean up after a `VACUUM` operation (zero or more `ambulkdelete` calls). This does not have to do anything beyond returning index statistics, but it might perform bulk cleanup such as reclaiming empty index pages. `stats` is whatever the last `ambulkdelete` call returned, or NULL if `ambulkdelete` was not called because no tuples needed to be deleted. If the result is not NULL it must be a palloc'd struct. The statistics it contains will be used to update `pg_class`, and will be reported by `VACUUM` if `VERBOSE` is given. It is OK to return NULL if the index was not changed at all during the `VACUUM` operation, but otherwise correct stats should be returned.

As of PostgreSQL 9.0, `amvacuumcleanup` will also be called at completion of an `ANALYZE` operation. In this case `stats` is always NULL and any return value will be ignored. This case can be distinguished by checking `info->analyze_only`. It is recommended that the access method do nothing except post-insert cleanup in such a call, and that only in an autovacuum worker process.

```
void
amcostestimate (PlannerInfo *root,
                IndexOptInfo *index,
                List *indexQuals,
                RelOptInfo *outer_rel,
                Cost *indexStartupCost,
                Cost *indexTotalCost,
                Selectivity *indexSelectivity,
                double *indexCorrelation);
```

Estimate the costs of an index scan. This function is described fully in *Section 51.6* (page 152), below.

```
bytea *
amoptions (ArrayType *reloptions,
           bool validate);
```

Parse and validate the reloptions array for an index. This is called only when a non-null reloptions array exists for the index. `reloptions` is a `text` array containing entries of the form *`name`* `=`*`value`*. The function should construct a `bytea` value, which will be copied into the `rd_options` field of the index's relcache entry. The data contents of the `bytea` value are open for the access method to define; most of the standard access methods use struct `StdRdOptions`. When `validate` is true, the function should report a suitable error message if any of the options are unrecognized or have invalid values; when `validate` is false, invalid entries should be silently ignored. (`validate` is false when loading options already stored in `pg_catalog`; an invalid entry could only be found if the access method has changed its rules for options, and in that case ignoring obsolete entries is appropriate.) It is OK to return NULL if default behavior is wanted.

The purpose of an index, of course, is to support scans for tuples matching an indexable `WHERE` condition, often called a *qualifier* or *scan key*. The semantics of index scanning are described more fully in *Section 51.3* (page 147), below. An index access method can support "plain" index scans, "bitmap" index scans, or both. The scan-related functions that an index access method must or may provide are:

```
IndexScanDesc
ambeginscan (Relation indexRelation,
             int nkeys,
             ScanKey key);
```

Begin a new scan. The `key` array (of length `nkeys`) describes the scan key(s) for the index scan. The result must be a palloc'd struct. For implementation reasons the index access method *must* create this struct by calling `RelationGetIndexScan()`. In most cases `ambeginscan` itself does little beyond making that call; the interesting parts of index-scan startup are in `amrescan`.

```
boolean
amgettuple (IndexScanDesc scan,
            ScanDirection direction);
```

Fetch the next tuple in the given scan, moving in the given direction (forward or backward in the index). Returns TRUE if a tuple was obtained, FALSE if no matching tuples remain. In the TRUE case the tuple TID is stored into the `scan` structure. Note that "success" means only that the index contains an entry that matches the scan keys, not that the tuple necessarily still exists in the heap or will pass the caller's snapshot test. On success, `amgettuple` must also set `scan->xs_recheck` to TRUE or FALSE. FALSE means it is certain that the index entry matches the scan keys. TRUE means this is not certain, and the conditions represented by the scan keys must be rechecked against the heap tuple after fetching it. This provision supports "lossy" index operators. Note that rechecking will extend only to the scan conditions; a partial index predicate (if any) is never rechecked by `amgettuple` callers.

The `amgettuple` function need only be provided if the access method supports "plain" index scans. If it doesn't, the `amgettuple` field in its `pg_am` row must be set to zero.

```
int64
amgetbitmap (IndexScanDesc scan,
             TIDBitmap *tbm);
```

Fetch all tuples in the given scan and add them to the caller-supplied TIDBitmap (that is, OR the set of tuple IDs into whatever set is already in the bitmap). The number of tuples fetched is returned (this might be just an approximate count, for instance some AMs do not detect duplicates). While inserting tuple IDs into the bitmap, `amgetbitmap` can indicate that rechecking of the scan conditions is required for specific tuple IDs. This is analogous to the `xs_recheck` output parameter of `amgettuple`. Note: in the current implementation, support for this feature is conflated with support for lossy storage of the bitmap itself, and therefore callers recheck both the scan conditions and the partial index predicate (if any) for recheckable tuples. That might not always be true, however. `amgetbitmap` and `amgettuple` cannot be used in the same index scan; there are other restrictions too when using `amgetbitmap`, as explained in *Section 51.3* (page 147).

The `amgetbitmap` function need only be provided if the access method supports "bitmap" index scans. If it doesn't, the `amgetbitmap` field in its `pg_am` row must be set to zero.

```
void
amrescan (IndexScanDesc scan,
          ScanKey key);
```

Restart the given scan, possibly with new scan keys (to continue using the old keys, NULL is passed for `key`). Note that it is not possible for the number of keys to be changed. In practice the restart feature is used when a new outer tuple is selected by a nested-loop join and so a new key comparison value is needed, but the scan key structure remains the same. This function is also called by `RelationGetIndexScan()`, so it is used for initial setup of an index scan as well as rescanning.

```
void
amendscan (IndexScanDesc scan);
```

End a scan and release resources. The `scan` struct itself should not be freed, but any locks or pins taken internally by the access method must be released.

```
void
ammarkpos (IndexScanDesc scan);
```

Mark current scan position. The access method need only support one remembered scan position per scan.

```
void
amrestrpos (IndexScanDesc scan);
```

Restore the scan to the most recently marked position.

By convention, the `pg_proc` entry for an index access method function should show the correct number of arguments, but declare them all as type `internal` (since most of the arguments have types that are not known to SQL, and we don't want users calling the functions directly anyway). The return type is declared as `void`, `internal`, or `boolean` as appropriate. The only exception is `amoptions`, which should be correctly declared as taking `text[]` and `bool` and returning `bytea`. This provision allows client code to execute `amoptions` to test validity of options settings.

51.3. Index Scanning

In an index scan, the index access method is responsible for regurgitating the TIDs of all the tuples it has been told about that match the *scan keys*. The access method is *not* involved in actually fetching those tuples from the index's parent table, nor in determining whether they pass the scan's time qualification test or other conditions.

A scan key is the internal representation of a `WHERE` clause of the form *`index_key operator constant`*, where the index key is one of the columns of the index and the operator is one of the members of the operator family associated with that index column. An index scan has zero or more scan keys, which are implicitly ANDed - the returned tuples are expected to satisfy all the indicated conditions.

The access method can report that the index is *lossy*, or requires rechecks, for a particular query. This implies that the index scan will return all the entries that pass the scan key, plus possibly additional entries that do not. The core system's index-scan machinery will then apply the index conditions again to the heap tuple to verify whether or not it really should be selected. If the recheck option is not specified, the index scan must return exactly the set of matching entries.

Note that it is entirely up to the access method to ensure that it correctly finds all and only the entries passing all the given scan keys. Also, the core system will simply hand off all the `WHERE` clauses that match the index keys and operator families, without any semantic analysis to determine whether they are redundant or contradictory. As an example, given `WHERE x > 4 AND x > 14` where `x` is a b-tree indexed column, it is left to the b-tree `amrescan` function to realize that the first scan key is redundant and can be discarded. The extent of preprocessing needed during `amrescan` will depend on the extent to which the index access method needs to reduce the scan keys to a "normalized" form.

Some access methods return index entries in a well-defined order, others do not. If entries are returned in sorted order, the access method should set `pg_am. amcanorder` true to indicate that it supports ordered scans. All such access methods must use btree-compatible strategy numbers for their equality and ordering operators.

The `amgettuple` function has a `direction` argument, which can be either `ForwardScanDirection` (the normal case) or `BackwardScanDirection`. If the first call after `amrescan` specifies `BackwardScanDirection` , then the set of matching index entries is to be scanned back-to-front rather than in the normal front-to-back direction, so `amgettuple` must return the last matching tuple in the index, rather than the first one as it normally would. (This will only occur for access methods that advertise they support ordered scans.) After the first call, `amgettuple` must be prepared to advance the scan in either direction from the most recently returned entry. (But if `pg_am. amcanbackward` is false, all subsequent calls will have the same direction as the first one.)

Access methods that support ordered scans must support "marking" a position in a scan and later returning to the marked position. The same position might be restored multiple times. However, only one position need be remembered per scan; a new `ammarkpos` call overrides the previously marked position. An access method that does not support ordered scans should still provide mark and restore functions in `pg_am`, but it is sufficient to have them throw errors if called.

Both the scan position and the mark position (if any) must be maintained consistently in the face of concurrent insertions or deletions in the index. It is OK if a freshly-inserted entry is not returned by a scan that would have found the entry if it had existed when the scan started, or for the scan to return such an entry upon rescanning or backing up even though it had not been returned the first time through. Similarly, a concurrent delete might or might not be reflected in the results of a scan. What is important is that insertions or deletions not cause the scan to miss or multiply return entries that were not themselves being inserted or deleted.

Instead of using `amgettuple`, an index scan can be done with `amgetbitmap` to fetch all tuples in one call. This can be noticeably more efficient than `amgettuple` because it allows avoiding lock/unlock cycles within the access method. In principle `amgetbitmap` should have the same effects as repeated `amgettuple` calls, but we impose several restrictions to simplify matters. First of all, `amgetbitmap` returns all tuples at once and marking or restoring scan positions isn't supported. Secondly, the tuples are returned in a bitmap which doesn't have any specific ordering, which is why `amgetbitmap` doesn't take a `direction` argument. Finally, `amgetbitmap` does not guarantee any locking of the returned tuples, with implications spelled out in *Section 51.4* (page 149).

Note that it is permitted for an access method to implement only `amgetbitmap` and not `amgettuple`, or vice versa, if its internal implementation is unsuited to one API or the other.

51.4. Index Locking Considerations

Index access methods must handle concurrent updates of the index by multiple processes. The core PostgreSQL system obtains `AccessShareLock` on the index during an index scan, and `RowExclusiveLock` when updating the index (including plain `VACUUM`). Since these lock types do not conflict, the access method is responsible for handling any fine-grained locking it might need. An exclusive lock on the index as a whole will be taken only during index creation, destruction, or `REINDEX`.

Building an index type that supports concurrent updates usually requires extensive and subtle analysis of the required behavior. For the b-tree and hash index types, you can read about the design decisions involved in `src/backend/access/nbtree/README` and `src/backend/access/hash/README`.

Aside from the index's own internal consistency requirements, concurrent updates create issues about consistency between the parent table (the *heap*) and the index. Because PostgreSQL separates accesses and updates of the heap from those of the index, there are windows in which the index might be inconsistent with the heap. We handle this problem with the following rules:

- A new heap entry is made before making its index entries. (Therefore a concurrent index scan is likely to fail to see the heap entry. This is okay because the index reader would be uninterested in an uncommitted row anyway. But see *Section* 51.5 - page 150.)
- When a heap entry is to be deleted (by `VACUUM`), all its index entries must be removed first.
- An index scan must maintain a pin on the index page holding the item last returned by `amgettuple`, and `ambulkdelete` cannot delete entries from pages that are pinned by other backends. The need for this rule is explained below.

Without the third rule, it is possible for an index reader to see an index entry just before it is removed by `VACUUM` , and then to arrive at the corresponding heap entry after that was removed by `VACUUM`. This creates no serious problems if that item number is still unused when the reader reaches it, since an empty item slot will be ignored by `heap_fetch()`. But what if a third backend has already re-used the item slot for something else? When using an MVCC-compliant snapshot, there is no problem because the new occupant of the slot is certain to be too new to pass the snapshot test. However, with a non-MVCC-compliant snapshot (such as `SnapshotNow`), it would be possible to accept and return a row that does not in fact match the scan keys. We could defend against this scenario by requiring the scan keys to be rechecked against the heap row in all cases, but that is too expensive. Instead, we use a pin on an index page as a proxy to indicate that the reader might still be "in flight" from the index entry to the matching heap entry. Making `ambulkdelete` block on such a pin ensures that `VACUUM` cannot delete the heap entry before the reader is done with it. This solution costs little in run time, and adds blocking overhead only in the rare cases where there actually is a conflict.

This solution requires that index scans be "synchronous": we have to fetch each heap tuple immediately after scanning the corresponding index entry. This is expensive for a number of reasons. An "asynchronous" scan in which we collect many TIDs from the index, and only visit the heap tuples sometime later, requires much less index locking overhead and can allow a more efficient heap access pattern. Per the above analysis, we must use the synchronous approach for non-MVCC-compliant snapshots, but an asynchronous scan is workable for a query using an MVCC snapshot.

In an `amgetbitmap` index scan, the access method does not keep an index pin on any of the returned tuples. Therefore it is only safe to use such scans with MVCC-compliant snapshots.

51.5. Index Uniqueness Checks

PostgreSQL enforces SQL uniqueness constraints using *unique indexes*, which are indexes that disallow multiple entries with identical keys. An access method that supports this feature sets `pg_am.amcanunique` true. (At present, only b-tree supports it.)

Because of MVCC, it is always necessary to allow duplicate entries to exist physically in an index: the entries might refer to successive versions of a single logical row. The behavior we actually want to enforce is that no MVCC snapshot could include two rows with equal index keys. This breaks down into the following cases that must be checked when inserting a new row into a unique index:

- If a conflicting valid row has been deleted by the current transaction, it's okay. (In particular, since an UPDATE always deletes the old row version before inserting the new version, this will allow an UPDATE on a row without changing the key.)
- If a conflicting row has been inserted by an as-yet-uncommitted transaction, the would-be inserter must wait to see if that transaction commits. If it rolls back then there is no conflict. If it commits without deleting the conflicting row again, there is a uniqueness violation. (In practice we just wait for the other transaction to end and then redo the visibility check in toto.)
- Similarly, if a conflicting valid row has been deleted by an as-yet-uncommitted transaction, the would-be inserter must wait for that transaction to commit or abort, and then repeat the test.

Furthermore, immediately before reporting a uniqueness violation according to the above rules, the access method must recheck the liveness of the row being inserted. If it is committed dead then no violation should be reported. (This case cannot occur during the ordinary scenario of inserting a row that's just been created by the current transaction. It can happen during `CREATE UNIQUE INDEX CONCURRENTLY`, however.)

We require the index access method to apply these tests itself, which means that it must reach into the heap to check the commit status of any row that is shown to have a duplicate key according to the index contents. This is without a doubt ugly and non-modular, but it saves redundant work: if we did a separate probe then the index lookup for a conflicting row would be essentially repeated while finding the place to insert the new row's index entry. What's more, there is no obvious way to avoid race conditions unless the conflict check is an integral part of insertion of the new index entry.

If the unique constraint is deferrable, there is additional complexity: we need to be able to insert an index entry for a new row, but defer any uniqueness-violation error until end of statement or even later. To avoid unnecessary repeat searches of the index, the index access method should do a preliminary uniqueness check during the initial insertion. If this shows that there is definitely no conflicting live tuple, we are done. Otherwise, we schedule a recheck to occur when it is time to enforce the constraint. If, at the time of the recheck, both the inserted tuple and some other tuple with the same key are live, then the error must be reported. (Note that for this purpose, "live" actually means "any tuple in the index entry's HOT chain is live".) To implement this, the `aminsert` function is passed a `checkUnique` parameter having one of the following values:

- `UNIQUE_CHECK_NO` indicates that no uniqueness checking should be done (this is not a unique index).
- `UNIQUE_CHECK_YES` indicates that this is a non-deferrable unique index, and the uniqueness check must be done immediately, as described above.
- `UNIQUE_CHECK_PARTIAL` indicates that the unique constraint is deferrable. PostgreSQL will use this mode to insert each row's index entry. The access method must allow duplicate entries into the index, and report any potential duplicates by returning FALSE from `aminsert`. For each row for which FALSE is returned, a deferred recheck will be scheduled.

  The access method must identify any rows which might violate the unique constraint, but it is not an error for it to report false positives. This allows the check to be done without waiting for other transactions to finish; conflicts reported here are not treated as errors and will be rechecked later, by which time they may no longer be conflicts.
- `UNIQUE_CHECK_EXISTING` indicates that this is a deferred recheck of a row that was reported as a potential uniqueness violation. Although this is implemented by calling `aminsert`, the access method must *not* insert a new index entry in this case. The index entry is already present. Rather, the access method must check to see if there is another live index entry. If so, and if the target row is also still live, report error.

It is recommended that in a `UNIQUE_CHECK_EXISTING` call, the access method further verify that the target row actually does have an existing entry in the index, and report error if not. This is a good idea because the index tuple values passed to `aminsert` will have been recomputed. If the index definition involves functions that are not really immutable, we might be checking the wrong area of the index. Checking that the target row is found in the recheck verifies that we are scanning for the same tuple values as were used in the original insertion.

51.6. Index Cost Estimation Functions

The amcostestimate function is given a list of WHERE clauses that have been determined to be usable with the index. It must return estimates of the cost of accessing the index and the selectivity of the WHERE clauses (that is, the fraction of parent-table rows that will be retrieved during the index scan). For simple cases, nearly all the work of the cost estimator can be done by calling standard routines in the optimizer; the point of having an amcostestimate function is to allow index access methods to provide index-type-specific knowledge, in case it is possible to improve on the standard estimates.

Each amcostestimate function must have the signature:

```
void
amcostestimate (PlannerInfo *root,
                IndexOptInfo *index,
                List *indexQuals,
                RelOptInfo *outer_rel,
                Cost *indexStartupCost,
                Cost *indexTotalCost,
                Selectivity *indexSelectivity,
                double *indexCorrelation);
```

The first four parameters are inputs:

root

The planner's information about the query being processed.

index

The index being considered.

indexQuals

List of index qual clauses (implicitly ANDed); a NIL list indicates no qualifiers are available. Note that the list contains expression trees, not ScanKeys.

outer_rel

If the index is being considered for use in a join inner indexscan, the planner's information about the outer side of the join. Otherwise NULL. When non-NULL, some of the qual clauses will be join clauses with this rel rather than being simple restriction clauses. Also, the cost estimator should expect that the index scan will be repeated for each row of the outer rel.

The last four parameters are pass-by-reference outputs:

*indexStartupCost

Set to cost of index start-up processing

*indexTotalCost

Set to total cost of index processing

*indexSelectivity

Set to index selectivity

*indexCorrelation

Set to correlation coefficient between index scan order and underlying table's order

Note that cost estimate functions must be written in C, not in SQL or any available procedural language, because they must access internal data structures of the planner/optimizer.

The index access costs should be computed using the parameters used by `src/backend/optimizer/path/costsize.c`: a sequential disk block fetch has cost `seq_page_cost`, a nonsequential fetch has cost `random_page_cost`, and the cost of processing one index row should usually be taken as `cpu_index_tuple_cost`. In addition, an appropriate multiple of `cpu_operator_cost` should be charged for any comparison operators invoked during index processing (especially evaluation of the indexQuals themselves).

The access costs should include all disk and CPU costs associated with scanning the index itself, but *not* the costs of retrieving or processing the parent-table rows that are identified by the index.

The "start-up cost" is the part of the total scan cost that must be expended before we can begin to fetch the first row. For most indexes this can be taken as zero, but an index type with a high start-up cost might want to set it nonzero.

The indexSelectivity should be set to the estimated fraction of the parent table rows that will be retrieved during the index scan. In the case of a lossy query, this will typically be higher than the fraction of rows that actually pass the given qual conditions.

The indexCorrelation should be set to the correlation (ranging between -1.0 and 1.0) between the index order and the table order. This is used to adjust the estimate for the cost of fetching rows from the parent table.

In the join case, the returned numbers should be averages expected for any one scan of the index.

Cost Estimation

A typical cost estimator will proceed as follows:

1. Estimate and return the fraction of parent-table rows that will be visited based on the given qual conditions. In the absence of any index-type-specific knowledge, use the standard optimizer function `clauselist_selectivity()`:

   ```
   *indexSelectivity = clauselist_selectivity(root, indexQuals,
                                              index->rel->relid,
                                              JOIN_INNER, NULL);
   ```

2. Estimate the number of index rows that will be visited during the scan. For many index types this is the same as indexSelectivity times the number of rows in the index, but it might be more. (Note that the index's size in pages and rows is available from the IndexOptInfo struct.)

3. Estimate the number of index pages that will be retrieved during the scan. This might be just indexSelectivity times the index's size in pages.

4. Compute the index access cost. A generic estimator might do this:

   ```
   /*
    * Our generic assumption is that the index pages will be read
    * sequentially, so they cost seq_page_cost each, not random_page_cost.
    * Also, we charge for evaluation of the indexquals at each index row.
    * All the costs are assumed to be paid incrementally during the scan.
    */
   cost_qual_eval(&index_qual_cost, indexQuals, root);
   *indexStartupCost = index_qual_cost.startup;
   *indexTotalCost = seq_page_cost * numIndexPages +
       (cpu_index_tuple_cost + index_qual_cost.per_tuple) * numIndexTuples;
   ```

   However, the above does not account for amortization of index reads across repeated index scans in the join case.

5. Estimate the index correlation. For a simple ordered index on a single field, this can be retrieved from pg_statistic. If the correlation is not known, the conservative estimate is zero (no correlation).

Examples of cost estimator functions can be found in `src/backend/utils/adt/selfuncs.c`.

Chapter 52. GiST Indexes

52.1. Introduction

GiST stands for Generalized Search Tree. It is a balanced, tree-structured access method, that acts as a base template in which to implement arbitrary indexing schemes. B-trees, R-trees and many other indexing schemes can be implemented in GiST.

One advantage of GiST is that it allows the development of custom data types with the appropriate access methods, by an expert in the domain of the data type, rather than a database expert.

Some of the information here is derived from the University of California at Berkeley's GiST Indexing Project *web site*[1] and Marcel Kornacker's thesis, *Access Methods for Next-Generation Database Systems*[2]. The GiST implementation in PostgreSQL is primarily maintained by Teodor Sigaev and Oleg Bartunov, and there is more information on their *web site*[3].

52.2. Extensibility

Traditionally, implementing a new index access method meant a lot of difficult work. It was necessary to understand the inner workings of the database, such as the lock manager and Write-Ahead Log. The GiST interface has a high level of abstraction, requiring the access method implementer only to implement the semantics of the data type being accessed. The GiST layer itself takes care of concurrency, logging and searching the tree structure.

This extensibility should not be confused with the extensibility of the other standard search trees in terms of the data they can handle. For example, PostgreSQL supports extensible B-trees and hash indexes. That means that you can use PostgreSQL to build a B-tree or hash over any data type you want. But B-trees only support range predicates (<, =, >), and hash indexes only support equality queries.

---

1 *http://gist.cs.berkeley.edu/*

2 *http://www.sai.msu.su/~megera/postgres/gist/papers/concurrency/access-methods-for-next-generation.pdf.gz*

3 *http://www.sai.msu.su/~megera/postgres/gist/*

So if you index, say, an image collection with a PostgreSQL B-tree, you can only issue queries such as "is imagex equal to imagey", "is imagex less than imagey" and "is imagex greater than imagey". Depending on how you define "equals", "less than" and "greater than" in this context, this could be useful. However, by using a GiST based index, you could create ways to ask domain-specific questions, perhaps "find all images of horses" or "find all over-exposed images".

All it takes to get a GiST access method up and running is to implement seven user-defined methods, which define the behavior of keys in the tree. Of course these methods have to be pretty fancy to support fancy queries, but for all the standard queries (B-trees, R-trees, etc.) they're relatively straightforward. In short, GiST combines extensibility along with generality, code reuse, and a clean interface.

52.3. Implementation

There are seven methods that an index operator class for GiST must provide. Correctness of the index is ensured by proper implementation of the `same`, `consistent` and `union` methods, while efficiency (size and speed) of the index will depend on the `penalty` and `picksplit` methods. The remaining two methods are `compress` and `decompress`, which allow an index to have internal tree data of a different type than the data it indexes. The leaves are to be of the indexed data type, while the other tree nodes can be of any C struct (but you still have to follow PostgreSQL datatype rules here, see about `varlena` for variable sized data). If the tree's internal data type exists at the SQL level, the `STORAGE` option of the `CREATE OPERATOR CLASS` command can be used.

`consistent`

> Given an index entry `p` and a query value `q`, this function determines whether the index entry is "consistent" with the query; that is, could the predicate "*indexed_column indexable_operator* `q`" be true for any row represented by the index entry? For a leaf index entry this is equivalent to testing the indexable condition, while for an internal tree node this determines whether it is necessary to scan the subtree of the index represented by the tree node. When the result is `true`, a `recheck` flag must also be returned. This indicates whether the predicate is certainly true or only possibly true. If `recheck` = `false` then the index has tested the predicate condition exactly, whereas if `recheck` = `true` the row is only a candidate match. In that case the system will automatically evaluate the *indexable_operator* against the actual row value to see if it is really a match. This convention allows GiST to support both lossless and lossy index structures.
>
> The SQL declaration of the function must look like this:

```
CREATE OR REPLACE FUNCTION my_consistent(internal,data_type,smallint,oid,internal)
RETURNS bool
```

```
AS 'MODULE_PATHNAME'
LANGUAGE C STRICT;
```

And the matching code in the C module could then follow this skeleton:

```
Datum       my_consistent(PG_FUNCTION_ARGS);
PG_FUNCTION_INFO_V1(my_consistent);

Datum
my_consistent(PG_FUNCTION_ARGS)
{
  GISTENTRY  *entry = (GISTENTRY *) PG_GETARG_POINTER(0);
  data_type  *query = PG_GETARG_DATA_TYPE_P(1);
  StrategyNumber strategy = (StrategyNumber) PG_GETARG_UINT16(2);
  /* Oid subtype = PG_GETARG_OID(3); */
  bool       *recheck = (bool *) PG_GETARG_POINTER(4);
  data_type  *key = DatumGetDataType(entry->key);
  bool        retval;

  /*
   * determine return value as a function of strategy, key and query.
   *
   * Use GIST_LEAF(entry) to know where you're called in the index tree,
   * which comes handy when supporting the = operator for example (you could
   * check for non empty union() in non-leaf nodes and equality in leaf
   * nodes).
   */

  *recheck = true;        /* or false if check is exact */

  PG_RETURN_BOOL(retval);
}
```

Here, `key` is an element in the index and `query` the value being looked up in the index. The `StrategyNumber` parameter indicates which operator of your operator class is being applied - it matches one of the operator numbers in the `CREATE OPERATOR CLASS` command. Depending on what operators you have included in the class, the data type of `query` could vary with the operator, but the above skeleton assumes it doesn't.

`union`

This method consolidates information in the tree. Given a set of entries, this function generates a new index entry that represents all the given entries.

The SQL declaration of the function must look like this:

```
CREATE OR REPLACE FUNCTION my_union(internal, internal)
RETURNS internal
AS 'MODULE_PATHNAME'
LANGUAGE C STRICT;
```

And the matching code in the C module could then follow this skeleton:

```
Datum       my_union(PG_FUNCTION_ARGS);
PG_FUNCTION_INFO_V1(my_union);

Datum
my_union(PG_FUNCTION_ARGS)
{
    GistEntryVector *entryvec = (GistEntryVector *) PG_GETARG_POINTER(0);
    GISTENTRY  *ent = entryvec->vector;
    data_type  *out,
               *tmp,
               *old;
    int         numranges,
                i = 0;

    numranges = entryvec->n;
    tmp = DatumGetDataType(ent[0].key);
    out = tmp;

    if (numranges == 1)
    {
        out = data_type_deep_copy(tmp);

        PG_RETURN_DATA_TYPE_P(out);
    }

    for (i = 1; i < numranges; i++)
    {
        old = out;
        tmp = DatumGetDataType(ent[i].key);
        out = my_union_implementation(out, tmp);
    }

    PG_RETURN_DATA_TYPE_P(out);
}
```

As you can see, in this skeleton we're dealing with a data type where `union(X, Y, Z) = union(union(X, Y), Z)`. It's easy enough to support data types where this is not the case, by implementing the proper union algorithm in this GiST support method.

The `union` implementation function should return a pointer to newly `palloc()` ed memory. You can't just return whatever the input is.

`compress`

Converts the data item into a format suitable for physical storage in an index page.

The SQL declaration of the function must look like this:

```
CREATE OR REPLACE FUNCTION my_compress(internal)
RETURNS internal
AS 'MODULE_PATHNAME'
LANGUAGE C STRICT;
```

And the matching code in the C module could then follow this skeleton:

```
Datum       my_compress(PG_FUNCTION_ARGS);
PG_FUNCTION_INFO_V1(my_compress);

Datum
my_compress(PG_FUNCTION_ARGS)
{
    GISTENTRY  *entry = (GISTENTRY *) PG_GETARG_POINTER(0);
    GISTENTRY  *retval;

    if (entry->leafkey)
    {
        /* replace entry->key with a compressed version */
        compressed_data_type *compressed_data = palloc(sizeof(compressed_data_type));

        /* fill *compressed_data from entry->key ... */

        retval = palloc(sizeof(GISTENTRY));
        gistentryinit(*retval, PointerGetDatum(compressed_data),
                      entry->rel, entry->page, entry->offset, FALSE);
    }
    else
    {
        /* typically we needn't do anything with non-leaf entries */
        retval = entry;
    }

    PG_RETURN_POINTER(retval);
}
```

You have to adapt *compressed_data_type* to the specific type you're converting to in order to compress your leaf nodes, of course.

Depending on your needs, you could also need to care about compressing `NULL` values in there, storing for example `(Datum) 0` like `gist_circle_compress` does.

`decompress`

The reverse of the `compress` method. Converts the index representation of the data item into a format that can be manipulated by the database.

The SQL declaration of the function must look like this:

```
CREATE OR REPLACE FUNCTION my_decompress(internal)
RETURNS internal
AS 'MODULE_PATHNAME'
LANGUAGE C STRICT;
```

And the matching code in the C module could then follow this skeleton:

```
Datum       my_decompress(PG_FUNCTION_ARGS);
PG_FUNCTION_INFO_V1(my_decompress);
```

```
Datum
my_decompress(PG_FUNCTION_ARGS)
{
    PG_RETURN_POINTER(PG_GETARG_POINTER(0));
}
```

The above skeleton is suitable for the case where no decompression is needed.

`penalty`

Returns a value indicating the "cost" of inserting the new entry into a particular branch of the tree. Items will be inserted down the path of least `penalty` in the tree.

The SQL declaration of the function must look like this:

```
CREATE OR REPLACE FUNCTION my_penalty(internal, internal, internal)
RETURNS internal
AS 'MODULE_PATHNAME'
LANGUAGE C STRICT;  -- in some cases penalty functions need not be strict
```

And the matching code in the C module could then follow this skeleton:

```
Datum       my_penalty(PG_FUNCTION_ARGS);
PG_FUNCTION_INFO_V1(my_penalty);

Datum
my_penalty(PG_FUNCTION_ARGS)
{
    GISTENTRY  *origentry = (GISTENTRY *) PG_GETARG_POINTER(0);
    GISTENTRY  *newentry = (GISTENTRY *) PG_GETARG_POINTER(1);
    float      *penalty = (float *) PG_GETARG_POINTER(2);
    data_type  *orig = DatumGetDataType(origentry->key);
    data_type  *new = DatumGetDataType(newentry->key);

    *penalty = my_penalty_implementation(orig, new);
    PG_RETURN_POINTER(penalty);
}
```

The `penalty` function is crucial to good performance of the index. It'll get used at insertion time to determine which branch to follow when choosing where to add the new entry in the tree. At query time, the more balanced the index, the quicker the lookup.

`picksplit`

When an index page split is necessary, this function decides which entries on the page are to stay on the old page, and which are to move to the new page.

The SQL declaration of the function must look like this:

```
CREATE OR REPLACE FUNCTION my_picksplit(internal, internal)
RETURNS internal
AS 'MODULE_PATHNAME'
LANGUAGE C STRICT;
```

And the matching code in the C module could then follow this skeleton:

```
Datum       my_picksplit(PG_FUNCTION_ARGS);
PG_FUNCTION_INFO_V1(my_picksplit);

Datum
my_picksplit(PG_FUNCTION_ARGS)
{
    GistEntryVector *entryvec = (GistEntryVector *) PG_GETARG_POINTER(0);
    OffsetNumber maxoff = entryvec->n - 1;
    GISTENTRY  *ent = entryvec->vector;
    GIST_SPLITVEC *v = (GIST_SPLITVEC *) PG_GETARG_POINTER(1);
    int         i,
                nbytes;
    OffsetNumber *left,
               *right;
    data_type  *tmp_union;
    data_type  *unionL;
    data_type  *unionR;
    GISTENTRY **raw_entryvec;

    maxoff = entryvec->n - 1;
    nbytes = (maxoff + 1) * sizeof(OffsetNumber);

    v->spl_left = (OffsetNumber *) palloc(nbytes);
    left = v->spl_left;
    v->spl_nleft = 0;

    v->spl_right = (OffsetNumber *) palloc(nbytes);
    right = v->spl_right;
    v->spl_nright = 0;

    unionL = NULL;
    unionR = NULL;

    /* Initialize the raw entry vector. */
    raw_entryvec = (GISTENTRY **) malloc(entryvec->n * sizeof(void *));
    for (i = FirstOffsetNumber; i <= maxoff; i = OffsetNumberNext(i))
        raw_entryvec[i] = &(entryvec->vector[i]);

    for (i = FirstOffsetNumber; i <= maxoff; i = OffsetNumberNext(i))
    {
        int         real_index = raw_entryvec[i] - entryvec->vector;

        tmp_union = DatumGetDataType(entryvec->vector[real_index].key);
        Assert(tmp_union != NULL);

       /*
        * Choose where to put the index entries and update unionL and unionR
        * accordingly. Append the entries to either v_spl_left or
        * v_spl_right, and care about the counters.
        */
```

```
        if (my_choice_is_left(unionL, curl, unionR, curr))
        {
            if (unionL == NULL)
                unionL = tmp_union;
            else
                unionL = my_union_implementation(unionL, tmp_union);

            *left = real_index;
            ++left;
            ++(v->spl_nleft);
        }
        else
        {
            /*
             * Same on the right
             */
        }
    }

    v->spl_ldatum = DataTypeGetDatum(unionL);
    v->spl_rdatum = DataTypeGetDatum(unionR);
    PG_RETURN_POINTER(v);
}
```

Like `penalty`, the `picksplit` function is crucial to good performance of the index. Designing suitable `penalty` and `picksplit` implementations is where the challenge of implementing well-performing GiST indexes lies.

`same`

Returns true if two index entries are identical, false otherwise.

The SQL declaration of the function must look like this:

```
CREATE OR REPLACE FUNCTION my_same(internal, internal, internal)
RETURNS internal
AS 'MODULE_PATHNAME'
LANGUAGE C STRICT;
```

And the matching code in the C module could then follow this skeleton:

```
Datum       my_same(PG_FUNCTION_ARGS);
PG_FUNCTION_INFO_V1(my_same);

Datum
my_same(PG_FUNCTION_ARGS)
{
    prefix_range *v1 = PG_GETARG_PREFIX_RANGE_P(0);
    prefix_range *v2 = PG_GETARG_PREFIX_RANGE_P(1);
    bool        *result = (bool *) PG_GETARG_POINTER(2);

    *result = my_eq(v1, v2);
    PG_RETURN_POINTER(result);
}
```

For historical reasons, the `same` function doesn't just return a Boolean result; instead it has to store the flag at the location indicated by the third argument.

52.4. Examples

The PostgreSQL source distribution includes several examples of index methods implemented using GiST. The core system currently provides text search support (indexing for `tsvector` and `tsquery`) as well as R-Tree equivalent functionality for some of the built-in geometric data types (see `src/backend/access/gist/gistproc.c`). The following `contrib` modules also contain GiST operator classes:

btree_gist

B-tree equivalent functionality for several data types

cube

Indexing for multidimensional cubes

hstore

Module for storing (key, value) pairs

intarray

RD-Tree for one-dimensional array of int4 values

ltree

Indexing for tree-like structures

pg_trgm

Text similarity using trigram matching

seg

Indexing for "float ranges"

52.5. Crash Recovery

Usually, replay of the WAL log is sufficient to restore the integrity of a GiST index following a database crash. However, there are some corner cases in which the index state is not fully rebuilt. The index will still be functionally correct, but there might be some performance degradation. When this occurs, the index can be repaired by `VACUUM`ing its table, or by rebuilding the index using `REINDEX`. In some cases a plain `VACUUM` is not sufficient, and either `VACUUM FULL` or `REINDEX` is needed. The need for one of these procedures is indicated by occurrence of this log message during crash recovery:

```
LOG:  index NNN/NNN/NNN needs VACUUM or REINDEX to finish crash recovery
```

or this log message during routine index insertions:

```
LOG:  index "FOO" needs VACUUM or REINDEX to finish crash recovery
```

If a plain `VACUUM` finds itself unable to complete recovery fully, it will return a notice:

```
NOTICE:  index "FOO" needs VACUUM FULL or REINDEX to finish crash recovery
```

Chapter 53. GIN Indexes

53.1. Introduction

GIN stands for Generalized Inverted Index. It is an index structure storing a set of (key, posting list) pairs, where a "posting list" is a set of rows in which the key occurs. Each indexed value can contain many keys, so the same row ID can appear in multiple posting lists.

It is generalized in the sense that a GIN index does not need to be aware of the operation that it accelerates. Instead, it uses custom strategies defined for particular data types.

One advantage of GIN is that it allows the development of custom data types with the appropriate access methods, by an expert in the domain of the data type, rather than a database expert. This is much the same advantage as using GiST.

The GIN implementation in PostgreSQL is primarily maintained by Teodor Sigaev and Oleg Bartunov. There is more information about GIN on their *website*[1].

53.2. Extensibility

The GIN interface has a high level of abstraction, requiring the access method implementer only to implement the semantics of the data type being accessed. The GIN layer itself takes care of concurrency, logging and searching the tree structure.

All it takes to get a GIN access method working is to implement four (or five) user-defined methods, which define the behavior of keys in the tree and the relationships between keys, indexed values, and indexable queries. In short, GIN combines extensibility with generality, code reuse, and a clean interface.

The four methods that an operator class for GIN must provide are:

int compare(Datum a, Datum b)

> Compares keys (not indexed values!) and returns an integer less than zero, zero, or greater than zero, indicating whether the first key is less than, equal to, or greater than the second.

[1] *http://www.sai.msu.su/~megera/wiki/Gin*

Datum *extractValue(Datum inputValue, int32 *nkeys)

Returns an array of keys given a value to be indexed. The number of returned keys must be stored into `*nkeys`.

Datum *extractQuery(Datum query, int32 *nkeys, StrategyNumber n, bool **pmatch, Pointer **extra_data)

Returns an array of keys given a value to be queried; that is, `query` is the value on the right-hand side of an indexable operator whose left-hand side is the indexed column. `n` is the strategy number of the operator within the operator class (see *Section 35.14.2* - Vol.III). Often, `extractQuery` will need to consult `n` to determine the data type of `query` and the key values that need to be extracted. The number of returned keys must be stored into `*nkeys`. If the query contains no keys then `extractQuery` should store 0 or -1 into `*nkeys`, depending on the semantics of the operator. 0 means that every value matches the `query` and a full-index scan should be performed (but see *Section 53.5* - page 169). -1 means that nothing can match the `query`, and so the index scan can be skipped entirely. `pmatch` is an output argument for use when partial match is supported. To use it, `extractQuery` must allocate an array of `*nkeys` Booleans and store its address at `*pmatch`. Each element of the array should be set to TRUE if the corresponding key requires partial match, FALSE if not. If `*pmatch` is set to NULL then GIN assumes partial match is not required. The variable is initialized to NULL before call, so this argument can simply be ignored by operator classes that do not support partial match. `extra_data` is an output argument that allows `extractQuery` to pass additional data to the `consistent` and `comparePartial` methods. To use it, `extractQuery` must allocate an array of `*nkeys` Pointers and store its address at `*extra_data`, then store whatever it wants to into the individual pointers. The variable is initialized to NULL before call, so this argument can simply be ignored by operator classes that do not require extra data. If `*extra_data` is set, the whole array is passed to the `consistent` method, and the appropriate element to the `comparePartial` method.

bool consistent(bool check[], StrategyNumber n, Datum query, int32 nkeys, Pointer extra_data[], bool *recheck)

Returns TRUE if the indexed value satisfies the query operator with strategy number `n` (or might satisfy, if the recheck indication is returned). The `check` array has length `nkeys`, which is the same as the number of keys previously returned by `extractQuery` for this `query` datum. Each element of the `check` array is TRUE if the indexed value contains the corresponding query key, ie, if (check[i] == TRUE) the i-th key of the `extractQuery` result array is present in the indexed value. The original `query` datum (not the extracted key array!) is passed in case the `consistent` method needs to consult it. `extra_data` is the extra-data array returned by `extractQuery`, or NULL if none. On success, `*recheck` should be set to TRUE if the heap tuple needs to be rechecked against the query operator, or FALSE if the index test is exact.

Optionally, an operator class for GIN can supply a fifth method:

int comparePartial(Datum partial_key, Datum key, StrategyNumber n, Pointer extra_data)

Compare a partial-match query to an index key. Returns an integer whose sign indicates the result: less than zero means the index key does not match the query, but the index scan should continue; zero means that the index key does match the query; greater than zero indicates that the index scan should stop because no more matches are possible. The strategy number `n` of the operator that generated the partial match query is provided, in case its semantics are needed to determine when to end the scan. Also, `extra_data` is the corresponding element of the extra-data array made by `extractQuery`, or NULL if none.

To support "partial match" queries, an operator class must provide the `comparePartial` method, and its `extractQuery` method must set the `pmatch` parameter when a partial-match query is encountered. See *Section 53.3.2* (page 168) for details.

53.3. Implementation

Internally, a GIN index contains a B-tree index constructed over keys, where each key is an element of the indexed value (a member of an array, for example) and where each tuple in a leaf page is either a pointer to a B-tree over heap pointers (PT, posting tree), or a list of heap pointers (PL, posting list) if the list is small enough.

53.3.1. GIN fast update technique

Updating a GIN index tends to be slow because of the intrinsic nature of inverted indexes: inserting or updating one heap row can cause many inserts into the index (one for each key extracted from the indexed value). As of PostgreSQL 9.0, GIN is capable of postponing much of this work by inserting new tuples into a temporary, unsorted list of pending entries. When the table is vacuumed, or if the pending list becomes too large (larger than *work_mem* - Vol.II), the entries are moved to the main GIN data structure using the same bulk insert techniques used during initial index creation. This greatly improves GIN index update speed, even counting the additional vacuum overhead. Moreover the overhead can be done by a background process instead of in foreground query processing.

The main disadvantage of this approach is that searches must scan the list of pending entries in addition to searching the regular index, and so a large list of pending entries will slow searches significantly. Another disadvantage is that, while most updates are fast, an update that causes the pending list to become "too large" will incur an immediate cleanup cycle and thus be much slower than other updates. Proper use of autovacuum can minimize both of these problems.

If consistent response time is more important than update speed, use of pending entries can be disabled by turning off the `FASTUPDATE` storage parameter for a GIN index. See CREATE INDEX for details.

53.3.2. Partial match algorithm

GIN can support "partial match" queries, in which the query does not determine an exact match for one or more keys, but the possible matches fall within a reasonably narrow range of key values (within the key sorting order determined by the `compare` support method). The `extractQuery` method, instead of returning a key value to be matched exactly, returns a key value that is the lower bound of the range to be searched, and sets the `pmatch` flag true. The key range is then searched using the `comparePartial` method. `comparePartial` must return zero for an actual match, less than zero for a non-match that is still within the range to be searched, or greater than zero if the index key is past the range that could match.

53.4. GIN tips and tricks

Create vs insert

> Insertion into a GIN index can be slow due to the likelihood of many keys being inserted for each value. So, for bulk insertions into a table it is advisable to drop the GIN index and recreate it after finishing bulk insertion.
>
> As of PostgreSQL 9.0, this advice is less necessary since delayed indexing is used (see *Section 53.3.1* - page 167 for details). But for very large updates it may still be best to drop and recreate the index.

maintenance_work_mem (Vol.II)

> Build time for a GIN index is very sensitive to the `maintenance_work_mem` setting; it doesn't pay to skimp on work memory during index creation.

work_mem (Vol.II)

> During a series of insertions into an existing GIN index that has `FASTUPDATE` enabled, the system will clean up the pending-entry list whenever it grows larger than `work_mem`. To avoid fluctuations in observed response time, it's desirable to have pending-list cleanup occur in the background (i.e., via autovacuum). Foreground cleanup operations can be avoided by increasing `work_mem` or making autovacuum more aggressive. However, enlarging `work_mem` means that if a foreground cleanup does occur, it will take even longer.

gin_fuzzy_search_limit (Vol.II)

The primary goal of developing GIN indexes was to create support for highly scalable, full-text search in PostgreSQL, and there are often situations when a full-text search returns a very large set of results. Moreover, this often happens when the query contains very frequent words, so that the large result set is not even useful. Since reading many tuples from the disk and sorting them could take a lot of time, this is unacceptable for production. (Note that the index search itself is very fast.)

To facilitate controlled execution of such queries GIN has a configurable soft upper limit on the number of rows returned, the `gin_fuzzy_search_limit` configuration parameter. It is set to 0 (meaning no limit) by default. If a non-zero limit is set, then the returned set is a subset of the whole result set, chosen at random.

"Soft" means that the actual number of returned results could differ slightly from the specified limit, depending on the query and the quality of the system's random number generator.

53.5. Limitations

GIN doesn't support full index scans. The reason for this is that `extractValue` is allowed to return zero keys, as for example might happen with an empty string or empty array. In such a case the indexed value will be unrepresented in the index. It is therefore impossible for GIN to guarantee that a scan of the index can find every row in the table.

Because of this limitation, when `extractQuery` returns `nkeys = 0` to indicate that all values match the query, GIN will emit an error. (If there are multiple ANDed indexable operators in the query, this happens only if they all return zero for `nkeys` .)

It is possible for an operator class to circumvent the restriction against full index scan. To do that, `extractValue` must return at least one (possibly dummy) key for every indexed value, and `extractQuery` must convert an unrestricted search into a partial-match query that will scan the whole index. This is inefficient but might be necessary to avoid corner-case failures with operators such as `LIKE` or subset inclusion.

GIN assumes that indexable operators are strict. This means that `extractValue` will not be called at all on a NULL value (so the value will go unindexed), and `extractQuery` will not be called on a NULL comparison value either (instead, the query is presumed to be unmatchable).

A possibly more serious limitation is that GIN cannot handle NULL keys - for example, an array containing a NULL cannot be handled except by ignoring the NULL.

53.6. Examples

The PostgreSQL source distribution includes GIN operator classes for `tsvector` and for one-dimensional arrays of all internal types. Prefix searching in `tsvector` is implemented using the GIN partial match feature. The following `contrib` modules also contain GIN operator classes:

btree_gin

B-tree equivalent functionality for several data types

hstore

Module for storing (key, value) pairs

intarray

Enhanced support for int[]

pg_trgm

Text similarity using trigram matching

Chapter 54. Database Physical Storage

This chapter provides an overview of the physical storage format used by PostgreSQL databases.

54.1. Database File Layout

This section describes the storage format at the level of files and directories.

All the data needed for a database cluster is stored within the cluster's data directory, commonly referred to as `PGDATA` (after the name of the environment variable that can be used to define it). A common location for `PGDATA` is `/var/lib/pgsql/data`. Multiple clusters, managed by different server instances, can exist on the same machine.

The `PGDATA` directory contains several subdirectories and control files, as shown in *Table 54-1* (see below). In addition to these required items, the cluster configuration files `postgresql.conf`, `pg_hba.conf`, and `pg_ident.conf` are traditionally stored in `PGDATA` (although in PostgreSQL 8.0 and later, it is possible to keep them elsewhere).

Item	Description
`PG_VERSION`	A file containing the major version number of PostgreSQL
`base`	Subdirectory containing per-database subdirectories
`global`	Subdirectory containing cluster-wide tables, such as `pg_database`
`pg_clog`	Subdirectory containing transaction commit status data
`pg_multixact`	Subdirectory containing multitransaction status data (used for shared row locks)
`pg_notify`	Subdirectory containing LISTEN/NOTIFY status data
`pg_stat_tmp`	Subdirectory containing temporary files for the statistics subsystem
`pg_subtrans`	Subdirectory containing subtransaction status data
`pg_tblspc`	Subdirectory containing symbolic links to tablespaces
`pg_twophase`	Subdirectory containing state files for prepared transactions
`pg_xlog`	Subdirectory containing WAL (Write Ahead Log) files
`postmaster.opts`	A file recording the command-line options the server was last started with

Item	Description
postmaster.pid	A lock file recording the current server PID and shared memory segment ID (not present after server shutdown)

Table 54-1. Contents of PGDATA

For each database in the cluster there is a subdirectory within `PGDATA/base`, named after the database's OID in `pg_database`. This subdirectory is the default location for the database's files; in particular, its system catalogs are stored there.

Each table and index is stored in a separate file, named after the table or index's *filenode* number, which can be found in `pg_class. relfilenode`. In addition to the main file (a/k/a main fork), each table and index has a *free space map* (see *Section 54.3* - page 175), which stores information about free space available in the relation. The free space map is stored in a file named with the filenode number plus the suffix `_fsm`. Tables also have a *visibility map*, stored in a fork with the suffix `_vm`, to track which pages are known to have no dead tuples. The visibility map is described further in *Section 54.4* (page 176).

Caution

Note that while a table's filenode often matches its OID, this is *not* necessarily the case; some operations, like `TRUNCATE`, `REINDEX`, `CLUSTER` and some forms of `ALTER TABLE`, can change the filenode while preserving the OID. Avoid assuming that filenode and table OID are the same. Also, for certain system catalogs including `pg_class` itself, `pg_class.relfilenode` contains zero. The actual filenode number of these catalogs is stored in a lower-level data structure, and can be obtained using the `pg_relation_filenode()` function.

When a table or index exceeds 1 GB, it is divided into gigabyte-sized *segments*. The first segment's file name is the same as the filenode; subsequent segments are named filenode.1, filenode.2, etc. This arrangement avoids problems on platforms that have file size limitations. (Actually, 1 GB is just the default segment size. The segment size can be adjusted using the configuration option `--with-segsize` when building PostgreSQL.) In principle, free space map and visibility map forks could require multiple segments as well, though this is unlikely to happen in practice.

A table that has columns with potentially large entries will have an associated *TOAST* table, which is used for out-of-line storage of field values that are too large to keep in the table rows proper. `pg_class.reltoastrelid` links from a table to its TOAST table, if any. See *Section 54.2* (page 173) for more information.

The contents of tables and indexes are discussed further in *Section 54.5* (page 176).

Tablespaces make the scenario more complicated. Each user-defined tablespace has a symbolic link inside the `PGDATA/pg_tblspc` directory, which points to the physical tablespace directory (i.e., the location specified in the tablespace's `CREATE TABLESPACE` command). This symbolic link is named after the tablespace's OID. Inside the physical tablespace directory there is a subdirectory with a name that depends on the PostgreSQL server version, such as `PG_9.0_201008051`. (The reason for using this subdirectory is so that successive versions of the database can use the same `CREATE TABLESPACE` location value without conflicts.) Within the version-specific subdirectory, there is a subdirectory for each database that has elements in the tablespace, named after the database's OID. Tables and indexes are stored within that directory, using the filenode naming scheme. The `pg_default` tablespace is not accessed through `pg_tblspc`, but corresponds to `PGDATA/base`. Similarly, the `pg_global` tablespace is not accessed through `pg_tblspc`, but corresponds to `PGDATA/global`.

The `pg_relation_filepath()` function shows the entire path (relative to `PGDATA`) of any relation. It is often useful as a substitute for remembering many of the above rules. But keep in mind that this function just gives the name of the first segment of the main fork of the relation — you may need to append a segment number and/or `_fsm` or `_vm` to find all the files associated with the relation.

Temporary files (for operations such as sorting more data than can fit in memory) are created within `PGDATA /base/pgsql_tmp`, or within a `pgsql_tmp` subdirectory of a tablespace directory if a tablespace other than `pg_default` is specified for them. The name of a temporary file has the form `pgsql_tmp`*`PPP`*` .`*`NNN`*, where *`PPP`* is the PID of the owning backend and *`NNN`* distinguishes different temporary files of that backend.

54.2. TOAST

This section provides an overview of TOAST (The Oversized-Attribute Storage Technique).

PostgreSQL uses a fixed page size (commonly 8 kB), and does not allow tuples to span multiple pages. Therefore, it is not possible to store very large field values directly. To overcome this limitation, large field values are compressed and/or broken up into multiple physical rows. This happens transparently to the user, with only small impact on most of the backend code. The technique is affectionately known as TOAST (or "the best thing since sliced bread").

Only certain data types support TOAST - there is no need to impose the overhead on data types that cannot produce large field values. To support TOAST , a data type must have a variable-length (*varlena*) representation, in which the first 32-bit word of any stored value contains the total length of the value in bytes (including itself). TOAST does not constrain the rest of the representation. All the C-level functions supporting a TOAST-able data type must be careful to handle TOASTed input values. (This is normally done by invoking `PG_DETOAST_DATUM` before doing anything with an input value, but in some cases more efficient approaches are possible.)

TOAST usurps two bits of the varlena length word (the high-order bits on big-endian machines, the low-order bits on little-endian machines), thereby limiting the logical size of any value of a TOAST-able data type to 1 GB (2^{30} - 1 bytes). When both bits are zero, the value is an ordinary un-TOASTed value of the data type, and the remaining bits of the length word give the total datum size (including length word) in bytes. When the highest-order or lowest-order bit is set, the value has only a single-byte header instead of the normal four-byte header, and the remaining bits give the total datum size (including length byte) in bytes. As a special case, if the remaining bits are all zero (which would be impossible for a self-inclusive length), the value is a pointer to out-of-line data stored in a separate TOAST table. (The size of a TOAST pointer is given in the second byte of the datum.) Values with single-byte headers aren't aligned on any particular boundary, either. Lastly, when the highest-order or lowest-order bit is clear but the adjacent bit is set, the content of the datum has been compressed and must be decompressed before use. In this case the remaining bits of the length word give the total size of the compressed datum, not the original data. Note that compression is also possible for out-of-line data but the varlena header does not tell whether it has occurred - the content of the TOAST pointer tells that, instead.

If any of the columns of a table are TOAST -able, the table will have an associated TOAST table, whose OID is stored in the table's `pg_class.reltoastrelid` entry. Out-of-line TOASTed values are kept in the TOAST table, as described in more detail below.

The compression technique used is a fairly simple and very fast member of the LZ family of compression techniques. See `src/backend/utils/adt/pg_lzcompress.c` for the details.

Out-of-line values are divided (after compression if used) into chunks of at most `TOAST_MAX_CHUNK_SIZE` bytes (by default this value is chosen so that four chunk rows will fit on a page, making it about 2000 bytes). Each chunk is stored as a separate row in the TOAST table for the owning table. Every TOAST table has the columns `chunk_id` (an OID identifying the particular TOASTed value), `chunk_seq` (a sequence number for the chunk within its value), and `chunk_data` (the actual data of the chunk). A unique index on `chunk_id` and `chunk_seq` provides fast retrieval of the values. A pointer datum representing an out-of-line TOASTed value therefore needs to store the OID of the TOAST table in which to look and the OID of the specific value (its `chunk_id`). For convenience, pointer datums also store the logical datum size (original uncompressed data length) and actual stored size (different if compression was applied). Allowing for the varlena header bytes, the total size of a TOAST pointer datum is therefore 18 bytes regardless of the actual size of the represented value.

The TOAST code is triggered only when a row value to be stored in a table is wider than `TOAST_TUPLE_THRESHOLD` bytes (normally 2 kB). The TOAST code will compress and/or move field values out-of-line until the row value is shorter than `TOAST_TUPLE_TARGET` bytes (also normally 2 kB) or no more gains can be had. During an UPDATE operation, values of unchanged fields are normally preserved as-is; so an UPDATE of a row with out-of-line values incurs no TOAST costs if none of the out-of-line values change.

The TOAST code recognizes four different strategies for storing TOAST -able columns:

- `PLAIN` prevents either compression or out-of-line storage; furthermore it disables use of single-byte headers for varlena types. This is the only possible strategy for columns of non-TOAST-able data types.
- `EXTENDED` allows both compression and out-of-line storage. This is the default for most TOAST-able data types. Compression will be attempted first, then out-of-line storage if the row is still too big.
- `EXTERNAL` allows out-of-line storage but not compression. Use of `EXTERNAL` will make substring operations on wide `text` and `bytea` columns faster (at the penalty of increased storage space) because these operations are optimized to fetch only the required parts of the out-of-line value when it is not compressed.
- `MAIN` allows compression but not out-of-line storage. (Actually, out-of-line storage will still be performed for such columns, but only as a last resort when there is no other way to make the row small enough to fit on a page.)

Each TOAST-able data type specifies a default strategy for columns of that data type, but the strategy for a given table column can be altered with `ALTER TABLE SET STORAGE`.

This scheme has a number of advantages compared to a more straightforward approach such as allowing row values to span pages. Assuming that queries are usually qualified by comparisons against relatively small key values, most of the work of the executor will be done using the main row entry. The big values of TOASTed attributes will only be pulled out (if selected at all) at the time the result set is sent to the client. Thus, the main table is much smaller and more of its rows fit in the shared buffer cache than would be the case without any out-of-line storage. Sort sets shrink also, and sorts will more often be done entirely in memory. A little test showed that a table containing typical HTML pages and their URLs was stored in about half of the raw data size including the TOAST table, and that the main table contained only about 10% of the entire data (the URLs and some small HTML pages). There was no run time difference compared to an un-TOASTed comparison table, in which all the HTML pages were cut down to 7 kB to fit.

54.3. Free Space Map

Each heap and index relation, except for hash indexes, has a Free Space Map (FSM) to keep track of available space in the relation. It's stored alongside the main relation data in a separate relation fork, named after the filenode number of the relation, plus a `_fsm` suffix. For example, if the filenode of a relation is 12345, the FSM is stored in a file called `12345_fsm`, in the same directory as the main relation file.

The Free Space Map is organized as a tree of FSM pages. The bottom level FSM pages store the free space available on each heap (or index) page, using one byte to represent each such page. The upper levels aggregate information from the lower levels.

Within each FSM page is a binary tree, stored in an array with one byte per node. Each leaf node represents a heap page, or a lower level FSM page. In each non-leaf node, the higher of its children's values is stored. The maximum value in the leaf nodes is therefore stored at the root.

See `src/backend/storage/freespace/README` for more details on how the FSM is structured, and how it's updated and searched. The `contrib/pg_freespacemap` module can be used to examine the information stored in free space maps (see *Section F.26* - page 388).

54.4. Visibility Map

Each heap relation has a Visibility Map (VM) to keep track of which pages contain only tuples that are known to be visible to all active transactions. It's stored alongside the main relation data in a separate relation fork, named after the filenode number of the relation, plus a `_vm` suffix. For example, if the filenode of a relation is 12345, the VM is stored in a file called `12345_vm`, in the same directory as the main relation file. Note that indexes do not have VMs.

The visibility map simply stores one bit per heap page. A set bit means that all tuples on the page are known to be visible to all transactions. This means that the page does not contain any tuples that need to be vacuumed; in future it might also be used to avoid visiting the page for visibility checks. The map is conservative in the sense that we make sure that whenever a bit is set, we know the condition is true, but if a bit is not set, it might or might not be true.

54.5. Database Page Layout

This section provides an overview of the page format used within PostgreSQL tables and indexes[1]. Sequences and TOAST tables are formatted just like a regular table.

In the following explanation, a *byte* is assumed to contain 8 bits. In addition, the term *item* refers to an individual data value that is stored on a page. In a table, an item is a row; in an index, an item is an index entry.

Every table and index is stored as an array of *pages* of a fixed size (usually 8 kB, although a different page size can be selected when compiling the server). In a table, all the pages are logically equivalent, so a particular item (row) can be stored in any page. In indexes, the first

[1] Actually, index access methods need not use this page format. All the existing index methods do use this basic format, but the data kept on index metapages usually doesn't follow the item layout rules.

page is generally reserved as a *metapage* holding control information, and there can be different types of pages within the index, depending on the index access method.

Table 54-2 (see below) shows the overall layout of a page. There are five parts to each page.

Item	Description
PageHeaderData	24 bytes long. Contains general information about the page, including free space pointers.
ItemIdData	Array of (offset,length) pairs pointing to the actual items. 4 bytes per item.
Free space	The unallocated space. New item pointers are allocated from the start of this area, new items from the end.
Items	The actual items themselves.
Special space	Index access method specific data. Different methods store different data. Empty in ordinary tables.

Table 54-2. Overall Page Layout

The first 24 bytes of each page consists of a page header (PageHeaderData). Its format is detailed in *Table 54-3* (see below). The first two fields track the most recent WAL entry related to this page. Next is a 2-byte field containing flag bits. This is followed by three 2-byte integer fields (`pd_lower`, `pd_upper`, and `pd_special`). These contain byte offsets from the page start to the start of unallocated space, to the end of unallocated space, and to the start of the special space. The next 2 bytes of the page header, `pd_pagesize_version`, store both the page size and a version indicator. Beginning with PostgreSQL 8.3 the version number is 4; PostgreSQL 8.1 and 8.2 used version number 3; PostgreSQL 8.0 used version number 2; PostgreSQL 7.3 and 7.4 used version number 1; prior releases used version number 0. (The basic page layout and header format has not changed in most of these versions, but the layout of heap row headers has.) The page size is basically only present as a cross-check; there is no support for having more than one page size in an installation. The last field is a hint that shows whether pruning the page is likely to be profitable: it tracks the oldest un-pruned XMAX on the page.

Field	Type	Length	Description
pd_lsn	XLogRecPtr	8 bytes	LSN: next byte after last byte of xlog record for last change to this page
pd_tli	uint16	2 bytes	TimeLineID of last change (only its lowest 16 bits)
pd_flags	uint16	2 bytes	Flag bits
pd_lower	LocationIndex	2 bytes	Offset to start of free space
pd_upper	LocationIndex	2 bytes	Offset to end of free space
pd_special	LocationIndex	2 bytes	Offset to start of special space
pd_pagesize_version	uint16	2 bytes	Page size and layout version number information
pd_prune_xid	TransactionId	4 bytes	Oldest unpruned XMAX on page, or zero if none

Table 54-3. PageHeaderData Layout

All the details can be found in `src/include/storage/bufpage.h`.

Following the page header are item identifiers (`ItemIdData`), each requiring four bytes. An item identifier contains a byte-offset to the start of an item, its length in bytes, and a few attribute bits which affect its interpretation. New item identifiers are allocated as needed from the beginning of the unallocated space. The number of item identifiers present can be determined by looking at `pd_lower`, which is increased to allocate a new identifier. Because an item identifier is never moved until it is freed, its index can be used on a long-term basis to reference an item, even when the item itself is moved around on the page to compact free space. In fact, every pointer to an item (`ItemPointer` , also known as `CTID`) created by PostgreSQL consists of a page number and the index of an item identifier.

The items themselves are stored in space allocated backwards from the end of unallocated space. The exact structure varies depending on what the table is to contain. Tables and sequences both use a structure named `HeapTupleHeaderData`, described below.

The final section is the "special section" which can contain anything the access method wishes to store. For example, b-tree indexes store links to the page's left and right siblings, as well as some other data relevant to the index structure. Ordinary tables do not use a special section at all (indicated by setting `pd_special` to equal the page size).

All table rows are structured in the same way. There is a fixed-size header (occupying 23 bytes on most machines), followed by an optional null bitmap, an optional object ID field, and the user data. The header is detailed in *Table 54-4* (see below). The actual user data (columns of the row) begins at the offset indicated by `t_hoff`, which must always be a multiple of the MAXALIGN distance for the platform. The null bitmap is only present if the *HEAP_HASNULL* bit is set in `t_infomask`. If it is present it begins just after the fixed header and occupies enough bytes to have one bit per data column (that is, `t_natts` bits altogether). In this list of bits, a 1 bit indicates not-null, a 0 bit is a null. When the bitmap is not present, all columns are assumed not-null. The object ID is only present if the *HEAP_HASOID* bit is set in `t_infomask`. If present, it appears just before the `t_hoff` boundary. Any padding needed to make `t_hoff` a MAXALIGN multiple will appear between the null bitmap and the object ID. (This in turn ensures that the object ID is suitably aligned.)

Field	Type	Length	Description
t_xmin	TransactionId	4 bytes	insert XID stamp
t_xmax	TransactionId	4 bytes	delete XID stamp
t_cid	CommandId	4 bytes	insert and/or delete CID stamp (overlays with t_xvac)
t_xvac	TransactionId	4 bytes	XID for VACUUM operation moving a row version
t_ctid	ItemPointerData	6 bytes	current TID of this or newer row version

Field	Type	Length	Description
t_infomask2	int16	2 bytes	number of attributes, plus various flag bits
t_infomask	uint16	2 bytes	various flag bits
t_hoff	uint8	1 byte	offset to user data

Table 54-4. HeapTupleHeaderData Layout

All the details can be found in `src/include/access/htup.h`.

Interpreting the actual data can only be done with information obtained from other tables, mostly `pg_attribute`. The key values needed to identify field locations are `attlen` and `attalign`. There is no way to directly get a particular attribute, except when there are only fixed width fields and no null values. All this trickery is wrapped up in the functions *heap_getattr*, *fastgetattr* and *heap_getsysattr*.

To read the data you need to examine each attribute in turn. First check whether the field is NULL according to the null bitmap. If it is, go to the next. Then make sure you have the right alignment. If the field is a fixed width field, then all the bytes are simply placed. If it's a variable length field (attlen = -1) then it's a bit more complicated. All variable-length datatypes share the common header structure `struct varlena`, which includes the total length of the stored value and some flag bits. Depending on the flags, the data can be either inline or in a TOAST table; it might be compressed, too (see *Section 54.2* - page 173).

Chapter 55. BKI Backend Interface

Backend Interface (BKI) files are scripts in a special language that is understood by the PostgreSQL backend when running in the "bootstrap" mode. The bootstrap mode allows system catalogs to be created and filled from scratch, whereas ordinary SQL commands require the catalogs to exist already. BKI files can therefore be used to create the database system in the first place. (And they are probably not useful for anything else.)

initdb uses a BKI file to do part of its job when creating a new database cluster. The input file used by initdb is created as part of building and installing PostgreSQL by a program named `genbki.pl`, which reads some specially formatted C header files in the `src/include/catalog/` directory of the source tree. The created BKI file is called `postgres.bki` and is normally installed in the `share` subdirectory of the installation tree.

Related information can be found in the documentation for initdb.

55.1. BKI File Format

This section describes how the PostgreSQL backend interprets BKI files. This description will be easier to understand if the `postgres.bki` file is at hand as an example.

BKI input consists of a sequence of commands. Commands are made up of a number of tokens, depending on the syntax of the command. Tokens are usually separated by whitespace, but need not be if there is no ambiguity. There is no special command separator; the next token that syntactically cannot belong to the preceding command starts a new one. (Usually you would put a new command on a new line, for clarity.) Tokens can be certain key words, special characters (parentheses, commas, etc.), numbers, or double-quoted strings. Everything is case sensitive.

Lines starting with `#` are ignored.

55.2. BKI Commands

`create` *`tablename`* *`tableoid`* [`bootstrap`] [`shared_relation`] [`without_oids`] [`rowtype_oid` *`oid`*] (*`name1`* = *`type1`* [, *`name2`* = *`type2`*, ...])

> Create a table named *`tablename`*, and having the OID *`tableoid`*, with the columns given in parentheses.

The following column types are supported directly by `bootstrap.c`: `bool`, `bytea` , `char` (1 byte), `name`, `int2`, `int4`, `regproc`, `regclass`, `regtype`, `text`, `oid`, `tid`, `xid`, `cid`, `int2vector`, `oidvector`, `_int4` (array), `_text` (array), `_oid` (array), `_char` (array), `_aclitem` (array). Although it is possible to create tables containing columns of other types, this cannot be done until after `pg_type` has been created and filled with appropriate entries. (That effectively means that only these column types can be used in bootstrapped tables, but non-bootstrap catalogs can contain any built-in type.)

When `bootstrap` is specified, the table will only be created on disk; nothing is entered into `pg_class`, `pg_attribute`, etc, for it. Thus the table will not be accessible by ordinary SQL operations until such entries are made the hard way (with `insert` commands). This option is used for creating `pg_class` etc themselves.

The table is created as shared if `shared_relation` is specified. It will have OIDs unless `without_oids` is specified. The table's row type OID (`pg_type` OID) can optionally be specified via the `rowtype_oid` clause; if not specified, an OID is automatically generated for it. (The `rowtype_oid` clause is useless if `bootstrap` is specified, but it can be provided anyway for documentation.)

`open` *`tablename`*

Open the table named *`tablename`* for insertion of data. Any currently open table is closed.

`close` [*`tablename`*]

Close the open table. The name of the table can be given as a cross-check, but this is not required.

`insert` [`OID =` *`oid_value`*] `(`*`value1 value2`* ... `)`

Insert a new row into the open table using *`value1`*, *`value2`*, etc., for its column values and *`oid_value`* for its OID. If *`oid_value`* is zero (0) or the clause is omitted, and the table has OIDs, then the next available OID is assigned.

NULL values can be specified using the special key word `_null_`. Values containing spaces must be double quoted.

`declare` [`unique`] `index` *`indexname indexoid`* `on` *`tablename`* `using` *`amname`* `(`*`opclass1 name1`* [, ...] `)`

Create an index named *`indexname`*, having OID *`indexoid`*, on the table named *`tablename`*, using the *`amname`* access method. The fields to index are called *`name1`*, *`name2`* etc., and the operator classes to use are *`opclass1`* , *`opclass2`* etc., respectively. The index file is created and appropriate catalog entries are made for it, but the index contents are not initialized by this command.

`declare toast` *`toasttableoid toastindexoid`* `on` *`tablename`*

Create a TOAST table for the table named *`tablename`*. The TOAST table is assigned OID *`toasttableoid`* and its index is assigned OID *`toastindexoid`*. As with `declare index`, filling of the index is postponed.

`build indices`

Fill in the indices that have previously been declared.

55.3. Structure of the Bootstrap BKI File

The `open` command cannot be used until the tables it uses exist and have entries for the table that is to be opened. (These minimum tables are `pg_class`, `pg_attribute`, `pg_proc`, and `pg_type`.) To allow those tables themselves to be filled, `create` with the `bootstrap` option implicitly opens the created table for data insertion.

Also, the `declare index` and `declare toast` commands cannot be used until the system catalogs they need have been created and filled in.

Thus, the structure of the `postgres.bki` file has to be:

1. create bootstrap one of the critical tables
2. insert data describing at least the critical tables

close

1. Repeat for the other critical tables.
2. create (without bootstrap) a noncritical table

open

1. insert desired data

close

1. Repeat for the other noncritical tables.
2. Define indexes and toast tables.

build indices

There are doubtless other, undocumented ordering dependencies.

55.4. Example

The following sequence of commands will create the table `test_table` with OID 420, having two columns `cola` and `colb` of type `int4` and `text`, respectively, and insert two rows into the table:

```
create test_table 420 (cola = int4, colb = text)
open test_table
insert OID=421 ( 1 "value1" )
insert OID=422 ( 2 _null_ )
close test_table
```

Chapter 56. How the Planner Uses Statistics

This chapter builds on the material covered in *Section 14.1* (Vol.I) and *Section 14.2* (Vol.I) to show some additional details about how the planner uses the system statistics to estimate the number of rows each part of a query might return. This is a significant part of the planning process, providing much of the raw material for cost calculation.

The intent of this chapter is not to document the code in detail, but to present an overview of how it works. This will perhaps ease the learning curve for someone who subsequently wishes to read the code.

56.1. Row Estimation Examples

The examples shown below use tables in the PostgreSQL regression test database. The outputs shown are taken from version 8.3. The behavior of earlier (or later) versions might vary. Note also that since `ANALYZE` uses random sampling while producing statistics, the results will change slightly after any new `ANALYZE`.

Let's start with a very simple query:

```
EXPLAIN SELECT * FROM tenk1;

                         QUERY PLAN
-------------------------------------------------------------
 Seq Scan on tenk1  (cost=0.00..458.00 rows=10000 width=244)
```

How the planner determines the cardinality of `tenk1` is covered in *Section 14.2* (Vol.I), but is repeated here for completeness. The number of pages and rows is looked up in `pg_class`:

```
SELECT relpages, reltuples FROM pg_class WHERE relname = 'tenk1';

 relpages | reltuples
----------+-----------
      358 |     10000
```

These numbers are current as of the last `VACUUM` or `ANALYZE` on the table. The planner then fetches the actual current number of pages in the table (this is a cheap operation, not requiring a table scan). If that is different from `relpages` then `reltuples` is scaled accordingly to arrive at a current number-of-rows estimate. In this case the values are correct so the rows estimate is the same as `reltuples`.

Let's move on to an example with a range condition in its `WHERE` clause:

```
EXPLAIN SELECT * FROM tenk1 WHERE unique1 < 1000;

                                   QUERY PLAN
--------------------------------------------------------------------------------
 Bitmap Heap Scan on tenk1  (cost=24.06..394.64 rows=1007 width=244)
   Recheck Cond: (unique1 < 1000)
   ->  Bitmap Index Scan on tenk1_unique1  (cost=0.00..23.80 rows=1007 width=0)
         Index Cond: (unique1 < 1000)
```

The planner examines the `WHERE` clause condition and looks up the selectivity function for the operator < in `pg_operator`. This is held in the column `oprrest`, and the entry in this case is `scalarltsel`. The `scalarltsel` function retrieves the histogram for `unique1` from `pg_statistics`. For manual queries it is more convenient to look in the simpler `pg_stats` view:

```
SELECT histogram_bounds FROM pg_stats
WHERE tablename='tenk1' AND attname='unique1';

                   histogram_bounds
------------------------------------------------------
 {0,993,1997,3050,4040,5036,5957,7057,8029,9016,9995}
```

Next the fraction of the histogram occupied by "< 1000" is worked out. This is the selectivity. The histogram divides the range into equal frequency buckets, so all we have to do is locate the bucket that our value is in and count *part* of it and *all* of the ones before. The value 1000 is clearly in the second bucket (993-1997). Assuming a linear distribution of values inside each bucket, we can calculate the selectivity as:

```
selectivity = (1 + (1000 - bucket[2].min)/(bucket[2].max - bucket[2].min))/num_buckets
            = (1 + (1000 - 993)/(1997 - 993))/10
            = 0.100697
```

that is, one whole bucket plus a linear fraction of the second, divided by the number of buckets. The estimated number of rows can now be calculated as the product of the selectivity and the cardinality of `tenk1`:

```
rows = rel_cardinality * selectivity
     = 10000 * 0.100697
     = 1007  (rounding off)
```

Next let's consider an example with an equality condition in its `WHERE` clause:

```
EXPLAIN SELECT * FROM tenk1 WHERE stringu1 = 'CRAAAA';

                        QUERY PLAN
----------------------------------------------------------
 Seq Scan on tenk1  (cost=0.00..483.00 rows=30 width=244)
   Filter: (stringu1 = 'CRAAAA'::name)
```

Again the planner examines the `WHERE` clause condition and looks up the selectivity function for `=`, which is `eqsel`. For equality estimation the histogram is not useful; instead the list of *most common values* (MCVs) is used to determine the selectivity. Let's have a look at the MCVs, with some additional columns that will be useful later:

```
SELECT null_frac, n_distinct, most_common_vals, most_common_freqs FROM pg_stats
WHERE tablename='tenk1' AND attname='stringu1';

null_frac         | 0
n_distinct        | 676
most_common_vals  | {EJAAAA,BBAAAA,CRAAAA,FCAAAA,FEAAAA,GSAAAA,JOAAAA,MCAAAA,NAAAAA,WGAAAA}
most_common_freqs | {0.00333333,0.003,0.003,0.003,0.003,0.003,0.003,0.003,0.003,0.003}
```

Since `CRAAAA` appears in the list of MCVs, the selectivity is merely the corresponding entry in the list of most common frequencies (MCFs):

```
selectivity = mcf[3]
            = 0.003
```

As before, the estimated number of rows is just the product of this with the cardinality of `tenk1`:

```
rows = 10000 * 0.003
     = 30
```

Now consider the same query, but with a constant that is not in the MCV list:

```
EXPLAIN SELECT * FROM tenk1 WHERE stringu1 = 'xxx';

                        QUERY PLAN
----------------------------------------------------------
 Seq Scan on tenk1  (cost=0.00..483.00 rows=15 width=244)
   Filter: (stringu1 = 'xxx'::name)
```

This is quite a different problem: how to estimate the selectivity when the value is *not* in the MCV list. The approach is to use the fact that the value is not in the list, combined with the knowledge of the frequencies for all of the MCVs:

```
selectivity = (1 - sum(mvf))/(num_distinct - num_mcv)
            = (1 - (0.00333333 + 0.003 + 0.003 + 0.003 + 0.003 + 0.003 +
                    0.003 + 0.003 + 0.003 + 0.003))/(676 - 10)
            = 0.0014559
```

That is, add up all the frequencies for the MCVs and subtract them from one, then divide by the number of *other* distinct values. This amounts to assuming that the fraction of the column that is not any of the MCVs is evenly distributed among all the other distinct values. Notice that there are no null values so we don't have to worry about those (otherwise we'd subtract the null fraction from the numerator as well). The estimated number of rows is then calculated as usual:

```
rows = 10000 * 0.0014559
     = 15  (rounding off)
```

The previous example with `unique1 < 1000` was an oversimplification of what `scalarltsel` really does; now that we have seen an example of the use of MCVs, we can fill in some more detail. The example was correct as far as it went, because since `unique1` is a unique column it has no MCVs (obviously, no value is any more common than any other value). For a non-unique column, there will normally be both a histogram and an MCV list, and *the histogram does not include the portion of the column population represented by the MCVs*. We do things this way because it allows more precise estimation. In this situation `scalarltsel` directly applies the condition (e.g., "< 1000") to each value of the MCV list, and adds up the frequencies of the MCVs for which the condition is true. This gives an exact estimate of the selectivity within the portion of the table that is MCVs. The histogram is then used in the same way as above to estimate the selectivity in the portion of the table that is not MCVs, and then the two numbers are combined to estimate the overall selectivity. For example, consider

```
EXPLAIN SELECT * FROM tenk1 WHERE stringu1 < 'IAAAAA';

                         QUERY PLAN
------------------------------------------------------------
 Seq Scan on tenk1  (cost=0.00..483.00 rows=3077 width=244)
   Filter: (stringu1 < 'IAAAAA'::name)
```

We already saw the MCV information for `stringu1`, and here is its histogram:

```
SELECT histogram_bounds FROM pg_stats
WHERE tablename='tenk1' AND attname='stringu1';

                                histogram_bounds
--------------------------------------------------------------------------------
 {AAAAAA,CQAAAA,FRAAAA,IBAAAA,KRAAAA,NFAAAA,PSAAAA,SGAAAA,VAAAAA,XLAAAA,ZZAAAA}
```

Checking the MCV list, we find that the condition `stringu1 < 'IAAAAA'` is satisfied by the first six entries and not the last four, so the selectivity within the MCV part of the population is

```
selectivity = sum(relevant mvfs)
            = 0.00333333 + 0.003 + 0.003 + 0.003 + 0.003 + 0.003
            = 0.01833333
```

Summing all the MCFs also tells us that the total fraction of the population represented by MCVs is 0.03033333, and therefore the fraction represented by the histogram is 0.96966667 (again, there are no nulls, else we'd have to exclude them here). We can see that the value `IAAAAA` falls nearly at the end of the third histogram bucket. Using some rather cheesy assumptions about the frequency of different characters, the planner arrives at the estimate 0.298387 for the portion of the histogram population that is less than `IAAAAA`. We then combine the estimates for the MCV and non-MCV populations:

```
selectivity = mcv_selectivity + histogram_selectivity * histogram_fraction
            = 0.01833333 + 0.298387 * 0.96966667
```

```
              = 0.307669

rows          = 10000 * 0.307669
              = 3077  (rounding off)
```

In this particular example, the correction from the MCV list is fairly small, because the column distribution is actually quite flat (the statistics showing these particular values as being more common than others are mostly due to sampling error). In a more typical case where some values are significantly more common than others, this complicated process gives a useful improvement in accuracy because the selectivity for the most common values is found exactly.

Now let's consider a case with more than one condition in the `WHERE` clause:

```
EXPLAIN SELECT * FROM tenk1 WHERE unique1 < 1000 AND stringu1 = 'xxx';

                                    QUERY PLAN
--------------------------------------------------------------------------------
 Bitmap Heap Scan on tenk1  (cost=23.80..396.91 rows=1 width=244)
   Recheck Cond: (unique1 < 1000)
   Filter: (stringu1 = 'xxx'::name)
   ->  Bitmap Index Scan on tenk1_unique1  (cost=0.00..23.80 rows=1007 width=0)
         Index Cond: (unique1 < 1000)
```

The planner assumes that the two conditions are independent, so that the individual selectivities of the clauses can be multiplied together:

```
selectivity = selectivity(unique1 < 1000) * selectivity(stringu1 = 'xxx')
            = 0.100697 * 0.0014559
            = 0.0001466

rows        = 10000 * 0.0001466
            = 1  (rounding off)
```

Notice that the number of rows estimated to be returned from the bitmap index scan reflects only the condition used with the index; this is important since it affects the cost estimate for the subsequent heap fetches.

Finally we will examine a query that involves a join:

```
EXPLAIN SELECT * FROM tenk1 t1, tenk2 t2
WHERE t1.unique1 < 50 AND t1.unique2 = t2.unique2;

                                    QUERY PLAN
--------------------------------------------------------------------------------
 Nested Loop  (cost=4.64..456.23 rows=50 width=488)
  -> Bitmap Heap Scan on tenk1 t1  (cost=4.64..142.17 rows=50 width=244)
       Recheck Cond: (unique1 < 50)
       ->  Bitmap Index Scan on tenk1_unique1  (cost=0.00..4.63 rows=50 width=0)
             Index Cond: (unique1 < 50)
  -> Index Scan using tenk2_unique2 on tenk2 t2  (cost=0.00..6.27 rows=1 width=244)
       Index Cond: (t2.unique2 = t1.unique2)
```

The restriction on `tenk1, unique1 < 50`, is evaluated before the nested-loop join. This is handled analogously to the previous range example. This time the value 50 falls into the first bucket of the `unique1` histogram:

```
selectivity = (0 + (50 - bucket[1].min)/(bucket[1].max - bucket[1].min))/num_buckets
            = (0 + (50 - 0)/(993 - 0))/10
            = 0.005035

rows        = 10000 * 0.005035
            = 50  (rounding off)
```

The restriction for the join is `t2.unique2 = t1.unique2`. The operator is just our familiar `=`, however the selectivity function is obtained from the `oprjoin` column of `pg_operator`, and is `eqjoinsel`. `eqjoinsel` looks up the statistical information for both `tenk2` and `tenk1`:

```
SELECT tablename, null_frac,n_distinct, most_common_vals FROM pg_stats
WHERE tablename IN ('tenk1', 'tenk2') AND attname='unique2';

tablename  | null_frac | n_distinct | most_common_vals
-----------+-----------+------------+------------------
 tenk1     |         0 |         -1 |
 tenk2     |         0 |         -1 |
```

In this case there is no MCV information for `unique2` because all the values appear to be unique, so we use an algorithm that relies only on the number of distinct values for both relations together with their null fractions:

```
selectivity = (1 - null_frac1) * (1 - null_frac2) * min(1/num_distinct1, 1/num_distinct2)
            = (1 - 0) * (1 - 0) / max(10000, 10000)
            = 0.0001
```

This is, subtract the null fraction from one for each of the relations, and divide by the maximum of the numbers of distinct values. The number of rows that the join is likely to emit is calculated as the cardinality of the Cartesian product of the two inputs, multiplied by the selectivity:

```
rows = (outer_cardinality * inner_cardinality) * selectivity
     = (50 * 10000) * 0.0001
     = 50
```

Had there been MCV lists for the two columns, `eqjoinsel` would have used direct comparison of the MCV lists to determine the join selectivity within the part of the column populations represented by the MCVs. The estimate for the remainder of the populations follows the same approach shown here.

Notice that we showed `inner_cardinality` as 10000, that is, the unmodified size of `tenk2` . It might appear from inspection of the `EXPLAIN` output that the estimate of join rows comes from 50 * 1, that is, the number of outer rows times the estimated number of rows obtained by each inner indexscan on `tenk2`. But this is not the case: the join relation size is estimated before any particular join plan has been considered. If everything is working well then the two ways of estimating the join size will produce about the same answer, but due to roundoff error and other factors they sometimes diverge significantly.

For those interested in further details, estimation of the size of a table (before any `WHERE` clauses) is done in `src/backend/optimizer/util/plancat.c`. The generic logic for clause selectivities is in `src/backend/optimizer/path/clausesel.c`. The operator-specific selectivity functions are mostly found in `src/backend/utils/adt/selfuncs.c`.

Part VIII. Appendixes

Appendix A. PostgreSQL Error Codes

All messages emitted by the PostgreSQL server are assigned five-character error codes that follow the SQL standard's conventions for "SQLSTATE" codes. Applications that need to know which error condition has occurred should usually test the error code, rather than looking at the textual error message. The error codes are less likely to change across PostgreSQL releases, and also are not subject to change due to localization of error messages. Note that some, but not all, of the error codes produced by PostgreSQL are defined by the SQL standard; some additional error codes for conditions not defined by the standard have been invented or borrowed from other databases.

According to the standard, the first two characters of an error code denote a class of errors, while the last three characters indicate a specific condition within that class. Thus, an application that does not recognize the specific error code can still be able to infer what to do from the error class.

Table A-1 (see below) lists all the error codes defined in PostgreSQL 9.0.3. (Some are not actually used at present, but are defined by the SQL standard.) The error classes are also shown. For each error class there is a "standard" error code having the last three characters `000`. This code is used only for error conditions that fall within the class but do not have any more-specific code assigned.

The PL/pgSQL condition name for each error code is the same as the phrase shown in the table, with underscores substituted for spaces. For example, code `22012`, DIVISION BY ZERO, has condition name `DIVISION_BY_ZERO`. Condition names can be written in either upper or lower case. (Note that PL/pgSQL does not recognize warning, as opposed to error, condition names; those are classes 00, 01, and 02.)

Error Code	Meaning	Condition Name
Class 00 - Successful Completion		
`00000`	SUCCESSFUL COMPLETION	successful_completion
Class 01 - Warning		
`01000`	WARNING	warning
`0100C`	DYNAMIC RESULT SETS RETURNED	dynamic_result_sets_returned

Error Code	Meaning	Condition Name
01008	IMPLICIT ZERO BIT PADDING	implicit_zero_bit_padding
01003	NULL VALUE ELIMINATED IN SET FUNCT	null_value_eliminated_in_set_function
01007	PRIVILEGE NOT GRANTED	privilege_not_granted
01006	PRIVILEGE NOT REVOKED	privilege_not_revoked
01004	STRING DATA RIGHT TRUNCATION	string_data_right_truncation
01P01	DEPRECATED FEATURE	deprecated_feature
Class 02 - No Data (this is also a warning class per the SQL standard)		
02000	NO DATA	no_data
02001	NO ADDITIONAL DYNAMIC RESULT SETS RETURNED	no_additional_dynamic_result_sets_returned
Class 03 - SQL Statement Not Yet Complete		
03000	SQL STATEMENT NOT YET COMPLETE	sql_statement_not_yet_complete
Class 08 - Connection Exception		
08000	CONNECTION EXCEPTION	connection_exception
08003	CONNECTION DOES NOT EXIST	connection_does_not_exist
08006	CONNECTION FAILURE	connection_failure
08001	SQLCLIENT UNABLE TO ESTABLISH SQLCONNECTION	sqlclient_unable_to_establish_sqlconnection
08004	SQLSERVER REJECTED ESTABLISHMENT OF SQLCONNECTION	sqlserver_rejected_establishment_of_sqlconnection
08007	TRANSACTION RESOLUTION UNKNOWN	transaction_resolution_unknown
08P01	PROTOCOL VIOLATION	protocol_violation
Class 09 - Triggered Action Exception		
09000	TRIGGERED ACTION EXCEPTION	triggered_action_exception
Class 0A - Feature Not Supported		
0A000	FEATURE NOT SUPPORTED	feature_not_supported
Class 0B - Invalid Transaction Initiation		
0B000	INVALID TRANSACTION INITIATION	invalid_transaction_initiation
Class 0F - Locator Exception		
0F000	LOCATOR EXCEPTION	locator_exception
0F001	INVALID LOCATOR SPECIFICATION	invalid_locator_specification
Class 0L - Invalid Grantor		
0L000	INVALID GRANTOR	invalid_grantor
0LP01	INVALID GRANT OPERATION	invalid_grant_operation

Error Code	Meaning	Condition Name
Class 0P - Invalid Role Specification		
0P000	INVALID ROLE SPECIFICATION	invalid_role_specification
Class 20 - Case Not Found		
20000	CASE NOT FOUND	case_not_found
Class 21 - Cardinality Violation		
21000	CARDINALITY VIOLATION	cardinality_violation
Class 22 - Data Exception		
22000	DATA EXCEPTION	data_exception
2202E	ARRAY SUBSCRIPT ERROR	array_subscript_error
22021	CHARACTER NOT IN REPERTOIRE	character_not_in_repertoire
22008	DATETIME FIELD OVERFLOW	datetime_field_overflow
22012	DIVISION BY ZERO	division_by_zero
22005	ERROR IN ASSIGNMENT	error_in_assignment
2200B	ESCAPE CHARACTER CONFLICT	escape_character_conflict
22022	INDICATOR OVERFLOW	indicator_overflow
22015	INTERVAL FIELD OVERFLOW	interval_field_overflow
2201E	INVALID ARGUMENT FOR LOGARITHM	invalid_argument_for_logarithm
22014	INVALID ARGUMENT FOR NTILE FUNCTION	invalid_argument_for_ntile_function
22016	INVALID ARGUMENT FOR NTH_VALUE FUNCTION	invalid_argument_for_nth_value_function
2201F	INVALID ARGUMENT FOR POWER FUNCTION	invalid_argument_for_power_function
2201G	INVALID ARGUMENT FOR WIDTH BUCKET FUNCTION	invalid_argument_for_width_bucket_function
22018	INVALID CHARACTER VALUE FOR CAST	invalid_character_value_for_cast
22007	INVALID DATETIME FORMAT	invalid_datetime_format
22019	INVALID ESCAPE CHARACTER	invalid_escape_character
2200D	INVALID ESCAPE OCTET	invalid_escape_octet
22025	INVALID ESCAPE SEQUENCE	invalid_escape_sequence
22P06	NONSTANDARD USE OF ESCAPE CHARACTER	nonstandard_use_of_escape_character
22010	INVALID INDICATOR PARAMETER VALUE	invalid_indicator_parameter_value
22023	INVALID PARAMETER VALUE	invalid_parameter_value
2201B	INVALID REGULAR EXPRESSION	invalid_regular_expression

Error Code	Meaning	Condition Name
2201W	INVALID ROW COUNT IN LIMIT CLAUSE	invalid_row_count_in_limit_clause
2201X	INVALID ROW COUNT IN RESULT OFFSET CLAUSE	invalid_row_count_in_result_offset_clause
22009	INVALID TIME ZONE DISPLACEMENT VALUE	invalid_time_zone_displacement_value
2200C	INVALID USE OF ESCAPE CHARACTER	invalid_use_of_escape_character
2200G	MOST SPECIFIC TYPE MISMATCH	most_specific_type_mismatch
22004	NULL VALUE NOT ALLOWED	null_value_not_allowed
22002	NULL VALUE NO INDICATOR PARAMETER	null_value_no_indicator_parameter
22003	NUMERIC VALUE OUT OF RANGE	numeric_value_out_of_range
22026	STRING DATA LENGTH MISMATCH	string_data_length_mismatch
22001	STRING DATA RIGHT TRUNCATION	string_data_right_truncation
22011	SUBSTRING ERROR	substring_error
22027	TRIM ERROR	trim_error
22024	UNTERMINATED C STRING	unterminated_c_string
2200F	ZERO LENGTH CHARACTER STRING	zero_length_character_string
22P01	FLOATING POINT EXCEPTION	floating_point_exception
22P02	INVALID TEXT REPRESENTATION	invalid_text_representation
22P03	INVALID BINARY REPRESENTATION	invalid_binary_representation
22P04	BAD COPY FILE FORMAT	bad_copy_file_format
22P05	UNTRANSLATABLE CHARACTER	untranslatable_character
2200L	NOT AN XML DOCUMENT	not_an_xml_document
2200M	INVALID XML DOCUMENT	invalid_xml_document
2200N	INVALID XML CONTENT	invalid_xml_content
2200S	INVALID XML COMMENT	invalid_xml_comment
2200T	INVALID XML PROCESSING INSTRUCTION	invalid_xml_processing_instruction
Class 23 - Integrity Constraint Violation		
23000	INTEGRITY CONSTRAINT VIOLATION	integrity_constraint_violation
23001	RESTRICT VIOLATION	restrict_violation
23502	NOT NULL VIOLATION	not_null_violation
23503	FOREIGN KEY VIOLATION	foreign_key_violation
23505	UNIQUE VIOLATION	unique_violation

Error Code	Meaning	Condition Name
23514	CHECK VIOLATION	check_violation
23P01	EXCLUSION VIOLATION	exclusion_violation
Class 24 - Invalid Cursor State		
24000	INVALID CURSOR STATE	invalid_cursor_state
Class 25 - Invalid Transaction State		
25000	INVALID TRANSACTION STATE	invalid_transaction_state
25001	ACTIVE SQL TRANSACTION	active_sql_transaction
25002	BRANCH TRANSACTION ALREADY ACTIVE	branch_transaction_already_active
25008	HELD CURSOR REQUIRES SAME ISOLATION LEVEL	held_cursor_requires_same_isolation_level
25003	INAPPROPRIATE ACCESS MODE FOR BRANCH TRANSACTION	inappropriate_access_mode_for_branch_transactio n
25004	INAPPROPRIATE ISOLATION LEVEL FOR BRANCH TRANSACTION	inappropriate_isolation_level_for_branch_transacti on
25005	NO ACTIVE SQL TRANSACTION FOR BRANCH TRANSACTION	no_active_sql_transaction_for_branch_transaction
25006	READ ONLY SQL TRANSACTION	read_only_sql_transaction
25007	SCHEMA AND DATA STATEMENT MIXING NOT SUPPORTED	schema_and_data_statement_mixing_not_support ed
25P01	NO ACTIVE SQL TRANSACTION	no_active_sql_transaction
25P02	IN FAILED SQL TRANSACTION	in_failed_sql_transaction
Class 26 - Invalid SQL Statement Name		
26000	INVALID SQL STATEMENT NAME	invalid_sql_statement_name
Class 27 - Triggered Data Change Violation		
27000	TRIGGERED DATA CHANGE VIOLATION	triggered_data_change_violation
Class 28 - Invalid Authorization Specification		
28000	INVALID AUTHORIZATION SPECIFICATION	invalid_authorization_specification
28P01	INVALID PASSWORD	invalid_password
Class 2B - Dependent Privilege Descriptors Still Exist		
2B000	DEPENDENT PRIVILEGE DESCRIPTORS STILL EXIST	dependent_privilege_descriptors_still_exist
2BP01	DEPENDENT OBJECTS STILL EXIST	dependent_objects_still_exist
Class 2D - Invalid Transaction Termination		
2D000	INVALID TRANSACTION TERMINATION	invalid_transaction_termination

Error Code	Meaning	Condition Name
Class 2F - SQL Routine Exception		
2F000	SQL ROUTINE EXCEPTION	sql_routine_exception
2F005	FUNCTION EXECUTED NO RETURN STATEMENT	function_executed_no_return_statement
2F002	MODIFYING SQL DATA NOT PERMITTED	modifying_sql_data_not_permitted
2F003	PROHIBITED SQL STATEMENT ATTEMPTED	prohibited_sql_statement_attempted
2F004	READING SQL DATA NOT PERMITTED	reading_sql_data_not_permitted
Class 34 - Invalid Cursor Name		
34000	INVALID CURSOR NAME	invalid_cursor_name
Class 38 - External Routine Exception		
38000	EXTERNAL ROUTINE EXCEPTION	external_routine_exception
38001	CONTAINING SQL NOT PERMITTED	containing_sql_not_permitted
38002	MODIFYING SQL DATA NOT PERMITTED	modifying_sql_data_not_permitted
38003	PROHIBITED SQL STATEMENT ATTEMPTED	prohibited_sql_statement_attempted
38004	READING SQL DATA NOT PERMITTED	reading_sql_data_not_permitted
Class 39 - External Routine Invocation Exception		
39000	EXTERNAL ROUTINE INVOCATION EXCEPTION	external_routine_invocation_exception
39001	INVALID SQLSTATE RETURNED	invalid_sqlstate_returned
39004	NULL VALUE NOT ALLOWED	null_value_not_allowed
39P01	TRIGGER PROTOCOL VIOLATED	trigger_protocol_violated
39P02	SRF PROTOCOL VIOLATED	srf_protocol_violated
Class 3B - Savepoint Exception		
3B000	SAVEPOINT EXCEPTION	savepoint_exception
3B001	INVALID SAVEPOINT SPECIFICATION	invalid_savepoint_specification
Class 3D - Invalid Catalog Name		
3D000	INVALID CATALOG NAME	invalid_catalog_name
Class 3F - Invalid Schema Name		
3F000	INVALID SCHEMA NAME	invalid_schema_name
Class 40 - Transaction Rollback		
40000	TRANSACTION ROLLBACK	transaction_rollback
40002	TRANSACTION INTEGRITY CONSTRAINT VIOLATION	transaction_integrity_constraint_violation

Error Code	Meaning	Condition Name
40001	SERIALIZATION FAILURE	serialization_failure
40003	STATEMENT COMPLETION UNKNOWN	statement_completion_unknown
40P01	DEADLOCK DETECTED	deadlock_detected
Class 42 - Syntax Error or Access Rule Violation		
42000	SYNTAX ERROR OR ACCESS RULE VIOLATION	syntax_error_or_access_rule_violation
42601	SYNTAX ERROR	syntax_error
42501	INSUFFICIENT PRIVILEGE	insufficient_privilege
42846	CANNOT COERCE	cannot_coerce
42803	GROUPING ERROR	grouping_error
42P20	WINDOWING ERROR	windowing_error
42P19	INVALID RECURSION	invalid_recursion
42830	INVALID FOREIGN KEY	invalid_foreign_key
42602	INVALID NAME	invalid_name
42622	NAME TOO LONG	name_too_long
42939	RESERVED NAME	reserved_name
42804	DATATYPE MISMATCH	datatype_mismatch
42P18	INDETERMINATE DATATYPE	indeterminate_datatype
42809	WRONG OBJECT TYPE	wrong_object_type
42703	UNDEFINED COLUMN	undefined_column
42883	UNDEFINED FUNCTION	undefined_function
42P01	UNDEFINED TABLE	undefined_table
42P02	UNDEFINED PARAMETER	undefined_parameter
42704	UNDEFINED OBJECT	undefined_object
42701	DUPLICATE COLUMN	duplicate_column
42P03	DUPLICATE CURSOR	duplicate_cursor
42P04	DUPLICATE DATABASE	duplicate_database
42723	DUPLICATE FUNCTION	duplicate_function
42P05	DUPLICATE PREPARED STATEMENT	duplicate_prepared_statement
42P06	DUPLICATE SCHEMA	duplicate_schema
42P07	DUPLICATE TABLE	duplicate_table
42712	DUPLICATE ALIAS	duplicate_alias
42710	DUPLICATE OBJECT	duplicate_object

Error Code	Meaning	Condition Name
42702	AMBIGUOUS COLUMN	ambiguous_column
42725	AMBIGUOUS FUNCTION	ambiguous_function
42P08	AMBIGUOUS PARAMETER	ambiguous_parameter
42P09	AMBIGUOUS ALIAS	ambiguous_alias
42P10	INVALID COLUMN REFERENCE	invalid_column_reference
42611	INVALID COLUMN DEFINITION	invalid_column_definition
42P11	INVALID CURSOR DEFINITION	invalid_cursor_definition
42P12	INVALID DATABASE DEFINITION	invalid_database_definition
42P13	INVALID FUNCTION DEFINITION	invalid_function_definition
42P14	INVALID PREPARED STATEMENT DEFINITION	invalid_prepared_statement_definition
42P15	INVALID SCHEMA DEFINITION	invalid_schema_definition
42P16	INVALID TABLE DEFINITION	invalid_table_definition
42P17	INVALID OBJECT DEFINITION	invalid_object_definition
Class 44 - WITH CHECK OPTION Violation		
44000	WITH CHECK OPTION VIOLATION	with_check_option_violation
Class 53 - Insufficient Resources		
53000	INSUFFICIENT RESOURCES	insufficient_resources
53100	DISK FULL	disk_full
53200	OUT OF MEMORY	out_of_memory
53300	TOO MANY CONNECTIONS	too_many_connections
Class 54 - Program Limit Exceeded		
54000	PROGRAM LIMIT EXCEEDED	program_limit_exceeded
54001	STATEMENT TOO COMPLEX	statement_too_complex
54011	TOO MANY COLUMNS	too_many_columns
54023	TOO MANY ARGUMENTS	too_many_arguments
Class 55 - Object Not In Prerequisite State		
55000	OBJECT NOT IN PREREQUISITE STATE	object_not_in_prerequisite_state
55006	OBJECT IN USE	object_in_use
55P02	CANT CHANGE RUNTIME PARAM	cant_change_runtime_param
55P03	LOCK NOT AVAILABLE	lock_not_available
Class 57 - Operator Intervention		
57000	OPERATOR INTERVENTION	operator_intervention

Error Code	Meaning	Condition Name
57014	QUERY CANCELED	query_canceled
57P01	ADMIN SHUTDOWN	admin_shutdown
57P02	CRASH SHUTDOWN	crash_shutdown
57P03	CANNOT CONNECT NOW	cannot_connect_now
Class 58 - System Error (errors external to PostgreSQL itself)		
58030	IO ERROR	io_error
58P01	UNDEFINED FILE	undefined_file
58P02	DUPLICATE FILE	duplicate_file
Class F0 - Configuration File Error		
F0000	CONFIG FILE ERROR	config_file_error
F0001	LOCK FILE EXISTS	lock_file_exists
Class P0 - PL/pgSQL Error		
P0000	PLPGSQL ERROR	plpgsql_error
P0001	RAISE EXCEPTION	raise_exception
P0002	NO DATA FOUND	no_data_found
P0003	TOO MANY ROWS	too_many_rows
Class XX - Internal Error		
XX000	INTERNAL ERROR	internal_error
XX001	DATA CORRUPTED	data_corrupted
XX002	INDEX CORRUPTED	index_corrupted

Table A-1. PostgreSQL Error Codes

Appendix B. Date/Time Support

PostgreSQL uses an internal heuristic parser for all date/time input support. Dates and times are input as strings, and are broken up into distinct fields with a preliminary determination of what kind of information can be in the field. Each field is interpreted and either assigned a numeric value, ignored, or rejected. The parser contains internal lookup tables for all textual fields, including months, days of the week, and time zones.

This appendix includes information on the content of these lookup tables and describes the steps used by the parser to decode dates and times.

B.1. Date/Time Input Interpretation

The date/time type inputs are all decoded using the following procedure.

1. Break the input string into tokens and categorize each token as a string, time, time zone, or number.
   1. If the numeric token contains a colon (:), this is a time string. Include all subsequent digits and colons.
   2. If the numeric token contains a dash (-), slash (/), or two or more dots (.), this is a date string which might have a text month. If a date token has already been seen, it is instead interpreted as a time zone name (e.g., America/New_York).
   3. If the token is numeric only, then it is either a single field or an ISO 8601 concatenated date (e.g., 19990113 for January 13, 1999) or time (e.g., 141516 for 14:15:16).
   4. If the token starts with a plus (+) or minus (-), then it is either a numeric time zone or a special field.
2. If the token is a text string, match up with possible strings:
   1. Do a binary-search table lookup for the token as a time zone abbreviation.
   2. If not found, do a similar binary-search table lookup to match the token as either a special string (e.g., today), day (e.g., Thursday), month (e.g., January), or noise word (e.g., at, on).
   3. If still not found, throw an error.

3. When the token is a number or number field:

    1. If there are eight or six digits, and if no other date fields have been previously read, then interpret as a "concatenated date" (e.g., 19990118 or 990118). The interpretation is YYYYMMDD or YYMMDD.

    2. If the token is three digits and a year has already been read, then interpret as day of year.

    3. If four or six digits and a year has already been read, then interpret as a time (HHMM or HHMMSS).

    4. If three or more digits and no date fields have yet been found, interpret as a year (this forces yy-mm-dd ordering of the remaining date fields).

    5. Otherwise the date field ordering is assumed to follow the DateStyle setting: mm-dd-yy, dd-mm-yy, or yy-mm-dd. Throw an error if a month or day field is found to be out of range.

4. If BC has been specified, negate the year and add one for internal storage. (There is no year zero in the Gregorian calendar, so numerically 1 BC becomes year zero.)

5. If BC was not specified, and if the year field was two digits in length, then adjust the year to four digits. If the field is less than 70, then add 2000, otherwise add 1900.

Tip

Gregorian years AD 1-99 can be entered by using 4 digits with leading zeros (e.g., `0099` is AD 99).

B.2. Date/Time Key Words

Table B-1 (see below) shows the tokens that are recognized as names of months.

Month	Abbreviations
January	Jan
February	Feb
March	Mar
April	Apr
May	
June	Jun
July	Jul
August	Aug
September	Sep, Sept

Month	Abbreviations
October	Oct
November	Nov
December	Dec

Table B-1. Month Names

Table B-2 (see below) shows the tokens that are recognized as names of days of the week.

Day	Abbreviations
Sunday	Sun
Monday	Mon
Tuesday	Tue, Tues
Wednesday	Wed, Weds
Thursday	Thu, Thur, Thurs
Friday	Fri
Saturday	Sat

Table B-2. Day of the Week Names

Table B-3 (see below) shows the tokens that serve various modifier purposes.

Identifier	Description
`AM`	Time is before 12:00
`AT`	Ignored
`JULIAN`, `JD`, `J`	Next field is Julian Day
`ON`	Ignored
`PM`	Time is on or after 12:00
`T`	Next field is time

Table B-3. Date/Time Field Modifiers

B.3. Date/Time Configuration Files

Since timezone abbreviations are not well standardized, PostgreSQL provides a means to customize the set of abbreviations accepted by the server. The *timezone_abbreviations* (Vol.II) run-time parameter determines the active set of abbreviations. While this parameter can be altered by any database user, the possible values for it are under the control of the database administrator - they are in fact names of configuration files stored in `.../share/timezonesets/` of the installation directory. By adding or altering files in that directory, the administrator can set local policy for timezone abbreviations.

`timezone_abbreviations` can be set to any file name found in `.../share/timezonesets/`, if the file's name is entirely alphabetic. (The prohibition against non-alphabetic characters in `timezone_abbreviations` prevents reading files outside the intended directory, as well as reading editor backup files and other extraneous files.)

A timezone abbreviation file can contain blank lines and comments beginning with `#`. Non-comment lines must have one of these formats:

```
time_zone_name offset
time_zone_name offset D
@INCLUDE file_name
@OVERRIDE
```

A *`time_zone_name`* is just the abbreviation being defined. The *`offset`* is the zone's offset in seconds from UTC, positive being east from Greenwich and negative being west. For example, -18000 would be five hours west of Greenwich, or North American east coast standard time. `D` indicates that the zone name represents local daylight-savings time rather than standard time. Since all known time zone offsets are on 15 minute boundaries, the number of seconds has to be a multiple of 900.

The `@INCLUDE` syntax allows inclusion of another file in the `.../share/timezonesets/` directory. Inclusion can be nested, to a limited depth.

The `@OVERRIDE` syntax indicates that subsequent entries in the file can override previous entries (i.e., entries obtained from included files). Without this, conflicting definitions of the same timezone abbreviation are considered an error.

In an unmodified installation, the file `Default` contains all the non-conflicting time zone abbreviations for most of the world. Additional files `Australia` and `India` are provided for those regions: these files first include the `Default` file and then add or modify timezones as needed.

For reference purposes, a standard installation also contains files `Africa.txt`, `America.txt`, etc, containing information about every time zone abbreviation known to be in use according to the `zoneinfo` timezone database. The zone name definitions found in these files can be copied and pasted into a custom configuration file as needed. Note that these files cannot be directly referenced as `timezone_abbreviations` settings, because of the dot embedded in their names.

Note

If an error occurs while reading the time zone data sets, no new value is applied but the old set is kept. If the error occurs while starting the database, startup fails.

> **Caution**
>
> Time zone abbreviations defined in the configuration file override non-timezone meanings built into PostgreSQL. For example, the `Australia` configuration file defines `SAT` (for South Australian Standard Time). When this file is active, `SAT` will not be recognized as an abbreviation for Saturday.

> **Caution**
>
> If you modify files in `.../share/timezonesets/`, it is up to you to make backups - a normal database dump will not include this directory.

B.4. History of Units

The Julian calendar was introduced by Julius Caesar in 45 BC. It was in common use in the Western world until the year 1582, when countries started changing to the Gregorian calendar. In the Julian calendar, the tropical year is approximated as 365 1/4 days = 365.25 days. This gives an error of about 1 day in 128 years.

The accumulating calendar error prompted Pope Gregory XIII to reform the calendar in accordance with instructions from the Council of Trent. In the Gregorian calendar, the tropical year is approximated as 365 + 97 / 400 days = 365.2425 days. Thus it takes approximately 3300 years for the tropical year to shift one day with respect to the Gregorian calendar.

The approximation 365+97/400 is achieved by having 97 leap years every 400 years, using the following rules:

Every year divisible by 4 is a leap year.
However, every year divisible by 100 is not a leap year.
However, every year divisible by 400 is a leap year after all.

So, 1700, 1800, 1900, 2100, and 2200 are not leap years. But 1600, 2000, and 2400 are leap years. By contrast, in the older Julian calendar all years divisible by 4 are leap years.

The papal bull of February 1582 decreed that 10 days should be dropped from October 1582 so that 15 October should follow immediately after 4 October. This was observed in Italy, Poland, Portugal, and Spain. Other Catholic countries followed shortly after, but Protestant countries were reluctant to change, and the Greek Orthodox countries didn't change until the start of the 20th century. The reform was observed by Great Britain and Dominions (including what is now the USA) in 1752. Thus 2 September 1752 was followed by 14 September 1752. This is why Unix systems have the `cal` program produce the following:

```
$ cal 9 1752
   September 1752
```

```
 S  M Tu  W Th  F  S
       1  2 14 15 16
17 18 19 20 21 22 23
24 25 26 27 28 29 30
```

The SQL standard states that "Within the definition of a 'datetime literal', the 'datetime value's are constrained by the natural rules for dates and times according to the Gregorian calendar". Dates between 1582-10-05 and 1582-10-14, although eliminated in some countries by Papal fiat, conform to "natural rules" and are hence valid dates. PostgreSQL follows the SQL standard's lead by counting dates exclusively in the Gregorian calendar, even for years before that calendar was in use.

Different calendars have been developed in various parts of the world, many predating the Gregorian system. For example, the beginnings of the Chinese calendar can be traced back to the 14th century BC. Legend has it that the Emperor Huangdi invented that calendar in 2637 BC. The People's Republic of China uses the Gregorian calendar for civil purposes. The Chinese calendar is used for determining festivals.

The "Julian Date" is unrelated to the "Julian calendar". The Julian Date system was invented by the French scholar Joseph Justus Scaliger (1540-1609) and probably takes its name from Scaliger's father, the Italian scholar Julius Caesar Scaliger (1484-1558). In the Julian Date system, each day has a sequential number, starting from JD 0 (which is sometimes called *the* Julian Date). JD 0 corresponds to 1 January 4713 BC in the Julian calendar, or 24 November 4714 BC in the Gregorian calendar. Julian Date counting is most often used by astronomers for labeling their nightly observations, and therefore a date runs from noon UTC to the next noon UTC, rather than from midnight to midnight: JD 0 designates the 24 hours from noon UTC on 1 January 4713 BC to noon UTC on 2 January 4713 BC.

Although PostgreSQL supports Julian Date notation for input and output of dates (and also uses them for some internal datetime calculations), it does not observe the nicety of having dates run from noon to noon. PostgreSQL treats a Julian Date as running from midnight to midnight.

Appendix C. SQL Key Words

Table C-1 (see below) lists all tokens that are key words in the SQL standard and in PostgreSQL 9.0.3. Background information can be found in *Section 4.1.1* (Vol.I).

SQL distinguishes between *reserved* and *non-reserved* key words. According to the standard, reserved key words are the only real key words; they are never allowed as identifiers. Non-reserved key words only have a special meaning in particular contexts and can be used as identifiers in other contexts. Most non-reserved key words are actually the names of built-in tables and functions specified by SQL. The concept of non-reserved key words essentially only exists to declare that some predefined meaning is attached to a word in some contexts.

In the PostgreSQL parser life is a bit more complicated. There are several different classes of tokens ranging from those that can never be used as an identifier to those that have absolutely no special status in the parser as compared to an ordinary identifier. (The latter is usually the case for functions specified by SQL.) Even reserved key words are not completely reserved in PostgreSQL, but can be used as column labels (for example, `SELECT 55 AS CHECK`, even though `CHECK` is a reserved key word).

In *Table C-1* (see below) in the column for PostgreSQL we classify as "non-reserved" those key words that are explicitly known to the parser but are allowed as column or table names. Some key words that are otherwise non-reserved cannot be used as function or data type names and are marked accordingly. (Most of these words represent built-in functions or data types with special syntax. The function or type is still available but it cannot be redefined by the user.) Labeled "reserved" are those tokens that are not allowed as column or table names. Some reserved key words are allowable as names for functions or data types; this is also shown in the table. If not so marked, a reserved key word is only allowed as an "AS" column label name.

As a general rule, if you get spurious parser errors for commands that contain any of the listed key words as an identifier you should try to quote the identifier to see if the problem goes away.

It is important to understand before studying *Table C-1* (see below) that the fact that a key word is not reserved in PostgreSQL does not mean that the feature related to the word is not implemented. Conversely, the presence of a key word does not indicate the existence of a feature.

Key Word	PostgreSQL	SQL:2008	SQL:2003	SQL:1999	SQL-92
A		non-reserved	non-reserved		
ABORT	non-reserved				
ABS		reserved	reserved	non-reserved	
ABSENT		non-reserved			
ABSOLUTE	non-reserved	non-reserved	non-reserved	reserved	reserved
ACCESS	non-reserved				
ACCORDING		non-reserved			
ACTION	non-reserved	non-reserved	non-reserved	reserved	reserved
ADA		non-reserved	non-reserved	non-reserved	non-reserved
ADD	non-reserved	non-reserved	non-reserved	reserved	reserved
ADMIN	non-reserved	non-reserved	non-reserved	reserved	
AFTER	non-reserved	non-reserved	non-reserved	reserved	
AGGREGATE	non-reserved			reserved	
ALIAS				reserved	
ALL	reserved	reserved	reserved	reserved	reserved
ALLOCATE		reserved	reserved	reserved	reserved
ALSO	non-reserved				
ALTER	non-reserved	reserved	reserved	reserved	reserved
ALWAYS	non-reserved	non-reserved	non-reserved		
ANALYSE	reserved				
ANALYZE	reserved				
AND	reserved	reserved	reserved	reserved	reserved
ANY	reserved	reserved	reserved	reserved	reserved
ARE		reserved	reserved	reserved	reserved

Key Word	PostgreSQL	SQL:2008	SQL:2003	SQL:1999	SQL-92
ARRAY	reserved	reserved	reserved	reserved	
ARRAY_AGG		reserved			
AS	reserved	reserved	reserved	reserved	reserved
ASC	reserved	non-reserved	non-reserved	reserved	reserved
ASENSITIVE		reserved	reserved	non-reserved	
ASSERTION	non-reserved	non-reserved	non-reserved	reserved	reserved
ASSIGNMENT	non-reserved	non-reserved	non-reserved	non-reserved	
ASYMMETRIC	reserved	reserved	reserved	non-reserved	
AT	non-reserved	reserved	reserved	reserved	reserved
ATOMIC		reserved	reserved	non-reserved	
ATTRIBUTE		non-reserved	non-reserved		
ATTRIBUTES		non-reserved	non-reserved		
AUTHORIZATION	reserved (can be function or type)	reserved	reserved	reserved	reserved
AVG		reserved	reserved	non-reserved	reserved
BACKWARD	non-reserved				
BASE64		non-reserved	non-reserved		
BEFORE	non-reserved	non-reserved	non-reserved	reserved	
BEGIN	non-reserved	reserved	reserved	reserved	reserved
BERNOULLI		non-reserved	non-reserved		
BETWEEN	non-reserved (cannot be function or type)	reserved	reserved	non-reserved	reserved
BIGINT	non-reserved (cannot be function or type)	reserved	reserved		
BINARY	reserved (can be function or type)	reserved	reserved	reserved	

Key Word	PostgreSQL	SQL:2008	SQL:2003	SQL:1999	SQL-92
BIT	non-reserved (cannot be function or type)			reserved	reserved
BITVAR				non-reserved	
BIT_LENGTH				non-reserved	reserved
BLOB		reserved	reserved	reserved	
BLOCKED		non-reserved	non-reserved		
BOM		non-reserved			
BOOLEAN	non-reserved (cannot be function or type)	reserved	reserved	reserved	
BOTH	reserved	reserved	reserved	reserved	reserved
BREADTH		non-reserved	non-reserved	reserved	
BY	non-reserved	reserved	reserved	reserved	reserved
C		non-reserved	non-reserved	non-reserved	non-reserved
CACHE	non-reserved				
CALL		reserved	reserved	reserved	
CALLED	non-reserved	reserved	reserved	non-reserved	
CARDINALITY		reserved	reserved	non-reserved	
CASCADE	non-reserved	non-reserved	non-reserved	reserved	reserved
CASCADED	non-reserved	reserved	reserved	reserved	reserved
CASE	reserved	reserved	reserved	reserved	reserved
CAST	reserved	reserved	reserved	reserved	reserved
CATALOG	non-reserved	non-reserved	non-reserved	reserved	reserved
CATALOG_NAME		non-reserved	non-reserved	non-reserved	non-reserved
CEIL		reserved	reserved		
CEILING		reserved	reserved		
CHAIN	non-reserved	non-reserved	non-reserved	non-reserved	

Key Word	PostgreSQL	SQL:2008	SQL:2003	SQL:1999	SQL-92
CHAR	non-reserved (cannot be function or type)	reserved	reserved	reserved	reserved
CHARACTER	non-reserved (cannot be function or type)	reserved	reserved	reserved	reserved
CHARACTERISTICS	non-reserved	non-reserved	non-reserved		
CHARACTERS		non-reserved	non-reserved		
CHARACTER_LENGTH		reserved	reserved	non-reserved	reserved
CHARACTER_SET_CATALOG		non-reserved	non-reserved	non-reserved	non-reserved
CHARACTER_SET_NAME		non-reserved	non-reserved	non-reserved	non-reserved
CHARACTER_SET_SCHEMA		non-reserved	non-reserved	non-reserved	non-reserved
CHAR_LENGTH		reserved	reserved	non-reserved	reserved
CHECK	reserved	reserved	reserved	reserved	reserved
CHECKED				non-reserved	
CHECKPOINT	non-reserved				
CLASS	non-reserved			reserved	
CLASS_ORIGIN		non-reserved	non-reserved	non-reserved	non-reserved
CLOB		reserved	reserved	reserved	
CLOSE	non-reserved	reserved	reserved	reserved	reserved
CLUSTER	non-reserved				
COALESCE	non-reserved (cannot be function or type)	reserved	reserved	non-reserved	reserved
COBOL		non-reserved	non-reserved	non-reserved	non-reserved
COLLATE	reserved	reserved	reserved	reserved	reserved
COLLATION		non-reserved	non-reserved	reserved	reserved
COLLATION_CATALOG		non-reserved	non-reserved	non-reserved	non-reserved
COLLATION_NAME		non-reserved	non-reserved	non-reserved	non-reserved

Key Word	PostgreSQL	SQL:2008	SQL:2003	SQL:1999	SQL-92
COLLATION_SCHEMA		non-reserved	non-reserved	non-reserved	non-reserved
COLLECT		reserved	reserved		
COLUMN	reserved	reserved	reserved	reserved	reserved
COLUMNS		non-reserved			
COLUMN_NAME		non-reserved	non-reserved	non-reserved	non-reserved
COMMAND_FUNCTION		non-reserved	non-reserved	non-reserved	non-reserved
COMMAND_FUNCTION_CODE		non-reserved	non-reserved	non-reserved	
COMMENT	non-reserved				
COMMENTS	non-reserved				
COMMIT	non-reserved	reserved	reserved	reserved	reserved
COMMITTED	non-reserved	non-reserved	non-reserved	non-reserved	non-reserved
COMPLETION				reserved	
CONCURRENTLY	reserved (can be function or type)				
CONDITION		reserved	reserved		
CONDITION_NUMBER		non-reserved	non-reserved	non-reserved	non-reserved
CONFIGURATION	non-reserved				
CONNECT		reserved	reserved	reserved	reserved
CONNECTION	non-reserved	non-reserved	non-reserved	reserved	reserved
CONNECTION_NAME		non-reserved	non-reserved	non-reserved	non-reserved
CONSTRAINT	reserved	reserved	reserved	reserved	reserved
CONSTRAINTS	non-reserved	non-reserved	non-reserved	reserved	reserved
CONSTRAINT_CATALOG		non-reserved	non-reserved	non-reserved	non-reserved
CONSTRAINT_NAME		non-reserved	non-reserved	non-reserved	non-reserved
CONSTRAINT_SCHEMA		non-reserved	non-reserved	non-reserved	non-reserved

Key Word	PostgreSQL	SQL:2008	SQL:2003	SQL:1999	SQL-92
CONSTRUCTOR		non-reserved	non-reserved	reserved	
CONTAINS		non-reserved	non-reserved	non-reserved	
CONTENT	non-reserved	non-reserved	non-reserved		
CONTINUE	non-reserved	non-reserved	non-reserved	reserved	reserved
CONTROL		non-reserved	non-reserved		
CONVERSION	non-reserved				
CONVERT		reserved	reserved	non-reserved	reserved
COPY	non-reserved				
CORR		reserved	reserved		
CORRESPONDING		reserved	reserved	reserved	reserved
COST	non-reserved				
COUNT		reserved	reserved	non-reserved	reserved
COVAR_POP		reserved	reserved		
COVAR_SAMP		reserved	reserved		
CREATE	reserved	reserved	reserved	reserved	reserved
CREATEDB	non-reserved				
CREATEROLE	non-reserved				
CREATEUSER	non-reserved				
CROSS	reserved (can be function or type)	reserved	reserved	reserved	reserved
CSV	non-reserved				
CUBE		reserved	reserved	reserved	
CUME_DIST		reserved	reserved		
CURRENT	non-reserved	reserved	reserved	reserved	reserved
CURRENT_CATALOG	reserved	reserved			
CURRENT_DATE	reserved	reserved	reserved	reserved	reserved
CURRENT_DEFAULT_ TRANSFORM_GROUP		reserved	reserved		
CURRENT_PATH		reserved	reserved	reserved	

Key Word	PostgreSQL	SQL:2008	SQL:2003	SQL:1999	SQL-92
CURRENT_ROLE	reserved	reserved	reserved	reserved	
CURRENT_SCHEMA	reserved (can be function or type)	reserved			
CURRENT_TIME	reserved	reserved	reserved	reserved	reserved
CURRENT_TIMESTAMP	reserved	reserved	reserved	reserved	reserved
CURRENT_TRANSFORM_ GROUP_FOR_TYPE		reserved	reserved		
CURRENT_USER	reserved	reserved	reserved	reserved	reserved
CURSOR	non-reserved	reserved	reserved	reserved	reserved
CURSOR_NAME		non-reserved	non-reserved	non-reserved	non-reserved
CYCLE	non-reserved	reserved	reserved	reserved	
DATA	non-reserved	non-reserved	non-reserved	reserved	non-reserved
DATABASE	non-reserved				
DATALINK		reserved	reserved		
DATE		reserved	reserved	reserved	reserved
DATETIME_INTERVAL_CODE		non-reserved	non-reserved	non-reserved	non-reserved
DATETIME_INTERVAL_ PRECISION		non-reserved	non-reserved	non-reserved	non-reserved
DAY	non-reserved	reserved	reserved	reserved	reserved
DB		non-reserved	non-reserved		
DEALLOCATE	non-reserved	reserved	reserved	reserved	reserved
DEC	non-reserved (cannot be function or type)	reserved	reserved	reserved	reserved
DECIMAL	non-reserved (cannot be function or type)	reserved	reserved	reserved	reserved
DECLARE	non-reserved	reserved	reserved	reserved	reserved
DEFAULT	reserved	reserved	reserved	reserved	reserved
DEFAULTS	non-reserved	non-reserved	non-reserved		
DEFERRABLE	reserved	non-reserved	non-reserved	reserved	reserved
DEFERRED	non-reserved	non-reserved	non-reserved	reserved	reserved

Key Word	PostgreSQL	SQL:2008	SQL:2003	SQL:1999	SQL-92
DEFINED		non-res.	non-res.	non-res.	
DEFINER	non-reserved	non-reserved	non-reserved	non-reserved	
DEGREE		non-reserved	non-reserved		
DELETE	non-reserved	reserved	reserved	reserved	reserved
DELIMITER	non-reserved				
DELIMITERS	non-reserved				
DENSE_RANK		reserved	reserved		
DEPTH		non-reserved	non-reserved	reserved	
DEREF		reserved	reserved	reserved	
DERIVED		non-reserved	non-reserved		
DESC	reserved	non-reserved	non-reserved	reserved	reserved
DESCRIBE		reserved	reserved	reserved	reserved
DESCRIPTOR		non-reserved	non-reserved	reserved	reserved
DESTROY				reserved	
DESTRUCTOR				reserved	
DETERMINISTIC		reserved	reserved	reserved	
DIAGNOSTICS		non-reserved	non-reserved	reserved	reserved
DICTIONARY	non-reserved			reserved	
DISABLE	non-reserved				
DISCARD	non-reserved				
DISCONNECT		reserved	reserved	reserved	reserved
DISPATCH		non-reserved	non-reserved	non-reserved	
DISTINCT	reserved	reserved	reserved	reserved	reserved
DLNEWCOPY		reserved	reserved		
DLPREVIOUSCOPY		reserved	reserved		
DLURLCOMPLETE		reserved	reserved		
DLURLCOMPLETEONLY		reserved	reserved		
DLURLCOMPLETEWRITE		reserved	reserved		

Key Word	PostgreSQL	SQL:2008	SQL:2003	SQL:1999	SQL-92
DLURLPATH		reserved	reserved		
DLURLPATHONLY		reserved	reserved		
DLURLPATHWRITE			reserved	reserved	
DLURLSCHEME			reserved	reserved	
DLURLSERVER			reserved	reserved	
DLVALUE			reserved	reserved	
DO	reserved		reserved	reserved	
DOCUMENT	non-reserved	non-reserved	non-reserved	reserved	
DOMAIN	non-reserved	non-reserved	non-reserved	reserved	reserved
DOUBLE	non-reserved	reserved	reserved	reserved	reserved
DROP	non-reserved	reserved	reserved	reserved	reserved
DYNAMIC		reserved	reserved	reserved	
DYNAMIC_FUNCTION		non-reserved	non-reserved	non-reserved	non-reserved
DYNAMIC_FUNCTION_CODE		non-reserved	non-reserved	non-reserved	
EACH	non-reserved	reserved	reserved	reserved	
ELEMENT		reserved	reserved		
ELSE	reserved	reserved	reserved	reserved	reserved
EMPTY		non-reserved			
ENABLE	non-reserved				
ENCODING	non-reserved	non-reserved			
ENCRYPTED	non-reserved				
END	reserved	reserved	reserved	reserved	reserved
END-EXEC		reserved	reserved	reserved	reserved
ENUM	non-reserved				
EQUALS		non-reserved	non-reserved	reserved	
ESCAPE	non-reserved	reserved	reserved	reserved	reserved
EVERY		reserved	reserved	reserved	
EXCEPT	reserved	reserved	reserved	reserved	reserved

Key Word	PostgreSQL	SQL:2008	SQL:2003	SQL:1999	SQL-92
EXCEPTION			non-reserved	reserved	reserved
EXCLUDE	non-reserved	non-reserved	non-reserved		
EXCLUDING	non-reserved	non-reserved	non-reserved		
EXCLUSIVE	non-reserved				
EXEC		reserved	reserved	reserved	reserved
EXECUTE	non-reserved	reserved	reserved	reserved	reserved
EXISTING				non-reserved	
EXISTS	non-reserved (cannot be function or type)	reserved	reserved	non-reserved	reserved
EXP		reserved	reserved		
EXPLAIN	non-reserved				
EXTERNAL	non-reserved	reserved	reserved	reserved	reserved
EXTRACT	non-reserved (cannot be function or type)	reserved	reserved	non-reserved	reserved
FALSE	reserved	reserved	reserved	reserved	reserved
FAMILY	non-reserved				
FETCH	reserved	reserved	reserved	reserved	reserved
FILE		non-reserved	non-reserved		
FILTER		reserved	reserved		
FINAL		non-reserved	non-reserved	non-reserved	
FIRST	non-reserved	non-res.	non-res.	reserved	reserved
FIRST_VALUE		reserved			
FLAG		non-reserved			
FLOAT	non-reserved (cannot be function or type)	reserved	reserved	reserved	reserved
FLOOR		reserved	reserved		
FOLLOWING	non-reserved	non-reserved	non-reserved		
FOR	reserved	reserved	reserved	reserved	reserved

Key Word	PostgreSQL	SQL:2008	SQL:2003	SQL:1999	SQL-92
FORCE	non-reserved				
FOREIGN	reserved	reserved	reserved	reserved	reserved
FORTRAN		non-reserved	non-reserved	non-reserved	non-reserved
FORWARD	non-reserved				
FOUND		non-reserved	non-reserved	reserved	reserved
FREE		reserved	reserved	reserved	
FREEZE	reserved (can be function or type)				
FROM	reserved	reserved	reserved	reserved	reserved
FS		non-reserved	non-reserved		
FULL	reserved (can be function or type)	reserved	reserved	reserved	reserved
FUNCTION	non-reserved	reserved	reserved	reserved	
FUNCTIONS	non-reserved				
FUSION		reserved	reserved		
G		non-reserved	non-reserved	non-reserved	
GENERAL		non-reserved	non-reserved	reserved	
GENERATED		non-reserved	non-reserved	non-reserved	
GET		reserved	reserved	reserved	reserved
GLOBAL	non-reserved	reserved	reserved	reserved	reserved
GO		non-reserved	non-reserved	reserved	reserved
GOTO		non-reserved	non-reserved	reserved	reserved
GRANT	reserved	reserved	reserved	reserved	reserved
GRANTED	non-reserved	non-res.	non-res.	non-res.	
GREATEST	non-reserved (cannot be function or type)				
GROUP	reserved	reserved	reserved	reserved	reserved
GROUPING		reserved	reserved	reserved	

Key Word	PostgreSQL	SQL:2008	SQL:2003	SQL:1999	SQL-92
HANDLER	non-reserved				
HAVING	reserved	reserved	reserved	reserved	reserved
HEADER	non-reserved				
HEX		non-reserved	non-reserved		
HIERARCHY		non-reserved	non-reserved	non-reserved	
HOLD	non-reserved	reserved	reserved	non-reserved	
HOST				reserved	
HOUR	non-reserved	reserved	reserved	reserved	reserved
ID		non-reserved			
IDENTITY	non-reserved	reserved	reserved	reserved	reserved
IF	non-reserved				
IGNORE		non-reserved		reserved	
ILIKE	reserved (can be function or type)				
IMMEDIATE	non-reserved	non-reserved	non-reserved	reserved	reserved
IMMUTABLE	non-reserved				
IMPLEMENTATION		non-reserved	non-reserved	non-reserved	
IMPLICIT	non-reserved				
IMPORT		reserved	reserved		
IN	reserved	reserved	reserved	reserved	reserved
INCLUDING	non-reserved	non-reserved	non-reserved		
INCREMENT	non-reserved	non-reserved	non-reserved		
INDENT		non-reserved			
INDEX	non-reserved				
INDEXES	non-reserved				
INDICATOR		reserved	reserved	reserved	reserved

Key Word	PostgreSQL	SQL:2008	SQL:2003	SQL:1999	SQL-92
INFIX				non-reserved	
INHERIT	non-reserved				
INHERITS	non-reserved				
INITIALIZE				reserved	
INITIALLY	reserved	non-reserved	non-reserved	reserved	reserved
INLINE	non-reserved				
INNER	reserved (can be function or type)	reserved	reserved	reserved	reserved
INOUT	non-reserved (cannot be function or type)	reserved	reserved	reserved	
INPUT	non-reserved	non-reserved	non-reserved	reserved	reserved
INSENSITIVE	non-reserved	reserved	reserved	non-reserved	reserved
INSERT	non-reserved	reserved	reserved	reserved	reserved
INSTANCE		non-reserved	non-reserved	non-reserved	
INSTANTIABLE		non-reserved	non-reserved	non-reserved	
INSTEAD	non-reserved	non-reserved			
INT	non-reserved (cannot be function or type)	reserved	reserved	reserved	reserved
INTEGER	non-reserved (cannot be function or type)	reserved	reserved	reserved	reserved
INTEGRITY		non-reserved	non-reserved		
INTERSECT	reserved	reserved	reserved	reserved	reserved
INTERSECTION		reserved	reserved		
INTERVAL	non-reserved (cannot be function or type)	reserved	reserved	reserved	reserved
INTO	reserved	reserved	reserved	reserved	reserved
INVOKER	non-reserved	non-reserved	non-reserved	non-reserved	
IS	reserved (can be function or type)	reserved	reserved	reserved	reserved

Key Word	PostgreSQL	SQL:2008	SQL:2003	SQL:1999	SQL-92
ISNULL	reserved (can be function or type)				
ISOLATION	non-reserved	non-res.	non-res.	reserved	reserved
ITERATE				reserved	
JOIN	reserved (can be function or type)	reserved	reserved	reserved	reserved
K		non-reserved	non-reserved	non-reserved	
KEY	non-reserved	non-reserved	non-reserved	reserved	reserved
KEY_MEMBER		non-reserved	non-reserved	non-reserved	
KEY_TYPE		non-reserved	non-reserved	non-reserved	
LAG		reserved			
LANGUAGE	non-reserved	reserved	reserved	reserved	reserved
LARGE	non-reserved	reserved	reserved	reserved	
LAST	non-reserved	non-reserved	non-reserved	reserved	reserved
LAST_VALUE		reserved			
LATERAL		reserved	reserved	reserved	
LC_COLLATE	non-reserved				
LC_CTYPE	non-reserved				
LEAD		reserved			
LEADING	reserved	reserved	reserved	reserved	reserved
LEAST	non-reserved (cannot be function or type)				
LEFT	reserved (can be function or type)	reserved	reserved	reserved	reserved
LENGTH		non-reserved	non-reserved	non-reserved	non-reserved
LESS				reserved	
LEVEL	non-reserved	non-reserved	non-reserved	reserved	reserved
LIBRARY		non-reserved	non-reserved		
LIKE	reserved (can be function or type)	reserved	reserved	reserved	reserved

Key Word	PostgreSQL	SQL:2008	SQL:2003	SQL:1999	SQL-92
LIKE_REGEX		reserved			
LIMIT	reserved	non-reserved	non-reserved	reserved	
LINK		non-reserved	non-reserved		
LISTEN	non-reserved				
LN		reserved	reserved		
LOAD	non-reserved				
LOCAL	non-reserved	reserved	reserved	reserved	reserved
LOCALTIME	reserved	reserved	reserved	reserved	
LOCALTIMESTAMP	reserved	reserved	reserved	reserved	
LOCATION	non-reserved	non-reserved			
LOCATOR		non-reserved	non-reserved	reserved	
LOCK	non-reserved				
LOGIN	non-reserved				
LOWER		reserved	reserved	non-reserved	reserved
M		non-reserved	non-reserved	non-reserved	
MAP		non-reserved	non-reserved	reserved	
MAPPING	non-reserved	non-reserved	non-reserved		
MATCH	non-reserved	reserved	reserved	reserved	reserved
MATCHED		non-reserved	non-reserved		
MAX		reserved	reserved	non-reserved	reserved
MAXVALUE	non-reserved	non-reserved	non-reserved		
MAX_CARDINALITY		reserved			
MEMBER		reserved	reserved		
MERGE		reserved	reserved		
MESSAGE_LENGTH		non-reserved	non-reserved	non-reserved	non-reserved

Key Word	PostgreSQL	SQL:2008	SQL:2003	SQL:1999	SQL-92
MESSAGE_OCTET_LENGTH		non-reserved	non-reserved	non-reserved	non-reserved
MESSAGE_TEXT		non-reserved	non-reserved	non-reserved	non-reserved
METHOD		reserved	reserved	non-reserved	
MIN		reserved	reserved	non-res.	reserved
MINUTE	non-reserved	reserved	reserved	reserved	reserved
MINVALUE	non-reserved	non-reserved	non-reserved		
MOD		reserved	reserved	non-reserved	
MODE	non-reserved				
MODIFIES		reserved	reserved	reserved	
MODIFY				reserved	
MODULE		reserved	reserved	reserved	reserved
MONTH	non-reserved	reserved	reserved	reserved	reserved
MORE		non-reserved	non-reserved	non-reserved	non-reserved
MOVE	non-reserved				
MULTISET		reserved	reserved		
MUMPS		non-reserved	non-reserved	non-reserved	non-reserved
NAME	non-reserved	non-reserved	non-reserved	non-reserved	non-reserved
NAMES	non-reserved	non-reserved	non-reserved	reserved	reserved
NAMESPACE		non-reserved			
NATIONAL	non-reserved (cannot be function or type)	reserved	reserved	reserved	reserved
NATURAL	reserved (can be function or type)	reserved	reserved	reserved	reserved
NCHAR	non-reserved (cannot be function or type)	reserved	reserved	reserved	reserved
NCLOB		reserved	reserved	reserved	
NESTING		non-reserved	non-reserved		

Key Word	PostgreSQL	SQL:2008	SQL:2003	SQL:1999	SQL-92
NEW		reserved	reserved	reserved	
NEXT	non-reserved	non-reserved	non-reserved	reserved	reserved
NFC		non-reserved			
NFD		non-reserved			
NFKC		non-reserved			
NFKD		non-reserved			
NIL		non-reserved			
NO	non-reserved	reserved	reserved	reserved	reserved
NOCREATEDB	non-reserved				
NOCREATEROLE	non-reserved				
NOCREATEUSER	non-reserved				
NOINHERIT	non-reserved				
NOLOGIN	non-reserved				
NONE	non-reserved (cannot be function or type)	reserved	reserved	reserved	
NORMALIZE		reserved	reserved		
NORMALIZED		non-reserved	non-reserved		
NOSUPERUSER	non-reserved				
NOT	reserved	reserved	reserved	reserved	reserved
NOTHING	non-reserved				
NOTIFY	non-reserved				
NOTNULL	reserved (can be function or type)				
NOWAIT	non-reserved				
NTH_VALUE		reserved			
NTILE		reserved			
NULL	reserved	reserved	reserved	reserved	reserved
NULLABLE		non-reserved	non-reserved	non-reserved	non-reserved

Key Word	PostgreSQL	SQL:2008	SQL:2003	SQL:1999	SQL-92
NULLIF	non-reserved (cannot be function or type)	reserved	reserved	non-reserved	reserved
NULLS	non-reserved	non-reserved	non-reserved		
NUMBER		non-reserved	non-reserved	non-reserved	non-reserved
NUMERIC	non-reserved (cannot be function or type)	reserved	reserved	reserved	reserved
OBJECT	non-reserved	non-reserved	non-reserved	reserved	
OCCURRENCES_REGEX		reserved			
OCTETS		non-reserved	non-reserved		
OCTET_LENGTH		reserved	reserved	non-reserved	reserved
OF	non-reserved	reserved	reserved	reserved	reserved
OFF	non-reserved	non-reserved	non-reserved	reserved	
OFFSET	reserved	reserved			
OIDS	non-reserved				
OLD		reserved	reserved	reserved	
ON	reserved	reserved	reserved	reserved	reserved
ONLY	reserved	reserved	reserved	reserved	reserved
OPEN		reserved	reserved	reserved	reserved
OPERATION				reserved	
OPERATOR	non-reserved				
OPTION	non-reserved	non-reserved	non-reserved	reserved	reserved
OPTIONS	non-reserved	non-reserved	non-reserved	non-reserved	
OR	reserved	reserved	reserved	reserved	reserved
ORDER	reserved	reserved	reserved	reserved	reserved
ORDERING		non-reserved	non-reserved		
ORDINALITY		non-reserved	non-reserved	reserved	
OTHERS		non-reserved	non-reserved		

Key Word	PostgreSQL	SQL:2008	SQL:2003	SQL:1999	SQL-92
OUT	non-reserved (cannot be function or type)	reserved	reserved	reserved	
OUTER	reserved (can be function or type)	reserved	reserved	reserved	reserved
OUTPUT		non-reserved	non-reserved	reserved	reserved
OVER	reserved (can be function or type)	reserved	reserved		
OVERLAPS	reserved (can be function or type)	reserved	reserved	non-reserved	reserved
OVERLAY	non-reserved (cannot be function or type)	reserved	reserved	non-reserved	
OVERRIDING		non-reserved	non-reserved	non-reserved	
OWNED	non-reserved				
OWNER	non-reserved				
P		non-reserved			
PAD		non-reserved	non-reserved	reserved	reserved
PARAMETER		reserved	reserved	reserved	
PARAMETERS				reserved	
PARAMETER_MODE		non-reserved	non-reserved	non-reserved	
PARAMETER_NAME		non-reserved	non-reserved	non-reserved	
PARAMETER_ORDINAL_POSITION		non-reserved	non-reserved	non-reserved	
PARAMETER_SPECIFIC_CATALOG		non-reserved	non-reserved	non-reserved	
PARAMETER_SPECIFIC_NAME		non-reserved	non-reserved	non-reserved	
PARAMETER_SPECIFIC_SCHEMA		non-reserved	non-reserved	non-reserved	
PARSER	non-reserved				
PARTIAL	non-reserved	non-reserved	non-reserved	reserved	reserved
PARTITION	non-reserved	reserved	reserved		

Key Word	PostgreSQL	SQL:2008	SQL:2003	SQL:1999	SQL-92
PASCAL		non-reserved	non-reserved	non-reserved	non-reserved
PASSING		non-reserved			
PASSTHROUGH		non-reserved	non-reserved		
PASSWORD	non-reserved				
PATH		non-reserved	non-reserved	reserved	
PERCENTILE_CONT		reserved	reserved		
PERCENTILE_DISC		reserved	reserved		
PERCENT_RANK		reserved	reserved		
PERMISSION		non-reserved	non-reserved		
PLACING	reserved	non-reserved	non-reserved		
PLANS	non-reserved				
PLI		non-reserved	non-reserved	non-reserved	non-reserved
POSITION	non-reserved (cannot be function or type)	reserved	reserved	non-reserved	reserved
POSITION_REGEX		reserved			
POSTFIX				reserved	
POWER		reserved	reserved		
PRECEDING	non-reserved	non-reserved	non-reserved		
PRECISION	non-reserved (cannot be function or type)	reserved	reserved	reserved	reserved
PREFIX				reserved	
PREORDER				reserved	
PREPARE	non-reserved	reserved	reserved	reserved	reserved
PREPARED	non-reserved				
PRESERVE	non-reserved	non-reserved	non-reserved	reserved	reserved
PRIMARY	reserved	reserved	reserved	reserved	reserved
PRIOR	non-reserved	non-reserved	non-reserved	reserved	reserved

Key Word	PostgreSQL	SQL:2008	SQL:2003	SQL:1999	SQL-92
PRIVILEGES	non-reserved	non-reserved	non-reserved	reserved	reserved
PROCEDURAL	non-reserved				
PROCEDURE	non-reserved	reserved	reserved	reserved	reserved
PUBLIC		non-reserved	non-reserved	reserved	reserved
QUOTE	non-reserved				
RANGE	non-reserved	reserved	reserved		
RANK		reserved	reserved		
READ	non-reserved	non-reserved	non-reserved	reserved	reserved
READS		reserved	reserved	reserved	
REAL	non-reserved (cannot be function or type)	reserved	reserved	reserved	reserved
REASSIGN	non-reserved				
RECHECK	non-reserved				
RECOVERY		non-reserved	non-reserved		
RECURSIVE	non-reserved	reserved	reserved	reserved	
REF		reserved	reserved	reserved	
REFERENCES	reserved	reserved	reserved	reserved	reserved
REFERENCING		reserved	reserved	reserved	
REGR_AVGX		reserved	reserved		
REGR_AVGY		reserved	reserved		
REGR_COUNT		reserved	reserved		
REGR_INTERCEPT		reserved	reserved		
REGR_R2		reserved	reserved		
REGR_SLOPE		reserved	reserved		
REGR_SXX		reserved	reserved		
REGR_SXY		reserved	reserved		
REGR_SYY		reserved	reserved		
REINDEX	non-reserved				
RELATIVE	non-reserved	non-reserved	non-reserved	reserved	reserved
RELEASE	non-reserved	reserved	reserved		

Key Word	PostgreSQL	SQL:2008	SQL:2003	SQL:1999	SQL-92
RENAME	non-reserved				
REPEATABLE	non-reserved	non-reserved	non-reserved	non-reserved	non-reserved
REPLACE	non-reserved				
REPLICA	non-reserved				
REQUIRING		non-reserved	non-reserved		
RESET	non-reserved				
RESPECT		non-reserved			
RESTART	non-reserved	non-reserved	non-reserved		
RESTORE		non-reserved	non-reserved		
RESTRICT	non-reserved	non-reserved	non-reserved	reserved	reserved
RESULT		reserved	reserved	reserved	
RETURN		reserved	reserved	reserved	
RETURNED_CARDINALITY		non-reserved	non-reserved		
RETURNED_LENGTH		non-res.	non-res.	non-res.	non-res.
RETURNED_OCTET_LENGTH		non-reserved	non-reserved	non-reserved	non-reserved
RETURNED_SQLSTATE		non-reserved	non-reserved	non-reserved	non-reserved
RETURNING	reserved	non-reserved			
RETURNS	non-reserved	reserved	reserved	reserved	
REVOKE	non-reserved	reserved	reserved	reserved	reserved
RIGHT	reserved (can be function or type)	reserved	reserved	reserved	reserved
ROLE	non-reserved	non-reserved	non-reserved	reserved	
ROLLBACK	non-reserved	reserved	reserved	reserved	reserved
ROLLUP		reserved	reserved	reserved	
ROUTINE		non-reserved	non-reserved	reserved	

Key Word	PostgreSQL	SQL:2008	SQL:2003	SQL:1999	SQL-92
ROUTINE_CATALOG		non-reserved	non-reserved	non-reserved	
ROUTINE_NAME		non-reserved	non-reserved	non-reserved	
ROUTINE_SCHEMA		non-reserved	non-reserved	non-reserved	
ROW	non-reserved (cannot be function or type)	reserved	reserved	reserved	
ROWS	non-reserved	reserved	reserved	reserved	reserved
ROW_COUNT		non-reserved	non-reserved	non-reserved	non-reserved
ROW_NUMBER		reserved	reserved		
RULE	non-reserved				
SAVEPOINT	non-reserved	reserved	reserved	reserved	
SCALE		non-reserved	non-reserved	non-reserved	non-reserved
SCHEMA	non-reserved	non-reserved	non-reserved	reserved	reserved
SCHEMA_NAME		non-reserved	non-reserved	non-reserved	non-reserved
SCOPE		reserved	reserved	reserved	
SCOPE_CATALOG		non-reserved	non-reserved		
SCOPE_NAME		non-reserved	non-reserved		
SCOPE_SCHEMA		non-reserved	non-reserved		
SCROLL	non-reserved	reserved	reserved	reserved	reserved
SEARCH	non-reserved	reserved	reserved	reserved	
SECOND	non-reserved	reserved	reserved	reserved	reserved
SECTION		non-reserved	non-reserved	reserved	reserved
SECURITY	non-reserved	non-reserved	non-reserved	non-reserved	
SELECT	reserved	reserved	reserved	reserved	reserved
SELECTIVE		non-reserved	non-reserved		

Key Word	PostgreSQL	SQL:2008	SQL:2003	SQL:1999	SQL-92
SELF		non-reserved	non-reserved	non-reserved	
SENSITIVE		reserved	reserved	non-reserved	
SEQUENCE	non-reserved	non-reserved	non-reserved	reserved	
SEQUENCES	non-reserved				
SERIALIZABLE	non-reserved	non-reserved	non-reserved	non-reserved	non-reserved
SERVER	non-reserved	non-reserved	non-reserved		
SERVER_NAME		non-reserved	non-reserved	non-reserved	non-reserved
SESSION	non-reserved	non-reserved	non-reserved	reserved	reserved
SESSION_USER	reserved	reserved	reserved	reserved	reserved
SET	non-reserved	reserved	reserved	reserved	reserved
SETOF	non-reserved (cannot be function or type)				
SETS		non-reserved	non-reserved	reserved	
SHARE	non-reserved				
SHOW	non-reserved				
SIMILAR	reserved (can be function or type)	reserved	reserved	non-reserved	
SIMPLE	non-reserved	non-reserved	non-reserved	non-reserved	
SIZE		non-res.	non-res.	reserved	reserved
SMALLINT	non-reserved (cannot be function or type)	reserved	reserved	reserved	reserved
SOME	reserved	reserved	reserved	reserved	reserved
SOURCE		non-reserved	non-reserved	non-reserved	
SPACE		non-reserved	non-reserved	reserved	reserved
SPECIFIC		reserved	reserved	reserved	
SPECIFICTYPE		reserved	reserved	reserved	

Key Word	PostgreSQL	SQL:2008	SQL:2003	SQL:1999	SQL-92
SPECIFIC_NAME		non-reserved	non-reserved	non-reserved	
SQL		reserved	reserved	reserved	reserved
SQLCODE					reserved
SQLERROR					reserved
SQLEXCEPTION		reserved	reserved	reserved	
SQLSTATE		reserved	reserved	reserved	reserved
SQLWARNING		reserved	reserved	reserved	
SQRT		reserved	reserved		
STABLE	non-reserved				
STANDALONE	non-reserved	non-reserved	non-reserved		
START	non-reserved	reserved	reserved	reserved	
STATE		non-reserved	non-reserved	reserved	
STATEMENT	non-reserved	non-reserved	non-reserved	reserved	
STATIC		reserved	reserved	reserved	
STATISTICS	non-reserved				
STDDEV_POP		reserved	reserved		
STDDEV_SAMP		reserved	reserved		
STDIN	non-reserved				
STDOUT	non-reserved				
STORAGE	non-reserved				
STRICT	non-reserved				
STRIP	non-reserved	non-reserved	non-reserved		
STRUCTURE		non-res.	non-res.	reserved	
STYLE		non-reserved	non-reserved	non-reserved	
SUBCLASS_ORIGIN		non-reserved	non-reserved	non-reserved	non-reserved
SUBLIST				non-reserved	
SUBMULTISET		reserved	reserved		
SUBSTRING	non-reserved (cannot be function or type)	reserved	reserved	non-reserved	reserved

Key Word	PostgreSQL	SQL:2008	SQL:2003	SQL:1999	SQL-92
SUBSTRING_REGEX		reserved			
SUM		reserved	reserved	non-reserved	reserved
SUPERUSER	non-reserved				
SYMMETRIC	reserved	reserved	reserved	non-reserved	
SYSID	non-reserved				
SYSTEM	non-reserved	reserved	reserved	non-reserved	
SYSTEM_USER		reserved	reserved	reserved	reserved
T		non-reserved			
TABLE	reserved	reserved	reserved	reserved	reserved
TABLES	non-reserved				
TABLESAMPLE		reserved	reserved		
TABLESPACE	non-reserved				
TABLE_NAME		non-reserved	non-reserved	non-reserved	non-reserved
TEMP	non-reserved				
TEMPLATE	non-reserved				
TEMPORARY	non-reserved	non-reserved	non-reserved	reserved	reserved
TERMINATE				reserved	
TEXT	non-reserved				
THAN				reserved	
THEN	reserved	reserved	reserved	reserved	reserved
TIES		non-reserved	non-reserved		
TIME	non-reserved (cannot be function or type)	reserved	reserved	reserved	reserved
TIMESTAMP	non-reserved (cannot be function or type)	reserved	reserved	reserved	reserved
TIMEZONE_HOUR		reserved	reserved	reserved	reserved
TIMEZONE_MINUTE		reserved	reserved	reserved	reserved
TO	reserved	reserved	reserved	reserved	reserved
TOKEN		non-reserved	non-reserved		

Key Word	PostgreSQL	SQL:2008	SQL:2003	SQL:1999	SQL-92
TOP_LEVEL_COUNT		non-reserved	non-reserved		
TRAILING	reserved	reserved	reserved	reserved	reserved
TRANSACTION	non-reserved	non-reserved	non-reserved	reserved	reserved
TRANSACTIONS_COMMITTED		non-reserved	non-reserved	non-reserved	
TRANSACTIONS_ROLLED_BACK		non-reserved	non-reserved	non-reserved	
TRANSACTION_ACTIVE		non-reserved	non-reserved	non-reserved	
TRANSFORM		non-reserved	non-reserved	non-reserved	
TRANSFORMS		non-reserved	non-reserved	non-reserved	
TRANSLATE		reserved	reserved	non-reserved	reserved
TRANSLATE_REGEX		reserved			
TRANSLATION		reserved	reserved	reserved	reserved
TREAT	non-reserved (cannot be function or type)	reserved	reserved	reserved	
TRIGGER	non-reserved	reserved	reserved	reserved	
TRIGGER_CATALOG		non-reserved	non-reserved	non-reserved	
TRIGGER_NAME		non-reserved	non-reserved	non-reserved	
TRIGGER_SCHEMA		non-reserved	non-reserved	non-reserved	
TRIM	non-reserved (cannot be function or type)	reserved	reserved	non-reserved	reserved
TRIM_ARRAY		reserved			
TRUE	reserved	reserved	reserved	reserved	reserved
TRUNCATE	non-reserved	reserved			
TRUSTED	non-reserved				
TYPE	non-reserved	non-reserved	non-reserved	non-reserved	non-reserved
UESCAPE		reserved	reserved		

Key Word	PostgreSQL	SQL:2008	SQL:2003	SQL:1999	SQL-92
UNBOUNDED	non-reserved	non-reserved	non-reserved		
UNCOMMITTED	non-reserved	non-reserved	non-reserved	non-reserved	non-reserved
UNDER		non-reserved	non-reserved	reserved	
UNENCRYPTED	non-reserved				
UNION	reserved	reserved	reserved	reserved	reserved
UNIQUE	reserved	reserved	reserved	reserved	reserved
UNKNOWN	non-reserved	reserved	reserved	reserved	reserved
UNLINK		non-reserved	non-reserved		
UNLISTEN	non-reserved				
UNNAMED		non-reserved	non-reserved	non-reserved	non-reserved
UNNEST		reserved	reserved	reserved	
UNTIL	non-reserved				
UNTYPED		non-reserved			
UPDATE	non-reserved	reserved	reserved	reserved	reserved
UPPER		reserved	reserved	non-reserved	reserved
URI		non-reserved			
USAGE		non-reserved	non-reserved	reserved	reserved
USER	reserved	reserved	reserved	reserved	reserved
USER_DEFINED_TYPE_CATALOG		non-reserved	non-reserved	non-reserved	
USER_DEFINED_TYPE_CODE		non-reserved	non-reserved		
USER_DEFINED_TYPE_NAME		non-reserved	non-reserved	non-reserved	
USER_DEFINED_TYPE_SCHEMA		non-reserved	non-reserved	non-reserved	
USING	reserved	reserved	reserved	reserved	reserved
VACUUM	non-reserved				

Key Word	PostgreSQL	SQL:2008	SQL:2003	SQL:1999	SQL-92
VALID	non-reserved	non-reserved			
VALIDATOR	non-reserved				
VALUE	non-reserved	reserved	reserved	reserved	reserved
VALUES	non-reserved (cannot be function or type)	reserved	reserved	reserved	reserved
VARBINARY		reserved			
VARCHAR	non-reserved (cannot be function or type)	reserved	reserved	reserved	reserved
VARIABLE				reserved	
VARIADIC	reserved				
VARYING	non-reserved	reserved	reserved	reserved	reserved
VAR_POP		reserved	reserved		
VAR_SAMP		reserved	reserved		
VERBOSE	reserved (can be function or type)				
VERSION	non-reserved	non-reserved	non-reserved		
VIEW	non-reserved	non-reserved	non-reserved	reserved	reserved
VOLATILE	non-reserved				
WHEN	reserved	reserved	reserved	reserved	reserved
WHENEVER		reserved	reserved	reserved	reserved
WHERE	reserved	reserved	reserved	reserved	reserved
WHITESPACE	non-reserved	non-reserved	non-reserved		
WIDTH_BUCKET		reserved	reserved		
WINDOW	reserved	reserved	reserved		
WITH	reserved	reserved	reserved	reserved	reserved
WITHIN		reserved	reserved		
WITHOUT	non-reserved	reserved	reserved	reserved	
WORK	non-reserved	non-reserved	non-reserved	reserved	reserved
WRAPPER	non-reserved	non-reserved	non-reserved		
WRITE	non-reserved	non-res.	non-res.	reserved	reserved
XML	non-reserved	reserved	reserved		

Key Word	PostgreSQL	SQL:2008	SQL:2003	SQL:1999	SQL-92
XMLAGG		reserved	reserved		
XMLATTRIBUTES	non-reserved (cannot be function or type)	reserved	reserved		
XMLBINARY		reserved	reserved		
XMLCAST		reserved			
XMLCOMMENT		reserved	reserved		
XMLCONCAT	non-reserved (cannot be function or type)	reserved	reserved		
XMLDECLARATION		non-reserved			
XMLDOCUMENT		reserved			
XMLELEMENT	non-reserved (cannot be function or type)	reserved	reserved		
XMLEXISTS		reserved			
XMLFOREST	non-reserved (cannot be function or type)	reserved	reserved		
XMLITERATE		reserved			
XMLNAMESPACES		reserved	reserved		
XMLPARSE	non-reserved (cannot be function or type)	reserved	reserved		
XMLPI	non-reserved (cannot be function or type)	reserved	reserved		
XMLQUERY		reserved			
XMLROOT	non-reserved (cannot be function or type)		reserved		
XMLSCHEMA		non-reserved			
XMLSERIALIZE	non-reserved (cannot be function or type)	reserved	reserved		
XMLTABLE		reserved			
XMLTEXT		reserved			
XMLVALIDATE		reserved			
YEAR	non-reserved	reserved	reserved	reserved	reserved
YES	non-reserved	non-reserved			
ZONE	non-reserved	non-res.	non-res.	reserved	reserved

Table C-1. SQL Key Words

Appendix D. SQL Conformance

This section attempts to outline to what extent PostgreSQL conforms to the current SQL standard. The following information is not a full statement of conformance, but it presents the main topics in as much detail as is both reasonable and useful for users.

The formal name of the SQL standard is ISO/IEC 9075 "Database Language SQL". A revised version of the standard is released from time to time; the most recent update appearing in 2008. The 2008 version is referred to as ISO/IEC 9075:2008, or simply as SQL:2008. The versions prior to that were SQL:2003, SQL:1999, and SQL-92. Each version replaces the previous one, so claims of conformance to earlier versions have no official merit. PostgreSQL development aims for conformance with the latest official version of the standard where such conformance does not contradict traditional features or common sense. The PostgreSQL project is not represented in the ISO/IEC 9075 Working Group during the preparation of the SQL standard releases, but even so, many of the features required by the SQL standard are supported, though sometimes with slightly differing syntax or function. Further moves towards conformance can be expected over time.

SQL-92 defined three feature sets for conformance: Entry, Intermediate, and Full. Most database management systems claiming SQL standard conformance were conforming at only the Entry level, since the entire set of features in the Intermediate and Full levels was either too voluminous or in conflict with legacy behaviors.

Starting with SQL:1999, the SQL standard defines a large set of individual features rather than the ineffectively broad three levels found in SQL-92. A large subset of these features represents the "Core" features, which every conforming SQL implementation must supply. The rest of the features are purely optional. Some optional features are grouped together to form "packages", which SQL implementations can claim conformance to, thus claiming conformance to particular groups of features.

The SQL:2008 and SQL:2003 standard versions are also split into a number of parts. Each is known by a shorthand name. Note that these parts are not consecutively numbered.

- ISO/IEC 9075-1 Framework (SQL/Framework)
- ISO/IEC 9075-2 Foundation (SQL/Foundation)

- ISO/IEC 9075-3 Call Level Interface (SQL/CLI)
- ISO/IEC 9075-4 Persistent Stored Modules (SQL/PSM)
- ISO/IEC 9075-9 Management of External Data (SQL/MED)
- ISO/IEC 9075-10 Object Language Bindings (SQL/OLB)
- ISO/IEC 9075-11 Information and Definition Schemas (SQL/Schemata)
- ISO/IEC 9075-13 Routines and Types using the Java Language (SQL/JRT)
- ISO/IEC 9075-14 XML-related specifications (SQL/XML)

The PostgreSQL core covers parts 1, 2, 9, 11, and 14. Part 3 is covered by the ODBC driver, and part 13 is covered by the PL/Java plug-in, but exact conformance is currently not being verified for these components. There are currently no implementations of parts 4 and 10 for PostgreSQL.

PostgreSQL supports most of the major features of SQL:2008. Out of 179 mandatory features required for full Core conformance, PostgreSQL conforms to at least 160. In addition, there is a long list of supported optional features. It might be worth noting that at the time of writing, no current version of any database management system claims full conformance to Core SQL:2008.

In the following two sections, we provide a list of those features that PostgreSQL supports, followed by a list of the features defined in SQL:2008 which are not yet supported in PostgreSQL. Both of these lists are approximate: There might be minor details that are nonconforming for a feature that is listed as supported, and large parts of an unsupported feature might in fact be implemented. The main body of the documentation always contains the most accurate information about what does and does not work.

Note

Feature codes containing a hyphen are subfeatures. Therefore, if a particular subfeature is not supported, the main feature is listed as unsupported even if some other subfeatures are supported.

D.1. Supported Features

Identifier	Package	Description	Comment
B012		Embedded C	
B021		Direct SQL	
E011	Core	Numeric data types	
E011-01	Core	INTEGER and SMALLINT data types	
E011-02	Core	REAL, DOUBLE PRECISION, and FLOAT data types	

Identifier	Package	Description	Comment
E011-03	Core	DECIMAL and NUMERIC data types	
E011-04	Core	Arithmetic operators	
E011-05	Core	Numeric comparison	
E011-06	Core	Implicit casting among the numeric data types	
E021	Core	Character data types	
E021-01	Core	CHARACTER data type	
E021-02	Core	CHARACTER VARYING data type	
E021-03	Core	Character literals	
E021-04	Core	CHARACTER_LENGTH function	trims trailing spaces from CHARACTER values before counting
E021-05	Core	OCTET_LENGTH function	
E021-06	Core	SUBSTRING function	
E021-07	Core	Character concatenation	
E021-08	Core	UPPER and LOWER functions	
E021-09	Core	TRIM function	
E021-10	Core	Implicit casting among the character string types	
E021-11	Core	POSITION function	
E021-12	Core	Character comparison	
E031	Core	Identifiers	
E031-01	Core	Delimited identifiers	
E031-02	Core	Lower case identifiers	
E031-03	Core	Trailing underscore	
E051	Core	Basic query specification	
E051-01	Core	SELECT DISTINCT	
E051-02	Core	GROUP BY clause	
E051-04	Core	GROUP BY can contain columns not in <select list>	
E051-05	Core	Select list items can be renamed	
E051-06	Core	HAVING clause	
E051-07	Core	Qualified * in select list	
E051-08	Core	Correlation names in the FROM clause	
E051-09	Core	Rename columns in the FROM clause	
E061	Core	Basic predicates and search conditions	

Identifier	Package	Description	Comment
E061-01	Core	Comparison predicate	
E061-02	Core	BETWEEN predicate	
E061-03	Core	IN predicate with list of values	
E061-04	Core	LIKE predicate	
E061-05	Core	LIKE predicate ESCAPE clause	
E061-06	Core	NULL predicate	
E061-07	Core	Quantified comparison predicate	
E061-08	Core	EXISTS predicate	
E061-09	Core	Subqueries in comparison predicate	
E061-11	Core	Subqueries in IN predicate	
E061-12	Core	Subqueries in quantified comparison predicate	
E061-13	Core	Correlated subqueries	
E061-14	Core	Search condition	
E071	Core	Basic query expressions	
E071-01	Core	UNION DISTINCT table operator	
E071-02	Core	UNION ALL table operator	
E071-03	Core	EXCEPT DISTINCT table operator	
E071-05	Core	Columns combined via table operators need not have exactly the same data type	
E071-06	Core	Table operators in subqueries	
E081-01	Core	SELECT privilege	
E081-02	Core	DELETE privilege	
E081-03	Core	INSERT privilege at the table level	
E081-04	Core	UPDATE privilege at the table level	
E081-05	Core	UPDATE privilege at the column level	
E081-06	Core	REFERENCES privilege at the table level	
E081-07	Core	REFERENCES privilege at the column level	
E081-08	Core	WITH GRANT OPTION	
E081-10	Core	EXECUTE privilege	
E091	Core	Set functions	
E091-01	Core	AVG	
E091-02	Core	COUNT	
E091-03	Core	MAX	
E091-04	Core	MIN	

Identifier	Package	Description	Comment
E091-05	Core	SUM	
E091-06	Core	ALL quantifier	
E091-07	Core	DISTINCT quantifier	
E101	Core	Basic data manipulation	
E101-01	Core	INSERT statement	
E101-03	Core	Searched UPDATE statement	
E101-04	Core	Searched DELETE statement	
E111	Core	Single row SELECT statement	
E121	Core	Basic cursor support	
E121-01	Core	DECLARE CURSOR	
E121-02	Core	ORDER BY columns need not be in select list	
E121-03	Core	Value expressions in ORDER BY clause	
E121-04	Core	OPEN statement	
E121-06	Core	Positioned UPDATE statement	
E121-07	Core	Positioned DELETE statement	
E121-08	Core	CLOSE statement	
E121-10	Core	FETCH statement implicit NEXT	
E121-17	Core	WITH HOLD cursors	
E131	Core	Null value support (nulls in lieu of values)	
E141	Core	Basic integrity constraints	
E141-01	Core	NOT NULL constraints	
E141-02	Core	UNIQUE constraints of NOT NULL columns	
E141-03	Core	PRIMARY KEY constraints	
E141-04	Core	Basic FOREIGN KEY constraint with the NO ACTION default for both referential delete action and referential update action	
E141-06	Core	CHECK constraints	
E141-07	Core	Column defaults	
E141-08	Core	NOT NULL inferred on PRIMARY KEY	
E141-10	Core	Names in a foreign key can be specified in any order	
E151	Core	Transaction support	
E151-01	Core	COMMIT statement	
E151-02	Core	ROLLBACK statement	
E152	Core	Basic SET TRANSACTION statement	

Identifier	Package	Description	Comment
E152-01	Core	SET TRANSACTION statement: ISOLATION LEVEL SERIALIZABLE clause	
E152-02	Core	SET TRANSACTION statement: READ ONLY and READ WRITE clauses	
E161	Core	SQL comments using leading double minus	
E171	Core	SQLSTATE support	
F021	Core	Basic information schema	
F021-01	Core	COLUMNS view	
F021-02	Core	TABLES view	
F021-03	Core	VIEWS view	
F021-04	Core	TABLE_CONSTRAINTS view	
F021-05	Core	REFERENTIAL_CONSTRAINTS view	
F021-06	Core	CHECK_CONSTRAINTS view	
F031	Core	Basic schema manipulation	
F031-01	Core	CREATE TABLE statement to create persistent base tables	
F031-02	Core	CREATE VIEW statement	
F031-03	Core	GRANT statement	
F031-04	Core	ALTER TABLE statement: ADD COLUMN clause	
F031-13	Core	DROP TABLE statement: RESTRICT clause	
F031-16	Core	DROP VIEW statement: RESTRICT clause	
F031-19	Core	REVOKE statement: RESTRICT clause	
F032		CASCADE drop behavior	
F033		ALTER TABLE statement: DROP COLUMN clause	
F034		Extended REVOKE statement	
F034-01		REVOKE statement performed by other than the owner of a schema object	
F034-02		REVOKE statement: GRANT OPTION FOR clause	
F034-03		REVOKE statement to revoke a privilege that the grantee has WITH GRANT OPTION	
F041	Core	Basic joined table	
F041-01	Core	Inner join (but not necessarily the INNER keyword)	
F041-02	Core	INNER keyword	
F041-03	Core	LEFT OUTER JOIN	
F041-04	Core	RIGHT OUTER JOIN	

Identifier	Package	Description	Comment
F041-05	Core	Outer joins can be nested	
F041-07	Core	The inner table in a left or right outer join can also be used in an inner join	
F041-08	Core	All comparison operators are supp. (rather than just =)	
F051	Core	Basic date and time	
F051-01	Core	DATE data type (including support of DATE literal)	
F051-02	Core	TIME data type (including support of TIME literal) with fractional seconds precision of at least 0	
F051-03	Core	TIMESTAMP data type (including support of TIMESTAMP literal) with fractional seconds precision of at least 0 and 6	
F051-04	Core	Comparison predicate on DATE, TIME, and TIMESTAMP data types	
F051-05	Core	Explicit CAST between datetime types and character string types	
F051-06	Core	CURRENT_DATE	
F051-07	Core	LOCALTIME	
F051-08	Core	LOCALTIMESTAMP	
F052	Enhanced datetime facilities	Intervals and datetime arithmetic	
F053		OVERLAPS predicate	
F081	Core	UNION and EXCEPT in views	
F111		Isolation levels other than SERIALIZABLE	
F111-01		READ UNCOMMITTED isolation level	
F111-02		READ COMMITTED isolation level	
F111-03		REPEATABLE READ isolation level	
F131	Core	Grouped operations	
F131-01	Core	WHERE, GROUP BY, and HAVING clauses supported in queries with grouped views	
F131-02	Core	Multle tables supported in queries with grouped views	
F131-03	Core	Set functions supported in queries with grouped views	
F131-04	Core	Subqueries with GROUP BY and HAVING clauses and grouped views	
F131-05	Core	Single row SELECT with GROUP BY and HAVING clauses and grouped views	
F171		Multiple schemas per user	

Identifier	Package	Description	Comment
F191	Enhanced integrity management	Referential delete actions	
F200		TRUNCATE TABLE statement	
F201	Core	CAST function	
F221	Core	Explicit defaults	
F222		INSERT statement: DEFAULT VALUES clause	
F231		Privilege tables	
F231-01		TABLE_PRIVILEGES view	
F231-02		COLUMN_PRIVILEGES view	
F231-03		USAGE_PRIVILEGES view	
F251		Domain support	
F261	Core	CASE expression	
F261-01	Core	Simple CASE	
F261-02	Core	Searched CASE	
F261-03	Core	NULLIF	
F261-04	Core	COALESCE	
F271		Compound character literals	
F281		LIKE enhancements	
F302		INTERSECT table operator	
F302-01		INTERSECT DISTINCT table operator	
F302-02		INTERSECT ALL table operator	
F304		EXCEPT ALL table operator	
F311-01	Core	CREATE SCHEMA	
F311-02	Core	CREATE TABLE for persistent base tables	
F311-03	Core	CREATE VIEW	
F311-05	Core	GRANT statement	
F321		User authorization	
F361		Subprogram support	
F381		Extended schema manipulation	
F381-01		ALTER TABLE statement: ALTER COLUMN clause	
F381-02		ALTER TABLE statement: ADD CONSTRAINT clause	
F381-03		ALTER TABLE statement: DROP CONSTRAINT clause	
F382		Alter column data type	
F391		Long identifiers	

Identifier	Package	Description	Comment
F392		Unicode escapes in identifiers	
F393		Unicode escapes in literals	
F401		Extended joined table	
F401-01		NATURAL JOIN	
F401-02		FULL OUTER JOIN	
F401-04		CROSS JOIN	
F402		Named column joins for LOBs, arrays, and multisets	
F411	Enhanced datetime facilities	Time zone specification	differences regarding literal interpretation
F421		National character	
F431		Read-only scrollable cursors	
F431-01		FETCH with explicit NEXT	
F431-02		FETCH FIRST	
F431-03		FETCH LAST	
F431-04		FETCH PRIOR	
F431-05		FETCH ABSOLUTE	
F431-06		FETCH RELATIVE	
F441		Extended set function support	
F442		Mixed column references in set functions	
F471	Core	Scalar subquery values	
F481	Core	Expanded NULL predicate	
F491	Enhanced integrity management	Constraint management	
F501	Core	Features and conformance views	
F501-01	Core	SQL_FEATURES view	
F501-02	Core	SQL_SIZING view	
F501-03	Core	SQL_LANGUAGES view	
F502		Enhanced documentation tables	
F502-01		SQL_SIZING_PROFILES view	
F502-02		SQL_IMPLEMENTATION_INFO view	
F502-03		SQL_PACKAGES view	
F531		Temporary tables	
F555	Enhanced datetime facilities	Enhanced seconds precision	

Identifier	Package	Description	Comment
F561		Full value expressions	
F571		Truth value tests	
F591		Derived tables	
F611		Indicator data types	
F651		Catalog name qualifiers	
F661		Simple tables	
F672		Retrospective check constraints	
F701	Enhanced integrity management	Referential update actions	
F711		ALTER domain	
F731		INSERT column privileges	
F761		Session management	
F762		CURRENT_CATALOG	
F763		CURRENT_SCHEMA	
F771		Connection management	
F781		Self-referencing operations	
F791		Insensitive cursors	
F801		Full set function	
F850		Top-level <order by clause> in <query expression>	
F851		<order by clause> in subqueries	
F852		Top-level <order by clause> in views	
F855		Nested <order by clause> in <query expression>	
F856		Nested <fetch first clause> in <query expression>	
F857		Top-level <fetch first clause> in <query expression>	
F858		<fetch first clause> in subqueries	
F859		Top-level <fetch first clause> in views	
F860		<fetch first row count> in <fetch first clause>	
F861		Top-level <result offset clause> in <query expression>	
F862		<result offset clause> in subqueries	
F863		Nested <result offset clause> in <query expression>	
F864		Top-level <result offset clause> in views	
F865		<offset row count> in <result offset clause>	
S071	Enhanced object support	SQL paths in function and type name resolution	
S092		Arrays of user-defined types	

Identifier	Package	Description	Comment
S095		Array constructors by query	
S096		Optional array bounds	
S098		ARRAY_AGG	
S111	Enhanced object support	ONLY in query expressions	
S201		SQL-invoked routines on arrays	
S201-01		Array parameters	
S201-02		Array as result type of functions	
S211	Enh. object support	User-defined cast functions	
T031		BOOLEAN data type	
T071		BIGINT data type	
T121		WITH (excluding RECURSIVE) in query expression	
T122		WITH (excluding RECURSIVE) in subquery	
T131		Recursive query	
T132		Recursive query in subquery	
T141		SIMILAR predicate	
T151		DISTINCT predicate	
T152		DISTINCT predicate with negation	
T171		LIKE clause in table definition	
T172		AS subquery clause in table definition	
T173		Extended LIKE clause in table definition	
T191	Enhanced integrity management	Referential action RESTRICT	
T201	Enhanced integrity management	Comparable data types for referential constraints	
T211-01	Active database, Enhanced integrity management	Triggers activated on UPDATE, INSERT, or DELETE of one base table	
T211-02	Active database, Enhanced integrity management	BEFORE triggers	
T211-03	Active database, Enhanced integrity management	AFTER triggers	
T211-04	Active database, Enhanced integrity management	FOR EACH ROW triggers	

Identifier	Package	Description	Comment
T211-05	Active database, Enhanced integrity management	Ability to specify a search condition that must be true before the trigger is invoked	
T211-07	Active database, Enhanced integrity management	TRIGGER privilege	
T212	Enhanced integrity management	Enhanced trigger capability	
T231		Sensitive cursors	
T241		START TRANSACTION statement	
T271		Savepoints	
T281		SELECT privilege with column granularity	
T312		OVERLAY function	
T321-01	Core	User-defined functions with no overloading	
T321-03	Core	Function invocation	
T321-06	Core	ROUTINES view	
T321-07	Core	PARAMETERS view	
T322	PSM	Overloading of SQL-invoked functions and procedures	
T323		Explicit security for external routines	
T351		Bracketed SQL comments (/*...*/ comments)	
T441		ABS and MOD functions	
T461		Symmetric BETWEEN predicate	
T501		Enhanced EXISTS predicate	
T551		Optional key words for default syntax	
T581		Regular expression substring function	
T591		UNIQUE constraints of possibly null columns	
T614		NTILE function	
T615		LEAD and LAG functions	
T617		FIRST_VALUE and LAST_VALUE function	
T621		Enhanced numeric functions	
T631	Core	IN predicate with one list element	
T651		SQL-schema statements in SQL routines	
T655		Cyclically dependent routines	
X010		XML type	
X011		Arrays of XML type	

Identifier	Package	Description	Comment
X016		Persistent XML values	
X020		XMLConcat	
X031		XMLElement	
X032		XMLForest	
X034		XMLAgg	
X035		XMLAgg: ORDER BY option	
X036		XMLComment	
X037		XMLPI	
X040		Basic table mapping	
X041		Basic table mapping: nulls absent	
X042		Basic table mapping: null as nil	
X043		Basic table mapping: table as forest	
X044		Basic table mapping: table as element	
X045		Basic table mapping: with target namespace	
X046		Basic table mapping: data mapping	
X047		Basic table mapping: metadata mapping	
X048		Basic table mapping: base64 encoding of binary strings	
X049		Basic table mapping: hex encoding of binary strings	
X050		Advanced table mapping	
X051		Advanced table mapping: nulls absent	
X052		Advanced table mapping: null as nil	
X053		Advanced table mapping: table as forest	
X054		Advanced table mapping: table as element	
X055		Advanced table mapping: target namespace	
X056		Advanced table mapping: data mapping	
X057		Advanced table mapping: metadata mapping	
X058		Adv. table mapping: base64 encoding of binary strings	
X059		Advanced table mapping: hex encoding of binary strings	
X060		XMLParse: Character string input and CONTENT option	
X061		XMLParse: Character string input and DOCUMENT option	
X070		XMLSerialize: Character string serialization and CONTENT option	

Identifier	Package	Description	Comment
X071		XMLSerialize: Character string serialization and DOCUMENT option	
X072		XMLSerialize: Character string serialization	
X090		XML document predicate	
X120		XML parameters in SQL routines	
X121		XML parameters in external routines	

Table D-1. SQL Conformance - Supported Features

D.2. Unsupported Features

The following features defined in SQL:2008 are not implemented in this release of PostgreSQL. In a few cases, equivalent functionality is available.

Identifier	Package	Description	Comment
B011		Embedded Ada	
B013		Embedded COBOL	
B014		Embedded Fortran	
B015		Embedded MUMPS	
B016		Embedded Pascal	
B017		Embedded PL/I	
B031		Basic dynamic SQL	
B032		Extended dynamic SQL	
B032-01		<describe input statement>	
B033		Untyped SQL-invoked function arguments	
B034		Dynamic specification of cursor attributes	
B035		Non-extended descriptor names	
B041		Extensions to embedded SQL exception declarations	
B051		Enhanced execution rights	
B111		Module language Ada	
B112		Module language C	
B113		Module language COBOL	
B114		Module language Fortran	
B115		Module language MUMPS	
B116		Module language Pascal	
B117		Module language PL/I	

Identifier	Package	Description	Comment
B121		Routine language Ada	
B122		Routine language C	
B123		Routine language COBOL	
B124		Routine language Fortran	
B125		Routine language MUMPS	
B126		Routine language Pascal	
B127		Routine language PL/I	
B128		Routine language SQL	
E081	Core	Basic Privileges	
E081-09	Core	USAGE privilege	
E153	Core	Updatable queries with subqueries	
E182	Core	Module language	
F121		Basic diagnostics management	
F121-01		GET DIAGNOSTICS statement	
F121-02		SET TRANSACTION statement: DIAGNOSTICS SIZE clause	
F122		Enhanced diagnostics management	
F123		All diagnostics	
F181	Core	Multiple module support	
F202		TRUNCATE TABLE: identity column restart option	
F262		Extended CASE expression	
F263		Comma-separated predicates in simple CASE expression	
F291		UNIQUE predicate	
F301		CORRESPONDING in query expressions	
F311	Core	Schema definition statement	
F311-04	Core	CREATE VIEW: WITH CHECK OPTION	
F312		MERGE statement	
F313		Enhanced MERGE statement	
F341		Usage tables	
F394		Optional normal form specification	
F403		Partitioned joined tables	
F451		Character set definition	
F461		Named character sets	

Identifier	Package	Description	Comment
F521	Enhanced integrity management	Assertions	
F641		Row and table constructors	
F671	Enhanced integrity management	Subqueries in CHECK	intentionally omitted
F690		Collation support	
F692		Enhanced collation support	
F693		SQL-session and client module collations	
F695		Translation support	
F696		Additional translation documentation	
F721		Deferrable constraints	foreign and unique keys only
F741		Referential MATCH types	no partial match yet
F751		View CHECK enhancements	
F812	Core	Basic flagging	
F813		Extended flagging	
F821		Local table references	
F831		Full cursor update	
F831-01		Updatable scrollable cursors	
F831-02		Updatable ordered cursors	
F841		LIKE_REGEX predicate	
F842		OCCURENCES_REGEX function	
F843		POSITION_REGEX function	
F844		SUBSTRING_REGEX function	
F845		TRANSLATE_REGEX function	
F846		Octet support in regular expression operators	
F847		Nonconstant regular expressions	
S011	Core	Distinct data types	
S011-01	Core	USER_DEFINED_TYPES view	
S023	Basic object support	Basic structured types	
S024	Enhanced object support	Enhanced structured types	
S025		Final structured types	
S026		Self-referencing structured types	
S027		Create method by specific method name	

Identifier	Package	Description	Comment
S028		Permutable UDT options list	
S041	Basic object support	Basic reference types	
S043	Enhanced object support	Enhanced reference types	
S051	Basic object support	Create table of type	
S081	Enh. object support	Subtables	
S091		Basic array support	partially supported
S091-01		Arrays of built-in data types	
S091-02		Arrays of distinct types	
S091-03		Array expressions	
S094		Arrays of reference types	
S097		Array element assignment	
S151	Basic object support	Type predicate	
S161	Enhanced object support	Subtype treatment	
S162		Subtype treatment for references	
S202		SQL-invoked routines on multisets	
S231	Enhanced object support	Structured type locators	
S232		Array locators	
S233		Multiset locators	
S241		Transform functions	
S242		Alter transform statement	
S251		User-defined orderings	
S261		Specific type method	
S271		Basic multiset support	
S272		Multisets of user-defined types	
S274		Multisets of reference types	
S275		Advanced multiset support	
S281		Nested collection types	
S291		Unique constraint on entire row	
S301		Enhanced UNNEST	
S401		Distinct types based on array types	
S402		Distinct types based on distinct types	

Identifier	Package	Description	Comment
S403		MAX_CARDINALITY	
S404		TRIM_ARRAY	
T011		Timestamp in Information Schema	
T021		BINARY and VARBINARY data types	
T022		Advanced support for BINARY and VARBINARY data types	
T023		Compound binary literal	
T024		Spaces in binary literals	
T041	Basic object support	Basic LOB data type support	
T041-01	Basic object support	BLOB data type	
T041-02	Basic object support	CLOB data type	
T041-03	Basic object support	POSITION, LENGTH, LOWER, TRIM, UPPER, and SUBSTRING functions for LOB data types	
T041-04	Basic object support	Concatenation of LOB data types	
T041-05	Basic object support	LOB locator: non-holdable	
T042		Extended LOB data type support	
T043		Multiplier T	
T044		Multiplier P	
T051		Row types	
T052		MAX and MIN for row types	
T053		Explicit aliases for all-fields reference	
T061		UCS support	
T101		Enhanced nullability determiniation	
T111		Updatable joins, unions, and columns	
T174		Identity columns	
T175		Generated columns	
T176		Sequence generator support	
T177		Sequence generator support: simple restart option	
T178		Identity columns: simple restart option	
T211	Active database, Enhanced integrity management	Basic trigger capability	
T211-06	Active database, Enhanced integrity management	Support for run-time rules for the interaction of triggers and constraints	

Identifier	Package	Description	Comment
T211-08	Active database, Enhanced integrity management	Multiple triggers for the same event are executed in the order in which they were created in the catalog	intentionally omitted
T213		INSTEAD OF triggers	
T251		SET TRANSACTION statement: LOCAL option	
T261		Chained transactions	
T272		Enhanced savepoint management	
T285		Enhanced derived column names	
T301		Functional dependencies	
T321	Core	Basic SQL-invoked routines	
T321-02	Core	User-defined stored procedures with no overloading	
T321-04	Core	CALL statement	
T321-05	Core	RETURN statement	
T324		Explicit security for SQL routines	
T325		Qualified SQL parameter references	
T326		Table functions	
T331		Basic roles	
T332		Extended roles	
T431	OLAP	Extended grouping capabilities	
T432		Nested and concatenated GROUPING SETS	
T433		Multiargument GROUPING function	
T434		GROUP BY DISTINCT	
T471		Result sets return value	
T491		LATERAL derived table	
T511		Transaction counts	
T541		Updatable table references	
T561		Holdable locators	
T571		Array-returning external SQL-invoked functions	
T572		Multiset-returning external SQL-invoked functions	
T601		Local cursor references	
T611	OLAP	Elementary OLAP operations	most forms supported
T612		Advanced OLAP operations	some forms supported

Identifier	Package	Description	Comment
T613		Sampling	
T616		Null treatment option for LEAD and LAG functions	
T618		NTH_VALUE function	function exists, but some options missing
T641		Multiple column assignment	only some syntax variants supported
T652		SQL-dynamic statements in SQL routines	
T653		SQL-schema statements in external routines	
T654		SQL-dynamic statements in external routines	
M001		Datalinks	
M002		Datalinks via SQL/CLI	
M003		Datalinks via Embedded SQL	
M004		Foreign data support	
M005		Foreign schema support	
M006		GetSQLString routine	
M007		TransmitRequest	
M009		GetOpts and GetStatistics routines	
M010		Foreign data wrapper support	
M011		Datalinks via Ada	
M012		Datalinks via C	
M013		Datalinks via COBOL	
M014		Datalinks via Fortran	
M015		Datalinks via M	
M016		Datalinks via Pascal	
M017		Datalinks via PL/I	
M018		Foreign data wrapper interface routines in Ada	
M019		Foreign data wrapper interface routines in C	
M020		Foreign data wrapper interface routines in COBOL	
M021		Foreign data wrapper interface routines in Fortran	
M022		Foreign data wrapper interface routines in MUMPS	
M023		Foreign data wrapper interface routines in Pascal	
M024		Foreign data wrapper interface routines in PL/I	
M030		SQL-server foreign data support	
M031		Foreign data wrapper general routines	

Identifier	Package	Description	Comment
X012		Multisets of XML type	
X013		Distinct types of XML type	
X014		Attributes of XML type	
X015		Fields of XML type	
X025		XMLCast	
X030		XMLDocument	
X038		XMLText	
X065		XMLParse: BLOB input and CONTENT option	
X066		XMLParse: BLOB input and DOCUMENT option	
X068		XMLSerialize: BOM	
X069		XMLSerialize: INDENT	
X073		XMLSerialize: BLOB serialization and CONTENT option	
X074		XMLSerialize: BLOB serialization and DOCUMENT option	
X075		XMLSerialize: BLOB serialization	
X076		XMLSerialize: VERSION	
X077		XMLSerialize: explicit ENCODING option	
X078		XMLSerialize: explicit XML declaration	
X080		Namespaces in XML publishing	
X081		Query-level XML namespace declarations	
X082		XML namespace declarations in DML	
X083		XML namespace declarations in DDL	
X084		XML namespace declarations in compound statements	
X085		Predefined namespace prefixes	
X086		XML namespace declarations in XMLTable	
X091		XML content predicate	
X096		XMLExists	
X100		Host language support for XML: CONTENT option	
X101		Host language support for XML: DOCUMENT option	
X110		Host language support for XML: VARCHAR mapping	
X111		Host language support for XML: CLOB mapping	
X112		Host language support for XML: BLOB mapping	
X113		Host language support for XML: STRIP WHITESPACE option	

Identifier	Package	Description	Comment
X114		Host language support for XML: PRESERVE WHITESPACE option	
X131		Query-level XMLBINARY clause	
X132		XMLBINARY clause in DML	
X133		XMLBINARY clause in DDL	
X134		XMLBINARY clause in compound statements	
X135		XMLBINARY clause in subqueries	
X141		IS VALID predicate: data-driven case	
X142		IS VALID predicate: ACCORDING TO clause	
X143		IS VALID predicate: ELEMENT clause	
X144		IS VALID predicate: schema location	
X145		IS VALID predicate outside check constraints	
X151		IS VALID predicate with DOCUMENT option	
X152		IS VALID predicate with CONTENT option	
X153		IS VALID predicate with SEQUENCE option	
X155		IS VALID predicate: NAMESPACE without ELEMENT clause	
X157		IS VALID predicate: NO NAMESPACE with ELEMENT clause	
X160		Basic Information Schema for registered XML Schemas	
X161		Advanced Information Schema for registered XML Schemas	
X170		XML null handling options	
X171		NIL ON NO CONTENT option	
X181		XML(DOCUMENT(UNTYPED)) type	
X182		XML(DOCUMENT(ANY)) type	
X190		XML(SEQUENCE) type	
X191		XML(DOCUMENT(XMLSCHEMA)) type	
X192		XML(CONTENT(XMLSCHEMA)) type	
X200		XMLQuery	
X201		XMLQuery: RETURNING CONTENT	
X202		XMLQuery: RETURNING SEQUENCE	
X203		XMLQuery: passing a context item	
X204		XMLQuery: initializing an XQuery variable	

Identifier	Package	Description	Comment
X205		XMLQuery: EMPTY ON EMPTY option	
X206		XMLQuery: NULL ON EMPTY option	
X211		XML 1.1 support	
X221		XML passing mechanism BY VALUE	
X222		XML passing mechanism BY REF	
X231		XML(CONTENT(UNTYPED)) type	
X232		XML(CONTENT(ANY)) type	
X241		RETURNING CONTENT in XML publishing	
X242		RETURNING SEQUENCE in XML publishing	
X251		Persistent XML values of XML(DOCUMENT(UNTYPED)) type	
X252		Persist. XML values of XML(DOCUMENT(ANY)) type	
X253		Persist.XML val. of XML(CONTENT(UNTYPED)) type	
X254		Persistent XML values of XML(CONTENT(ANY)) type	
X255		Persistent XML values of XML(SEQUENCE) type	
X256		Persistent XML values of XML(DOCUMENT(XMLSCHEMA)) type	
X257		Persistent XML values of XML(CONTENT(XMLSCHEMA)) type	
X260		XML type: ELEMENT clause	
X261		XML type: NAMESPACE without ELEMENT clause	
X263		XML type: NO NAMESPACE with ELEMENT clause	
X264		XML type: schema location	
X271		XMLValidate: data-driven case	
X272		XMLValidate: ACCORDING TO clause	
X273		XMLValidate: ELEMENT clause	
X274		XMLValidate: schema location	
X281		XMLValidate: with DOCUMENT option	
X282		XMLValidate with CONTENT option	
X283		XMLValidate with SEQUENCE option	
X284		XMLValidate NAMESPACE without ELEMENT clause	
X286		XMLValidate: NO NAMESPACE with ELEMENT clause	
X300		XMLTable	

Identifier	Package	Description	Comment
X301		XMLTable: derived column list option	
X302		XMLTable: ordinality column option	
X303		XMLTable: column default option	
X304		XMLTable: passing a context item	
X305		XMLTable: initializing an XQuery variable	
X400		Name and identifier mapping	

Table D-2. SQL Conformance - Unsupported Features

Appendix E. Release Notes

The release notes contain the significant changes in each PostgreSQL release, with major features and migration issues listed at the top. The release notes do not contain changes that affect only a few users or changes that are internal and therefore not user-visible. For example, the optimizer is improved in almost every release, but the improvements are usually observed by users as simply faster queries.

A complete list of changes for each release can be obtained by viewing the *Git* (page 442) logs for each release. The *pgsql-committers email list*[1] records all source code changes as well. There is also a *web interface*[2] that shows changes to specific files.

The name appearing next to each item represents the major developer for that item. Of course all changes involve community discussion and patch review, so each item is truly a community effort.

E.1. Release 9.0.3

Release date: 2011-01-31

This release contains a variety of fixes from 9.0.2. For information about new features in the 9.0 major release, see *Section E.4* (page 269).

E.1.1. Migration to Version 9.0.3

A dump/restore is not required for those running 9.0.X.

E.1.2. Changes

- Before exiting walreceiver, ensure all the received WAL is fsync'd to disk (Heikki Linnakangas)

  Otherwise the standby server could replay some un-synced WAL, conceivably leading to data corruption if the system crashes just at that point.

[1] *http://archives.postgresql.org/pgsql-committers/*

[2] *http://anoncvs.postgresql.org/cvsweb.cgi/pgsql/*

- Avoid excess fsync activity in walreceiver (Heikki Linnakangas)
- Make `ALTER TABLE` revalidate uniqueness and exclusion constraints when needed (Noah Misch)

  This was broken in 9.0 by a change that was intended to suppress revalidation during `VACUUM FULL` and `CLUSTER`, but unintentionally affected `ALTER TABLE` as well.
- Fix EvalPlanQual for `UPDATE` of an inheritance tree in which the tables are not all alike (Tom Lane)

  Any variation in the table row types (including dropped columns present in only some child tables) would confuse the EvalPlanQual code, leading to misbehavior or even crashes. Since EvalPlanQual is only executed during concurrent updates to the same row, the problem was only seen intermittently.
- Avoid failures when `EXPLAIN` tries to display a simple-form `CASE` expression (Tom Lane)

  If the `CASE`'s test expression was a constant, the planner could simplify the `CASE` into a form that confused the expression-display code, resulting in "unexpected CASE WHEN clause" errors.
- Fix assignment to an array slice that is before the existing range of subscripts (Tom Lane)

  If there was a gap between the newly added subscripts and the first pre-existing subscript, the code miscalculated how many entries needed to be copied from the old array's null bitmap, potentially leading to data corruption or crash.
- Avoid unexpected conversion overflow in planner for very distant date values (Tom Lane)

  The `date` type supports a wider range of dates than can be represented by the `timestamp` types, but the planner assumed it could always convert a date to timestamp with impunity.
- Fix PL/Python crash when an array contains null entries (Alex Hunsaker)
- Remove ecpg's fixed length limit for constants defining an array dimension (Michael Meskes)
- Fix erroneous parsing of `tsquery` values containing `... & !(subexpression) | ...` (Tom Lane)

  Queries containing this combination of operators were not executed correctly. The same error existed in `contrib/intarray`'s `query_int` type and `contrib/ltree`'s `ltxtquery` type.

- Fix buffer overrun in `contrib/intarray`'s input function for the `query_int` type (Apple)

  This bug is a security risk since the function's return address could be overwritten. Thanks to Apple Inc's security team for reporting this issue and supplying the fix. (CVE-2010-4015)
- Fix bug in `contrib/seg`'s GiST picksplit algorithm (Alexander Korotkov)

  This could result in considerable inefficiency, though not actually incorrect answers, in a GiST index on a `seg` column. If you have such an index, consider `REINDEX`ing it after installing this update. (This is identical to the bug that was fixed in `contrib/cube` in the previous update.)

E.2. Release 9.0.2

Release date: 2010-12-16

This release contains a variety of fixes from 9.0.1. For information about new features in the 9.0 major release, see *Section E.4* (page 269).

E.2.1. Migration to Version 9.0.2

A dump/restore is not required for those running 9.0.X.

E.2.2. Changes

- Force the default `wal_sync_method` to be `fdatasync` on Linux (Tom Lane, Marti Raudsepp)

  The default on Linux has actually been `fdatasync` for many years, but recent kernel changes caused PostgreSQL to choose `open_datasync` instead. This choice did not result in any performance improvement, and caused outright failures on certain filesystems, notably `ext4` with the `data=journal` mount option.
- Fix "too many KnownAssignedXids" error during Hot Standby replay (Heikki Linnakangas)
- Fix race condition in lock acquisition during Hot Standby (Simon Riggs)
- Avoid unnecessary conflicts during Hot Standby (Simon Riggs)

  This fixes some cases where replay was considered to conflict with standby queries (causing delay of replay or possibly cancellation of the queries), but there was no real conflict.
- Fix assorted bugs in WAL replay logic for GIN indexes (Tom Lane)

  This could result in "bad buffer id: 0" failures or corruption of index contents during replication.

- Fix recovery from base backup when the starting checkpoint WAL record is not in the same WAL segment as its redo point (Jeff Davis)
- Fix corner-case bug when streaming replication is enabled immediately after creating the master database cluster (Heikki Linnakangas)
- Fix persistent slowdown of autovacuum workers when multiple workers remain active for a long time (Tom Lane)

  The effective `vacuum_cost_limit` for an autovacuum worker could drop to nearly zero if it processed enough tables, causing it to run extremely slowly.
- Fix long-term memory leak in autovacuum launcher (Alvaro Herrera)
- Avoid failure when trying to report an impending transaction wraparound condition from outside a transaction (Tom Lane)

  This oversight prevented recovery after transaction wraparound got too close, because database startup processing would fail.
- Add support for detecting register-stack overrun on `IA64` (Tom Lane)
- The `IA64` architecture has two hardware stacks. Full prevention of stack-overrun failures requires checking both.
- Add a check for stack overflow in `copyObject()` (Tom Lane)

  Certain code paths could crash due to stack overflow given a sufficiently complex query.
- Fix detection of page splits in temporary GiST indexes (Heikki Linnakangas)

  It is possible to have a "concurrent" page split in a temporary index, if for example there is an open cursor scanning the index when an insertion is done. GiST failed to detect this case and hence could deliver wrong results when execution of the cursor continued.
- Fix error checking during early connection processing (Tom Lane)

  The check for too many child processes was skipped in some cases, possibly leading to postmaster crash when attempting to add the new child process to fixed-size arrays.
- Improve efficiency of window functions (Tom Lane)

  Certain cases where a large number of tuples needed to be read in advance, but `work_mem` was large enough to allow them all to be held in memory, were unexpectedly slow. `percent_rank()`, `cume_dist()` and `ntile()` in particular were subject to this problem.
- Avoid memory leakage while `ANALYZE`'ing complex index expressions (Tom Lane)
- Ensure an index that uses a whole-row Var still depends on its table (Tom Lane)

An index declared like `create index i on t (foo(t.*))` would not automatically get dropped when its table was dropped.

- Add missing support in `DROP OWNED BY` for removing foreign data wrapper/server privileges belonging to a user (Heikki Linnakangas)
- Do not "inline" a SQL function with multiple `OUT` parameters (Tom Lane)

  This avoids a possible crash due to loss of information about the expected result rowtype.
- Fix crash when inline-ing a set-returning function whose argument list contains a reference to an inline-able user function (Tom Lane)
- Behave correctly if `ORDER BY`, `LIMIT`, `FOR UPDATE`, or `WITH` is attached to the `VALUES` part of `INSERT ... VALUES` (Tom Lane)
- Make the `OFF` keyword unreserved (Heikki Linnakangas)

  This prevents problems with using `off` as a variable name in PL/pgSQL. That worked before 9.0, but was now broken because PL/pgSQL now treats all core reserved words as reserved.
- Fix constant-folding of `COALESCE()` expressions (Tom Lane)

  The planner would sometimes attempt to evaluate sub-expressions that in fact could never be reached, possibly leading to unexpected errors.
- Fix "could not find pathkey item to sort" planner failure with comparison of whole-row Vars (Tom Lane)
- Fix postmaster crash when connection acceptance (`accept()` or one of the calls made immediately after it) fails, and the postmaster was compiled with GSSAPI support (Alexander Chernikov)
- Retry after receiving an invalid response packet from a RADIUS authentication server (Magnus Hagander)

  This fixes a low-risk potential denial of service condition.
- Fix missed unlink of temporary files when `log_temp_files` is active (Tom Lane)

  If an error occurred while attempting to emit the log message, the unlink was not done, resulting in accumulation of temp files.
- Add print functionality for `InhRelation` nodes (Tom Lane)

  This avoids a failure when `debug_print_parse` is enabled and certain types of query are executed.
- Fix incorrect calculation of distance from a point to a horizontal line segment (Tom Lane)

  This bug affected several different geometric distance-measurement operators.

- Fix incorrect calculation of transaction status in ecpg (Itagaki Takahiro)
- Fix errors in psql's Unicode-escape support (Tom Lane)
- Speed up parallel pg_restore when the archive contains many large objects (blobs) (Tom Lane)
- Fix PL/pgSQL's handling of "simple" expressions to not fail in recursion or error-recovery cases (Tom Lane)
- Fix PL/pgSQL's error reporting for no-such-column cases (Tom Lane)

  As of 9.0, it would sometimes report "missing FROM-clause entry for table foo" when "record foo has no field bar" would be more appropriate.
- Fix PL/Python to honor typmod (i.e., length or precision restrictions) when assigning to tuple fields (Tom Lane)

  This fixes a regression from 8.4.
- Fix PL/Python's handling of set-returning functions (Jan Urbanski)

  Attempts to call SPI functions within the iterator generating a set result would fail.
- Fix bug in `contrib/cube`'s GiST picksplit algorithm (Alexander Korotkov)

  This could result in considerable inefficiency, though not actually incorrect answers, in a GiST index on a `cube` column. If you have such an index, consider `REINDEX`ing it after installing this update.
- Don't emit "identifier will be truncated" notices in `contrib/dblink` except when creating new connections (Itagaki Takahiro)
- Fix potential coredump on missing public key in `contrib/pgcrypto` (Marti Raudsepp)
- Fix buffer overrun in `contrib/pg_upgrade` (Hernan Gonzalez)
- Fix memory leak in `contrib/xml2`'s XPath query functions (Tom Lane)
- Update time zone data files to tzdata release 2010o for DST law changes in Fiji and Samoa; also historical corrections for Hong Kong.

E.3. Release 9.0.1

Release date: 2010-10-04

This release contains a variety of fixes from 9.0.0. For information about new features in the 9.0 major release, see *Section E.4* (page 269).

E.3.1. Migration to Version 9.0.1

A dump/restore is not required for those running 9.0.X.

E.3.2. Changes

- Use a separate interpreter for each calling SQL userid in PL/Perl and PL/Tcl (Tom Lane)

  This change prevents security problems that can be caused by subverting Perl or Tcl code that will be executed later in the same session under another SQL user identity (for example, within a `SECURITY DEFINER` function). Most scripting languages offer numerous ways that that might be done, such as redefining standard functions or operators called by the target function. Without this change, any SQL user with Perl or Tcl language usage rights can do essentially anything with the SQL privileges of the target function's owner.

  The cost of this change is that intentional communication among Perl and Tcl functions becomes more difficult. To provide an escape hatch, PL/PerlU and PL/TclU functions continue to use only one interpreter per session. This is not considered a security issue since all such functions execute at the trust level of a database superuser already.

  It is likely that third-party procedural languages that claim to offer trusted execution have similar security issues. We advise contacting the authors of any PL you are depending on for security-critical purposes.

  Our thanks to Tim Bunce for pointing out this issue (CVE-2010-3433).
- Improve `pg_get_expr()` security fix so that the function can still be used on the output of a sub-select (Tom Lane)
- Fix incorrect placement of placeholder evaluation (Tom Lane)

  This bug could result in query outputs being non-null when they should be null, in cases where the inner side of an outer join is a sub-select with non-strict expressions in its output list.
- Fix join removal's handling of placeholder expressions (Tom Lane)
- Fix possible duplicate scans of `UNION ALL` member relations (Tom Lane)
- Prevent infinite loop in ProcessIncomingNotify() after unlistening (Jeff Davis)
- Prevent show_session_authorization() from crashing within autovacuum processes (Tom Lane)
- Re-allow input of Julian dates prior to 0001-01-01 AD (Tom Lane)

  Input such as `'J100000'::date` worked before 8.4, but was unintentionally broken by added error-checking.
- Make psql recognize `DISCARD ALL` as a command that should not be encased in a transaction block in autocommit-off mode (Itagaki Takahiro)
- Update build infrastructure and documentation to reflect the source code repository's move from CVS to Git (Magnus Hagander and others)

E.4. Release 9.0

Release date: 2010-09-20

E.4.1. Overview

This release of PostgreSQL adds features that have been requested for years, such as easy-to-use replication, a mass permission-changing facility, and anonymous code blocks. While past major releases have been conservative in their scope, this release shows a bold new desire to provide facilities that new and existing users of PostgreSQL will embrace. This has all been done with few incompatibilities. Major enhancements include:

- Built-in replication based on log shipping. This advance consists of two features: Streaming Replication, allowing continuous archive (WAL) files to be streamed over a network connection to a standby server, and Hot Standby, allowing continuous archive standby servers to execute read-only queries. The net effect is to support a single master with multiple read-only slave servers.
- Easier database object permissions management. `GRANT/REVOKE IN SCHEMA` supports mass permissions changes on existing objects, while ALTER DEFAULT PRIVILEGES allows control of privileges for objects created in the future. Large objects (BLOBs) now support permissions management as well.
- Broadly enhanced stored procedure support. The DO statement supports ad-hoc or "anonymous" code blocks. Functions can now be called using named parameters. *PL/pgSQL* is now installed by default, and *PL/Perl* and *PL/Python* have been enhanced in several ways, including support for Python3.
- Full support for *64-bit* Windows.
- More advanced reporting queries, including additional windowing options (`PRECEDING` and `FOLLOWING`) and the ability to control the order in which values are fed to aggregate functions.
- New trigger features, including SQL-standard-compliant *per-column triggers* and conditional trigger execution.
- *Deferrable unique constraints*. Mass updates to unique keys are now possible without trickery.
- *Exclusion constraints*. These provide a generalized version of unique constraints, allowing enforcement of complex conditions.
- New and enhanced security features, including RADIUS authentication, LDAP authentication improvements, and a new contrib module `passwordcheck` for testing password strength.

- New high-performance implementation of the `LISTEN`/`NOTIFY` feature. Pending events are now stored in a memory-based queue rather than a table. Also, a "payload" string can be sent with each event, rather than transmitting just an event name as before.
- New implementation of `VACUUM FULL`. This command now rewrites the entire table and indexes, rather than moving individual rows to compact space. It is substantially faster in most cases, and no longer results in index bloat.
- New contrib module `pg_upgrade` to support in-place upgrades from 8.3 or 8.4 to 9.0.
- Multiple performance enhancements for specific types of queries, including elimination of unnecessary joins. This helps optimize some automatically-generated queries, such as those produced by object-relational mappers (ORMs).
- `EXPLAIN` enhancements. The output is now available in JSON, XML, or YAML format, and includes buffer utilization and other data not previously available.
- `hstore` improvements, including new functions and greater data capacity.

The above items are explained in more detail in the sections below.

E.4.2. Migration to Version 9.0

A dump/restore using pg_dump, or use of pg_upgrade, is required for those wishing to migrate data from any previous release.

Version 9.0 contains a number of changes that selectively break backwards compatibility in order to support new features and code quality improvements. In particular, users who make extensive use of PL/pgSQL, Point-In-Time Recovery (PITR), or Warm Standby should test their applications because of slight user-visible changes in those areas. Observe the following incompatibilities:

E.4.2.1. Server Settings

- Remove server parameter `add_missing_from`, which was defaulted to off for many years (Tom Lane)
- Remove server parameter `regex_flavor`, which was defaulted to `advanced` for many years (Tom Lane)
- `archive_mode` now only affects `archive_command`; a new setting, `wal_level`, affects the contents of the write-ahead log (Heikki Linnakangas)
- `log_temp_files` now uses default file size units of kilobytes (Robert Haas)

E.4.2.2. Queries

- When querying a *parent table*, do not do any separate permission checks on child tables scanned as part of the query (Peter Eisentraut)

The SQL standard specifies this behavior, and it is also much more convenient in practice than the former behavior of checking permissions on each child as well as the parent.

E.4.2.3. Data Types

- `bytea` output now appears in hex format by default (Peter Eisentraut)

  The server parameter `bytea_output` can be used to select the traditional output format if needed for compatibility.
- Array input now considers only plain ASCII whitespace characters to be potentially ignorable; it will never ignore non-ASCII characters, even if they are whitespace according to some locales (Tom Lane)

  This avoids some corner cases where array values could be interpreted differently depending on the server's locale settings.
- Improve standards compliance of `SIMILAR TO` patterns and SQL-style `substring()` patterns (Tom Lane)

  This includes treating `?` and `{...}` as pattern metacharacters, while they were simple literal characters before; that corresponds to new features added in SQL:2008. Also, `^` and `$` are now treated as simple literal characters; formerly they were treated as metacharacters, as if the pattern were following POSIX rather than SQL rules. Also, in SQL-standard `substring()`, use of parentheses for nesting no longer interferes with capturing of a substring. Also, processing of bracket expressions (character classes) is now more standards-compliant.
- Reject negative length values in 3-parameter `substring()` for bit strings, per the SQL standard (Tom Lane)
- Make `date_trunc` truncate rather than round when reducing precision of fractional seconds (Tom Lane)

  The code always acted this way for integer-based dates/times. Now float-based dates/times behave similarly.

E.4.2.4. Object Renaming

- Tighten enforcement of column name consistency during `RENAME` when a child table inherits the same column from multiple unrelated parents (KaiGai Kohei)
- No longer automatically rename indexes and index columns when the underlying table columns are renamed (Tom Lane)

  Administrators can still rename such indexes and columns manually. This change will require an update of the JDBC driver, and possibly other drivers, so that unique indexes are correctly recognized after a rename.

- `CREATE OR REPLACE FUNCTION` can no longer change the declared names of function parameters (Pavel Stehule)

  In order to avoid creating ambiguity in named-parameter calls, it is no longer allowed to change the aliases for input parameters in the declaration of an existing function (although names can still be assigned to previously unnamed parameters). You now have to `DROP` and recreate the function to do that.

E.4.2.5. PL/pgSQL

- PL/pgSQL now throws an error if a variable name conflicts with a column name used in a query (Tom Lane)

  The former behavior was to bind ambiguous names to PL/pgSQL variables in preference to query columns, which often resulted in surprising misbehavior. Throwing an error allows easy detection of ambiguous situations. Although it's recommended that functions encountering this type of error be modified to remove the conflict, the old behavior can be restored if necessary via the configuration parameter `plpgsql.variable_conflict`, or via the per-function option `#variable_conflict`.

- PL/pgSQL no longer allows variable names that match certain SQL reserved words (Tom Lane)

  This is a consequence of aligning the PL/pgSQL parser to match the core SQL parser more closely. If necessary, variable names can be double-quoted to avoid this restriction.

- PL/pgSQL now requires columns of composite results to match the expected type modifier as well as base type (Pavel Stehule, Tom Lane)

  For example, if a column of the result type is declared as `NUMERIC(30,2)`, it is no longer acceptable to return a `NUMERIC` of some other precision in that column. Previous versions neglected to check the type modifier and would thus allow result rows that didn't actually conform to the declared restrictions.

- PL/pgSQL now treats selection into composite fields more consistently (Tom Lane)

  Formerly, a statement like `SELECT ... INTO` *`rec.fld`* `FROM ...` was treated as a scalar assignment even if the record field *`fld`* was of composite type. Now it is treated as a record assignment, the same as when the `INTO` target is a regular variable of composite type. So the values to be assigned to the field's subfields should be written as separate columns of the `SELECT` list, not as a `ROW(...)` construct as in previous versions.

  If you need to do this in a way that will work in both 9.0 and previous releases, you can write something like *`rec.fld`* `:= ROW(...) FROM ...`.

- Remove PL/pgSQL's `RENAME` declaration (Tom Lane)

  Instead of `RENAME`, use `ALIAS`, which can now create an alias for any variable, not only dollar sign parameter names (such as `$1`) as before.

E.4.2.6. Other Incompatibilities

Version 9.0 has an unprecedented number of new major features, and over 200 enhancements, improvements, new commands, new functions, and other changes.

E.4.3. Changes

Below you will find a detailed account of the changes between PostgreSQL 9.0 and the previous major release.

E.4.3.1. Server

E.4.3.1.1. Continuous Archiving and Streaming Replication

PostgreSQL's existing standby-server capability has been expanded both to support read-only queries on standby servers and to greatly reduce the lag between master and standby servers. For many users, this will be a useful and low-administration form of replication, either for high availability or for horizontal scalability.

- Allow a standby server to accept read-only queries (Simon Riggs, Heikki Linnakangas)

  This feature is called Hot Standby. There are new `postgresql.conf` and `recovery.conf` settings to control this feature, as well as extensive *documentation* (See Section 25.5 - Vol.II).

- Allow write-ahead log (WAL) data to be streamed to a standby server (Fujii Masao, Heikki Linnakangas)

  This feature is called Streaming Replication. Previously WAL data could be sent to standby servers only in units of entire WAL files (normally 16 megabytes each). Streaming Replication eliminates this inefficiency and allows updates on the master to be propagated to standby servers with very little delay. There are new `postgresql.conf` and `recovery.conf` settings to control this feature, as well as extensive *documentation* (See Section 25.2.5 - Vol.II).

- Add `pg_last_xlog_receive_location()` and `pg_last_xlog_replay_location()`, which can be used to monitor standby server WAL activity (Simon Riggs, Fujii Masao, Heikki Linnakangas)

E.4.3.1.2. Performance

- Allow per-tablespace values to be set for sequential and random page cost estimates (`seq_page_cost`/`random_page_cost`) via `ALTER TABLESPACE ... SET/RESET` (Robert Haas)
- Improve performance and reliability of EvalPlanQual rechecks in join queries (Tom Lane)

  `UPDATE`, `DELETE`, and `SELECT FOR UPDATE/SHARE` queries that involve joins will now behave much better when encountering freshly-updated rows.
- Improve performance of `TRUNCATE` when the table was created or truncated earlier in the same transaction (Tom Lane)
- Improve performance of finding inheritance child tables (Tom Lane)

E.4.3.1.3. Optimizer

- Remove unnecessary *outer joins* (Robert Haas)

  Outer joins where the inner side is unique and not referenced above the join are unnecessary and are therefore now removed. This will accelerate many automatically generated queries, such as those created by object-relational mappers (ORMs).
- Allow `IS NOT NULL` restrictions to use indexes (Tom Lane)

  This is particularly useful for finding `MAX()`/`MIN()` values in indexes that contain many null values.
- Improve the optimizer's choices about when to use materialize nodes, and when to use sorting versus hashing for `DISTINCT` (Tom Lane)
- Improve the optimizer's equivalence detection for expressions involving `boolean <>` operators (Tom Lane)

E.4.3.1.4. GEQO

- Use the same random seed every time GEQO plans a query (Andres Freund)

  While the Genetic Query Optimizer (GEQO) still selects random plans, it now always selects the same random plans for identical queries, thus giving more consistent performance. You can modify `geqo_seed` to experiment with alternative plans.
- Improve GEQO plan selection (Tom Lane)

  This avoids the rare error "failed to make a valid plan", and should also improve planning speed.

E.4.3.1.5. Optimizer Statistics

- Improve `ANALYZE` to support inheritance-tree statistics (Tom Lane)

  This is particularly useful for partitioned tables. However, autovacuum does not yet automatically re-analyze parent tables when child tables change.
- Improve *autovacuum*'s detection of when re-analyze is necessary (Tom Lane)
- Improve optimizer's estimation for greater/less-than comparisons (Tom Lane)

  When looking up statistics for greater/less-than comparisons, if the comparison value is in the first or last histogram bucket, use an index (if available) to fetch the current actual column minimum or maximum. This greatly improves the accuracy of estimates for comparison values near the ends of the data range, particularly if the range is constantly changing due to addition of new data.
- Allow setting of number-of-distinct-values statistics using `ALTER TABLE` (Robert Haas)

  This allows users to override the estimated number or percentage of distinct values for a column. This statistic is normally computed by `ANALYZE`, but the estimate can be poor, especially on tables with very large numbers of rows.

E.4.3.1.6. Authentication

- Add support for RADIUS (Remote Authentication Dial In User Service) authentication (Magnus Hagander)
- Allow LDAP (Lightweight Directory Access Protocol) authentication to operate in "search/bind" mode (Robert Fleming, Magnus Hagander)

  This allows the user to be looked up first, then the system uses the DN (Distinguished Name) returned for that user.
- Add `samehost` and `samenet` designations to `pg_hba.conf` (Stef Walter)

  These match the server's IP address and subnet address respectively.
- Pass trusted SSL root certificate names to the client so the client can return an appropriate client certificate (Craig Ringer)

E.4.3.1.7. Monitoring

- Add the ability for clients to set an *application name*, which is displayed in `pg_stat_activity` (Dave Page)

  This allows administrators to characterize database traffic and troubleshoot problems by source application.
- Add a SQLSTATE option (`%e`) to `log_line_prefix` (Guillaume Smet)

  This allows users to compile statistics on errors and messages by error code number.

- Write to the Windows event log in UTF16 encoding (Itagaki Takahiro)

  Now there is true multilingual support for PostgreSQL log messages on Windows.

E.4.3.1.8. Statistics Counters

- Add `pg_stat_reset_shared('bgwriter')` to reset the cluster-wide shared statistics for the background writer (Greg Smith)
- Add `pg_stat_reset_single_table_counters()` and `pg_stat_reset_single_function_counters()` to allow resetting the statistics counters for individual tables and functions (Magnus Hagander)

E.4.3.1.9. Server Settings

- Allow setting of configuration parameters based on *database/role combinations* (Alvaro Herrera)

  Previously only per-database and per-role settings were possible, not combinations. All role and database settings are now stored in the new `pg_db_role_setting` system catalog. A new psql command `\drds` shows these settings. The legacy system views `pg_roles`, `pg_shadow`, and `pg_user` do not show combination settings, and therefore no longer completely represent the configuration for a user or database.

- Add server parameter `bonjour`, which controls whether a Bonjour-enabled server advertises itself via Bonjour (Tom Lane)

  The default is off, meaning it does not advertise. This allows packagers to distribute Bonjour-enabled builds without worrying that individual users might not want the feature.

- Add server parameter `enable_material`, which controls the use of materialize nodes in the optimizer (Robert Haas)

  The default is on. When off, the optimizer will not add materialize nodes purely for performance reasons, though they will still be used when necessary for correctness.

- Change server parameter `log_temp_files` to use default file size units of kilobytes (Robert Haas)

  Previously this setting was interpreted in bytes if no units were specified.

- Log changes of parameter values when `postgresql.conf` is reloaded (Peter Eisentraut)

  This lets administrators and security staff audit changes of database settings, and is also very convenient for checking the effects of `postgresql.conf` edits.

- Properly enforce superuser permissions for custom server parameters (Tom Lane)

Non-superusers can no longer issue `ALTER ROLE/DATABASE SET` for parameters that are not currently known to the server. This allows the server to correctly check that superuser-only parameters are only set by superusers. Previously, the `SET` would be allowed and then ignored at session start, making superuser-only custom parameters much less useful than they should be.

E.4.3.2. Queries

- Perform `SELECT FOR UPDATE/SHARE` processing after applying `LIMIT`, so the number of rows returned is always predictable (Tom Lane)

  Previously, changes made by concurrent transactions could cause a `SELECT FOR UPDATE` to unexpectedly return fewer rows than specified by its `LIMIT`. `FOR UPDATE` in combination with `ORDER BY` can still produce surprising results, but that can be corrected by placing `FOR UPDATE` in a subquery.
- Allow mixing of traditional and SQL-standard `LIMIT/OFFSET` syntax (Tom Lane)
- Extend the supported frame options in *window functions* (Hitoshi Harada)

  Frames can now start with `CURRENT ROW`, and the `ROWS` *n* `PRECEDING/FOLLOWING` options are now supported.
- Make `SELECT INTO` and `CREATE TABLE AS` return row counts to the client in their command tags (Boszormenyi Zoltan)

  This can save an entire round-trip to the client, allowing result counts and pagination to be calculated without an additional `COUNT` query.

E.4.3.2.1. E. Unicode Strings

- Support Unicode surrogate pairs (dual 16-bit representation) in `U&` strings and identifiers (Peter Eisentraut)
- Support Unicode escapes in `E'...'` strings (Marko Kreen)

E.4.3.3. Object Manipulation

- Speed up `CREATE DATABASE` by deferring flushes to disk (Andres Freund, Greg Stark)
- Allow *comments* on columns of tables, views, and composite types only, not other relation types such as indexes and TOAST tables (Tom Lane)
- Allow the creation of *enumerated types* containing no values (Bruce Momjian)
- Let values of columns having storage type `MAIN` remain on the main heap page unless the row cannot fit on a page (Kevin Grittner)

  Previously `MAIN` values were forced out to TOAST tables until the row size was less than one-quarter of the page size.

E.4.3.3.1. ALTER TABLE

- Implement `IF EXISTS` for `ALTER TABLE DROP COLUMN` and `ALTER TABLE DROP CONSTRAINT` (Andres Freund)
- Allow `ALTER TABLE` commands that rewrite tables to skip WAL logging (Itagaki Takahiro)

  Such operations either produce a new copy of the table or are rolled back, so WAL archiving can be skipped, unless running in continuous archiving mode. This reduces I/O overhead and improves performance.
- Fix failure of `ALTER TABLE table ADD COLUMN col serial` when done by non-owner of table (Tom Lane)

E.4.3.3.2. CREATE TABLE

- Add support for copying `COMMENTS` and `STORAGE` settings in `CREATE TABLE ... LIKE` commands (Itagaki Takahiro)
- Add a shortcut for copying all properties in `CREATE TABLE ... LIKE` commands (Itagaki Takahiro)
- Add the SQL-standard `CREATE TABLE ... OF type` command (Peter Eisentraut)

  This allows creation of a table that matches an existing composite type. Additional constraints and defaults can be specified in the command.

E.4.3.3.3. Constraints

- Add *deferrable unique constraints* (Dean Rasheed)

  This allows mass updates, such as `UPDATE tab SET col = col + 1`, to work reliably on columns that have unique indexes or are marked as primary keys. If the constraint is specified as `DEFERRABLE` it will be checked at the end of the statement, rather than after each row is updated. The constraint check can also be deferred until the end of the current transaction, allowing such updates to be spread over multiple SQL commands.
- Add *exclusion constraints* (Jeff Davis)

  Exclusion constraints generalize uniqueness constraints by allowing arbitrary comparison operators, not just equality. They are created with the `CREATE TABLE CONSTRAINT ... EXCLUDE` clause. The most common use of exclusion constraints is to specify that column entries must not overlap, rather than simply not be equal. This is useful for time periods and other ranges, as well as arrays. This feature enhances checking of data integrity for many calendaring, time-management, and scientific applications.

- Improve uniqueness-constraint violation error messages to report the values causing the failure (Itagaki Takahiro)

  For example, a uniqueness constraint violation might now report `Key (x)=(2) already exists`.

E.4.3.3.4. Object Permissions

- Add the ability to make mass permission changes across a whole schema using the new `GRANT/REVOKE IN SCHEMA` clause (Petr Jelinek)

  This simplifies management of object permissions and makes it easier to utilize database roles for application data security.
- Add `ALTER DEFAULT PRIVILEGES` command to control privileges of objects created later (Petr Jelinek)

  This greatly simplifies the assignment of object privileges in a complex database application. Default privileges can be set for tables, views, sequences, and functions. Defaults may be assigned on a per-schema basis, or database-wide.
- Add the ability to control large object (BLOB) permissions with `GRANT/REVOKE` (KaiGai Kohei)

  Formerly, any database user could read or modify any large object. Read and write permissions can now be granted and revoked per large object, and the ownership of large objects is tracked.

E.4.3.4. Utility Operations

- Make `LISTEN/NOTIFY` store pending events in a memory queue, rather than in a system table (Joachim Wieland)

  This substantially improves performance, while retaining the existing features of transactional support and guaranteed delivery.
- Allow `NOTIFY` to pass an optional "payload" string to listeners (Joachim Wieland)

  This greatly improves the usefulness of `LISTEN/NOTIFY` as a general-purpose event queue system.
- Allow `CLUSTER` on all per-database system catalogs (Tom Lane)

  Shared catalogs still cannot be clustered.

E.4.3.4.1. COPY

- Accept `COPY ... CSV FORCE QUOTE *` (Itagaki Takahiro)

  Now `*` can be used as shorthand for "all columns" in the `FORCE QUOTE` clause.

- Add new `COPY` syntax that allows options to be specified inside parentheses (Robert Haas, Emmanuel Cecchet)

  This allows greater flexibility for future `COPY` options. The old syntax is still supported, but only for pre-existing options.

E.4.3.4.2. EXPLAIN

- Allow `EXPLAIN` to output in XML, JSON, or YAML format (Robert Haas, Greg Sabino Mullane)

  The new output formats are easily machine-readable, supporting the development of new tools for analysis of `EXPLAIN` output.
- Add new `BUFFERS` option to report query buffer usage during `EXPLAIN ANALYZE` (Itagaki Takahiro)

  This allows better query profiling for individual queries. Buffer usage is no longer reported in the output for *log_statement_stats* and related settings.
- Add hash usage information to `EXPLAIN` output (Robert Haas)
- Add new `EXPLAIN` syntax that allows options to be specified inside parentheses (Robert Haas)

  This allows greater flexibility for future `EXPLAIN` options. The old syntax is still supported, but only for pre-existing options.

E.4.3.4.3. VACUUM

- Change `VACUUM FULL` to rewrite the entire table and rebuild its indexes, rather than moving individual rows around to compact space (Itagaki Takahiro, Tom Lane)

  The previous method was usually slower and caused index bloat. Note that the new method will use more disk space transiently during `VACUUM FULL`; potentially as much as twice the space normally occupied by the table and its indexes.
- Add new `VACUUM` syntax that allows options to be specified inside parentheses (Itagaki Takahiro)

  This allows greater flexibility for future `VACUUM` options. The old syntax is still supported, but only for pre-existing options.

E.4.3.4.4. Indexes

- Allow an index to be named automatically by omitting the index name in `CREATE INDEX` (Tom Lane)
- By default, multicolumn indexes are now named after all their columns; and index expression columns are now named based on their expressions (Tom Lane)

- Reindexing shared system catalogs is now fully transactional and crash-safe (Tom Lane)

  Formerly, reindexing a shared index was only allowed in standalone mode, and a crash during the operation could leave the index in worse condition than it was before.
- Add `point_ops` operator class for GiST (Teodor Sigaev)

  This feature permits GiST indexing of `point` columns. The index can be used for several types of queries such as *`point <@ polygon`* (point is in polygon). This should make many PostGIS queries faster.
- Use red-black binary trees for GIN index creation (Teodor Sigaev)

  Red-black trees are self-balancing. This avoids slowdowns in cases where the input is in nonrandom order.

E.4.3.5. Data Types

- Allow `bytea` values to be written in hex notation (Peter Eisentraut)

  The server parameter `bytea_output` controls whether hex or traditional format is used for `bytea` output. Libpq's `PQescapeByteaConn()` function automatically uses the hex format when connected to PostgreSQL 9.0 or newer servers.

  The new hex format will be directly compatible with more applications that use binary data, allowing them to store and retrieve it without extra conversion. It is also significantly faster to read and write than the traditional format.
- Allow server parameter *extra_float_digits* to be increased to `3` (Tom Lane)

  The previous maximum `extra_float_digits` setting was `2`. There are cases where 3 digits are needed to dump and restore `float4` values exactly. pg_dump will now use the setting of 3 when dumping from a server that allows it.
- Tighten input checking for `int2vector` values (Caleb Welton)

E.4.3.5.1. Full Text Search

- Add prefix support in `synonym` dictionaries (Teodor Sigaev)
- Add *filtering* dictionaries (Teodor Sigaev)

  Filtering dictionaries allow tokens to be modified then passed to subsequent dictionaries.
- Allow underscores in email-address tokens (Teodor Sigaev)
- Use more standards-compliant rules for parsing URL tokens (Tom Lane)

E.4.3.6. Functions

- Allow function calls to supply parameter names and match them to named parameters in the function definition (Pavel Stehule)

  For example, if a function is defined to take parameters `a` and `b`, it can be called with `func(a := 7, b := 12)` or `func(b := 12, a := 7)`.
- Support locale-specific *regular expression* processing with UTF-8 server encoding (Tom Lane)

  Locale-specific regular expression functionality includes case-insensitive matching and locale-specific character classes. Previously, these features worked correctly for non-ASCII characters only if the database used a single-byte server encoding (such as LATIN1). They will still misbehave in multi-byte encodings other than UTF-8.
- Add support for scientific notation in `to_char()` (EEEE specification) (Pavel Stehule, Brendan Jurd)
- Make `to_char()` honor `FM` (fill mode) in `Y`, `YY`, and `YYY` specifications (Bruce Momjian, Tom Lane)

  It was already honored by `YYYY`.
- Fix `to_char()` to output localized numeric and monetary strings in the correct encoding on Windows (Hiroshi Inoue, Itagaki Takahiro, Bruce Momjian)
- Correct calculations of "overlaps" and "contains" operations for polygons (Teodor Sigaev)

  The polygon `&&` (overlaps) operator formerly just checked to see if the two polygons' bounding boxes overlapped. It now does a more correct check. The polygon `@>` and `<@` (contains/contained by) operators formerly checked to see if one polygon's vertexes were all contained in the other; this can wrongly report "true" for some non-convex polygons. Now they check that all line segments of one polygon are contained in the other.

E.4.3.6.1. Aggregates

- Allow aggregate functions to use `ORDER BY` (Andrew Gierth)

  For example, this is now supported: `array_agg(a ORDER BY b)`. This is useful with aggregates for which the order of input values is significant, and eliminates the need to use a nonstandard subquery to determine the ordering.
- Multi-argument aggregate functions can now use `DISTINCT` (Andrew Gierth)
- Add the `string_agg()` aggregate function to combine values into a single string (Pavel Stehule)

- Aggregate functions that are called with `DISTINCT` are now passed NULL values if the aggregate transition function is not marked as `STRICT` (Andrew Gierth)

  For example, `agg(DISTINCT x)` might pass a NULL `x` value to `agg()`. This is more consistent with the behavior in non-`DISTINCT` cases.

E.4.3.6.2. Bit Strings

- Add `get_bit()` and `set_bit()` functions for `bit` strings, mirroring those for `bytea` (Leonardo F)
- Implement `OVERLAY()` (replace) for `bit` strings and `bytea` (Leonardo F)

E.4.3.6.3. Object Information Functions

- Add `pg_table_size()` and `pg_indexes_size()` to provide a more user-friendly interface to the `pg_relation_size()` function (Bernd Helmle)
- Add `has_sequence_privilege()` for sequence permission checking (Abhijit Menon-Sen)
- Update the *information_schema* views to conform to SQL:2008 (Peter Eisentraut)
- Make the `information_schema` views correctly display maximum octet lengths for `char` and `varchar` columns (Peter Eisentraut)
- Speed up `information_schema` privilege views (Joachim Wieland)

E.4.3.6.4. Function and Trigger Creation

- Support execution of anonymous code blocks using the DO statement (Petr Jelinek, Joshua Tolley, Hannu Valtonen)

  This allows execution of server-side code without the need to create and delete a temporary function definition. Code can be executed in any language for which the user has permissions to define a function.
- Implement SQL-standard-compliant *per-column triggers* (Itagaki Takahiro)

  Such triggers are fired only when the specified column(s) are affected by the query, e.g. appear in an `UPDATE`'s `SET` list.
- Add the `WHEN` clause to `CREATE TRIGGER` to allow control over whether a trigger is fired (Itagaki Takahiro)

  While the same type of check can always be performed inside the trigger, doing it in an external `WHEN` clause can have performance benefits.

E.4.3.7. Server-Side Languages

- Add the `OR REPLACE` clause to `CREATE LANGUAGE` (Tom Lane)

  This is helpful to optionally install a language if it does not already exist, and is particularly helpful now that PL/pgSQL is installed by default.

E.4.3.7.1. PL/pgSQL Server-Side Language

- Install PL/pgSQL by default (Bruce Momjian)

  The language can still be removed from a particular database if the administrator has security or performance concerns about making it available.

- Improve handling of cases where PL/pgSQL variable names conflict with identifiers used in queries within a function (Tom Lane)

  The default behavior is now to throw an error when there is a conflict, so as to avoid surprising behaviors. This can be modified, via the configuration parameter `plpgsql.variable_conflict` or the per-function option `#variable_conflict`, to allow either the variable or the query-supplied column to be used. In any case PL/pgSQL will no longer attempt to substitute variables in places where they would not be syntactically valid.

- Make PL/pgSQL use the main lexer, rather than its own version (Tom Lane)

  This ensures accurate tracking of the main system's behavior for details such as string escaping. Some user-visible details, such as the set of keywords considered reserved in PL/pgSQL, have changed in consequence.

- Avoid throwing an unnecessary error for an invalid record reference (Tom Lane)

  An error is now thrown only if the reference is actually fetched, rather than whenever the enclosing expression is reached. For example, many people have tried to do this in triggers:

  ```
  if TG_OP = 'INSERT' and NEW.col1 = ... then
  ```

  This will now actually work as expected.

- Improve PL/pgSQL's ability to handle row types with dropped columns (Pavel Stehule)

- Allow input parameters to be assigned values within PL/pgSQL functions (Steve Prentice)

  Formerly, input parameters were treated as being declared `CONST`, so the function's code could not change their values. This restriction has been removed to simplify porting of functions from other DBMSes that do not impose the equivalent restriction. An input parameter now acts like a local variable initialized to the passed-in value.

- Improve error location reporting in PL/pgSQL (Tom Lane)
- Add *count* and `ALL` options to `MOVE FORWARD`/`BACKWARD` in PL/pgSQL (Pavel Stehule)
- Allow PL/pgSQL's `WHERE CURRENT OF` to use a cursor variable (Tom Lane)
- Allow PL/pgSQL's `OPEN` *cursor* `FOR EXECUTE` to use parameters (Pavel Stehule, Itagaki Takahiro)

  This is accomplished with a new `USING` clause.

E.4.3.7.2. PL/Perl Server-Side Language

- Add new PL/Perl functions: `quote_literal()`, `quote_nullable()`, `quote_ident()`, `encode_bytea()`, `decode_bytea()`, `looks_like_number()`, `encode_array_literal()`, `encode_array_constructor()` (Tim Bunce)
- Add server parameter `plperl.on_init` to specify a PL/Perl initialization function (Tim Bunce)

  `plperl.on_plperl_init` and `plperl.on_plperlu_init` are also available for initialization that is specific to the trusted or untrusted language respectively.
- Support `END` blocks in PL/Perl (Tim Bunce)

  `END` blocks do not currently allow database access.
- Allow `use strict` in PL/Perl (Tim Bunce)

  Perl `strict` checks can also be globally enabled with the new server parameter `plperl.use_strict`.
- Allow `require` in PL/Perl (Tim Bunce)

  This basically tests to see if the module is loaded, and if not, generates an error. It will not allow loading of modules that the administrator has not preloaded via the initialization parameters.
- Allow `use feature` in PL/Perl if Perl version 5.10 or later is used (Tim Bunce)
- Verify that PL/Perl return values are valid in the server encoding (Andrew Dunstan)

E.4.3.7.3. PL/Python Server-Side Language

- Add Unicode support in PL/Python (Peter Eisentraut)

  Strings are automatically converted from/to the server encoding as necessary.
- Improve `bytea` support in PL/Python (Caleb Welton)

  `Bytea` values passed into PL/Python are now represented as binary, rather than the PostgreSQL `bytea` text format. `Bytea` values containing null bytes are now also output properly from PL/Python. Passing of boolean, integer, and float values was also improved.

- Support *arrays* as parameters and return values in PL/Python (Peter Eisentraut)
- Improve mapping of SQL domains to Python types (Peter Eisentraut)
- Add Python 3 support to PL/Python (Peter Eisentraut)

  The new server-side language is called `plpython3u`. This cannot be used in the same session with the Python 2 server-side language.
- Improve error location and exception reporting in PL/Python (Peter Eisentraut)

E.4.3.8. Client Applications

- Add an `--analyze-only` option to `vacuumdb`, to analyze without vacuuming (Bruce Momjian)

E.4.3.8.1. psql

- Add support for quoting/escaping the values of psql variables as SQL strings or identifiers (Pavel Stehule, Robert Haas)

  For example, `:'var'` will produce the value of `var` quoted and properly escaped as a literal string, while `:"var"` will produce its value quoted and escaped as an identifier.
- Ignore a leading UTF-8-encoded Unicode byte-order marker in script files read by psql (Itagaki Takahiro)

  This is enabled when the client encoding is UTF-8. It improves compatibility with certain editors, mostly on Windows, that insist on inserting such markers.
- Fix `psql --file -` to properly honor `--single-transaction` (Bruce Momjian)
- Avoid overwriting of psql's command-line history when two psql sessions are run concurrently (Tom Lane)
- Improve psql's tab completion support (Itagaki Takahiro)
- Show `\timing` output when it is enabled, regardless of "quiet" mode (Peter Eisentraut)

psql Display

- Improve display of wrapped columns in psql (Roger Leigh)

  This behavior is now the default. The previous formatting is available by using `\pset linestyle old-ascii`.
- Allow psql to use fancy Unicode line-drawing characters via `\pset linestyle unicode` (Roger Leigh)

psql \d Commands

- Make `\d` show child tables that inherit from the specified parent (Damien Clochard)

  `\d` shows only the number of child tables, while `\d+` shows the names of all child tables.
- Show definitions of index columns in `\d index_name` (Khee Chin)

  The definition is useful for expression indexes.
- Show a view's defining query only in `\d+`, not in `\d` (Peter Eisentraut)

  Always including the query was deemed overly verbose.

E.4.3.8.2. pg_dump

- Make pg_dump/pg_restore `--clean` also remove large objects (Itagaki Takahiro)
- Fix pg_dump to properly dump large objects when `standard_conforming_strings` is enabled (Tom Lane)

  The previous coding could fail when dumping to an archive file and then generating script output from pg_restore.
- pg_restore now emits large-object data in hex format when generating script output (Tom Lane)

  This could cause compatibility problems if the script is then loaded into a pre-9.0 server. To work around that, restore directly to the server, instead.
- Allow pg_dump to dump comments attached to columns of composite types (Taro Minowa (Higepon))
- Make pg_dump `--verbose` output the pg_dump and server versions in text output mode (Jim Cox, Tom Lane)

  These were already provided in custom output mode.
- pg_restore now complains if any command-line arguments remain after the switches and optional file name (Tom Lane)

  Previously, it silently ignored any such arguments.

E.4.3.8.3. pg_ctl

- Allow pg_ctl to be used safely to start the postmaster during a system reboot (Tom Lane)

  Previously, pg_ctl's parent process could have been mistakenly identified as a running postmaster based on a stale postmaster lock file, resulting in a transient failure to start the database.
- Give pg_ctl the ability to initialize the database (by invoking initdb) (Zdenek Kotala)

E.4.3.9. Development Tools

E.4.3.9.1. libpq

- Add new libpq functions `PQconnectdbParams()` and `PQconnectStartParams()` (Guillaume Lelarge)

  These functions are similar to `PQconnectdb()` and `PQconnectStart()` except that they accept a null-terminated array of connection options, rather than requiring all options to be provided in a single string.
- Add libpq functions `PQescapeLiteral()` and `PQescapeIdentifier()` (Robert Haas)

  These functions return appropriately quoted and escaped SQL string literals and identifiers. The caller is not required to pre-allocate the string result, as is required by `PQescapeStringConn()`.
- Add support for a per-user service file (`.pg_service.conf`), which is checked before the site-wide service file (Peter Eisentraut)
- Properly report an error if the specified libpq service cannot be found (Peter Eisentraut)
- Add *TCP keepalive settings* in libpq (Tollef Fog Heen, Fujii Masao, Robert Haas)

  Keepalive settings were already supported on the server end of TCP connections.
- Avoid extra system calls to block and unblock `SIGPIPE` in libpq, on platforms that offer alternative methods (Jeremy Kerr)
- When a `.pgpass`-supplied password fails, mention where the password came from in the error message (Bruce Momjian)
- Load all SSL certificates given in the client certificate file (Tom Lane)

  This improves support for indirectly-signed SSL certificates.

E.4.3.9.2. ecpg

- Add SQLDA (SQL Descriptor Area) support to ecpg (Boszormenyi Zoltan)
- Add the `DESCRIBE` *[* `OUTPUT` *]* statement to ecpg (Boszormenyi Zoltan)
- Add an *ECPGtransactionStatus* function to return the current transaction status (Bernd Helmle)
- Add the `string` data type in ecpg Informix-compatibility mode (Boszormenyi Zoltan)
- Allow ecpg to use `new` and `old` variable names without restriction (Michael Meskes)
- Allow ecpg to use variable names in `free()` (Michael Meskes)

- Make `ecpg_dynamic_type()` return zero for non-SQL3 data types (Michael Meskes)

  Previously it returned the negative of the data type OID. This could be confused with valid type OIDs, however.
- Support `long long` types on platforms that already have 64-bit `long` (Michael Meskes)

ecpg Cursors

- Add out-of-scope cursor support in ecpg's native mode (Boszormenyi Zoltan)

  This allows `DECLARE` to use variables that are not in scope when `OPEN` is called. This facility already existed in ecpg's Informix-compatibility mode.
- Allow dynamic cursor names in ecpg (Boszormenyi Zoltan)
- Allow ecpg to use noise words `FROM` and `IN` in `FETCH` and `MOVE` (Boszormenyi Zoltan)

E.4.3.10. Build Options

- Enable client thread safety by default (Bruce Momjian)

  The thread-safety option can be disabled with `configure --disable-thread-safety`.
- Add support for controlling the Linux out-of-memory killer (Alex Hunsaker, Tom Lane)

  Now that `/proc/self/oom_adj` allows disabling of the Linux out-of-memory (OOM) killer, it's recommendable to disable OOM kills for the postmaster. It may then be desirable to re-enable OOM kills for the postmaster's child processes. The new compile-time option `LINUX_OOM_ADJ` allows the killer to be reactivated for child processes.

E.4.3.10.1. Makefiles

- New `Makefile` targets `world`, `install-world`, and `installcheck-world` (Andrew Dunstan)

  These are similar to the existing `all`, `install`, and `installcheck` targets, but they also build the HTML documentation, build and test `contrib`, and test server-side languages and ecpg.
- Add data and documentation installation location control to PGXS Makefiles (Mark Cave-Ayland)
- Add Makefile rules to build the PostgreSQL documentation as a single HTML file or as a single plain-text file (Peter Eisentraut, Bruce Momjian)

E.4.3.10.2. Windows

- Support compiling on *64-bit* Windows and running in 64-bit mode (Tsutomu Yamada, Magnus Hagander)

  This allows for large shared memory sizes on Windows.
- Support server builds using Visual Studio 2008 (Magnus Hagander)

E.4.3.11. Source Code

- Distribute prebuilt documentation in a subdirectory tree, rather than as tar archive files inside the distribution tarball (Peter Eisentraut)

  For example, the prebuilt HTML documentation is now in `doc/src/sgml/html/`; the manual pages are packaged similarly.
- Make the server's lexer reentrant (Tom Lane)

  This was needed for use of the lexer by PL/pgSQL.
- Improve speed of memory allocation (Tom Lane, Greg Stark)
- User-defined constraint triggers now have entries in `pg_constraint` as well as `pg_trigger` (Tom Lane)

  Because of this change, `pg_constraint.pgconstrname` is now redundant and has been removed.
- Add system catalog columns `pg_constraint.conindid` and `pg_trigger.tgconstrindid` to better document the use of indexes for constraint enforcement (Tom Lane)
- Allow multiple conditions to be communicated to backends using a single operating system signal (Fujii Masao)

  This allows new features to be added without a platform-specific constraint on the number of signal conditions.
- Improve source code test coverage, including `contrib`, PL/Python, and PL/Perl (Peter Eisentraut, Andrew Dunstan)
- Remove the use of flat files for system table bootstrapping (Tom Lane, Alvaro Herrera)

  This improves performance when using many roles or databases, and eliminates some possible failure conditions.
- Automatically generate the initial contents of `pg_attribute` for "bootstrapped" catalogs (John Naylor)

  This greatly simplifies changes to these catalogs.

- Split the processing of `INSERT`/`UPDATE`/`DELETE` operations out of `execMain.c` (Marko Tiikkaja)

  Updates are now executed in a separate ModifyTable node. This change is necessary infrastructure for future improvements.
- Simplify translation of psql's SQL help text (Peter Eisentraut)
- Reduce the lengths of some file names so that all file paths in the distribution tarball are less than 100 characters (Tom Lane)

  Some decompression programs have problems with longer file paths.
- Add a new `ERRCODE_INVALID_PASSWORD` `SQLSTATE` error code (Bruce Momjian)
- With authors' permissions, remove the few remaining personal source code copyright notices (Bruce Momjian)

  The personal copyright notices were insignificant but the community occasionally had to answer questions about them.
- Add new documentation *Section 14.5* (Vol.I) about running PostgreSQL in non-durable mode to improve performance (Bruce Momjian)
- Restructure the HTML documentation `Makefile` rules to make their dependency checks work correctly, avoiding unnecessary rebuilds (Peter Eisentraut)
- Use DocBook XSL stylesheets for man page building, rather than Docbook2X (Peter Eisentraut)

  This changes the set of tools needed to build the man pages.
- Improve PL/Perl code structure (Tim Bunce)
- Improve error context reports in PL/Perl (Alexey Klyukin)

E.4.3.11.1. New Build Requirements

Note that these requirements do not apply when building from a distribution tarball, since tarballs include the files that these programs are used to build.

- Require Autoconf 2.63 to build configure (Peter Eisentraut)
- Require Flex 2.5.31 or later to build from a CVS checkout (Tom Lane)
- Require Perl version 5.8 or later to build from a CVS checkout (John Naylor, Andrew Dunstan)

E.4.3.11.2. Portability

- Use a more modern API for Bonjour (Tom Lane)

  Bonjour support now requires OS X 10.3 or later. The older API has been deprecated by Apple.

- Add spinlock support for the SuperH architecture (Nobuhiro Iwamatsu)
- Allow non-GCC compilers to use inline functions if they support them (Kurt Harriman)
- Remove support for platforms that don't have a working 64-bit integer data type (Tom Lane)
- Restructure use of `LDFLAGS` to be more consistent across platforms (Tom Lane)

  `LDFLAGS` is now used for linking both executables and shared libraries, and we add on `LDFLAGS_EX` when linking executables, or `LDFLAGS_SL` when linking shared libraries.

E.4.3.11.3. Server Programming

- Make backend header files safe to include in C++ (Kurt Harriman, Peter Eisentraut)

  These changes remove keyword conflicts that previously made C++ usage difficult in backend code. However, there are still other complexities when using C++ for backend functions. `extern "C" { }` is still necessary in appropriate places, and memory management and error handling are still problematic.
- Add `AggCheckCallContext()` for use in detecting if a C function is being called as an aggregate (Hitoshi Harada)
- Change calling convention for `SearchSysCache()` and related functions to avoid hard-wiring the maximum number of cache keys (Robert Haas)

  Existing calls will still work for the moment, but can be expected to break in 9.1 or later if not converted to the new style.
- Require calls of `fastgetattr()` and `heap_getattr()` backend macros to provide a non-NULL fourth argument (Robert Haas)
- Custom typanalyze functions should no longer rely on `VacAttrStats.attr` to determine the type of data they will be passed (Tom Lane)

  This was changed to allow collection of statistics on index columns for which the storage type is different from the underlying column data type. There are new fields that tell the actual datatype being analyzed.

E.4.3.11.4. Server Hooks

- Add parser hooks for processing ColumnRef and ParamRef nodes (Tom Lane)
- Add a ProcessUtility hook so loadable modules can control utility commands (Itagaki Takahiro)

E.4.3.11.5. Binary Upgrade Support

- Add `contrib/pg_upgrade` to support in-place upgrades (Bruce Momjian)

  This avoids the requirement of dumping/reloading the database when upgrading to a new major release of PostgreSQL, thus reducing downtime by orders of magnitude. It supports upgrades to 9.0 from PostgreSQL 8.3 and 8.4.
- Add support for preserving relation `relfilenode` values during binary upgrades (Bruce Momjian)
- Add support for preserving `pg_type` and `pg_enum` OIDs during binary upgrades (Bruce Momjian)
- Move data files within tablespaces into PostgreSQL-version-specific subdirectories (Bruce Momjian)

  This simplifies binary upgrades.

E.4.3.12. Contrib

- Add multithreading option (`-j`) to `contrib/pgbench` (Itagaki Takahiro)

  This allows multiple CPUs to be used by pgbench, reducing the risk of pgbench itself becoming the test bottleneck.
- Add `\shell` and `\setshell` meta commands to `contrib/pgbench` (Michael Paquier)
- New features for `contrib/dict_xsyn` (Sergey Karpov)

  The new options are `matchorig`, `matchsynonyms`, and `keepsynonyms`.
- Add full text dictionary `contrib/unaccent` (Teodor Sigaev)

  This filtering dictionary removes accents from letters, which makes full-text searches over multiple languages much easier.
- Add `dblink_get_notify()` to `contrib/dblink` (Marcus Kempe)

  This allows asynchronous notifications in dblink.
- Improve `contrib/dblink`'s handling of dropped columns (Tom Lane)

  This affects `dblink_build_sql_insert()` and related functions. These functions now number columns according to logical not physical column numbers.
- Greatly increase `contrib/hstore`'s data length limit, and add B-tree and hash support so `GROUP BY` and `DISTINCT` operations are possible on `hstore` columns (Andrew Gierth)

  New functions and operators were also added. These improvements make `hstore` a full-function key-value store embedded in PostgreSQL.

- Add `contrib/passwordcheck` to support site-specific password strength policies (Laurenz Albe)

  The source code of this module should be modified to implement site-specific password policies.

- Add `contrib/pg_archivecleanup` tool (Simon Riggs)

  This is designed to be used in the `archive_cleanup_command` server parameter, to remove no-longer-needed archive files.

- Add query text to `contrib/auto_explain` output (Andrew Dunstan)
- Add buffer access counters to `contrib/pg_stat_statements` (Itagaki Takahiro)
- Update `contrib/start-scripts/linux` to use `/proc/self/oom_adj` to disable the Linux *out-of-memory* (OOM) killer (Alex Hunsaker, Tom Lane)

Appendix F. Additional Supplied Modules

This appendix contains information regarding the modules that can be found in the `contrib` directory of the PostgreSQL distribution. These include porting tools, analysis utilities, and plug-in features that are not part of the core PostgreSQL system, mainly because they address a limited audience or are too experimental to be part of the main source tree. This does not preclude their usefulness.

When building from the source distribution, these modules are not built automatically, unless you build the "world" target (see *Section 15.5 - Step 2* - Vol.II). You can build and install all of them by running:

When building from the source distribution, these modules are not built automatically. You can build and install all of them by running:

```
gmake
gmake install
```

in the `contrib` directory of a configured source tree; or to build and install just one selected module, do the same in that module's subdirectory. Many of the modules have regression tests, which can be executed by running:

```
gmake installcheck
```

once you have a PostgreSQL server running. (Note that `gmake check` is not supported; you must have an operational database server to perform these tests, and you must have built and installed the module(s) to be tested.)

If you are using a pre-packaged version of PostgreSQL, these modules are typically made available as a separate subpackage, such as `postgresql-contrib`.

Many modules supply new user-defined functions, operators, or types. To make use of one of these modules, after you have installed the code you need to register the new objects in the database system by running the SQL commands in the `.sql` file supplied by the module. For example,

```
psql -d dbname -f SHAREDIR/contrib/module.sql
```

Here, *`SHAREDIR`* means the installation's "share" directory (`pg_config --sharedir` will tell you what this is). In most cases the script must be run by a database superuser.

You need to run the .sql file in each database that you want the module's facilities to be available in. Alternatively, run it in database template1 so that the module will be copied into subsequently-created databases by default.

You can modify the first command in the .sql file to determine which schema within the database the module's objects will be created in. By default, they will be placed in public.

After a major-version upgrade of PostgreSQL, run the installation script again, even though the module's objects might have been brought forward from the old installation by dump and restore. This ensures that any new functions will be available and any needed corrections will be applied.

F.1. adminpack

adminpack provides a number of support functions which pgAdmin and other administration and management tools can use to provide additional functionality, such as remote management of server log files.

F.1.1. Functions implemented

The functions implemented by adminpack can only be run by a superuser. Here's a list of these functions:

```
int8 pg_catalog.pg_file_write(fname text, data text, append bool)
bool pg_catalog.pg_file_rename(oldname text, newname text, archivename text)
bool pg_catalog.pg_file_rename(oldname text, newname text)
bool pg_catalog.pg_file_unlink(fname text)
setof record pg_catalog.pg_logdir_ls()

/* Renaming of existing backend functions for pgAdmin compatibility */
int8 pg_catalog.pg_file_read(fname text, data text, append bool)
bigint pg_catalog.pg_file_length(text)
int4 pg_catalog.pg_logfile_rotate()
```

F.2. auto_explain

The auto_explain module provides a means for logging execution plans of slow statements automatically, without having to run EXPLAIN by hand. This is especially helpful for tracking down un-optimized queries in large applications.

The module provides no SQL-accessible functions. To use it, simply load it into the server. You can load it into an individual session:

```
LOAD 'auto_explain';
```

(You must be superuser to do that.) More typical usage is to preload it into all sessions by including auto_explain in shared_preload_libraries (Vol.II) in postgresql.conf .

Then you can track unexpectedly slow queries no matter when they happen. Of course there is a price in overhead for that.

F.2.1. Configuration parameters

There are several configuration parameters that control the behavior of `auto_explain`. Note that the default behavior is to do nothing, so you must set at least `auto_explain.log_min_duration` if you want any results.

`auto_explain.log_min_duration (integer)`

> `auto_explain.log_min_duration` is the minimum statement execution time, in milliseconds, that will cause the statement's plan to be logged. Setting this to zero logs all plans. Minus-one (the default) disables logging of plans. For example, if you set it to `250ms` then all statements that run 250ms or longer will be logged. Only superusers can change this setting.

`auto_explain.log_analyze (boolean)`

> `auto_explain.log_analyze` causes `EXPLAIN ANALYZE` output, rather than just `EXPLAIN` output, to be printed when an execution plan is logged. This parameter is off by default. Only superusers can change this setting.

> **Note**
>
> When this parameter is on, per-plan-node timing occurs for all statements executed, whether or not they run long enough to actually get logged. This can have extremely negative impact on performance.

`auto_explain.log_verbose (boolean)`

> `auto_explain.log_verbose` causes `EXPLAIN VERBOSE` output, rather than just `EXPLAIN` output, to be printed when an execution plan is logged. This parameter is off by default. Only superusers can change this setting.

`auto_explain.log_buffers` (boolean)

> `auto_explain.log_buffers` causes `EXPLAIN (ANALYZE, BUFFERS)` output, rather than just `EXPLAIN` output, to be printed when an execution plan is logged. This parameter is off by default. Only superusers can change this setting. This parameter has no effect unless `auto_explain.log_analyze` parameter is set.

`auto_explain.log_format` (enum)

> `auto_explain.log_format` selects the `EXPLAIN` output format to be used. The allowed values are `text`, `xml`, `json`, and `yaml`. The default is text. Only superusers can change this setting.

`auto_explain.log_nested_statements (boolean)`

> `auto_explain.log_nested_statements` causes nested statements (statements executed inside a function) to be considered for logging. When it is off, only top-level query plans are logged. This parameter is off by default. Only superusers can change this setting.

In order to set these parameters in your `postgresql.conf` file, you will need to add `auto_explain` to `custom_variable_classes` (Vol.II). Typical usage might be:

```
# postgresql.conf
shared_preload_libraries = 'auto_explain'

custom_variable_classes = 'auto_explain'
auto_explain.log_min_duration = '3s'
```

F.2.2. Example

```
postgres=# LOAD 'auto_explain';
postgres=# SET auto_explain.log_min_duration = 0;
postgres=# SELECT count(*)
            FROM pg_class, pg_index
           WHERE oid = indrelid AND indisunique;
```

This might produce log output such as:

```
LOG:  duration: 3.651 ms  plan:
  Query Text: SELECT count(*)
              FROM pg_class, pg_index
              WHERE oid = indrelid AND indisunique;
  Aggregate  (cost=16.79..16.80 rows=1 width=0)
                                 (actual time=3.626..3.627 rows=1 loops=1)
    ->  Hash Join  (cost=4.17..16.55 rows=92 width=0)
                                (actual time=3.349..3.594 rows=92 loops=1)
          Hash Cond: (pg_class.oid = pg_index.indrelid)
          ->  Seq Scan on pg_class  (cost=0.00..9.55 rows=255 width=4)
                               (actual time=0.016..0.140 rows=255 loops=1)
          ->  Hash  (cost=3.02..3.02 rows=92 width=4)
                                (actual time=3.238..3.238 rows=92 loops=1)
                Buckets: 1024  Batches: 1  Memory Usage: 4kB
                ->  Seq Scan on pg_index  (cost=0.00..3.02 rows=92 width=4)
                                (actual time=0.008..3.187 rows=92 loops=1)
                      Filter: indisunique
```

F.2.3. Author

Takahiro Itagaki *<itagaki.takahiro@oss.ntt.co.jp>*

F.3. btree_gin

`btree_gin` provides sample GIN operator classes that implement B-tree equivalent behavior for the data types int2, int4, int8, float4, float8, timestamp with time zone, timestamp without time zone, time with time zone, time without time zone, date, interval, oid, money, "char", varchar, text, bytea, bit, varbit, macaddr, inet, and cidr.

In general, these operator classes will not outperform the equivalent standard B-tree index methods, and they lack one major feature of the standard B-tree code: the ability to enforce uniqueness. However, they are useful for GIN testing and as a base for developing other GIN operator classes. Also, for queries that test both a GIN-indexable column and a B-tree-indexable column, it might be more efficient to create a multicolumn GIN index that uses one of these operator classes than to create two separate indexes that would have to be combined via bitmap ANDing.

F.3.1. Example usage

```
CREATE TABLE test (a int4);
-- create index
CREATE INDEX testidx ON test USING gin (a);
-- query
SELECT * FROM test WHERE a < 10;
```

F.3.2. Authors

Teodor Sigaev (<`teodor@stack.net`>) and Oleg Bartunov (<`oleg@sai.msu.su`>). See *http://www.sai.msu.su/~megera/oddmuse/index.cgi/Gin* for additional information.

F.4. btree_gist

`btree_gist` provides sample GiST operator classes that implement B-tree equivalent behavior for the data types `int2`, `int4`, `int8`, `float4`, `float8`, `numeric`, `timestamp with time zone`, `timestamp without time zone`, `time with time zone`, `time without time zone`, `date`, `interval`, `oid`, `money`, `char`, `varchar`, `text`, `bytea`, `bit`, `varbit`, `macaddr`, `inet`, and `cidr`.

In general, these operator classes will not outperform the equivalent standard B-tree index methods, and they lack one major feature of the standard B-tree code: the ability to enforce uniqueness. However, they are useful for GiST testing and as a base for developing other GiST operator classes.

F.4.1. Example usage

```
CREATE TABLE test (a int4);
-- create index
CREATE INDEX testidx ON test USING gist (a);
-- query
SELECT * FROM test WHERE a < 10;
```

F.4.2. Authors

Teodor Sigaev (<*teodor@stack.net*>) , Oleg Bartunov (<*oleg@sai.msu.su*>), and Janko Richter (<*jankorichter@yahoo.de*>). See *http://www.sai.msu.su/~megera/postgres/gist/* for additional information.

F.5. chkpass

This module implements a data type `chkpass` that is designed for storing encrypted passwords. Each password is automatically converted to encrypted form upon entry, and is always stored encrypted. To compare, simply compare against a clear text password and the comparison function will encrypt it before comparing.

There are provisions in the code to report an error if the password is determined to be easily crackable. However, this is currently just a stub that does nothing.

If you precede an input string with a colon, it is assumed to be an already-encrypted password, and is stored without further encryption. This allows entry of previously-encrypted passwords.

On output, a colon is prepended. This makes it possible to dump and reload passwords without re-encrypting them. If you want the encrypted password without the colon then use the `raw()` function. This allows you to use the type with things like Apache's Auth_PostgreSQL module.

The encryption uses the standard Unix function `crypt()`, and so it suffers from all the usual limitations of that function; notably that only the first eight characters of a password are considered.

Note that the chkpass data type is not indexable.

Sample usage:

```
test=# create table test (p chkpass);
CREATE TABLE
test=# insert into test values ('hello');
INSERT 0 1
test=# select * from test;
       p
----------------
 :dVGkpXdOrE3ko
(1 row)

test=# select raw(p) from test;
      raw
---------------
 dVGkpXdOrE3ko
(1 row)
```

```
test=# select p = 'hello' from test;
 ?column?
----------
 t
(1 row)

test=# select p = 'goodbye' from test;
 ?column?
----------
 f
(1 row)
```

F.5.1. Author

D'Arcy J.M. Cain (<*darcy@druid.net*>)

F.6. citext

The `citext` module provides a case-insensitive character string type, `citext`. Essentially, it internally calls `lower` when comparing values. Otherwise, it behaves almost exactly like `text`.

F.6.1. Rationale

The standard approach to doing case-insensitive matches in PostgreSQL has been to use the `lower` function when comparing values, for example

```
SELECT * FROM tab WHERE lower(col) = LOWER(?);
```

This works reasonably well, but has a number of drawbacks:

- It makes your SQL statements verbose, and you always have to remember to use `lower` on both the column and the query value.
- It won't use an index, unless you create a functional index using `lower`.
- If you declare a column as `UNIQUE` or `PRIMARY KEY`, the implicitly generated index is case-sensitive. So it's useless for case-insensitive searches, and it won't enforce uniqueness case-insensitively.

The `citext` data type allows you to eliminate calls to `lower` in SQL queries, and allows a primary key to be case-insensitive. `citext` is locale-aware, just like `text`, which means that the comparison of uppercase and lowercase characters is dependent on the rules of the `LC_CTYPE` locale setting. Again, this behavior is identical to the use of `lower` in queries. But because it's done transparently by the datatype, you don't have to remember to do anything special in your queries.

F.6.2. How to Use It

Here's a simple example of usage:

```
CREATE TABLE users (
    nick CITEXT PRIMARY KEY,
    pass TEXT   NOT NULL
);

INSERT INTO users VALUES ( 'larry',  md5(random()::text) );
INSERT INTO users VALUES ( 'Tom',    md5(random()::text) );
INSERT INTO users VALUES ( 'Damian', md5(random()::text) );
INSERT INTO users VALUES ( 'NEAL',   md5(random()::text) );
INSERT INTO users VALUES ( 'Bjern',  md5(random()::text) );

SELECT * FROM users WHERE nick = 'Larry';
```

The `SELECT` statement will return one tuple, even though the `nick` column was set to larry and the query was for Larry.

F.6.3. String Comparison Behavior

In order to emulate a case-insensitive collation as closely as possible, there are `citext`-specific versions of a number of the comparison operators and functions. So, for example, the regular expression operators `~` and `~*` exhibit the same behavior when applied to `citext`: they both compare case-insensitively. The same is true for `!~` and `!~*`, as well as for the `LIKE` operators `~~` and `~~*`, and `!~~` and `!~~*`. If you'd like to match case-sensitively, you can always cast to `text` before comparing.

Similarly, all of the following functions perform matching case-insensitively if their arguments are `citext`:

- `regexp_replace()`
- `regexp_split_to_array()`
- `regexp_split_to_table()`
- `replace()`
- `split_part()`
- `strpos()`
- `translate()`

For the regexp functions, if you want to match case-sensitively, you can specify the "c" flag to force a case-sensitive match. Otherwise, you must cast to `text` before using one of these functions if you want case-sensitive behavior.

F.6.4. Limitations

- `citext`'s behavior depends on the `LC_CTYPE` setting of your database. How it compares values is therefore determined when initdb is run to create the cluster. It is not truly case-insensitive in the terms defined by the Unicode standard. Effectively, what this means is that, as long as you're happy with your collation, you should be happy with `citext`'s comparisons. But if you have data in different languages stored in your database, users of one language may find their query results are not as expected if the collation is for another language.
- `citext` is not as efficient as `text` because the operator functions and the B-tree comparison functions must make copies of the data and convert it to lower case for comparisons. It is, however, slightly more efficient than using `lower` to get case-insensitive matching.
- `citext` doesn't help much if you need data to compare case-sensitively in some contexts and case-insensitively in other contexts. The standard answer is to use the `text` type and manually use the `lower` function when you need to compare case-insensitively; this works all right if case-insensitive comparison is needed only infrequently. If you need case-insensitive most of the time and case-sensitive infrequently, consider storing the data as `citext` and explicitly casting the column to `text` when you want case-sensitive comparison. In either situation, you will need two indexes if you want both types of searches to be fast.
- The schema containing the `citext` operators must be in the current `search_path` (typically `public`); if it is not, a normal case-sensitive `text` comparison is performed.

F.6.5. Author

David E. Wheeler <*david@kineticode.com*>

Inspired by the original citext module by Donald Fraser.

F.7. cube

This module implements a data type `cube` for representing multidimensional cubes.

F.7.1. Syntax

Table F-1 (see below) shows the valid external representations for the `cube` type. *x*, *y*, etc. denote floating-point numbers.

x	**A one-dimensional point (or, zero-length one-dimensional interval)**
(*x*)	Same as above
x1, *x2*,...,*xn*	A point in n-dimensional space, represented internally as a zero-volume cube
(*x1*, *x2*,...,*xn*)	Same as above

x	A one-dimensional point (or, zero-length one-dimensional interval)
(x),(y)	A one-dimensional interval starting at x and ending at y or vice versa; the order does not matter
[(x),(y)]	Same as above
(x1,...,xn),(y1 ,...,yn)	An n-dimensional cube represented by a pair of its diagonally opposite corners
[(x1,...,xn),(y1,...,yn)]	Same as above

Table F-1. Cube external representations

It does not matter which order the opposite corners of a cube are entered in. The `cube` functions automatically swap values if needed to create a uniform "lower left - upper right" internal representation.

White space is ignored, so `[(x),(y)]` is the same as `[ ( x ), ( y ) ]`.

F.7.2. Precision

Values are stored internally as 64-bit floating point numbers. This means that numbers with more than about 16 significant digits will be truncated.

F.7.3. Usage

The `cube` module includes a GiST index operator class for `cube` values. The operators supported by the GiST operator class are shown in *Table F-2* (see below).

Operator	Description
a = b	The cubes a and b are identical.
a && b	The cubes a and b overlap.
a @> b	The cube a contains the cube b.
a <@ b	The cube a is contained in the cube b.

Table F-2. Cube GiST operators

(Before PostgreSQL 8.2, the containment operators @> and <@ were respectively called @ and ~. These names are still available, but are deprecated and will eventually be retired. Notice that the old names are reversed from the convention formerly followed by the core geometric datatypes!)

The standard B-tree operators are also provided, for example

Operator	Description
[a, b] < [c, d]	Less than
[a, b] > [c, d]	Greater than

These operators do not make a lot of sense for any practical purpose but sorting. These operators first compare (a) to (c), and if these are equal, compare (b) to (d). That results in reasonably good sorting in most cases, which is useful if you want to use ORDER BY with this type.

Table F-3 (see below) shows the available functions.

`cube(float8) returns cube`	Makes a one dimensional cube with both coordinates the same. `cube(1) == '(1)'`
`cube(float8, float8) returns cube`	Makes a one dimensional cube. `cube(1,2) == '(1),(2)'`
`cube(float8[]) returns cube`	Makes a zero-volume cube using the coordinates defined by the array. `cube(ARRAY[1,2]) == '(1,2)'`
`cube(float8[], float8[]) returns cube`	Makes a cube with upper right and lower left coordinates as defined by the two arrays, which must be of the same length. `cube('{1,2}'::float[], '{3,4}'::float[]) == '(1,2),(3,4)'`
`cube(cube, float8) returns cube`	Makes a new cube by adding a dimension on to an existing cube with the same values for both parts of the new coordinate. This is useful for building cubes piece by piece from calculated values. `cube('(1)',2) == '(1,2),(1,2)'`
`cube(cube, float8, float8) returns cube`	Makes a new cube by adding a dimension on to an existing cube. This is useful for building cubes piece by piece from calculated values. `cube('(1,2)',3,4) == '(1,3),(2,4)'`
`cube_dim(cube) returns int`	Returns the number of dimensions of the cube
`cube_ll_coord(cube, int) returns double`	Returns the n'th coordinate value for the lower left corner of a cube
`cube_ur_coord(cube, int) returns double`	Returns the n'th coordinate value for the upper right corner of a cube
`cube_is_point(cube) returns bool`	Returns true if a cube is a point, that is, the two defining corners are the same.
`cube_distance(cube, cube) returns double`	Returns the distance between two cubes. If both cubes are points, this is the normal distance function.
`cube_subset(cube, int[]) returns cube`	Makes a new cube from an existing cube, using a list of dimension indexes from an array. Can be used to find both the LL and UR coordinates of a single dimension, e.g. `cube_subset(cube('(1,3,5),(6,7,8)'), ARRAY[2]) = '(3),(7)'`. Or can be used to drop dimensions, or reorder them as desired, e.g. `cube_subset(cube('(1,3,5),(6,7,8)'), ARRAY[3,2,1,1]) = '(5, 3, 1, 1),(8, 7, 6, 6)'`.
`cube_union(cube, cube) returns cube`	Produces the union of two cubes
`cube_inter(cube, cube) returns cube`	Produces the intersection of two cubes
`cube_enlarge(cube c,`	Increases the size of a cube by a specified radius in at least n dimensions. If the

`double r, int n) returns cube`	radius is negative the cube is shrunk instead. This is useful for creating bounding boxes around a point for searching for nearby points. All defined dimensions are changed by the radius r. LL coordinates are decreased by r and UR coordinates are increased by r. If a LL coordinate is increased to larger than the corresponding UR coordinate (this can only happen when r < 0) than both coordinates are set to their average. If n is greater than the number of defined dimensions and the cube is being increased (r >= 0) then 0 is used as the base for the extra coordinates.

Table F-3. Cube functions

F.7.4. Defaults

I believe this union:

```
select cube_union('(0,5,2),(2,3,1)', '0');
cube_union
-------------------
(0, 0, 0),(2, 5, 2)
(1 row)
```

does not contradict common sense, neither does the intersection

```
select cube_inter('(0,-1),(1,1)', '(-2),(2)');
cube_inter
-------------
(0, 0),(1, 0)
(1 row)
```

In all binary operations on differently-dimensioned cubes, I assume the lower-dimensional one to be a Cartesian projection, i. e., having zeroes in place of coordinates omitted in the string representation. The above examples are equivalent to:

```
cube_union('(0,5,2),(2,3,1)','(0,0,0),(0,0,0)');
cube_inter('(0,-1),(1,1)','(-2,0),(2,0)');
```

The following containment predicate uses the point syntax, while in fact the second argument is internally represented by a box. This syntax makes it unnecessary to define a separate point type and functions for (box,point) predicates.

```
select cube_contains('(0,0),(1,1)', '0.5,0.5');
cube_contains
--------------
t
(1 row)
```

F.7.5. Notes

For examples of usage, see the regression test `sql/cube.sql`.

To make it harder for people to break things, there is a limit of 100 on the number of dimensions of cubes. This is set in `cubedata.h` if you need something bigger.

F.7.6. Credits

Original author: Gene Selkov, Jr. `<selkovjr@mcs.anl.gov>`, Mathematics and Computer Science Division, Argonne National Laboratory.

My thanks are primarily to Prof. Joe Hellerstein (*http://db.cs.berkeley.edu/jmh/*) for elucidating the gist of the GiST (*http://gist.cs.berkeley.edu/*), and to his former student, Andy Dong (*http://best.me.berkeley.edu/~adong/*), for his example written for Illustra, *http://best.berkeley.edu/~adong/rtree/index.html*. I am also grateful to all Postgres developers, present and past, for enabling myself to create my own world and live undisturbed in it. And I would like to acknowledge my gratitude to Argonne Lab and to the U.S. Department of Energy for the years of faithful support of my database research.

Minor updates to this package were made by Bruno Wolff III `<bruno@wolff.to>` in August/September of 2002. These include changing the precision from single precision to double precision and adding some new functions.

Additional updates were made by Joshua Reich `<josh@root.net>` in July 2006. These include `cube(float8[], float8[])` and cleaning up the code to use the V1 call protocol instead of the deprecated V0 protocol.

F.8. dblink

`dblink` is a module which supports connections to other PostgreSQL databases from within a database session.

---

dblink_connect

Name

dblink_connect -- opens a persistent connection to a remote database

Synopsis

```
dblink_connect(text connstr) returns text
dblink_connect(text connname, text connstr) returns text
```

Description

`dblink_connect()` establishes a connection to a remote PostgreSQL database. The server and database to be contacted are identified through a standard libpq connection string. Optionally, a name can be assigned to the connection. Multiple named connections can be open at once, but only one unnamed connection is permitted at a time. The connection will persist until closed or until the database session is ended.

The connection string may also be the name of an existing foreign server. It is recommended to use the `postgresql_fdw_validator` when defining the corresponding foreign-data wrapper. See the example below, as well as the following: CREATE FOREIGN DATA WRAPPER , CREATE SERVER, CREATE USER MAPPING

Arguments

`conname`

The name to use for this connection; if omitted, an unnamed connection is opened, replacing any existing unnamed connection.

`connstr`

libpq-style connection info string, for example `hostaddr=127.0.0.1 port=5432 dbname=mydb user=postgres password=mypasswd`. For details see `PQconnectdb` in *Section 31.1* (Vol.II).

Return Value

Returns status, which is always `OK` (since any error causes the function to throw an error instead of returning).

Notes

Only superusers may use `dblink_connect` to create non-password-authenticated connections. If non-superusers need this capability, use `dblink_connect_u` instead.

It is unwise to choose connection names that contain equal signs, as this opens a risk of confusion with connection info strings in other `dblink` functions.

Example

```
SELECT dblink_connect('dbname=postgres');
 dblink_connect
----------------
 OK
(1 row)

SELECT dblink_connect('myconn', 'dbname=postgres');
 dblink_connect
----------------
 OK
(1 row)

-- FOREIGN DATA WRAPPER functionality
-- Note: local connection must require password authentication for this to
--       work properly
--       Otherwise, you will receive the following error from dblink_connect():
--       ----------------------------------------------------------------------
--       ERROR:  password is required
--       DETAIL: Non-superuser cannot connect if the server does not request
--               a password.
--       HINT:   Target server's authentication method must be changed.
CREATE USER dblink_regression_test WITH PASSWORD 'secret';
```

```
CREATE FOREIGN DATA WRAPPER postgresql VALIDATOR postgresql_fdw_validator;
CREATE SERVER fdtest FOREIGN DATA WRAPPER postgresql OPTIONS
                            (hostaddr '127.0.0.1', dbname 'contrib_regression');

CREATE USER MAPPING FOR dblink_regression_test SERVER fdtest OPTIONS
                             (user 'dblink_regression_test', password 'secret');
GRANT USAGE ON FOREIGN SERVER fdtest TO dblink_regression_test;
GRANT SELECT ON TABLE foo TO dblink_regression_test;

\set ORIGINAL_USER :USER
\c - dblink_regression_test
SELECT dblink_connect('myconn', 'fdtest');
 dblink_connect
----------------
 OK
(1 row)

SELECT * FROM dblink('myconn','SELECT * FROM foo') AS t(a int, b text, c text[]);
 a  | b |       c
----+---+---------------
  0 | a | {a0,b0,c0}
  1 | b | {a1,b1,c1}
  2 | c | {a2,b2,c2}
  3 | d | {a3,b3,c3}
  4 | e | {a4,b4,c4}
  5 | f | {a5,b5,c5}
  6 | g | {a6,b6,c6}
  7 | h | {a7,b7,c7}
  8 | i | {a8,b8,c8}
  9 | j | {a9,b9,c9}
 10 | k | {a10,b10,c10}
(11 rows)

\c - :ORIGINAL_USER
REVOKE USAGE ON FOREIGN SERVER fdtest FROM dblink_regression_test;
REVOKE SELECT ON TABLE foo FROM  dblink_regression_test;
DROP USER MAPPING FOR dblink_regression_test SERVER fdtest;
DROP USER dblink_regression_test;
DROP SERVER fdtest;
DROP FOREIGN DATA WRAPPER postgresql;
```

dblink_connect_u

Name

dblink_connect_u -- opens a persistent connection to a remote database, insecurely

Synopsis

```
dblink_connect_u(text connstr) returns text
dblink_connect_u(text connname, text connstr) returns text
```

Description

`dblink_connect_u()` is identical to `dblink_connect()`, except that it will allow non-superusers to connect using any authentication method.

If the remote server selects an authentication method that does not involve a password, then impersonation and subsequent escalation of privileges can occur, because the session will appear to have originated from the user as which the local PostgreSQL server runs. Also, even if the remote server does demand a password, it is possible for the password to be supplied from the server environment, such as a `~/.pgpass` file belonging to the server's user. This opens not only a risk of impersonation, but the possibility of exposing a password to an untrustworthy remote server. Therefore, `dblink_connect_u()` is initially installed with all privileges revoked from `PUBLIC`, making it un-callable except by superusers. In some situations it may be appropriate to grant `EXECUTE` permission for `dblink_connect_u()` to specific users who are considered trustworthy, but this should be done with care. It is also recommended that any `~/.pgpass` file belonging to the server's user *not* contain any records specifying a wildcard host name.

For further details see `dblink_connect()`.

dblink_disconnect

Name

dblink_disconnect -- closes a persistent connection to a remote database

Synopsis

```
dblink_disconnect() returns text
dblink_disconnect(text connname) returns text
```

Description

`dblink_disconnect()` closes a connection previously opened by `dblink_connect()`. The form with no arguments closes an unnamed connection.

Arguments

`conname`

The name of a named connection to be closed.

Return Value

Returns status, which is always `OK` (since any error causes the function to throw an error instead of returning).

Example

```
SELECT dblink_disconnect();
 dblink_disconnect
-------------------
 OK
(1 row)

SELECT dblink_disconnect('myconn');
 dblink_disconnect
-------------------
 OK
(1 row)
```

dblink

Name

dblink -- executes a query in a remote database

Synopsis

```
dblink(text connname, text sql [, bool fail_on_error]) returns setof record
dblink(text connstr, text sql [, bool fail_on_error]) returns setof record
dblink(text sql [, bool fail_on_error]) returns setof record
```

Description

`dblink` executes a query (usually a `SELECT`, but it can be any SQL statement that returns rows) in a remote database.

When two `text` arguments are given, the first one is first looked up as a persistent connection's name; if found, the command is executed on that connection. If not found, the first argument is treated as a connection info string as for `dblink_connect`, and the indicated connection is made just for the duration of this command.

Arguments

`conname`

Name of the connection to use; omit this parameter to use the unnamed connection.

`connstr`

A connection info string, as previously described for `dblink_connect`.

`sql`

The SQL query that you wish to execute in the remote database, for example `select * from foo`.

`fail_on_error`

If true (the default when omitted) then an error thrown on the remote side of the connection causes an error to also be thrown locally. If false, the remote error is locally reported as a NOTICE, and the function returns no rows.

Return Value

The function returns the row(s) produced by the query. Since `dblink` can be used with any query, it is declared to return `record`, rather than specifying any particular set of columns. This means that you must specify the expected set of columns in the calling query - otherwise PostgreSQL would not know what to expect. Here is an example:

```
SELECT *
    FROM dblink('dbname=mydb', 'select proname, prosrc from pg_proc')
      AS t1(proname name, prosrc text)
    WHERE proname LIKE 'bytea%';
```

The "alias" part of the `FROM` clause must specify the column names and types that the function will return. (Specifying column names in an alias is actually standard SQL syntax, but specifying column types is a PostgreSQL extension.) This allows the system to understand what `*` should expand to, and what `proname` in the `WHERE` clause refers to, in advance of trying to execute the function. At runtime, an error will be thrown if the actual query result from the remote database does not have the same number of columns shown in the `FROM` clause. The column names need not match, however, and `dblink` does not insist on exact type matches either. It will succeed so long as the returned data strings are valid input for the column type declared in the `FROM` clause.

Notes

`dblink` fetches the entire remote query result before returning any of it to the local system. If the query is expected to return a large number of rows, it's better to open it as a cursor with `dblink_open` and then fetch a manageable number of rows at a time.

A convenient way to use `dblink` with predetermined queries is to create a view. This allows the column type information to be buried in the view, instead of having to spell it out in every query. For example,

```
CREATE VIEW myremote_pg_proc AS
  SELECT *
    FROM dblink('dbname=postgres', 'select proname, prosrc from pg_proc')
    AS t1(proname name, prosrc text);

SELECT * FROM myremote_pg_proc WHERE proname LIKE 'bytea%';
```

Example

```
SELECT * FROM dblink('dbname=postgres', 'select proname, prosrc from pg_proc')
```

```
  AS t1(proname name, prosrc text) WHERE proname LIKE 'bytea%';
  proname    |   prosrc
------------+------------
 byteacat    | byteacat
 byteaeq     | byteaeq
 bytealt     | bytealt
 byteale     | byteale
 byteagt     | byteagt
 byteage     | byteage
 byteane     | byteane
 byteacmp    | byteacmp
 bytealike   | bytealike
 byteanlike  | byteanlike
 byteain     | byteain
 byteaout    | byteaout
(12 rows)

SELECT dblink_connect('dbname=postgres');
 dblink_connect
----------------
 OK
(1 row)

SELECT * FROM dblink('select proname, prosrc from pg_proc')
  AS t1(proname name, prosrc text) WHERE proname LIKE 'bytea%';
  proname    |   prosrc
------------+------------
 byteacat    | byteacat
 byteaeq     | byteaeq
 bytealt     | bytealt
 byteale     | byteale
 byteagt     | byteagt
 byteage     | byteage
 byteane     | byteane
 byteacmp    | byteacmp
 bytealike   | bytealike
 byteanlike  | byteanlike
 byteain     | byteain
 byteaout    | byteaout
(12 rows)

SELECT dblink_connect('myconn', 'dbname=regression');
 dblink_connect
----------------
 OK
(1 row)

SELECT * FROM dblink('myconn', 'select proname, prosrc from pg_proc')
  AS t1(proname name, prosrc text) WHERE proname LIKE 'bytea%';
  proname    |   prosrc
------------+------------
 bytearecv   | bytearecv
 byteasend   | byteasend
```

```
 byteale    | byteale
 byteagt    | byteagt
 byteage    | byteage
 byteane    | byteane
 byteacmp   | byteacmp
 bytealike  | bytealike
 byteanlike | byteanlike
 byteacat   | byteacat
 byteaeq    | byteaeq
 bytealt    | bytealt
 byteain    | byteain
 byteaout   | byteaout
(14 rows)
```

dblink_exec

Name

dblink_exec -- executes a command in a remote database

Synopsis

```
dblink_exec(text connname, text sql [, bool fail_on_error]) returns text
dblink_exec(text connstr, text sql [, bool fail_on_error]) returns text
dblink_exec(text sql [, bool fail_on_error]) returns text
```

Description

`dblink_exec` executes a command (that is, any SQL statement that doesn't return rows) in a remote database.

When two `text` arguments are given, the first one is first looked up as a persistent connection's name; if found, the command is executed on that connection. If not found, the first argument is treated as a connection info string as for `dblink_connect`, and the indicated connection is made just for the duration of this command.

Arguments

`conname`

Name of the connection to use; omit this parameter to use the unnamed connection.

`connstr`

A connection info string, as previously described for `dblink_connect`.

`sql`

The SQL command that you wish to execute in the remote database, for example `insert into foo values(0,'a','{"a0","b0","c0"}')`.

`fail_on_error`

If true (the default when omitted) then an error thrown on the remote side of the connection causes an error to also be thrown locally. If false, the remote error is locally reported as a NOTICE, and the function's return value is set to `ERROR` .

Return Value

Returns status, either the command's status string or `ERROR`.

Example

```
SELECT dblink_connect('dbname=dblink_test_slave');
 dblink_connect
----------------
 OK
(1 row)

SELECT dblink_exec('insert into foo values(21,''z'',''{"a0","b0","c0"}'');');
   dblink_exec
-----------------
 INSERT 943366 1
(1 row)

SELECT dblink_connect('myconn', 'dbname=regression');
 dblink_connect
----------------
 OK
(1 row)

SELECT dblink_exec('myconn', 'insert into foo values(21,''z'',''{"a0","b0","c0"}'');');
   dblink_exec
------------------
 INSERT 6432584 1
(1 row)

SELECT dblink_exec('myconn', 'insert into pg_class values (''foo'')',false);
NOTICE:  sql error
DETAIL:  ERROR:  null value in column "relnamespace" violates not-null constraint

 dblink_exec
-------------
 ERROR
(1 row)
```

dblink_open

Name

dblink_open -- opens a cursor in a remote database

Synopsis

```
dblink_open(text cursorname, text sql [, bool fail_on_error]) returns text
dblink_open(text connname, text cursorname, text sql [, bool fail_on_error])
                                                                returns text
```

Description

`dblink_open()` opens a cursor in a remote database. The cursor can subsequently be manipulated with `dblink_fetch()` and `dblink_close()`.

Arguments

`conname`

Name of the connection to use; omit this parameter to use the unnamed connection.

`cursorname`

The name to assign to this cursor.

`sql`

The `SELECT` statement that you wish to execute in the remote database, for example `select * from pg_class`.

`fail_on_error`

If true (the default when omitted) then an error thrown on the remote side of the connection causes an error to also be thrown locally. If false, the remote error is locally reported as a NOTICE, and the function's return value is set to `ERROR` .

Return Value

Returns status, either `OK` or `ERROR`.

Notes

Since a cursor can only persist within a transaction, `dblink_open` starts an explicit transaction block (`BEGIN`) on the remote side, if the remote side was not already within a transaction. This transaction will be closed again when the matching `dblink_close` is executed. Note that if you use `dblink_exec` to change data between `dblink_open` and `dblink_close`, and then an error occurs or you use `dblink_disconnect` before `dblink_close` , your change *will be lost* because the transaction will be aborted.

Example

```
SELECT dblink_connect('dbname=postgres');
 dblink_connect
----------------
 OK
(1 row)
```

```
SELECT dblink_open('foo', 'select proname, prosrc from pg_proc');
 dblink_open
-------------
 OK
(1 row)
```

dblink_fetch

Name

dblink_fetch -- returns rows from an open cursor in a remote database

Synopsis

```
dblink_fetch(text cursorname, int howmany [, bool fail_on_error])
                                              returns setof record
dblink_fetch(text connname, text cursorname, int howmany [, bool
                                 fail_on_error]) returns setof record
```

Description

`dblink_fetch` fetches rows from a cursor previously established by `dblink_open` .

Arguments

`conname`

Name of the connection to use; omit this parameter to use the unnamed connection.

`cursorname`

The name of the cursor to fetch from.

`howmany`

The maximum number of rows to retrieve. The next `howmany` rows are fetched, starting at the current cursor position, moving forward. Once the cursor has reached its end, no more rows are produced.

`fail_on_error`

If true (the default when omitted) then an error thrown on the remote side of the connection causes an error to also be thrown locally. If false, the remote error is locally reported as a NOTICE, and the function returns no rows.

Return Value

The function returns the row(s) fetched from the cursor. To use this function, you will need to specify the expected set of columns, as previously discussed for `dblink`.

Notes

On a mismatch between the number of return columns specified in the `FROM` clause, and the actual number of columns returned by the remote cursor, an error will be thrown. In this event, the remote cursor is still advanced by as many rows as it would have been if the error had not occurred. The same is true for any other error occurring in the local query after the remote `FETCH` has been done.

Example

```
SELECT dblink_connect('dbname=postgres');
 dblink_connect
----------------
 OK
(1 row)

SELECT dblink_open('foo', 'select proname, prosrc from pg_proc where
                                                          proname like ''bytea%''');
 dblink_open
------------
 OK
(1 row)

SELECT * FROM dblink_fetch('foo', 5) AS (funcname name, source text);
 funcname |  source
----------+----------
 byteacat | byteacat
 byteacmp | byteacmp
 byteaeq  | byteaeq
 byteage  | byteage
 byteagt  | byteagt
(5 rows)

SELECT * FROM dblink_fetch('foo', 5) AS (funcname name, source text);
 funcname  |  source
-----------+-----------
 byteain   | byteain
 byteale   | byteale
 bytealike | bytealike
 bytealt   | bytealt
 byteane   | byteane
(5 rows)

SELECT * FROM dblink_fetch('foo', 5) AS (funcname name, source text);
  funcname  |   source
------------+------------
 byteanlike | byteanlike
 byteaout   | byteaout
(2 rows)

SELECT * FROM dblink_fetch('foo', 5) AS (funcname name, source text);
 funcname | source
----------+--------
(0 rows)
```

dblink_close

Name

dblink_close -- closes a cursor in a remote database

Synopsis

```
dblink_close(text cursorname [, bool fail_on_error]) returns text
dblink_close(text connname, text cursorname [, bool fail_on_error])
                                                          returns text
```

Description

`dblink_close` closes a cursor previously opened with `dblink_open`.

Arguments

`conname`

Name of the connection to use; omit this parameter to use the unnamed connection.

`cursorname`

The name of the cursor to close.

`fail_on_error`

If true (the default when omitted) then an error thrown on the remote side of the connection causes an error to also be thrown locally. If false, the remote error is locally reported as a NOTICE, and the function's return value is set to `ERROR` .

Return Value

Returns status, either `OK` or `ERROR`.

Notes

If `dblink_open` started an explicit transaction block, and this is the last remaining open cursor in this connection, `dblink_close` will issue the matching `COMMIT`.

Example

```
SELECT dblink_connect('dbname=postgres');
 dblink_connect
----------------
 OK
(1 row)

SELECT dblink_open('foo', 'select proname, prosrc from pg_proc');
 dblink_open
-------------
 OK
(1 row)
```

```
SELECT dblink_close('foo');
 dblink_close
--------------
 OK
(1 row)
```

dblink_get_connections

Name

dblink_get_connections -- returns the names of all open named dblink connections

Synopsis

```
dblink_get_connections() returns text[]
```

Description

`dblink_get_connections` returns an array of the names of all open named `dblink` connections.

Return Value

Returns a text array of connection names, or NULL if none.

Example

```
SELECT dblink_get_connections();
```

dblink_error_message

Name

dblink_error_message -- gets last error message on the named connection

Synopsis

```
dblink_error_message(text connname) returns text
```

Description

`dblink_error_message` fetches the most recent remote error message for a given connection.

Arguments

`conname`

Name of the connection to use.

Return Value

Returns last error message, or an empty string if there has been no error in this connection.

Example

```
SELECT dblink_error_message('dtest1');
```

dblink_send_query

Name

dblink_send_query -- sends an async query to a remote database

Synopsis

```
dblink_send_query(text connname, text sql) returns int
```

Description

`dblink_send_query` sends a query to be executed asynchronously, that is, without immediately waiting for the result. There must not be an async query already in progress on the connection.

After successfully dispatching an async query, completion status can be checked with `dblink_is_busy`, and the results are ultimately collected with `dblink_get_result`. It is also possible to attempt to cancel an active async query using `dblink_cancel_query`.

Arguments

`conname`

Name of the connection to use.

`sql`

The SQL statement that you wish to execute in the remote database, for example `select * from pg_class`.

Return Value

Returns 1 if the query was successfully dispatched, 0 otherwise.

Example

```
SELECT dblink_send_query('dtest1', 'SELECT * FROM foo WHERE f1 < 3');
```

dblink_is_busy

Name

dblink_is_busy -- checks if connection is busy with an async query

Synopsis

```
dblink_is_busy(text connname) returns int
```

Description

`dblink_is_busy` tests whether an async query is in progress.

Arguments

`conname`

Name of the connection to check.

Return Value

Returns 1 if connection is busy, 0 if it is not busy. If this function returns 0, it is guaranteed that `dblink_get_result` will not block.

Example

```
SELECT dblink_is_busy('dtest1');
```

---

dblink_get_notify

Name

dblink_get_notify - retrieve async notifications on a connection

Synopsis

```
dblink_get_notify() returns setof (notify_name text, be_pid int, extra text)
dblink_get_notify(text connname) returns setof (notify_name text, be_pid int,
                                                                extra text)
```

Description

`dblink_get_notify` retrieves notifications on either the unnamed connection, or on a named connection if specified. To receive notifications via dblink, `LISTEN` must first be issued, using `dblink_exec`. For details see LISTEN and NOTIFY.

Arguments

`conname`

The name of a named connection to get notifications on.

Return Value

Returns `setof (notify_name text, be_pid int, extra text)`, or an empty set if none.

Example

```
SELECT dblink_exec('LISTEN virtual');
 dblink_exec
-------------
 LISTEN
(1 row)

SELECT * FROM dblink_get_notify();
 notify_name | be_pid | extra
-------------+--------+-------
(0 rows)

NOTIFY virtual;
NOTIFY

SELECT * FROM dblink_get_notify();
 notify_name | be_pid | extra
-------------+--------+-------
 virtual     |   1229 |
(1 row)
```

dblink_get_result

Name

dblink_get_result -- gets an async query result

Synopsis

```
dblink_get_result(text connname [, bool fail_on_error]) returns setof record
```

Description

`dblink_get_result` collects the results of an asynchronous query previously sent with `dblink_send_query`. If the query is not already completed, `dblink_get_result` will wait until it is.

Arguments

`conname`

Name of the connection to use.

`fail_on_error`

If true (the default when omitted) then an error thrown on the remote side of the connection causes an error to also be thrown locally. If false, the remote error is locally reported as a NOTICE, and the function returns no rows.

Return Value

For an async query (that is, a SQL statement returning rows), the function returns the row(s) produced by the query. To use this function, you will need to specify the expected set of columns, as previously discussed for `dblink`.

For an async command (that is, a SQL statement not returning rows), the function returns a single row with a single text column containing the command's status string. It is still necessary to specify that the result will have a single text column in the calling `FROM` clause.

Notes

This function *must* be called if `dblink_send_query` returned 1. It must be called once for each query sent, and one additional time to obtain an empty set result, before the connection can be used again.

Example

```
contrib_regression=# SELECT dblink_connect('dtest1', 'dbname=contrib_regression');
 dblink_connect
----------------
 OK
(1 row)

contrib_regression=# SELECT * FROM
contrib_regression-# dblink_send_query('dtest1', 'select * from foo
                                                              where f1 < 3') AS t1;
 t1
----
  1
(1 row)

contrib_regression=# SELECT * FROM dblink_get_result('dtest1') AS t1(f1 int,
                                                              f2 text, f3 text[]);
 f1 | f2 |     f3
----+----+------------
  0 | a  | {a0,b0,c0}
  1 | b  | {a1,b1,c1}
  2 | c  | {a2,b2,c2}
(3 rows)

contrib_regression=# SELECT * FROM dblink_get_result('dtest1') AS t1(f1 int,
                                                              f2 text, f3 text[]);
 f1 | f2 | f3
----+----+----
(0 rows)

contrib_regression=# SELECT * FROM
contrib_regression-# dblink_send_query('dtest1', 'select * from foo
                              where f1 < 3; select * from foo where f1 > 6') AS t1;
```

```
 t1
----
  1
(1 row)

contrib_regression=# SELECT * FROM dblink_get_result('dtest1') AS t1(f1 int,
                                                      f2 text, f3 text[]);
 f1 | f2 |     f3
----+----+------------
  0 | a  | {a0,b0,c0}
  1 | b  | {a1,b1,c1}
  2 | c  | {a2,b2,c2}
(3 rows)

contrib_regression=# SELECT * FROM dblink_get_result('dtest1') AS t1(f1 int,
                                                      f2 text, f3 text[]);
 f1 | f2 |      f3
----+----+---------------
  7 | h  | {a7,b7,c7}
  8 | i  | {a8,b8,c8}
  9 | j  | {a9,b9,c9}
 10 | k  | {a10,b10,c10}
(4 rows)

contrib_regression=# SELECT * FROM dblink_get_result('dtest1') AS t1(f1 int,
                                                      f2 text, f3 text[]);
 f1 | f2 | f3
----+----+----
(0 rows)
```

dblink_cancel_query

Name

dblink_cancel_query -- cancels any active query on the named connection

Synopsis

```
dblink_cancel_query(text connname) returns text
```

Description

`dblink_cancel_query` attempts to cancel any query that is in progress on the named connection. Note that this is not certain to succeed (since, for example, the remote query might already have finished). A cancel request simply improves the odds that the query will fail soon. You must still complete the normal query protocol, for example by calling `dblink_get_result`.

Arguments

`conname`

Name of the connection to use.

Return Value

Returns `OK` if the cancel request has been sent, or the text of an error message on failure.

Example

```
SELECT dblink_cancel_query('dtest1');
```

dblink_get_pkey

Name

dblink_get_pkey -- returns the positions and field names of a relation's primary key fields

Synopsis

```
dblink_get_pkey(text relname) returns setof dblink_pkey_results
```

Description

`dblink_get_pkey` provides information about the primary key of a relation in the local database. This is sometimes useful in generating queries to be sent to remote databases.

Arguments

`relname`

Name of a local relation, for example `foo` or `myschema.mytab`. Include double quotes if the name is mixed-case or contains special characters, for example `"FooBar"`; without quotes, the string will be folded to lower case.

Return Value

Returns one row for each primary key field, or no rows if the relation has no primary key. The result rowtype is defined as

```
CREATE TYPE dblink_pkey_results AS (position int, colname text);
```

The `position` column simply runs from 1 to *N*; it is the number of the field within the primary key, not the number within the table's columns.

Example

```
CREATE TABLE foobar (
    f1 int,
```

```
    f2 int,
    f3 int,
    PRIMARY KEY (f1, f2, f3)
);
CREATE TABLE

SELECT * FROM dblink_get_pkey('foobar');
 position | colname
----------+---------
        1 | f1
        2 | f2
        3 | f3
(3 rows)
```

dblink_build_sql_insert

Name

dblink_build_sql_insert -- builds an INSERT statement using a local tuple, replacing the primary key field values with alternative supplied values

Synopsis

```
dblink_build_sql_insert(text relname,
                        int2vector primary_key_attnums,
                        integer num_primary_key_atts,
                        text[] src_pk_att_vals_array,
                        text[] tgt_pk_att_vals_array) returns text
```

Description

`dblink_build_sql_insert` can be useful in doing selective replication of a local table to a remote database. It selects a row from the local table based on primary key, and then builds a SQL `INSERT` command that will duplicate that row, but with the primary key values replaced by the values in the last argument. (To make an exact copy of the row, just specify the same values for the last two arguments.)

Arguments

`relname`

Name of a local relation, for example `foo` or `myschema.mytab`. Include double quotes if the name is mixed-case or contains special characters, for example `"FooBar"`; without quotes, the string will be folded to lower case.

`primary_key_attnums`

Attribute numbers (1-based) of the primary key fields, for example `1 2`.

`num_primary_key_atts`

The number of primary key fields.

`src_pk_att_vals_array`

Values of the primary key fields to be used to look up the local tuple. Each field is represented in text form. An error is thrown if there is no local row with these primary key values.

`tgt_pk_att_vals_array`

Values of the primary key fields to be placed in the resulting `INSERT` command. Each field is represented in text form.

Return Value

Returns the requested SQL statement as text.

Notes

As of PostgreSQL 9.0, the attribute numbers in `primary_key_attnums` are interpreted as logical column numbers, corresponding to the column's position in `SELECT * FROM relname`. Previous versions interpreted the numbers as physical column positions. There is a difference if any column(s) to the left of the indicated column have been dropped during the lifetime of the table.

Example

```
SELECT dblink_build_sql_insert('foo', '1 2', 2, '{"1", "a"}', '{"1", "b''a"}');
             dblink_build_sql_insert
--------------------------------------------------
 INSERT INTO foo(f1,f2,f3) VALUES('1','b''a','1')
(1 row)
```

dblink_build_sql_delete

Name

dblink_build_sql_delete -- builds a DELETE statement using supplied values for primary key field values

Synopsis

```
dblink_build_sql_delete(text relname,
                        int2vector primary_key_attnums,
                        integer num_primary_key_atts,
                        text[] tgt_pk_att_vals_array) returns text
```

Description

`dblink_build_sql_delete` can be useful in doing selective replication of a local table to a remote database. It builds a SQL `DELETE` command that will delete the row with the given primary key values.

Arguments

`relname`

Name of a local relation, for example `foo` or `myschema.mytab`. Include double quotes if the name is mixed-case or contains special characters, for example `"FooBar"`; without quotes, the string will be folded to lower case.

`primary_key_attnums`

Attribute numbers (1-based) of the primary key fields, for example `1 2`.

`num_primary_key_atts`

The number of primary key fields.

`tgt_pk_att_vals_array`

Values of the primary key fields to be used in the resulting `DELETE` command. Each field is represented in text form.

Return Value

Returns the requested SQL statement as text.

Notes

As of PostgreSQL 9.0, the attribute numbers in `primary_key_attnums` are interpreted as logical column numbers, corresponding to the column's position in `SELECT * FROM relname`. Previous versions interpreted the numbers as physical column positions. There is a difference if any column(s) to the left of the indicated column have been dropped during the lifetime of the table.

Example

```
SELECT dblink_build_sql_delete('"MyFoo"', '1 2', 2, '{"1", "b"}');
           dblink_build_sql_delete
---------------------------------------------
 DELETE FROM "MyFoo" WHERE f1='1' AND f2='b'
(1 row)
```

dblink_build_sql_update

Name

dblink_build_sql_update -- builds an UPDATE statement using a local tuple, replacing the primary key field values with alternative supplied values

Synopsis

```
dblink_build_sql_update(text relname,
                        int2vector primary_key_attnums,
```

```
integer num_primary_key_atts,
text[] src_pk_att_vals_array,
text[] tgt_pk_att_vals_array) returns text
```

Description

`dblink_build_sql_update` can be useful in doing selective replication of a local table to a remote database. It selects a row from the local table based on primary key, and then builds a SQL `UPDATE` command that will duplicate that row, but with the primary key values replaced by the values in the last argument. (To make an exact copy of the row, just specify the same values for the last two arguments.) The `UPDATE` command always assigns all fields of the row - the main difference between this and `dblink_build_sql_insert` is that it's assumed that the target row already exists in the remote table.

Arguments

`relname`

Name of a local relation, for example `foo` or `myschema.mytab`. Include double quotes if the name is mixed-case or contains special characters, for example `"FooBar"`; without quotes, the string will be folded to lower case.

`primary_key_attnums`

Attribute numbers (1-based) of the primary key fields, for example `1 2`.

`num_primary_key_atts`

The number of primary key fields.

`src_pk_att_vals_array`

Values of the primary key fields to be used to look up the local tuple. Each field is represented in text form. An error is thrown if there is no local row with these primary key values.

`tgt_pk_att_vals_array`

Values of the primary key fields to be placed in the resulting `UPDATE` command. Each field is represented in text form.

Return Value

Returns the requested SQL statement as text.

Notes

As of PostgreSQL 9.0, the attribute numbers in `primary_key_attnums` are interpreted as logical column numbers, corresponding to the column's position in `SELECT * FROM relname`. Previous versions interpreted the numbers as physical column positions. There is a difference if any column(s) to the left of the indicated column have been dropped during the lifetime of the table.

Example

```
SELECT dblink_build_sql_update('foo', '1 2', 2, '{"1", "a"}', '{"1", "b"}');
                    dblink_build_sql_update
-------------------------------------------------------------
 UPDATE foo SET f1='1',f2='b',f3='1' WHERE f1='1' AND f2='b'
(1 row)
```

F.9. dict_int

`dict_int` is an example of an add-on dictionary template for full-text search. The motivation for this example dictionary is to control the indexing of integers (signed and unsigned), allowing such numbers to be indexed while preventing excessive growth in the number of unique words, which greatly affects the performance of searching.

F.9.1. Configuration

The dictionary accepts two options:

- The `maxlen` parameter specifies the maximum number of digits allowed in an integer word. The default value is 6.
- The `rejectlong` parameter specifies whether an overlength integer should be truncated or ignored. If `rejectlong` is `false` (the default), the dictionary returns the first `maxlen` digits of the integer. If `rejectlong` is `true`, the dictionary treats an overlength integer as a stop word, so that it will not be indexed. Note that this also means that such an integer cannot be searched for.

F.9.2. Usage

Running the installation script creates a text search template `intdict_template` and a dictionary `intdict` based on it, with the default parameters. You can alter the parameters, for example

```
mydb# ALTER TEXT SEARCH DICTIONARY intdict (MAXLEN = 4, REJECTLONG = true);
ALTER TEXT SEARCH DICTIONARY
```

or create new dictionaries based on the template.

To test the dictionary, you can try

```
mydb# select ts_lexize('intdict', '12345678');
 ts_lexize
-----------
 {123456}
```

but real-world usage will involve including it in a text search configuration as described in *Chapter 12* (Vol.I). That might look like this:

```
ALTER TEXT SEARCH CONFIGURATION english
    ALTER MAPPING FOR int, uint WITH intdict;
```

F.10. dict_xsyn

`dict_xsyn` (Extended Synonym Dictionary) is an example of an add-on dictionary template for full-text search. This dictionary type replaces words with groups of their synonyms, and so makes it possible to search for a word using any of its synonyms.

F.10.1. Configuration

A `dict_xsyn` dictionary accepts the following options:

- `matchorig` controls whether the original word is accepted by the dictionary. Default is `true`.
- `matchsynonyms` controls whether the synonyms are accepted by the dictionary. Default is `false`.
- `keeporig` controls whether the original word is included in the dictionary's output. Default is `true`.
- `keepsynonyms` controls whether the synonyms are included in the dictionary's output. Default is `true`.
- `rules` is the base name of the file containing the list of synonyms. This file must be stored in `$SHAREDIR/tsearch_data/` (where `$SHAREDIR` means the PostgreSQL installation's shared-data directory). Its name must end in `.rules` (which is not to be included in the `rules` parameter).

The rules file has the following format:

- Each line represents a group of synonyms for a single word, which is given first on the line. Synonyms are separated by whitespace, thus:
  ```
  word syn1 syn2 syn3
  ```
- The sharp (`#`) sign is a comment delimiter. It may appear at any position in a line. The rest of the line will be skipped.

Look at `xsyn_sample.rules`, which is installed in `$SHAREDIR/tsearch_data/`, for an example.

F.10.2. Usage

Running the installation script creates a text search template `xsyn_template` and a dictionary `xsyn` based on it, with default parameters. You can alter the parameters, for example

```
mydb# ALTER TEXT SEARCH DICTIONARY xsyn (RULES='my_rules', KEEPORIG=false);
ALTER TEXT SEARCH DICTIONARY
```

or create new dictionaries based on the template.

To test the dictionary, you can try

```
mydb=# SELECT ts_lexize('xsyn', 'word');
      ts_lexize
-----------------------
 {syn1,syn2,syn3}

mydb# ALTER TEXT SEARCH DICTIONARY xsyn (RULES='my_rules', KEEPORIG=true);
ALTER TEXT SEARCH DICTIONARY

mydb=# SELECT ts_lexize('xsyn', 'word');
      ts_lexize
-----------------------
 {word,syn1,syn2,syn3}

mydb# ALTER TEXT SEARCH DICTIONARY xsyn (RULES='my_rules', KEEPORIG=false,
                                                              MATCHSYNONYMS=true);
ALTER TEXT SEARCH DICTIONARY

mydb=# SELECT ts_lexize('xsyn', 'syn1');
      ts_lexize
-----------------------
 {syn1,syn2,syn3}

mydb# ALTER TEXT SEARCH DICTIONARY xsyn (RULES='my_rules', KEEPORIG=true,
                                        MATCHORIG=false, KEEPSYNONYMS=false);
ALTER TEXT SEARCH DICTIONARY

mydb=# SELECT ts_lexize('xsyn', 'syn1');
      ts_lexize
-----------------------
 {word}
```

Real-world usage will involve including it in a text search configuration as described in *Chapter 12* (Vol.I) . That might look like this:

```
ALTER TEXT SEARCH CONFIGURATION english
    ALTER MAPPING FOR word, asciiword WITH xsyn, english_stem;
```

F.11. earthdistance

The `earthdistance` module provides two different approaches to calculating great circle distances on the surface of the Earth. The one described first depends on the `cube` package (which *must* be installed before `earthdistance` can be installed). The second one is based on the built-in `point` datatype, using longitude and latitude for the coordinates.

In this module, the Earth is assumed to be perfectly spherical. (If that's too inaccurate for you, you might want to look at the *PostGIS*[1] project.)

[1] *http://www.postgis.org/*

F.11.1. Cube-based earth distances

Data is stored in cubes that are points (both corners are the same) using 3 coordinates representing the x, y, and z distance from the center of the Earth. A domain `earth` over `cube` is provided, which includes constraint checks that the value meets these restrictions and is reasonably close to the actual surface of the Earth.

The radius of the Earth is obtained from the `earth()` function. It is given in meters. But by changing this one function you can change the module to use some other units, or to use a different value of the radius that you feel is more appropriate.

This package has applications to astronomical databases as well. Astronomers will probably want to change `earth()` to return a radius of `180/pi()` so that distances are in degrees.

Functions are provided to support input in latitude and longitude (in degrees), to support output of latitude and longitude, to calculate the great circle distance between two points and to easily specify a bounding box usable for index searches.

The following functions are provided:

Function	Returns	Description
`earth()`	`float8`	Returns the assumed radius of the Earth.
`sec_to_gc(float8)`	`float8`	Converts the normal straight line (secant) distance between between two points on the surface of the Earth to the great circle distance between them.
`gc_to_sec(float8)`	`float8`	Converts the great circle distance between two points on the surface of the Earth to the normal straight line (secant) distance between them.
`ll_to_earth(float8, float8)`	`earth`	Returns the location of a point on the surface of the Earth given its latitude (argument 1) and longitude (argument 2) in degrees.
`latitude(earth)`	`float8`	Returns the latitude in degrees of a point on the surface of the Earth.
`longitude(earth)`	`float8`	Returns the longitude in degrees of a point on the surface of the Earth.
`earth_distance(earth, earth)`	`float8`	Returns the great circle distance between two points on the surface of the Earth.
`earth_box(earth, float8)`	`cube`	Returns a box suitable for an indexed search using the cube `@>` operator for points within a given great circle distance of a location. Some points in this box are further than the specified great circle distance from the location, so a second check using `earth_distance` should be included in the query.

Table F-4. Cube-based earthdistance functions

F.11.2. Point-based earth distances

The second part of the module relies on representing Earth locations as values of type `point`, in which the first component is taken to represent longitude in degrees, and the second component is taken to represent latitude in degrees. Points are taken as (longitude, latitude) and not vice versa because longitude is closer to the intuitive idea of x-axis and latitude to y-axis.

A single operator is provided:

Operator	Returns	Description
`point <@> point`	`float8`	Gives the distance in statute miles between two points on the Earth's surface.

Table F-5. Point-based earthdistance operators

Note that unlike the `cube`-based part of the module, units are hardwired here: changing the `earth()` function will not affect the results of this operator.

One disadvantage of the longitude/latitude representation is that you need to be careful about the edge conditions near the poles and near +/- 180 degrees of longitude. The `cube`-based representation avoids these discontinuities.

F.12. fuzzystrmatch

The `fuzzystrmatch` module provides several functions to determine similarities and distance between strings.

> **Caution**
>
> At present, `fuzzystrmatch` does not work well with multibyte encodings (such as UTF-8).

F.12.1. Soundex

The Soundex system is a method of matching similar-sounding names by converting them to the same code. It was initially used by the United States Census in 1880, 1900, and 1910. Note that Soundex is not very useful for non-English names.

The `fuzzystrmatch` module provides two functions for working with Soundex codes:

```
soundex(text) returns text
difference(text, text) returns int
```

The `soundex` function converts a string to its Soundex code. The `difference` function converts two strings to their Soundex codes and then reports the number of matching code positions. Since Soundex codes have four characters, the result ranges from zero to four, with zero being no match and four being an exact match. (Thus, the function is misnamed - `similarity` would have been a better name.)

Here are some usage examples:

```
SELECT soundex('hello world!');

SELECT soundex('Anne'), soundex('Ann'), difference('Anne', 'Ann');
SELECT soundex('Anne'), soundex('Andrew'), difference('Anne', 'Andrew');
SELECT soundex('Anne'), soundex('Margaret'), difference('Anne', 'Margaret');

CREATE TABLE s (nm text);

INSERT INTO s VALUES ('john');
INSERT INTO s VALUES ('joan');
INSERT INTO s VALUES ('wobbly');
INSERT INTO s VALUES ('jack');

SELECT * FROM s WHERE soundex(nm) = soundex('john');

SELECT * FROM s WHERE difference(s.nm, 'john') > 2;
```

F.12.2. Levenshtein

This function calculates the Levenshtein distance between two strings:

```
levenshtein(text source, text target, int ins_cost, int del_cost, int sub_cost) returns int
levenshtein(text source, text target) returns int
```

Both `source` and `target` can be any non-null string, with a maximum of 255 bytes. The cost parameters specify how much to charge for a character insertion, deletion, or substitution, respectively. You can omit the cost parameters, as in the second version of the function; in that case they all default to 1.

Examples:

```
test=# SELECT levenshtein('GUMBO', 'GAMBOL');
 levenshtein
-------------
           2
(1 row)

test=# SELECT levenshtein('GUMBO', 'GAMBOL', 2,1,1);
 levenshtein
-------------
           3
(1 row)
```

F.12.3. Metaphone

Metaphone, like Soundex, is based on the idea of constructing a representative code for an input string. Two strings are then deemed similar if they have the same codes.

This function calculates the metaphone code of an input string:

```
metaphone(text source, int max_output_length) returns text
```

`source` has to be a non-null string with a maximum of 255 characters. `max_output_length` sets the maximum length of the output metaphone code; if longer, the output is truncated to this length.

Example:

```
test=# SELECT metaphone('GUMBO', 4);
 metaphone
-----------
 KM
(1 row)
```

F.12.4. Double Metaphone

The Double Metaphone system computes two "sounds like" strings for a given input string - a "primary" and an "alternate". In most cases they are the same, but for non-English names especially they can be a bit different, depending on pronunciation. These functions compute the primary and alternate codes:

```
dmetaphone(text source) returns text
dmetaphone_alt(text source) returns text
```

There is no length limit on the input strings.

Example:

```
test=# select dmetaphone('gumbo');
 dmetaphone
------------
 KMP
(1 row)
```

F.13. hstore

This module implements the `hstore` data type for storing sets of key/value pairs within a single PostgreSQL value. This can be useful in various scenarios, such as rows with many attributes that are rarely examined, or semi-structured data. Keys and values are simply text strings.

F.13.1. hstore External Representation

The text representation of an `hstore`, used for input and output, includes zero or more *key* => *value* pairs separated by commas. Some examples:

```
k => v
foo => bar, baz => whatever
"1-a" => "anything at all"
```

The order of the pairs is not significant (and may not be reproduced on output). Whitespace between pairs or around the => sign is ignored. Double-quote keys and values that include whitespace, commas, =s or >s. To include a double quote or a backslash in a key or value, escape it with a backslash.

Each key in an `hstore` is unique. If you declare an `hstore` with duplicate keys, only one will be stored in the `hstore` and there is no guarantee as to which will be kept:

```
SELECT 'a=>1,a=>2'::hstore;
  hstore
----------
 "a"=>"1"
```

A value (but not a key) can be an SQL `NULL`. For example:

```
key => NULL
```

The `NULL` keyword is case-insensitive. Double-quote the `NULL` to treat it as the ordinary string "NULL".

Note

Keep in mind that the `hstore` text format, when used for input, applies *before* any required quoting or escaping. If you are passing an `hstore` literal via a parameter, then no additional processing is needed. But if you're passing it as a quoted literal constant, then any single-quote characters and (depending on the setting of the `standard_conforming_strings` configuration parameter) backslash characters need to be escaped correctly. See *Section 4.1.2.1* (Vol.II) for more on the handling of string constants.

On output, double quotes always surround keys and values, even when it's not strictly necessary.

F.13.2. hstore Operators and Functions

<table>
<tr><th>Operator</th><th>Description</th><th>Example</th><th>Result</th></tr>
<tr><td><code>hstore -> text</code></td><td>get value for key (<code>NULL</code> if not present)</td><td><code>'a=>x, b=>y'::hstore -> 'a'</code></td><td><code>x</code></td></tr>
<tr><td><code>hstore -> text[]</code></td><td>get values for keys (<code>NULL</code> if not present)</td><td><code>'a=>x, b=>y, c=>z'::hstore -> ARRAY['c','a']</code></td><td><code>{"z","x"}</code></td></tr>
<tr><td><code>text => text</code></td><td>make single-pair <code>hstore</code></td><td><code>'a' => 'b'</code></td><td><code>"a"=>"b"</code></td></tr>
<tr><td><code>hstore || hstore</code></td><td>concatenate <code>hstore</code>s</td><td><code>'a=>b, c=>d'::hstore || 'c=>x, d=>q'::hstore</code></td><td><code>"a"=>"b", "c"=>"x", "d"=>"q"</code></td></tr>
<tr><td><code>hstore ? text</code></td><td>does <code>hstore</code> contain key?</td><td><code>'a=>1'::hstore ? 'a'</code></td><td><code>t</code></td></tr>
<tr><td><code>hstore ?& text[]</code></td><td>does <code>hstore</code> contain all specified keys?</td><td><code>'a=>1,b=>2'::hstore ?& ARRAY['a','b']</code></td><td><code>t</code></td></tr>
</table>

<table>
<tr><th>Operator</th><th>Description</th><th>Example</th><th>Result</th></tr>
<tr><td>hstore ?| text[]</td><td>does hstore contain any of the specified keys?</td><td>'a=>1,b=>2'::hstore ?| ARRAY['b','c']</td><td>t</td></tr>
<tr><td>hstore @> hstore</td><td>does left operand contain right?</td><td>'a=>b, b=>1, c=>NULL'::hstore @> 'b=>1'</td><td>t</td></tr>
<tr><td>hstore <@ hstore</td><td>is left operand contained in right?</td><td>'a=>c'::hstore <@ 'a=>b, b=>1, c=>NULL'</td><td>f</td></tr>
<tr><td>hstore - text</td><td>delete key from left operand</td><td>'a=>1, b=>2, c=>3'::hstore - 'b'::text</td><td>"a"=>"1", "c"=>"3"</td></tr>
<tr><td>hstore - text[]</td><td>delete keys from left operand</td><td>'a=>1, b=>2, c=>3'::hstore - ARRAY['a','b']</td><td>"c"=>"3"</td></tr>
<tr><td>hstore - hstore</td><td>delete matching pairs from left operand</td><td>'a=>1, b=>2, c=>3'::hstore - 'a=>4, b=>2'::hstore</td><td>"a"=>"1", "c"=>"3"</td></tr>
<tr><td>record #= hstore</td><td>replace fields in record with matching values from hstore</td><td>see Examples section</td><td></td></tr>
<tr><td>%% hstore</td><td>convert hstore to array of alternating keys and values</td><td>%% 'a=>foo, b=>bar'::hstore</td><td>{a,foo,b,bar}</td></tr>
<tr><td>%# hstore</td><td>convert hstore to two-dimensional key/value array</td><td>%# 'a=>foo, b=>bar'::hstore</td><td>{{a,foo},{b,bar}}</td></tr>
</table>

Table F-6. hstore Operators

Note

Prior to PostgreSQL 8.2, the containment operators @> and <@ were called @ and ~, respectively. These names are still available, but are deprecated and will eventually be removed. Notice that the old names are reversed from the convention formerly followed by the core geometric data types!

Note

The => operator is deprecated and may be removed in a future release. Use the `hstore(text, text)` function instead.

<table>
<tr><th>Function</th><th>Return Type</th><th>Description</th><th>Example</th><th>Result</th></tr>
<tr><td>hstore(record)</td><td>hstore</td><td>construct an hstore from a record or row</td><td>hstore(ROW(1,2))</td><td>f1=>1, f2=>2</td></tr>
<tr><td>hstore(text[])</td><td>hstore</td><td>construct an hstore from an array, which may</td><td>hstore(ARRAY['a', '1','b','2']) || hstore(ARRAY[['c', '3'],['d','4']])</td><td>a=>1, b=>2, c=>3, d=>4</td></tr>
</table>

Function	Return Type	Description	Example	Result
		be either a key/value array, or a two-dimensional array		
`hstore (text[], text[])`	`hstore`	construct an `hstore` from separate key and value arrays	`hstore(ARRAY['a', 'b'],ARRAY['1','2'])`	`"a"=>"1", "b"=>"2"`
`hstore(text, text)`	`hstore`	make single-item `hstore`	`hstore('a', 'b')`	`"a"=>"b"`
`akeys(hstore)`	`text[]`	get `hstore`'s keys as an array	`akeys('a=>1,b=>2')`	`{a,b}`
`skeys(hstore)`	`setof text`	get `hstore`'s keys as a set	`skeys('a=>1,b=>2')`	`a` `b`
`avals(hstore)`	`text[]`	get `hstore`'s values as an array	`avals('a=>1,b=>2')`	`{1,2}`
`svals(hstore)`	`setof text`	get `hstore`'s values as a set	`svals('a=>1,b=>2')`	`1` `2`
`hstore_to_array (hstore)`	`text[]`	get `hstore`'s keys and values as an array of alternating keys and values	`hstore_to_array ('a=>1,b=>2')`	`{a,1, b,2}`
`hstore_to_matrix (hstore)`	`text[]`	get `hstore`'s keys and values as a two-dimensional array	`hstore_to_matrix ('a=>1,b=>2')`	`{{a,1}, {b,2}}`
`slice (hstore, text[])`	`hstore`	extract a subset of an `hstore`	`slice('a=>1,b=>2, c=>3'::hstore, ARRAY['b','c','x'])`	`"b"=>"2", "c"=>"3"`

`each(hstore)`	`setof(key text, value text)`	get `hstore`'s keys and values as a set	`select * from each('a=>1,b=>2')`	`key|value`
				`---+-----`
				` a | 1`
				` b | 2`

`exist(hstore,text)`	`boolean`	does `hstore` contain key?	`exist('a=>1','a')`	`t`
`defined(hstore,text)`	`boolean`	does `hstore` contain non-`NULL` value for key?	`defined('a=>NULL','a')`	`f`
`delete(hstore,text)`	`hstore`	delete pair with matching key	`delete ('a=>1,b=>2','b')`	`"a"=>"1"`
`delete (hstore,text[])`	`hstore`	delete pairs with matching keys	`delete('a=>1,b=>2, c=>3',ARRAY['a','b'])`	`"c"=>"3"`

Function	Return Type	Description	Example	Result
`delete (hstore,hstore)`	`hstore`	delete pairs matching those in the second argument	`delete('a=>1,b=>2', 'a=>4,b=>2'::hstore)`	`"a"=>"1"`
`populate_record (record,hstore)`	`record`	replace fields in `record` with matching values from `hstore`	see Examples section	

Table F-7. `hstore` Functions

> **Note**
>
> The function `populate_record` is actually declared with `anyelement`, not `record`, as its first argument, but it will reject non-record types with a run-time error.

F.13.3. Indexes

`hstore` has GiST and GIN index support for the `@>`, `?`, `?&` and `?|` operators. For example:

```
CREATE INDEX hidx ON testhstore USING GIST (h);

CREATE INDEX hidx ON testhstore USING GIN (h);
```

`hstore` also supports `btree` or `hash` indexes for the `=` operator. This allows `hstore` columns to be declared `UNIQUE`, or to be used in `GROUP BY`, `ORDER BY` or `DISTINCT` expressions. The sort ordering for `hstore` values is not particularly useful, but these indexes may be useful for equivalence lookups. Create indexes for `=` comparisons as follows:

```
CREATE INDEX hidx ON testhstore USING BTREE (h);

CREATE INDEX hidx ON testhstore USING HASH (h);
```

F.13.4. Examples

Add a key, or update an existing key with a new value:

```
UPDATE tab SET h = h || ('c' => '3');
```

Delete a key:

```
UPDATE tab SET h = delete(h, 'k1');
```

Convert a `record` to an `hstore`:

```
CREATE TABLE test (col1 integer, col2 text, col3 text);
INSERT INTO test VALUES (123, 'foo', 'bar');

SELECT hstore(t) FROM test AS t;
                   hstore
---------------------------------------------
 "col1"=>"123", "col2"=>"foo", "col3"=>"bar"
(1 row)
```

Convert an `hstore` to a predefined `record` type:

```
CREATE TABLE test (col1 integer, col2 text, col3 text);

SELECT * FROM populate_record(null::test,
                              '"col1"=>"456", "col2"=>"zzz"');
 col1 | col2 | col3
------+------+------
  456 | zzz  |
(1 row)
```

Modify an existing record using the values from an `hstore`:

```
CREATE TABLE test (col1 integer, col2 text, col3 text);
INSERT INTO test VALUES (123, 'foo', 'bar');

SELECT (r).* FROM (SELECT t #= '"col3"=>"baz"' AS r FROM test t) s;
 col1 | col2 | col3
------+------+------
  123 | foo  | baz
(1 row)
```

F.13.5. Statistics

The `hstore` type, because of its intrinsic liberality, could contain a lot of different keys. Checking for valid keys is the task of the application. The following examples demonstrate several techniques for checking keys and obtaining statistics.

Simple example:

```
SELECT * FROM each('aaa=>bq, b=>NULL, ""=>1');
```

Using a table:

```
SELECT (each(h)).key, (each(h)).value INTO stat FROM testhstore;
```

Online statistics:

```
SELECT key, count(*) FROM
  (SELECT (each(h)).key FROM testhstore) AS stat
  GROUP BY key
  ORDER BY count DESC, key;
    key     | count
-----------+-------
 line      |   883
 query     |   207
 pos       |   203
 node      |   202
 space     |   197
 status    |   195
 public    |   194
 title     |   190
 org       |   189
...................
```

F.13.6. Compatibility

When upgrading from older versions, always load the new version of this module into the database before restoring a dump. Otherwise, many new features will be unavailable.

As of PostgreSQL 9.0, `hstore` uses a different internal representation than previous versions. This presents no obstacle for dump/restore upgrades since the text representation (used in the dump) is unchanged.

In the event of a binary upgrade, upward compatibility is maintained by having the new code recognize old-format data. This will entail a slight performance penalty when processing data that has not yet been modified by the new code. It is possible to force an upgrade of all values in a table column by doing an `UPDATE` statement as follows:

```
UPDATE tablename SET hstorecol = hstorecol || '';
```

Another way to do it is:

```
ALTER TABLE tablename ALTER hstorecol TYPE hstore USING hstorecol || '';
```

The `ALTER TABLE` method requires an exclusive lock on the table, but does not result in bloating the table with old row versions.

F.13.7. Authors

Oleg Bartunov *<oleg@sai.msu.su>*, Moscow, Moscow University, Russia

Teodor Sigaev *<teodor@sigaev.ru>*, Moscow, Delta-Soft Ltd., Russia

Additional enhancements by Andrew Gierth *<andrew@tao11.riddles.org.uk>*, United Kingdom

F.14. intagg

The `intagg` module provides an integer aggregator and an enumerator. `intagg` is now obsolete, because there are built-in functions that provide a superset of its capabilities. However, the module is still provided as a compatibility wrapper around the built-in functions.

F.14.1. Functions

The aggregator is an aggregate function `int_array_aggregate(integer)` that produces an integer array containing exactly the integers it is fed. This is a wrapper around `array_agg`, which does the same thing for any array type.

The enumerator is a function `int_array_enum(integer[])` that returns `setof integer`. It is essentially the reverse operation of the aggregator: given an array of integers, expand it into a set of rows. This is a wrapper around `unnest`, which does the same thing for any array type.

F.14.2. Sample Uses

Many database systems have the notion of a one to many table. Such a table usually sits between two indexed tables, for example:

```
CREATE TABLE left (id INT PRIMARY KEY, ...);
CREATE TABLE right (id INT PRIMARY KEY, ...);
CREATE TABLE one_to_many(left INT REFERENCES left, right INT REFERENCES right);
```

It is typically used like this:

```
SELECT right.* from right JOIN one_to_many ON (right.id = one_to_many.right)
  WHERE one_to_many.left = item;
```

This will return all the items in the right hand table for an entry in the left hand table. This is a very common construct in SQL.

Now, this methodology can be cumbersome with a very large number of entries in the `one_to_many` table. Often, a join like this would result in an index scan and a fetch for each right hand entry in the table for a particular left hand entry. If you have a very dynamic system, there is not much you can do. However, if you have some data which is fairly static, you can create a summary table with the aggregator.

```
CREATE TABLE summary AS
  SELECT left, int_array_aggregate(right) AS right
  FROM one_to_many
  GROUP BY left;
```

This will create a table with one row per left item, and an array of right items. Now this is pretty useless without some way of using the array; that's why there is an array enumerator. You can do

```
SELECT left, int_array_enum(right) FROM summary WHERE left = item;
```

The above query using `int_array_enum` produces the same results as

```
SELECT left, right FROM one_to_many WHERE left = item;
```

The difference is that the query against the summary table has to get only one row from the table, whereas the direct query against `one_to_many` must index scan and fetch a row for each entry.

On one system, an `EXPLAIN` showed a query with a cost of 8488 was reduced to a cost of 329. The original query was a join involving the `one_to_many` table, which was replaced by:

```
SELECT right, count(right) FROM
  (SELECT left, int_array_enum(right) AS right
    FROM summary JOIN (SELECT left FROM left_table WHERE left = item) AS lefts
         ON (summary.left = lefts.left)
  ) AS list
  GROUP BY right
  ORDER BY count DESC;
```

F.15. intarray

The `intarray` module provides a number of useful functions and operators for manipulating one-dimensional arrays of integers. There is also support for indexed searches using some of the operators.

F.15.1. `intarray` Functions and Operators

Function	Return Type	Description	Example	Result
`icount(int[])`	`int`	number of elements in array	`icount('{1,2,3}'::int[])`	`3`
`sort(int[], text dir)`	`int[]`	sort array - `dir` must be `asc` or `desc`	`sort('{1,2,3}'::int[], 'desc')`	`{3,2,1}`
`sort(int[])`	`int[]`	sort in ascending order	`sort(array[11,77,44])`	`{11,44,77}`
`sort_asc(int[])`	`int[]`	sort in ascending order		
`sort_desc(int[])`	`int[]`	sort in descending order		
`uniq(int[])`	`int[]`	remove adjacent duplicates	`uniq(sort('{1,2,3,2,1}'::int[]))`	`{1,2,3}`
`idx(int[], int item)`	`int`	index of first element matching `item` (0 if none)	`idx(array[11,22,33,22,11], 22)`	`2`
`subarray(int[], int start, int len)`	`int[]`	portion of array starting at position `start`, len `elements`	`subarray('{1,2,3,2,1}'::int[], 2, 3)`	`{2,3,2}`
`subarray(int[], int start)`	`int[]`	portion of array starting at position `start`	`subarray('{1,2,3,2,1}'::int[], 2)`	`{2,3,2,1}`
`intset(int)`	`int[]`	make single-element array	`intset(42)`	`{42}`

Table F-8. `intarray` Functions

Operator	Returns	Description
`int[] && int[]`	`boolean`	overlap - `true` if arrays have at least one common element
`int[] @> int[]`	`boolean`	contains - `true` if left array contains right array
`int[] <@ int[]`	`boolean`	contained - `true` if left array is contained in right array
`# int[]`	`int`	number of elements in array
`int[] # int`	`int`	index (same as `idx` function)
`int[] + int`	`int[]`	push element onto array (add it to end of array)
`int[] + int[]`	`int[]`	array concatenation (right array added to the end of left one)
`int[] - int`	`int[]`	remove entries matching right argument from array
`int[] - int[]`	`int[]`	remove elements of right array from left

<table>
<tr><th>Operator</th><th>Returns</th><th>Description</th></tr>
<tr><td><code>int[] | int</code></td><td><code>int[]</code></td><td>union of arguments</td></tr>
<tr><td><code>int[] | int[]</code></td><td><code>int[]</code></td><td>union of arrays</td></tr>
<tr><td><code>int[] & int[]</code></td><td><code>int[]</code></td><td>intersection of arrays</td></tr>
<tr><td><code>int[] @@ query_int</code></td><td><code>boolean</code></td><td><code>true</code> if array satisfies query (see below)</td></tr>
<tr><td><code>query_int ~~ int[]</code></td><td><code>boolean</code></td><td><code>true</code> if array satisfies query (commutator of <code>@@</code>)</td></tr>
</table>

Table F-9. `intarray` Operators

(Before PostgreSQL 8.2, the containment operators `@>` and `<@` were respectively called `@` and `~`. These names are still available, but are deprecated and will eventually be retired. Notice that the old names are reversed from the convention formerly followed by the core geometric datatypes!)

The containment operators `@>` and `<@` are approximately equivalent to PostgreSQL's built-in operators of the same names, except that they work only on integer arrays while the built-in operators work for any array type. An important difference is that `intarray`'s operators do not consider an empty array to be contained in anything else. This is consistent with the behavior of GIN-indexed queries, but not with the usual mathematical definition of containment.

The `@@` and `~~` operators test whether an array satisfies a *query* , which is expressed as a value of a specialized data type `query_int`. A *query* consists of integer values that are checked against the elements of the array, possibly combined using the operators `&` (AND), `|` (OR), and `!` (NOT). Parentheses can be used as needed. For example, the query `1&(2|3)` matches arrays that contain 1 and also contain either 2 or 3.

F.15.2. Index Support

`intarray` provides index support for the `&&`, `@>`, `<@`, and `@@` operators, as well as regular array equality.

Two GiST index operator classes are provided: `gist__int_ops` (used by default) is suitable for small- to medium-size data sets, while `gist__intbig_ops` uses a larger signature and is more suitable for indexing large data sets (i.e., columns containing a large number of distinct array values). The implementation uses an RD-tree data structure with built-in lossy compression.

There is also a non-default GIN operator class `gin__int_ops` supporting the same operators.

The choice between GiST and GIN indexing depends on the relative performance characteristics of GiST and GIN, which are discussed elsewhere. As a rule of thumb, a GIN index is faster to search than a GiST index, but slower to build or update; so GIN is better suited for static data and GiST for often-updated data.

F.15.3. Example

```
-- a message can be in one or more

"sections"
CREATE TABLE message (mid INT PRIMARY KEY, sections INT[], ...);

-- create specialized index
CREATE INDEX message_rdtree_idx ON message USING GIST (sections gist__int_ops);

-- select messages in section 1 OR 2 - OVERLAP operator
SELECT message.mid FROM message WHERE message.sections && '{1,2}';

-- select messages in sections 1 AND 2 - CONTAINS operator
SELECT message.mid FROM message WHERE message.sections @> '{1,2}';

-- the same, using QUERY operator
SELECT message.mid FROM message WHERE message.sections @@ '1&2'::query_int;
```

F.15.4. Benchmark

The source directory `contrib/intarray/bench` contains a benchmark test suite. To run:

```
cd .../bench
createdb TEST
psql TEST < ../_int.sql
./create_test.pl | psql TEST
./bench.pl
```

The `bench.pl` script has numerous options, which are displayed when it is run without any arguments.

F.15.5. Authors

All work was done by Teodor Sigaev (<*teodor@sigaev.ru*>) and Oleg Bartunov (<*oleg@sai.msu.su*>). See *http://www.sai.msu.su/~megera/postgres/gist/* for additional information. Andrey Oktyabrski did a great work on adding new functions and operations.

F.16. isn

The `isn` module provides data types for the following international product numbering standards: EAN13, UPC, ISBN (books), ISMN (music), and ISSN (serials). Numbers are validated on input, and correctly hyphenated on output.

F.16.1. Data types

Table F-10 (see below) shows the data types provided by the `isn` module.

Data type	Description
`EAN13`	European Article Numbers, always displayed in the EAN13 display format
`ISBN13`	International Standard Book Numbers to be displayed in the new EAN13 display format
`ISMN13`	International Standard Music Numbers to be displayed in the new EAN13 display format
`ISSN13`	International Standard Serial Numbers to be displayed in the new EAN13 display format
`ISBN`	International Standard Book Numbers to be displayed in the old short display format
`ISMN`	International Standard Music Numbers to be displayed in the old short display format
`ISSN`	International Standard Serial Numbers to be displayed in the old short display format
`UPC`	Universal Product Codes

Table F-10. `isn` data types

Some notes:

1. ISBN13, ISMN13, ISSN13 numbers are all EAN13 numbers.
2. EAN13 numbers aren't always ISBN13, ISMN13 or ISSN13 (some are).

Some ISBN13 numbers can be displayed as ISBN.

Some ISMN13 numbers can be displayed as ISMN.

Some ISSN13 numbers can be displayed as ISSN.

UPC numbers are a subset of the EAN13 numbers (they are basically EAN13 without the first `0` digit).

All UPC, ISBN, ISMN and ISSN numbers can be represented as EAN13 numbers.

Internally, all these types use the same representation (a 64-bit integer), and all are interchangeable. Multiple types are provided to control display formatting and to permit tighter validity checking of input that is supposed to denote one particular type of number.

The `ISBN`, `ISMN`, and `ISSN` types will display the short version of the number (ISxN 10) whenever it's possible, and will show ISxN 13 format for numbers that do not fit in the short version. The `EAN13`, `ISBN13`, `ISMN13` and `ISSN13` types will always display the long version of the ISxN (EAN13).

F.16.2. Casts

The `isn` module provides the following pairs of type casts:

- ISBN13 <=> EAN13
- ISMN13 <=> EAN13
- ISSN13 <=> EAN13
- ISBN <=> EAN13
- ISMN <=> EAN13

- ISSN <=> EAN13
- UPC <=> EAN13
- ISBN <=> ISBN13
- ISMN <=> ISMN13
- ISSN <=> ISSN13

When casting from `EAN13` to another type, there is a run-time check that the value is within the domain of the other type, and an error is thrown if not. The other casts are simply relabelings that will always succeed.

F.16.3. Functions and Operators

The `isn` module provides the standard comparison operators, plus B-tree and hash indexing support for all these datatypes. In addition there are several specialized functions; shown in *Table F-11* (see below). In this table, `isn` means any one of the module's data types.

Function	Returns	Description
`isn_weak(boolean)`	`boolean`	Sets the weak input mode (returns new setting)
`isn_weak()`	`boolean`	Gets the current status of the weak mode
`make_valid(isn)`	`isn`	Validates an invalid number (clears the invalid flag)
`is_valid(isn)`	`boolean`	Checks for the presence of the invalid flag

Table F-11. `isn` functions

Weak mode is used to be able to insert invalid data into a table. Invalid means the check digit is wrong, not that there are missing numbers.

Why would you want to use the weak mode? Well, it could be that you have a huge collection of ISBN numbers, and that there are so many of them that for weird reasons some have the wrong check digit (perhaps the numbers were scanned from a printed list and the OCR got the numbers wrong, perhaps the numbers were manually captured... who knows). Anyway, the point is you might want to clean the mess up, but you still want to be able to have all the numbers in your database and maybe use an external tool to locate the invalid numbers in the database so you can verify the information and validate it more easily; so for example you'd want to select all the invalid numbers in the table.

When you insert invalid numbers in a table using the weak mode, the number will be inserted with the corrected check digit, but it will be displayed with an exclamation mark (`!`) at the end, for example `0-11-000322-5!`. This invalid marker can be checked with the `is_valid` function and cleared with the `make_valid` function.

You can also force the insertion of invalid numbers even when not in the weak mode, by appending the `!` character at the end of the number.

Another special feature is that during input, you can write ? in place of the check digit, and the correct check digit will be inserted automatically.

F.16.4. Examples

```
--Using the types directly:
SELECT isbn('978-0-393-04002-9');
SELECT isbn13('0901690546');
SELECT issn('1436-4522');

--Casting types:
-- note that you can only cast from ean13 to another type when the
-- number would be valid in the realm of the target type;
-- thus, the following will NOT work: select isbn(ean13('0220356483481'));
-- but these will:
SELECT upc(ean13('0220356483481'));
SELECT ean13(upc('220356483481'));

--Create a table with a single column to hold ISBN numbers:
CREATE TABLE test (id isbn);
INSERT INTO test VALUES('9780393040029');

--Automatically calculate check digits (observe the '?'):
INSERT INTO test VALUES('220500896?');
INSERT INTO test VALUES('978055215372?');

SELECT issn('3251231?');
SELECT ismn('979047213542?');

--Using the weak mode:
SELECT isn_weak(true);
INSERT INTO test VALUES('978-0-11-000533-4');
INSERT INTO test VALUES('9780141219307');
INSERT INTO test VALUES('2-205-00876-X');
SELECT isn_weak(false);

SELECT id FROM test WHERE NOT is_valid(id);
UPDATE test SET id = make_valid(id) WHERE id = '2-205-00876-X!';

SELECT * FROM test;

SELECT isbn13(id) FROM test;
```

F.16.5. Bibliography

The information to implement this module was collected from several sites, including:

- *http://www.isbn-international.org/*
- *http://www.issn.org/*
- *http://www.ismn-international.org/*
- *http://www.wikipedia.org/*

The prefixes used for hyphenation were also compiled from:

- *http://www.gs1.org/productssolutions/idkeys/support/prefix_list.html*
- *http://www.isbn-international.org/en/identifiers.html*
- *http://www.ismn-international.org/ranges.html*

Care was taken during the creation of the algorithms and they were meticulously verified against the suggested algorithms in the official ISBN, ISMN, ISSN User Manuals.

F.16.6. Author

German Mendez Bravo (Kronuz), 2004 - 2006

This module was inspired by Garrett A. Wollman's isbn_issn code.

F.17. lo

The `lo` module provides support for managing Large Objects (also called LOs or BLOBs). This includes a data type `lo` and a trigger `lo_manage`.

F.17.1. Rationale

One of the problems with the JDBC driver (and this affects the ODBC driver also), is that the specification assumes that references to BLOBs (Binary Large OBjects) are stored within a table, and if that entry is changed, the associated BLOB is deleted from the database.

As PostgreSQL stands, this doesn't occur. Large objects are treated as objects in their own right; a table entry can reference a large object by OID, but there can be multiple table entries referencing the same large object OID, so the system doesn't delete the large object just because you change or remove one such entry.

Now this is fine for PostgreSQL-specific applications, but standard code using JDBC or ODBC won't delete the objects, resulting in orphan objects - objects that are not referenced by anything, and simply occupy disk space.

The `lo` module allows fixing this by attaching a trigger to tables that contain LO reference columns. The trigger essentially just does a `lo_unlink` whenever you delete or modify a value referencing a large object. When you use this trigger, you are assuming that there is only one database reference to any large object that is referenced in a trigger-controlled column!

The module also provides a data type `lo`, which is really just a domain of the `oid` type. This is useful for differentiating database columns that hold large object references from those that are OIDs of other things. You don't have to use the `lo` type to use the trigger, but it may be convenient to use it to keep track of which columns in your database represent large objects that you are managing with the trigger. It is also rumored that the ODBC driver gets confused if you don't use `lo` for BLOB columns.

F.17.2. How to Use It

Here's a simple example of usage:

```
CREATE TABLE image (title TEXT, raster lo);

CREATE TRIGGER t_raster BEFORE UPDATE OR DELETE ON image
  FOR EACH ROW EXECUTE PROCEDURE lo_manage(raster);
```

For each column that will contain unique references to large objects, create a `BEFORE UPDATE OR DELETE` trigger, and give the column name as the sole trigger argument. If you need multiple `lo` columns in the same table, create a separate trigger for each one, remembering to give a different name to each trigger on the same table.

F.17.3. Limitations

- Dropping a table will still orphan any objects it contains, as the trigger is not executed. You can avoid this by preceding the `DROP TABLE` with `DELETE FROM` *`table`*.

  `TRUNCATE` has the same hazard.

  If you already have, or suspect you have, orphaned large objects, see the `contrib/vacuumlo` module (*Section F.41* - page 433) to help you clean them up. It's a good idea to run vacuumlo occasionally as a back-stop to the `lo_manage` trigger.
- Some frontends may create their own tables, and will not create the associated trigger(s). Also, users may not remember (or know) to create the triggers.

F.17.4. Author

Peter Mount *<peter@retep.org.uk>*

F.18. ltree

This module implements a data type `ltree` for representing labels of data stored in a hierarchical tree-like structure. Extensive facilities for searching through label trees are provided.

F.18.1. Definitions

A *label* is a sequence of alphanumeric characters and underscores (for example, in C locale the characters `A-Za-z0-9_` are allowed). Labels must be less than 256 bytes long.

Examples: `42`, `Personal_Services`

A *label path* is a sequence of zero or more labels separated by dots, for example `L1.L2.L3`, representing a path from the root of a hierarchical tree to a particular node. The length of a label path must be less than 65Kb, but keeping it under 2Kb is preferable. In practice this is not a major limitation; for example, the longest label path in the DMOZ catalogue (*http://www.dmoz.org*) is about 240 bytes.

Example: `Top.Countries.Europe.Russia`

The `ltree` module provides several datatypes:

- `ltree` stores a label path.
- `lquery` represents a regular-expression-like pattern for matching `ltree` values. A simple word matches that label within a path. A star symbol (`*`) matches zero or more labels. For example:

  ```
  foo         Match the exact label path foo
  *.foo.*     Match any label path containing the label foo
  *.foo       Match any label path whose last label is foo
  ```

  Star symbols can also be quantified to restrict how many labels they can match:

  ```
  *{n}        Match exactly n labels
  *{n,}       Match at least n labels
  *{n,m}      Match at least n but not more than m labels
  *{,m}       Match at most m labels - same as  *{0,m}
  ```

  There are several modifiers that can be put at the end of a non-star label in `lquery` to make it match more than just the exact match:

  ```
  @           Match case-insensitively, for example a@ matches A
  *           Match any label with this prefix, for example foo* matches foobar
  %           Match initial underscore-separated words
  ```

  The behavior of `%` is a bit complicated. It tries to match words rather than the entire label. For example `foo_bar%` matches `foo_bar_baz` but not `foo_barbaz`. If combined with `*`, prefix matching applies to each word separately, for example `foo_bar%*` matches `foo1_bar2_baz` but not `foo1_br2_baz`.

  Also, you can write several possibly-modified labels separated with `|` (OR) to match any of those labels, and you can put `!` (NOT) at the start to match any label that doesn't match any of the alternatives.

  Here's an annotated example of `lquery`:

  ```
      Top.*{0,2}.sport*@.!football|tennis.Russ*|Spain
      a.  b.     c.      d.                e.
  ```

  This query will match any label path that:

  - begins with the label `Top`
  - and next has zero to two labels before
  - a label beginning with the case-insensitive prefix `sport`

  - then a label not matching `football` nor `tennis`
  - and then ends with a label beginning with `Russ` or exactly matching `Spain`.

- `ltxtquery` represents a full-text-search-like pattern for matching `ltree` values. An `ltxtquery` value contains words, possibly with the modifiers `@`, `*`, `%` at the end; the modifiers have the same meanings as in `lquery` . Words can be combined with `&` (AND), `|` (OR), `!` (NOT), and parentheses. The key difference from `lquery` is that `ltxtquery` matches words without regard to their position in the label path.

  Here's an example `ltxtquery`:

  ```
  Europe & Russia*@ & !Transportation
  ```

  This will match paths that contain the label `Europe` and any label beginning with `Russia` (case-insensitive), but not paths containing the label `Transportation`. The location of these words within the path is not important. Also, when `%` is used, the word can be matched to any underscore-separated word within a label, regardless of position.

Note

`ltxtquery` allows whitespace between symbols, but `ltree` and `lquery` do not.

F.18.2. Operators and Functions

Type `ltree` has the usual comparison operators =, <>, <, >, <=, >=. Comparison sorts in the order of a tree traversal, with the children of a node sorted by label text. In addition, there are the following specialized operators:

Operator	Returns	Description
`ltree @> ltree`	`boolean`	is left argument an ancestor of right (or equal)?
`ltree <@ ltree`	`boolean`	is left argument a descendant of right (or equal)?
`ltree ~ lquery`	`boolean`	does `ltree` match `lquery`?
`lquery ~ ltree`	`boolean`	does `ltree` match `lquery`?
`ltree ? lquery[]`	`boolean`	does `ltree` match any `lquery` in array?
`lquery[] ? ltree`	`boolean`	does `ltree` match any `lquery` in array?
`ltree @ ltxtquery`	`boolean`	does `ltree` match `ltxtquery`?
`ltxtquery @ ltree`	`boolean`	does `ltree` match `ltxtquery`?
`ltree || ltree`	`ltree`	concatenate `ltree` paths
`ltree || text`	`ltree`	convert text to `ltree` and concatenate
`text || ltree`	`ltree`	convert text to `ltree` and concatenate
`ltree[] @> ltree`	`boolean`	does array contain an ancestor of `ltree`?

Operator	Returns	Description
`ltree<@ltree[]`	boolean	does array contain an ancestor of `ltree`?
`ltree[] <@ltree`	boolean	does array contain a descendant of `ltree`?
`ltree@>ltree[]`	boolean	does array contain a descendant of `ltree`?
`ltree[] ~ lquery`	boolean	does array contain any path matching `lquery`?
`lquery~ltree[]`	boolean	does array contain any path matching `lquery`?
`ltree[] ? lquery[]`	boolean	does `ltree` array contain any path matching any `lquery` ?
`lquery[] ? ltree[]`	boolean	does `ltree` array contain any path matching any `lquery` ?
`ltree[] @ ltxtquery`	boolean	does array contain any path matching `ltxtquery`?
`ltxtquery@ltree[]`	boolean	does array contain any path matching `ltxtquery`?
`ltree[] ?@>ltree`	ltree	first array entry that is an ancestor of `ltree`; NULL if none
`ltree[] ?<@ltree`	ltree	first array entry that is a descendant of `ltree`; NULL if none
`ltree[] ?~lquery`	ltree	first array entry that matches `lquery`; NULL if none
`ltree[] ?@ ltxtquery`	ltree	first array entry that matches `ltxtquery`; NULL if none

Table F-12. `ltree` Operators

The operators `<@`, `@>` , `@` and `~` have analogues `^<@`, `^@>`, `^@`, `^~`, which are the same except they do not use indexes. These are useful only for testing purposes.

The following functions are available:

Function	Return Type	Description	Example	Result
`subltree(ltree, int start, int end)`	ltree	subpath of `ltree` from position `start` to position `end`-1 (counting from 0)	`subltree('Top.Child1.Child2',1,2)`	Child1
`subpath(ltree, int offset, int len)`	ltree	subpath of `ltree` starting at position `offset`, length `len`. If `offset` is negative, subpath starts that far from the end of the path. If `len` is negative, leaves that many labels off the end of the path.	`subpath('Top.Child1.Child2',0,2)`	Top.Child1
`subpath(ltree, int offset)`	ltree	subpath of `ltree` starting at position `offset`, extending to end of path. If `offset` is negative, subpath starts that far from the end of the path.	`subpath('Top.Child1.Child2',1)`	Child1.Child2
`nlevel(ltree)`	integer	number of labels in path	`nlevel('Top.Child1.Child2')`	3

Function	Return Type	Description	Example	Result
`index(ltree a, ltree b)`	`integer`	position of first occurrence of `b` in `a`; -1 if not found	`index('0.1.2.3.5.4.5.6.8.5.6.8','5.6')`	`6`
`index(ltree a, ltree b, int offset)`	`integer`	position of first occurrence of `b` in `a`, searching starting at `offset`; negative `offset` means start `-offset` labels from the end of the path	`index('0.1.2.3.5.4.5.6.8.5.6.8','5.6',-4)`	`9`
`text2ltree(text)`	`ltree`	cast `text` to `ltree`		
`ltree2text(ltree)`	`text`	cast `ltree` to `text`		
`lca(ltree, ltree, ...)`	`ltree`	lowest common ancestor, i.e., longest common prefix of paths (up to 8 arguments supported)	`lca('1.2.2.3','1.2.3.4.5.6')`	`1.2`
`lca(ltree[])`	`ltree`	lowest common ancestor, i.e., longest common prefix of paths	`lca(array['1.2.2.3'::ltree,'1.2.3'])`	`1.2`

Table F-13. `ltree` Functions

F.18.3. Indexes

`ltree` supports several types of indexes that can speed up the indicated operators:

- B-tree index over `ltree`: `<`, `<=`, `=`, `>=`, `>`
- GiST index over `ltree`: `<`, `<=`, `=`, `>=`, `>`, `@>`, `<@`, `@`, `~`, `?`

  Example of creating such an index:

  ```
  CREATE INDEX path_gist_idx ON test USING GIST (path);
  ```

- GiST index over ltree[]: `ltree[] <@ ltree`, `ltree @> ltree[]`, `@`, `~`, `?`

  Example of creating such an index:

  ```
  CREATE INDEX path_gist_idx ON test USING GIST (array_path);
  ```

Note

This index type is lossy.

F.18.4. Example

This example uses the following data (also available in file `contrib/ltree/ltreetest.sql` in the source distribution):

```
CREATE TABLE test (path ltree);
INSERT INTO test VALUES ('Top');
```

```
INSERT INTO test VALUES ('Top.Science');
INSERT INTO test VALUES ('Top.Science.Astronomy');
INSERT INTO test VALUES ('Top.Science.Astronomy.Astrophysics');
INSERT INTO test VALUES ('Top.Science.Astronomy.Cosmology');
INSERT INTO test VALUES ('Top.Hobbies');
INSERT INTO test VALUES ('Top.Hobbies.Amateurs_Astronomy');
INSERT INTO test VALUES ('Top.Collections');
INSERT INTO test VALUES ('Top.Collections.Pictures');
INSERT INTO test VALUES ('Top.Collections.Pictures.Astronomy');
INSERT INTO test VALUES ('Top.Collections.Pictures.Astronomy.Stars');
INSERT INTO test VALUES ('Top.Collections.Pictures.Astronomy.Galaxies');
INSERT INTO test VALUES ('Top.Collections.Pictures.Astronomy.Astronauts');
CREATE INDEX path_gist_idx ON test USING gist(path);
CREATE INDEX path_idx ON test USING btree(path);
```

Now, we have a table `test` populated with data describing the hierarchy shown below:

```
                        Top
                     /   |  \
             Science Hobbies Collections
                 /       |              \
        Astronomy   Amateurs_Astronomy Pictures
           /  \                            |
Astrophysics  Cosmology                Astronomy
                                        /  |    \
                                 Galaxies Stars Astronauts
```

We can do inheritance:

```
ltreetest=> SELECT path FROM test WHERE path <@ 'Top.Science';
                path
------------------------------------
 Top.Science
 Top.Science.Astronomy
 Top.Science.Astronomy.Astrophysics
 Top.Science.Astronomy.Cosmology
(4 rows)
```

Here are some examples of path matching:

```
ltreetest=> SELECT path FROM test WHERE path ~ '*.Astronomy.*';
                     path
-----------------------------------------------
 Top.Science.Astronomy
 Top.Science.Astronomy.Astrophysics
 Top.Science.Astronomy.Cosmology
 Top.Collections.Pictures.Astronomy
 Top.Collections.Pictures.Astronomy.Stars
 Top.Collections.Pictures.Astronomy.Galaxies
 Top.Collections.Pictures.Astronomy.Astronauts
(7 rows)
```

```
ltreetest=> SELECT path FROM test WHERE path ~ '*.!pictures@.*.Astronomy.*';
                path
------------------------------------
```

```
 Top.Science.Astronomy
 Top.Science.Astronomy.Astrophysics
 Top.Science.Astronomy.Cosmology
(3 rows)
```

Here are some examples of full text search:

```
ltreetest=> SELECT path FROM test WHERE path @ 'Astro*% & !pictures@';
                path
------------------------------------
 Top.Science.Astronomy
 Top.Science.Astronomy.Astrophysics
 Top.Science.Astronomy.Cosmology
 Top.Hobbies.Amateurs_Astronomy
(4 rows)

ltreetest=> SELECT path FROM test WHERE path @ 'Astro* & !pictures@';
                path
------------------------------------
 Top.Science.Astronomy
 Top.Science.Astronomy.Astrophysics
 Top.Science.Astronomy.Cosmology
(3 rows)
```

Path construction using functions:

```
ltreetest=> SELECT subpath(path,0,2)||'Space'||subpath(path,2) FROM test
                                            WHERE path <@ 'Top.Science.Astronomy';
                 ?column?
------------------------------------------
 Top.Science.Space.Astronomy
 Top.Science.Space.Astronomy.Astrophysics
 Top.Science.Space.Astronomy.Cosmology
(3 rows)
```

We could simplify this by creating a SQL function that inserts a label at a specified position in a path:

```
CREATE FUNCTION ins_label(ltree, int, text) RETURNS ltree
    AS 'select subpath($1,0,$2) || $3 || subpath($1,$2);'
    LANGUAGE SQL IMMUTABLE;

ltreetest=> SELECT ins_label(path,2,'Space') FROM test
                                            WHERE path <@ 'Top.Science.Astronomy';
                ins_label
------------------------------------------
 Top.Science.Space.Astronomy
 Top.Science.Space.Astronomy.Astrophysics
 Top.Science.Space.Astronomy.Cosmology
(3 rows)
```

F.18.5. Authors

All work was done by Teodor Sigaev (<`teodor@stack.net`>) and Oleg Bartunov (<`oleg@sai.msu.su`>). See *http://www.sai.msu.su/~megera/postgres/gist/* for additional information. Authors would like to thank Eugeny Rodichev for helpful discussions. Comments and bug reports are welcome.

F.19. oid2name

oid2name is a utility program that helps administrators to examine the file structure used by PostgreSQL. To make use of it, you need to be familiar with the database file structure, which is described in *Chapter 54* (page 171).

> **Note**
>
> The name "oid2name" is historical, and is actually rather misleading, since most of the time when you use it, you will really be concerned with tables' filenode numbers (which are the file names visible in the database directories). Be sure you understand the difference between table OIDs and table filenodes!

F.19.1. Overview

oid2name connects to a target database and extracts OID, filenode, and/or table name information. You can also have it show database OIDs or tablespace OIDs.

F.19.2. oid2name Options

oid2name accepts the following command-line arguments:

`-o` *`oid`*

: show info for table with OID *`oid`*

`-f` *`filenode`*

: show info for table with filenode *`filenode`*

`-t` *`tablename_pattern`*

: show info for table(s) matching *`tablename_pattern`*

`-s`

: show tablespace OIDs

`-S`

: include system objects (those in `information_schema`, `pg_toast` and `pg_catalog` schemas)

`-i`

: include indexes and sequences in the listing

`-x`

: display more information about each object shown: tablespace name, schema name, and OID

`-q`

omit headers (useful for scripting)

`-d` *`database`*

database to connect to

`-H` *`host`*

database server's host

`-p` *`port`*

database server's port

`-U` *`username`*

user name to connect as

`-P` *`password`*

password (deprecated — putting this on the command line is a security hazard)

To display specific tables, select which tables to show by using `-o`, `-f` and/or `-t`. `-o` takes an OID, `-f` takes a filenode, and `-t` takes a table name (actually, it's a `LIKE` pattern, so you can use things like `foo%`). You can use as many of these options as you like, and the listing will include all objects matched by any of the options. But note that these options can only show objects in the database given by `-d`.

If you don't give any of `-o`, `-f` or `-t`, but do give `-d`, it will list all tables in the database named by `-d`. In this mode, the `-S` and `-i` options control what gets listed.

If you don't give `-d` either, it will show a listing of database OIDs. Alternatively you can give `-s` to get a tablespace listing.

F.19.3. Examples

```
$ # what's in this database server, anyway?
$ oid2name
All databases:
    Oid  Database Name  Tablespace
----------------------------------
  17228       alvherre  pg_default
  17255     regression  pg_default
  17227      template0  pg_default
      1      template1  pg_default

$ oid2name -s
All tablespaces:
     Oid  Tablespace Name
-------------------------
    1663       pg_default
    1664        pg_global
```

```
  155151        fastdisk
  155152         bigdisk

$ # OK, let's look into database alvherre
$ cd $PGDATA/base/17228

$ # get top 10 db objects in the default tablespace, ordered by size
$ ls -lS * | head -10
-rw-------  1 alvherre alvherre 136536064 sep 14 09:51 155173
-rw-------  1 alvherre alvherre  17965056 sep 14 09:51 1155291
-rw-------  1 alvherre alvherre   1204224 sep 14 09:51 16717
-rw-------  1 alvherre alvherre    581632 sep  6 17:51 1255
-rw-------  1 alvherre alvherre    237568 sep 14 09:50 16674
-rw-------  1 alvherre alvherre    212992 sep 14 09:51 1249
-rw-------  1 alvherre alvherre    204800 sep 14 09:51 16684
-rw-------  1 alvherre alvherre    196608 sep 14 09:50 16700
-rw-------  1 alvherre alvherre    163840 sep 14 09:50 16699
-rw-------  1 alvherre alvherre    122880 sep  6 17:51 16751

$ # I wonder what file 155173 is ...
$ oid2name -d alvherre -f 155173
From database "alvherre":
  Filenode  Table Name
----------------------
    155173    accounts

$ # you can ask for more than one object
$ oid2name -d alvherre -f 155173 -f 1155291
From database "alvherre":
  Filenode     Table Name
-------------------------
    155173       accounts
   1155291  accounts_pkey

$ # you can mix the options, and get more details with -x
$ oid2name -d alvherre -t accounts -f 1155291 -x
From database "alvherre":
  Filenode     Table Name      Oid  Schema  Tablespace
------------------------------------------------------
    155173       accounts   155173  public  pg_default
   1155291  accounts_pkey  1155291  public  pg_default

$ # show disk space for every db object
$ du [0-9]* |
> while read SIZE FILENODE
> do
>   echo "$SIZE       `oid2name -q -d alvherre -i -f $FILENODE`"
> done
16           1155287  branches_pkey
16           1155289  tellers_pkey
17561           1155291  accounts_pkey
...
```

```
$ # same, but sort by size
$ du [0-9]* | sort -rn | while read SIZE FN
> do
>   echo "$SIZE   `oid2name -q -d alvherre -f $FN`"
> done
133466              155173    accounts
17561             1155291  accounts_pkey
1177               16717  pg_proc_proname_args_nsp_index
...

$ # If you want to see what's in tablespaces, use the pg_tblspc directory
$ cd $PGDATA/pg_tblspc
$ oid2name -s
All tablespaces:
     Oid  Tablespace Name
-------------------------
    1663       pg_default
    1664        pg_global
  155151         fastdisk
  155152          bigdisk

$ # what databases have objects in tablespace "fastdisk"?
$ ls -d 155151/*
155151/17228/  155151/PG_VERSION

$ # Oh, what was database 17228 again?
$ oid2name
All databases:
    Oid  Database Name  Tablespace
----------------------------------
  17228       alvherre  pg_default
  17255     regression  pg_default
  17227      template0  pg_default
      1      template1  pg_default

$ # Let's see what objects does this database have in the tablespace.
$ cd 155151/17228
$ ls -l
total 0
-rw-------  1 postgres postgres 0 sep 13 23:20 155156

$ # OK, this is a pretty small table ... but which one is it?
$ oid2name -d alvherre -f 155156
From database "alvherre":
  Filenode  Table Name
----------------------
    155156         foo
```

F.19.4. Limitations

oid2name requires a running database server with non-corrupt system catalogs. It is therefore of only limited use for recovering from catastrophic database corruption situations.

F.19.5. Author

B. Palmer *<bpalmer@crimelabs.net>*

F.20. pageinspect

The `pageinspect` module provides functions that allow you to inspect the contents of database pages at a low level, which is useful for debugging purposes. All of these functions may be used only by superusers.

F.20.1. Functions

`get_raw_page(relname text, fork text, blkno int) returns bytea`

> `get_raw_page` reads the specified block of the named table and returns a copy as a `bytea` value. This allows a single time-consistent copy of the block to be obtained. *`fork`* should be `'main'` for the main data fork, or `'fsm'` for the free space map, or `'vm'` for the visibility map.

`get_raw_page(relname text, blkno int) returns bytea`

> A shorthand version of `get_raw_page`, for reading from the main fork. Equivalent to `get_raw_page(relname, 'main', blkno)`

`page_header(page bytea) returns record`

> `page_header` shows fields that are common to all PostgreSQL heap and index pages.
>
> A page image obtained with `get_raw_page` should be passed as argument. For example:

```
test=# SELECT * FROM page_header(get_raw_page('pg_class', 0));
    lsn    | tli | flags | lower | upper | special | pagesize | version | prune_xid
-----------+-----+-------+-------+-------+---------+----------+---------+-----------
0/24A1B50  |   1 |     1 |   232 |   368 |    8192 |     8192 |       4 |         0
```

> The returned columns correspond to the fields in the `PageHeaderData` struct. See `src/include/storage/bufpage.h` for details.

`heap_page_items(page bytea) returns setof record`

> `heap_page_items` shows all line pointers on a heap page. For those line pointers that are in use, tuple headers are also shown. All tuples are shown, whether or not the tuples were visible to an MVCC snapshot at the time the raw page was copied.
>
> A heap page image obtained with `get_raw_page` should be passed as argument. For example:
>
> ```
> test=# SELECT * FROM heap_page_items(get_raw_page('pg_class', 0));
> ```
>
> See src/include/storage/itemid.h and src/include/access/htup.h for explanations of the fields returned.

`bt_metap(relname text) returns record`

`bt_metap` returns information about a B-tree index's metapage. For example:

```
test=# SELECT * FROM bt_metap('pg_cast_oid_index');
-[ RECORD 1 ]-----
magic     | 340322
version   | 2
root      | 1
level     | 0
fastroot  | 1
fastlevel | 0
```

`bt_page_stats(relname text, blkno int) returns record`

`bt_page_stats` returns summary information about single pages of B-tree indexes. For example:

```
test=# SELECT * FROM bt_page_stats('pg_cast_oid_index', 1);
-[ RECORD 1 ]-+-----
blkno         | 1
type          | l
live_items    | 256
dead_items    | 0
avg_item_size | 12
page_size     | 8192
free_size     | 4056
btpo_prev     | 0
btpo_next     | 0
btpo          | 0
btpo_flags    | 3
```

`bt_page_items(relname text, blkno int) returns setof record`

`bt_page_items` returns detailed information about all of the items on a B-tree index page. For example:

```
test=# SELECT * FROM bt_page_items('pg_cast_oid_index', 1);
 itemoffset |  ctid   | itemlen | nulls | vars |    data
------------+---------+---------+-------+------+-------------
          1 | (0,1)   |      12 | f     | f    | 23 27 00 00
          2 | (0,2)   |      12 | f     | f    | 24 27 00 00
          3 | (0,3)   |      12 | f     | f    | 25 27 00 00
          4 | (0,4)   |      12 | f     | f    | 26 27 00 00
          5 | (0,5)   |      12 | f     | f    | 27 27 00 00
          6 | (0,6)   |      12 | f     | f    | 28 27 00 00
          7 | (0,7)   |      12 | f     | f    | 29 27 00 00
          8 | (0,8)   |      12 | f     | f    | 2a 27 00 00
```

`fsm_page_contents(page bytea) returns text`

`fsm_page_contents` shows the internal node structure of a FSM page. The output is a multiline string, with one line per node in the binary tree within the page. Only those nodes that are not zero are printed. The so-called "next" pointer, which points to the next slot to be returned from the page, is also printed.

See `src/backend/storage/freespace/README` for more information on the structure of an FSM page.

F.21. passwordcheck

The `passwordcheck` module checks users' passwords whenever they are set with CREATE ROLE or ALTER ROLE. If a password is considered too weak, it will be rejected and the command will terminate with an error.

To enable this module, add `'$libdir/passwordcheck'` to *shared_preload_libraries* in `postgresql.conf`, then restart the server.

You can adapt this module to your needs by changing the source code. For example, you can use *CrackLib*[2] to check passwords — this only requires uncommenting two lines in the `Makefile` and rebuilding the module. (We cannot include CrackLib by default for license reasons.) Without CrackLib, the module enforces a few simple rules for password strength, which you can modify or extend as you see fit.

> **Caution**
>
> To prevent unencrypted passwords from being sent across the network, written to the server log or otherwise stolen by a database administrator, PostgreSQL allows the user to supply pre-encrypted passwords. Many client programs make use of this functionality and encrypt the password before sending it to the server.
>
> This limits the usefulness of the `passwordcheck` module, because in that case it can only try to guess the password. For this reason, `passwordcheck` is not recommendable if your security requirements are high. It is more secure to use an external authentication method such as Kerberos (see *Chapter 19* - Vol.II) than to rely on passwords within the database.
>
> Alternatively, you could modify `passwordcheck` to reject pre-encrypted passwords, but forcing users to set their passwords in clear text carries its own security risks.

F.22. pg_archivecleanup

pg_archivecleanup is designed to be used as an `archive_cleanup_command` to clean up WAL file archives when running as a standby server (see *Section 25.2* - Vol.II). pg_archivecleanup can also be used as a standalone program to clean WAL file archives.

pg_archivecleanup features include:

- Written in C, so very portable and easy to install

[2] *http://sourceforge.net/projects/cracklib/*

- Easy-to-modify source code, with specifically designated sections to modify for your own needs

F.22.1. Usage

To configure a standby server to use pg_archivecleanup, put this into its `recovery.conf` configuration file:

```
archive_cleanup_command = 'pg_archivecleanup archivelocation %r'
```

where *`archivelocation`* is the directory from which WAL segment files should be removed.

When used within *archive_cleanup_command*, all WAL files logically preceding the value of the `%r` argument will be removed from *`archivelocation`*. This minimizes the number of files that need to be retained, while preserving crash-restart capability. Use of this parameter is appropriate if the *`archivelocation`* is a transient staging area for this particular standby server, but *not* when the *`archivelocation`* is intended as a long-term WAL archive area, or when multiple standby servers are recovering from the same archive location.

The full syntax of pg_archivecleanup's command line is

```
pg_archivecleanup [ option ... ] archivelocation restartwalfile
```

When used as a standalone program all WAL files logically preceding the `restartwalfile` will be removed *`archivelocation`*. In this mode, if you specify a `.backup` file name, then only the file prefix will be used as the `restartwalfile`. This allows you to remove all WAL files archived prior to a specific base backup without error. For example, the following example will remove all files older than WAL file name `000000010000003700000010`:

```
pg_archivecleanup -d archive 000000010000003700000010.00000020.backup
```

```
pg_archivecleanup:  keep WAL file "archive/000000010000003700000010" and later
pg_archivecleanup:  removing file "archive/00000001000000370000000F"
pg_archivecleanup:  removing file "archive/00000001000000370000000E"
```

pg_archivecleanup assumes that *`archivelocation`* is a directory readable and writable by the server-owning user.

F.22.2. pg_archivecleanup Options

pg_archivecleanup accepts the following command-line arguments:

`-d`

Print lots of debug logging output on `stderr`.

F.22.3. Examples

On Linux or Unix systems, you might use:

```
archive_cleanup_command = 'pg_archivecleanup -d /mnt/standby/archive
                                                              %r 2>>cleanup.log'
```

where the archive directory is physically located on the standby server, so that the `archive_command` is accessing it across NFS, but the files are local to the standby. This will:

- produce debugging output in `cleanup.log`
- remove no-longer-needed files from the archive directory

F.22.4. Supported server versions

pg_archivecleanup is designed to work with PostgreSQL 8.0 and later when used as a standalone utility, or with PostgreSQL 9.0 and later when used as an archive cleanup command.

F.22.5. Author

Simon Riggs <*simon@2ndquadrant.com*>

F.23. pgbench

pgbench is a simple program for running benchmark tests on PostgreSQL. It runs the same sequence of SQL commands over and over, possibly in multiple concurrent database sessions, and then calculates the average transaction rate (transactions per second). By default, pgbench tests a scenario that is loosely based on TPC-B, involving five `SELECT`, `UPDATE`, and `INSERT` commands per transaction. However, it is easy to test other cases by writing your own transaction script files.

Typical output from pgbench looks like:

```
transaction type: TPC-B (sort of)
scaling factor: 10
query mode: simple
number of clients: 10
number of threads: 1
number of transactions per client: 1000
number of transactions actually processed: 10000/10000
tps = 85.184871 (including connections establishing)
tps = 85.296346 (excluding connections establishing)
```

The first six lines report some of the most important parameter settings. The next line reports the number of transactions completed and intended (the latter being just the product of number of clients and number of transactions per client); these will be equal unless the run failed before completion. The last two lines report the TPS rate, figured with and without counting the time to start database sessions.

F.23.1. Overview

The default TPC-B-like transaction test requires specific tables to be set up beforehand. pgbench should be invoked with the `-i` (initialize) option to create and populate these tables. (When you are testing a custom script, you don't need this step, but will instead need to do whatever setup your test needs.) Initialization looks like:

```
pgbench -i [ other-options ] dbname
```

where *dbname* is the name of the already-created database to test in. (You may also need `-h`, `-p`, and/or `-U` options to specify how to connect to the database server.)

Caution

> `pgbench -i` creates four tables `pgbench_accounts`, `pgbench_branches`, `pgbench_history`, and `pgbench_tellers`, destroying any existing tables of these names. Be very careful to use another database if you have tables having these names!

At the default "scale factor" of 1, the tables initially contain this many rows:

```
table                    # of rows
---------------------------------
pgbench_branches         1
pgbench_tellers          10
pgbench_accounts         100000
pgbench_history          0
```

You can (and, for most purposes, probably should) increase the number of rows by using the `-s` (scale factor) option. The `-F` (fillfactor) option might also be used at this point.

Once you have done the necessary setup, you can run your benchmark with a command that doesn't include `-i`, that is

```
pgbench [ options ] dbname
```

In nearly all cases, you'll need some options to make a useful test. The most important options are `-c` (number of clients), `-t` (number of transactions), `-T` (time limit), and `-f` (specify a custom script file). See below for a full list.

Section F.23.2 (page 368) shows options that are used during database initialization, while *Section F.23.2* (page 368) shows options that are used while running benchmarks, and *Section F.23.4* (page 370) shows options that are useful in both cases.

F.23.2. pgbench Initialization Options

pgbench accepts the following command-line initialization arguments:

`-F` *`fillfactor`*

> Create the `pgbench_accounts`, `pgbench_tellers` and `pgbench_branches` tables with the given fillfactor. Default is 100.

`-i`

Required to invoke initialization mode.

`-s` *`scale_factor`*

Multiply the number of rows generated by the scale factor. For example, `-s 100` will create 10,000,000 rows in the `pgbench_accounts` table. Default is 1.

F.23.3. pgbench Benchmarking Options

pgbench accepts the following command-line benchmarking arguments:

`-c` *`clients`*

Number of clients simulated, that is, number of concurrent database sessions. Default is 1.

`-C`

Establish a new connection for each transaction, rather than doing it just once per client session. This is useful to measure the connection overhead.

`-d`

Print debugging output.

`-D` *`varname=value`*

Define a variable for use by a custom script (see below). Multiple `-D` options are allowed.

`-f` *`filename`*

Read transaction script from *`filename`*. See below for details. `-N`, `-S`, and `-f` are mutually exclusive.

`-j` *`threads`*

Number of worker threads within pgbench. Using more than one thread can be helpful on multi-CPU machines. The number of clients must be a multiple of the number of threads, since each thread is given the same number of client sessions to manage. Default is 1.

`-l`

Write the time taken by each transaction to a log file. See below for details.

`-M` *`querymode`*

Protocol to use for submitting queries to the server:

- `simple`: use simple query protocol.

- `extended`: use extended query protocol.
- `prepared`: use extended query protocol with prepared statements.

The default is simple query protocol. (See *Chapter 46* – Vol.V for more information.)

`-n`

Perform no vacuuming before running the test. This option is *necessary* if you are running a custom test scenario that does not include the standard tables `pgbench_accounts`, `pgbench_branches`, `pgbench_history`, and `pgbench_tellers`.

`-N`

Do not update `pgbench_tellers` and `pgbench_branches`. This will avoid update contention on these tables, but it makes the test case even less like TPC-B.

`-s` *`scale_factor`*

Report the specified scale factor in pgbench's output. With the built-in tests, this is not necessary; the correct scale factor will be detected by counting the number of rows in the `pgbench_branches` table. However, when testing custom benchmarks (-`f` option), the scale factor will be reported as 1 unless this option is used.

`-S`

Perform select-only transactions instead of TPC-B-like test.

`-t` *`transactions`*

Number of transactions each client runs. Default is 10.

`-T` *`seconds`*

Run the test for this many seconds, rather than a fixed number of transactions per client. `-t` and `-T` are mutually exclusive.

`-v`

Vacuum all four standard tables before running the test. With neither `-n` nor `-v`, pgbench will vacuum the `pgbench_tellers` and `pgbench_branches` tables, and will truncate `pgbench_history`.

F.23.4. pgbench Common Options

pgbench accepts the following command-line common arguments:

`-h` *`hostname`*

The database server's host name

`-p` *`port`*

The database server's port number

`-U login`

The user name to connect as

F.23.5. What is the "transaction" actually performed in pgbench?

The default transaction script issues seven commands per transaction:

1. `BEGIN;`
2. `UPDATE pgbench_accounts SET abalance = abalance + :delta WHERE aid = :aid;`
3. `SELECT abalance FROM pgbench_accounts WHERE aid = :aid;`
4. `UPDATE pgbench_tellers SET tbalance = tbalance + :delta WHERE tid = :tid;`
5. `UPDATE pgbench_branches SET bbalance = bbalance + :delta WHERE bid = :bid;`
6. `INSERT INTO pgbench_history (tid, bid, aid, delta, mtime) VALUES (:tid, :bid, :aid, :delta, CURRENT_TIMESTAMP);`
7. `END;`

If you specify `-N`, steps 4 and 5 aren't included in the transaction. If you specify `-S`, only the `SELECT` is issued.

F.23.6. Custom Scripts

pgbench has support for running custom benchmark scenarios by replacing the default transaction script (described above) with a transaction script read from a file (`-f` option). In this case a "transaction" counts as one execution of a script file. You can even specify multiple scripts (multiple `-f` options), in which case a random one of the scripts is chosen each time a client session starts a new transaction.

The format of a script file is one SQL command per line; multiline SQL commands are not supported. Empty lines and lines beginning with `--` are ignored. Script file lines can also be "meta commands", which are interpreted by pgbench itself, as described below.

There is a simple variable-substitution facility for script files. Variables can be set by the command-line `-D` option, explained above, or by the meta commands explained below. In addition to any variables preset by `-D` command-line options, the variable `scale` is preset to the current scale factor. Once set, a variable's value can be inserted into a SQL command by writing `:` *`variablename`*. When running more than one client session, each session has its own set of variables.

Script file meta commands begin with a backslash (\). Arguments to a meta command are separated by white space. These meta commands are supported:

`\set varname operand1 [ operator operand2 ]`

Sets variable *varname* to a calculated integer value. Each *operand* is either an integer constant or a `:` *variablename* reference to a variable having an integer value. The *operator* can be `+`, `-`, `*`, or `/`.

Example:

```
\set ntellers 10 * :scale
```

`\setrandom` *varname min max*

Sets variable *varname* to a random integer value between the limits *min* and *max* inclusive. Each limit can be either an integer constant or a `:` *variablename* reference to a variable having an integer value.

Example:

```
\setrandom aid 1 :naccounts
```

`\sleep` *number* `[ us | ms | s ]`

Causes script execution to sleep for the specified duration in microseconds (`us`), milliseconds (`ms`) or seconds (`s`). If the unit is omitted then seconds are the default. *number* can be either an integer constant or a `:` *variablename* reference to a variable having an integer value.

Example:

```
\sleep 10 ms
```

`\setshell` *varname command* `[` *argument* `... ]`

Sets variable *varname* to the result of the shell command *command*. The command must return an integer value through its standard output.

argument can be either a text constant or a `:`*variablename* reference to a variable of any types. If you want to use *argument* starting with colons, you need to add an additional colon at the beginning of *argument*.

Example:

```
\setshell variable_to_be_assigned command literal_argument :variable
                                              ::literal_starting_with_colon
```

`\shell` *command* `[` *argument* `... ]`

Same as `\setshell`, but the result is ignored.

Example:

```
\shell command literal_argument :variable ::literal_starting_with_colon
```

As an example, the full definition of the built-in TPC-B-like transaction is:

```
\set nbranches :scale
\set ntellers 10 * :scale
\set naccounts 100000 * :scale
\setrandom aid 1 :naccounts
```

```
\setrandom bid 1 :nbranches
\setrandom tid 1 :ntellers
\setrandom delta -5000 5000
BEGIN;
UPDATE pgbench_accounts SET abalance = abalance + :delta WHERE aid = :aid;
SELECT abalance FROM pgbench_accounts WHERE aid = :aid;
UPDATE pgbench_tellers SET tbalance = tbalance + :delta WHERE tid = :tid;
UPDATE pgbench_branches SET bbalance = bbalance + :delta WHERE bid = :bid;
INSERT INTO pgbench_history (tid, bid, aid, delta, mtime) VALUES (:tid, :bid, :aid,
:delta, CURRENT_TIMESTAMP);
END;
```

This script allows each iteration of the transaction to reference different, randomly-chosen rows. (This example also shows why it's important for each client session to have its own variables - otherwise they'd not be independently touching different rows.)

F.23.7. Per-transaction logging

With the `-l` option, pgbench writes the time taken by each transaction to a log file. The log file will be named `pgbench_log.`*`nnn`*, where *`nnn`* is the PID of the pgbench process. If the `-j` option is 2 or higher, creating multiple worker threads, each will have its own log file. The first worker will use the same name for its log file as in the standard single worker case. The additional log files for the other workers will be named `pgbench_log.`*`nnn`*`.`*`mmm`*, where *`mmm`* is a sequential number for each worker starting with 1.

The format of the log is:

```
client_id transaction_no time file_no time_epoch time_us
```

where *`time`* is the elapsed transaction time in microseconds, *`file_no`* identifies which script file was used (useful when multiple scripts were specified with `-f`), and *`time_epoch`*/ *`time_us`* are a UNIX epoch format timestamp and an offset in microseconds (suitable for creating a ISO 8601 timestamp with fractional seconds) showing when the transaction completed.

Here are example outputs:

```
0 199 2241 0 1175850568 995598
0 200 2465 0 1175850568 998079
0 201 2513 0 1175850569 608
0 202 2038 0 1175850569 2663
```

F.23.8. Good Practices

It is very easy to use pgbench to produce completely meaningless numbers. Here are some guidelines to help you get useful results.

In the first place, *never* believe any test that runs for only a few seconds. Use the `-t` or `-T` option to make the run last at least a few minutes, so as to average out noise. In some cases you could need hours to get numbers that are reproducible. It's a good idea to try the test run a few times, to find out if your numbers are reproducible or not.

For the default TPC-B-like test scenario, the initialization scale factor (`-s`) should be at least as large as the largest number of clients you intend to test (`-c`); else you'll mostly be measuring update contention. There are only `-s` rows in the `pgbench_branches` table, and every transaction wants to update one of them, so `-c` values in excess of `-s` will undoubtedly result in lots of transactions blocked waiting for other transactions.

The default test scenario is also quite sensitive to how long it's been since the tables were initialized: accumulation of dead rows and dead space in the tables changes the results. To understand the results you must keep track of the total number of updates and when vacuuming happens. If autovacuum is enabled it can result in unpredictable changes in measured performance.

A limitation of pgbench is that it can itself become the bottleneck when trying to test a large number of client sessions. This can be alleviated by running pgbench on a different machine from the database server, although low network latency will be essential. It might even be useful to run several pgbench instances concurrently, on several client machines, against the same database server.

F.24. pg_buffercache

The `pg_buffercache` module provides a means for examining what's happening in the shared buffer cache in real time.

The module provides a C function `pg_buffercache_pages` that returns a set of records, plus a view `pg_buffercache` that wraps the function for convenient use.

By default public access is revoked from both of these, just in case there are security issues lurking.

F.24.1. The `pg_buffercache` view

The definitions of the columns exposed by the view are shown in *Table F-14* (see below).

Name	Type	References	Description
`bufferid`	`integer`		ID, in the range 1.. `shared_buffers`
`relfilenode`	`oid`	`pg_class.relfilenode`	Filenode number of the relation
`reltablespace`	`oid`	`pg_tablespace.oid`	Tablespace OID of the relation
`reldatabase`	`oid`	`pg_database.oid`	Database OID of the relation
`relblocknumber`	`bigint`		Page number within the relation
`relforknumber`	`smallint`		Fork number within the relation

Name	Type	References	Description
isdirty	boolean		Is the page dirty?
usagecount	smallint		Page LRU count

Table F-14. pg_buffercache Columns

There is one row for each buffer in the shared cache. Unused buffers are shown with all fields null except bufferid. Shared system catalogs are shown as belonging to database zero.

Because the cache is shared by all the databases, there will normally be pages from relations not belonging to the current database. This means that there may not be matching join rows in pg_class for some rows, or that there could even be incorrect joins. If you are trying to join against pg_class, it's a good idea to restrict the join to rows having reldatabase equal to the current database's OID or zero.

When the pg_buffercache view is accessed, internal buffer manager locks are taken for long enough to copy all the buffer state data that the view will display. This ensures that the view produces a consistent set of results, while not blocking normal buffer activity longer than necessary. Nonetheless there could be some impact on database performance if this view is read often.

F.24.2. Sample output

```
regression=# SELECT c.relname, count(*) AS buffers
             FROM pg_buffercache b INNER JOIN pg_class c
             ON b.relfilenode = pg_relation_filenode(c.oid) AND
                b.reldatabase IN (0, (SELECT oid FROM pg_database
                                      WHERE datname = current_database()))
             GROUP BY c.relname
             ORDER BY 2 DESC
             LIMIT 10;

             relname             | buffers
---------------------------------+---------
 tenk2                           |     345
 tenk1                           |     141
 pg_proc                         |      46
 pg_class                        |      45
 pg_attribute                    |      43
 pg_class_relname_nsp_index      |      30
 pg_proc_proname_args_nsp_index  |      28
 pg_attribute_relid_attnam_index |      26
 pg_depend                       |      22
 pg_depend_reference_index       |      20
(10 rows)
```

F.24.3. Authors

Mark Kirkwood <*markir@paradise.net.nz*>

Design suggestions: Neil Conway <*neilc@samurai.com*>

Debugging advice: Tom Lane <*tgl@sss.pgh.pa.us*>

F.25. pgcrypto

The `pgcrypto` module provides cryptographic functions for PostgreSQL.

F.25.1. General hashing functions

F.25.1.1. `digest()`

```
digest(data text, type text) returns bytea
digest(data bytea, type text) returns bytea
```

Computes a binary hash of the given `data`. `type` is the algorithm to use. Standard algorithms are `md5`, `sha1`, `sha224`, `sha256`, `sha384` and `sha512`. If `pgcrypto` was built with OpenSSL, more algorithms are available, as detailed in *Table F-18* (page 385).

If you want the digest as a hexadecimal string, use `encode()` on the result. For example:

```
CREATE OR REPLACE FUNCTION sha1(bytea) returns text AS $$
  SELECT encode(digest($1, 'sha1'), 'hex')
$$ LANGUAGE SQL STRICT IMMUTABLE;
```

F.25.1.2. `hmac()`

```
hmac(data text, key text, type text) returns bytea
hmac(data bytea, key text, type text) returns bytea
```

Calculates hashed MAC for `data` with key `key`. `type` is the same as in `digest()`.

This is similar to `digest()` but the hash can only be recalculated knowing the key. This prevents the scenario of someone altering data and also changing the hash to match.

If the key is larger than the hash block size it will first be hashed and the result will be used as key.

F.25.2. Password hashing functions

The functions `crypt()` and `gen_salt()` are specifically designed for hashing passwords. `crypt()` does the hashing and `gen_salt()` prepares algorithm parameters for it.

The algorithms in `crypt()` differ from usual hashing algorithms like MD5 or SHA1 in the following respects:

1. They are slow. As the amount of data is so small, this is the only way to make brute-forcing passwords hard.
2. They use a random value, called the *salt*, so that users having the same password will have different encrypted passwords. This is also an additional defense against reversing the algorithm.
3. They include the algorithm type in the result, so passwords hashed with different algorithms can co-exist.
4. Some of them are adaptive - that means when computers get faster, you can tune the algorithm to be slower, without introducing incompatibility with existing passwords.

Table F-15 (see below) lists the algorithms supported by the `crypt()` function.

Algorithm	Max password length	Adaptive?	Salt bits	Description
`bf`	72	yes	128	Blowfish-based, variant 2a
`md5`	unlimited	no	48	MD5-based crypt
`xdes`	8	yes	24	Extended DES
`des`	8	no	12	Original UNIX crypt

Table F-15. Supported algorithms for `crypt()`

F.25.2.1. `crypt()`

```
crypt(password text, salt text) returns text
```

Calculates a crypt(3)-style hash of `password`. When storing a new password, you need to use `gen_salt()` to generate a new `salt` value. To check a password, pass the stored hash value as `salt`, and test whether the result matches the stored value.

Example of setting a new password:

```
UPDATE ... SET pswhash = crypt('new password', gen_salt('md5'));
```

Example of authentication:

```
SELECT pswhash = crypt('entered password', pswhash) FROM ... ;
```

This returns `true` if the entered password is correct.

F.25.2.2. `gen_salt()`

```
gen_salt(type text [, iter_count integer ]) returns text
```

Generates a new random salt string for use in `crypt()`. The salt string also tells `crypt()` which algorithm to use.

The `type` parameter specifies the hashing algorithm. The accepted types are: `des`, `xdes`, `md5` and `bf`.

The `iter_count` parameter lets the user specify the iteration count, for algorithms that have one. The higher the count, the more time it takes to hash the password and therefore the more time to break it. Although with too high a count the time to calculate a hash may be several years - which is somewhat impractical. If the `iter_count` parameter is omitted, the default iteration count is used. Allowed values for `iter_count` depend on the algorithm and are shown in *Table F-16* (see below).

Algorithm	Default	Min	Max
`xdes`	725	1	16777215
`bf`	6	4	31

Table F-16. Iteration counts for `crypt()`

For `xdes` there is an additional limitation that the iteration count must be an odd number.

To pick an appropriate iteration count, consider that the original DES crypt was designed to have the speed of 4 hashes per second on the hardware of that time. Slower than 4 hashes per second would probably dampen usability. Faster than 100 hashes per second is probably too fast.

Table F-17 (see below) gives an overview of the relative slowness of different hashing algorithms. The table shows how much time it would take to try all combinations of characters in an 8-character password, assuming that the password contains either only lowercase letters, or upper- and lower-case letters and numbers. In the `crypt-bf` entries, the number after a slash is the `iter_count` parameter of `gen_salt`.

Algorithm	Hashes/sec	For `[a-z]`	For `[A-Za-z0-9]`
`crypt-bf/8`	28	246 years	251322 years
`crypt-bf/7`	57	121 years	123457 years
`crypt-bf/6`	112	62 years	62831 years
`crypt-bf/5`	211	33 years	33351 years
`crypt-md5`	2681	2.6 years	2625 years
`crypt-des`	362837	7 days	19 years
`sha1`	590223	4 days	12 years
`md5`	2345086	1 day	3 years

Table F-17. Hash algorithm speeds

Notes:

- The machine used is a 1.5GHz Pentium 4.
- `crypt-des` and `crypt-md5` algorithm numbers are taken from John the Ripper v1.6.38 `-test` output.
- `md5` numbers are from mdcrack 1.2.
- `sha1` numbers are from lcrack-20031130-beta.
- `crypt-bf` numbers are taken using a simple program that loops over 1000 8-character passwords. That way I can show the speed with different numbers of iterations. For reference: `john -test` shows 213 loops/sec for `crypt-bf/5`. (The very small difference in results is in accordance with the fact that the `crypt-bf` implementation in `pgcrypto` is the same one used in John the Ripper.)

Note that "try all combinations" is not a realistic exercise. Usually password cracking is done with the help of dictionaries, which contain both regular words and various mutations of them. So, even somewhat word-like passwords could be cracked much faster than the above numbers suggest, while a 6-character non-word-like password may escape cracking. Or not.

F.25.3. PGP encryption functions

The functions here implement the encryption part of the OpenPGP (RFC 4880) standard. Supported are both symmetric-key and public-key encryption.

An encrypted PGP message consists of 2 parts, or *packets*:

- Packet containing a session key - either symmetric-key or public-key encrypted.
- Packet containing data encrypted with the session key.

When encrypting with a symmetric key (i.e., a password):

1. The given password is hashed using a String2Key (S2K) algorithm. This is rather similar to `crypt()` algorithms - purposefully slow and with random salt - but it produces a full-length binary key.
2. If a separate session key is requested, a new random key will be generated. Otherwise the S2K key will be used directly as the session key.
3. If the S2K key is to be used directly, then only S2K settings will be put into the session key packet. Otherwise the session key will be encrypted with the S2K key and put into the session key packet.

When encrypting with a public key:

1. A new random session key is generated.
2. It is encrypted using the public key and put into the session key packet.

In either case the data to be encrypted is processed as follows:

1. Optional data-manipulation: compression, conversion to UTF-8, and/or conversion of line-endings.
2. The data is prefixed with a block of random bytes. This is equivalent to using a random IV.
3. An SHA1 hash of the random prefix and data is appended.
4. All this is encrypted with the session key and placed in the data packet.

F.25.3.1. pgp_sym_encrypt()

```
pgp_sym_encrypt(data text, psw text [, options text ]) returns bytea
pgp_sym_encrypt_bytea(data bytea, psw text [, options text ]) returns bytea
```

Encrypt `data` with a symmetric PGP key `psw`. The `options` parameter can contain option settings, as described below.

F.25.3.2. pgp_sym_decrypt()

```
pgp_sym_decrypt(msg bytea, psw text [, options text ]) returns text
pgp_sym_decrypt_bytea(msg bytea, psw text [, options text ]) returns bytea
```

Decrypt a symmetric-key-encrypted PGP message.

Decrypting bytea data with `pgp_sym_decrypt` is disallowed. This is to avoid outputting invalid character data. Decrypting originally textual data with `pgp_sym_decrypt_bytea` is fine.

The `options` parameter can contain option settings, as described below.

F.25.3.3. pgp_pub_encrypt()

```
pgp_pub_encrypt(data text, key bytea [, options text ]) returns bytea
pgp_pub_encrypt_bytea(data bytea, key bytea [, options text ]) returns bytea
```

Encrypt `data` with a public PGP key `key`. Giving this function a secret key will produce a error.

The `options` parameter can contain option settings, as described below.

F.25.3.4. pgp_pub_decrypt()

```
pgp_pub_decrypt(msg bytea, key bytea [, psw text [, options text ]])
                                                        returns text
pgp_pub_decrypt_bytea(msg bytea, key bytea [, psw text [, options text ]])
                                                        returns bytea
```

Decrypt a public-key-encrypted message. `key` must be the secret key corresponding to the public key that was used to encrypt. If the secret key is password-protected, you must give the password in `psw`. If there is no password, but you want to specify options, you need to give an empty password.

Decrypting bytea data with `pgp_pub_decrypt` is disallowed. This is to avoid outputting invalid character data. Decrypting originally textual data with `pgp_pub_decrypt_bytea` is fine.

The `options` parameter can contain option settings, as described below.

F.25.3.5. pgp_key_id()

```
pgp_key_id(bytea) returns text
```

`pgp_key_id` extracts the key ID of a PGP public or secret key. Or it gives the key ID that was used for encrypting the data, if given an encrypted message.

It can return 2 special key IDs:

- `SYMKEY`

  The message is encrypted with a symmetric key.

- `ANYKEY`

  The message is public-key encrypted, but the key ID has been removed. That means you will need to try all your secret keys on it to see which one decrypts it. `pgcrypto` itself does not produce such messages.

Note that different keys may have the same ID. This is rare but a normal event. The client application should then try to decrypt with each one, to see which fits - like handling `ANYKEY`.

F.25.3.6. armor(), dearmor()

```
armor(data bytea) returns text
dearmor(data text) returns bytea
```

These functions wrap/unwrap binary data into PGP ASCII-armor format, which is basically Base64 with CRC and additional formatting.

F.25.3.7. Options for PGP functions

Options are named to be similar to GnuPG. An option's value should be given after an equal sign; separate options from each other with commas. For example:

```
pgp_sym_encrypt(data, psw, 'compress-algo=1, cipher-algo=aes256')
```

All of the options except `convert-crlf` apply only to encrypt functions. Decrypt functions get the parameters from the PGP data.

The most interesting options are probably `compress-algo` and `unicode-mode`. The rest should have reasonable defaults.

F.25.3.7.1. cipher-algo

Which cipher algorithm to use.

```
Values: bf, aes128, aes192, aes256 (OpenSSL-only: 3des, cast5)
Default: aes128
Applies to: pgp_sym_encrypt, pgp_pub_encrypt
```

F.25.3.7.2. compress-algo

Which compression algorithm to use. Only available if PostgreSQL was built with zlib.

```
Values:
  0 - no compression
  1 - ZIP compression
  2 - ZLIB compression (= ZIP plus meta-data and block CRCs)
Default: 0
Applies to: pgp_sym_encrypt, pgp_pub_encrypt
```

F.25.3.7.3. compress-level

How much to compress. Higher levels compress smaller but are slower. 0 disables compression.

```
Values: 0, 1-9
Default: 6
Applies to: pgp_sym_encrypt, pgp_pub_encrypt
```

F.25.3.7.4. convert-crlf

Whether to convert `\n` into `\r\n` when encrypting and `\r\n` to `\n` when decrypting. RFC 4880 specifies that text data should be stored using `\r\n` line-feeds. Use this to get fully RFC-compliant behavior.

```
Values: 0, 1
Default: 0
Applies to: pgp_sym_encrypt, pgp_pub_encrypt, pgp_sym_decrypt, pgp_pub_decrypt
```

F.25.3.7.5. disable-mdc

Do not protect data with SHA-1. The only good reason to use this option is to achieve compatibility with ancient PGP products, predating the addition of SHA-1 protected packets to RFC 4880. Recent gnupg.org and pgp.com software supports it fine.

```
Values: 0, 1
Default: 0
Applies to: pgp_sym_encrypt, pgp_pub_encrypt
```

F.25.3.7.6. enable-session-key

Use separate session key. Public-key encryption always uses a separate session key; this is for symmetric-key encryption, which by default uses the S2K key directly.

```
Values: 0, 1
Default: 0
Applies to: pgp_sym_encrypt
```

F.25.3.7.7. s2k-mode

Which S2K algorithm to use.

```
Values:
  0 - Without salt.  Dangerous!
  1 - With salt but with fixed iteration count.
  3 - Variable iteration count.
Default: 3
Applies to: pgp_sym_encrypt
```

F.25.3.7.8. s2k-digest-algo

Which digest algorithm to use in S2K calculation.

```
Values: md5, sha1
Default: sha1
Applies to: pgp_sym_encrypt
```

F.25.3.7.9. s2k-cipher-algo

Which cipher to use for encrypting separate session key.

```
Values: bf, aes, aes128, aes192, aes256
Default: use cipher-algo
Applies to: pgp_sym_encrypt
```

F.25.3.7.10. unicode-mode

Whether to convert textual data from database internal encoding to UTF-8 and back. If your database already is UTF-8, no conversion will be done, but the message will be tagged as UTF-8. Without this option it will not be.

```
Values: 0, 1
Default: 0
Applies to: pgp_sym_encrypt, pgp_pub_encrypt
```

F.25.3.8. Generating PGP keys with GnuPG

To generate a new key:

```
gpg --gen-key
```

The preferred key type is "DSA and Elgamal".

For RSA encryption you must create either DSA or RSA sign-only key as master and then add an RSA encryption subkey with `gpg --edit-key`.

To list keys:

```
gpg --list-secret-keys
```

To export a public key in ASCII-armor format:

```
gpg -a --export KEYID > public.key
```

To export a secret key in ASCII-armor format:

```
gpg -a --export-secret-keys KEYID > secret.key
```

You need to use `dearmor()` on these keys before giving them to the PGP functions. Or if you can handle binary data, you can drop `-a` from the command.

For more details see `man gpg`, *The GNU Privacy Handbook*[3] and other documentation on *http://www.gnupg.org*.

F.25.3.9. Limitations of PGP code

- No support for signing. That also means that it is not checked whether the encryption subkey belongs to the master key.
- No support for encryption key as master key. As such practice is generally discouraged, this should not be a problem.
- No support for several subkeys. This may seem like a problem, as this is common practice. On the other hand, you should not use your regular GPG/PGP keys with `pgcrypto`, but create new ones, as the usage scenario is rather different.

F.25.4. Raw encryption functions

These functions only run a cipher over data; they don't have any advanced features of PGP encryption. Therefore they have some major problems:

1. They use user key directly as cipher key.
2. They don't provide any integrity checking, to see if the encrypted data was modified.
3. They expect that users manage all encryption parameters themselves, even IV.
4. They don't handle text.

So, with the introduction of PGP encryption, usage of raw encryption functions is discouraged.

```
encrypt(data bytea, key bytea, type text) returns bytea
decrypt(data bytea, key bytea, type text) returns bytea

encrypt_iv(data bytea, key bytea, iv bytea, type text) returns bytea
decrypt_iv(data bytea, key bytea, iv bytea, type text) returns bytea
```

[3] *http://www.gnupg.org/gph/en/manual.html*

Encrypt/decrypt data using the cipher method specified by `type`. The syntax of the `type` string is:

```
algorithm [ - mode ] [ /pad: padding ]
```

where *`algorithm`* is one of:

- `bf` - Blowfish
- `aes` - AES (Rijndael-128)

and *`mode`* is one of:

- `cbc` - next block depends on previous (default)
- `ecb` - each block is encrypted separately (for testing only)

and *`padding`* is one of:

- `pkcs` - data may be any length (default)
- `none` - data must be multiple of cipher block size

So, for example, these are equivalent:

```
encrypt(data, 'fooz', 'bf')
encrypt(data, 'fooz', 'bf-cbc/pad:pkcs')
```

In `encrypt_iv` and `decrypt_iv`, the `iv` parameter is the initial value for the CBC mode; it is ignored for ECB. It is clipped or padded with zeroes if not exactly block size. It defaults to all zeroes in the functions without this parameter.

F.25.5. Random-data functions

```
gen_random_bytes(count integer) returns bytea
```

Returns `count` cryptographically strong random bytes. At most 1024 bytes can be extracted at a time. This is to avoid draining the randomness generator pool.

F.25.6. Notes

F.25.6.1. Configuration

`pgcrypto` configures itself according to the findings of the main PostgreSQL `configure` script. The options that affect it are `--with-zlib` and `--with-openssl`.

When compiled with zlib, PGP encryption functions are able to compress data before encrypting.

When compiled with OpenSSL, there will be more algorithms available. Also public-key encryption functions will be faster as OpenSSL has more optimized BIGNUM functions.

Functionality	Built-in	With OpenSSL
MD5	yes	yes
SHA1	yes	yes
SHA224/256/384/512	yes	yes (Note 1)
Other digest algorithms	no	yes (Note 2)
Blowfish	yes	yes
AES	yes	yes (Note 3)
DES/3DES/CAST5	no	yes
Raw encryption	yes	yes
PGP Symmetric encryption	yes	yes
PGP Public-Key encryption	yes	yes

Table F-18. Summary of functionality with and without OpenSSL

Notes:

1. SHA2 algorithms were added to OpenSSL in version 0.9.8. For older versions, `pgcrypto` will use built-in code.
2. Any digest algorithm OpenSSL supports is automatically picked up. This is not possible with ciphers, which need to be supported explicitly.
3. AES is included in OpenSSL since version 0.9.7. For older versions, `pgcrypto` will use built-in code.

F.25.6.2. NULL handling

As is standard in SQL, all functions return NULL, if any of the arguments are NULL. This may create security risks on careless usage.

F.25.6.3. Security limitations

All `pgcrypto` functions run inside the database server. That means that all the data and passwords move between `pgcrypto` and client applications in clear text. Thus you must:

1. Connect locally or use SSL connections.
2. Trust both system and database administrator.

If you cannot, then better do crypto inside client application.

F.25.6.4. Useful reading

- *http://www.gnupg.org/gph/en/manual.html*

  The GNU Privacy Handbook.

- *http://www.openwall.com/crypt/*

  Describes the crypt-blowfish algorithm.
- *http://www.stack.nl/~galactus/remailers/passphrase-faq.html*

  How to choose a good password.
- *http://world.std.com/~reinhold/diceware.html*

  Interesting idea for picking passwords.
- *http://www.interhack.net/people/cmcurtin/snake-oil-faq.html*

  Describes good and bad cryptography.

F.25.6.5. Technical references

- *http://www.ietf.org/rfc/rfc4880.txt*

  OpenPGP message format.
- *http://www.ietf.org/rfc/rfc1321.txt*

  The MD5 Message-Digest Algorithm.
- *http://www.ietf.org/rfc/rfc2104.txt*

  HMAC: Keyed-Hashing for Message Authentication.
- *http://www.usenix.org/events/usenix99/provos.html*

  Comparison of crypt-des, crypt-md5 and bcrypt algorithms.
- *http://csrc.nist.gov/cryptval/des.htm*

  Standards for DES, 3DES and AES.
- *http://en.wikipedia.org/wiki/Fortuna_(PRNG)*

  Description of Fortuna CSPRNG.
- *http://jlcooke.ca/random/*

  Jean-Luc Cooke Fortuna-based /dev/random driver for Linux.
- *http://research.cyber.ee/~lipmaa/crypto/*

  Collection of cryptology pointers.

F.25.7. Author

Marko Kreen `<markokr@gmail.com>`

`pgcrypto` uses code from the following sources:

Algorithm	Author	Source origin
DES crypt	David Burren and others	FreeBSD libcrypt
MD5 crypt	Poul-Henning Kamp	FreeBSD libcrypt
Blowfish crypt	Solar Designer	www.openwall.com
Blowfish cipher	Simon Tatham	PuTTY
Rijndael cipher	Brian Gladman	OpenBSD sys/crypto
MD5 and SHA1	WIDE Project	KAME kame/sys/crypto
SHA256/384/512	Aaron D. Gifford	OpenBSD sys/crypto
BIGNUM math	Michael J. Fromberger	dartmouth.edu/~sting/sw/imath

F.26. pg_freespacemap

The `pg_freespacemap` module provides a means for examining the free space map (FSM). It provides a function called `pg_freespace`, or two overloaded functions, to be precise. The functions show the value recorded in the free space map for a given page, or for all pages in the relation.

By default public access is revoked from the functions, just in case there are security issues lurking.

F.26.1. Functions

`pg_freespace(rel regclass IN, blkno bigint IN) returns int2`

> Returns the amount of free space on the page of the relation, specified by `blkno`, according to the FSM.

`pg_freespace(rel regclass IN, blkno OUT bigint, avail OUT int2)`

> Displays the amount of free space on each page of the relation, according to the FSM. A set of `(blkno bigint, avail int2)` tuples is returned, one tuple for each page in the relation.

The values stored in the free space map are not exact. They're rounded to precision of 1/256th of BLCKSZ (32 bytes with default BLCKSZ), and they're not kept fully up-to-date as tuples are inserted and updated.

For indexes, what is tracked is entirely-unused pages, rather than free space within pages. Therefore, the values are not meaningful, just whether a page is full or empty.

Note

> The interface was changed in version 9.0, to reflect the new FSM implementation introduced in the same version.

F.26.2. Sample output

```
postgres=# SELECT * FROM pg_freespace('foo');
 blkno | avail
-------+-------
     0 |     0
     1 |     0
     2 |     0
     3 |    32
     4 |   704
     5 |   704
     6 |   704
     7 |  1216
     8 |   704
     9 |   704
    10 |   704
    11 |   704
    12 |   704
    13 |   704
    14 |   704
    15 |   704
    16 |   704
    17 |   704
    18 |   704
    19 |  3648
(20 rows)
postgres=# SELECT * FROM pg_freespace('foo', 7);
 pg_freespace
--------------
         1216
(1 row)
```

F.26.3. Author

Original version by Mark Kirkwood *<markir@paradise.net.nz>*. Rewritten in version 9.0 to suit new FSM implementation by Heikki Linnakangas *<heikki@enterprisedb.com>*

F.27. pgrowlocks

The `pgrowlocks` module provides a function to show row locking information for a specified table.

F.27.1. Overview

```
pgrowlocks(text) returns setof record
```

The parameter is the name of a table. The result is a set of records, with one row for each locked row within the table. The output columns are shown in *Table F-19* (see below).

Name	Type	Description
locked_row	tid	Tuple ID (TID) of locked row
lock_type	text	`Shared` for shared lock, or `Exclusive` for exclusive lock
locker	xid	Transaction ID of locker, or multixact ID if multi-transaction
multi	boolean	True if locker is a multi-transaction
xids	xid[]	Transaction IDs of lockers (more than one if multi-transaction)
pids	integer[]	Process IDs of locking backends (more than one if multi-transaction)

Table F-19. `pgrowlocks` **output columns**

`pgrowlocks` takes `AccessShareLock` for the target table and reads each row one by one to collect the row locking information. This is not very speedy for a large table. Note that:

1. If the table as a whole is exclusive-locked by someone else, `pgrowlocks` will be blocked.
2. `pgrowlocks` is not guaranteed to produce a self-consistent snapshot. It is possible that a new row lock is taken, or an old lock is freed, during its execution.

`pgrowlocks` does not show the contents of locked rows. If you want to take a look at the row contents at the same time, you could do something like this:

```
SELECT * FROM accounts AS a, pgrowlocks('accounts') AS p
  WHERE p.locked_row = a.ctid;
```

Be aware however that (as of PostgreSQL 8.3) such a query will be very inefficient.

F.27.2. Sample output

```
test=# SELECT * FROM pgrowlocks('t1');
 locked_row | lock_type | locker | multi |   xids    |     pids
------------+-----------+--------+-------+-----------+---------------
      (0,1) | Shared    |     19 | t     | {804,805} | {29066,29068}
      (0,2) | Shared    |     19 | t     | {804,805} | {29066,29068}
      (0,3) | Exclusive |    804 | f     | {804}     | {29066}
      (0,4) | Exclusive |    804 | f     | {804}     | {29066}
(4 rows)
```

F.27.3. Author

Tatsuo Ishii

F.28. pg_standby

pg_standby supports creation of a "warm standby" database server. It is designed to be a production-ready program, as well as a customizable template should you require specific modifications.

pg_standby is designed to be a waiting `restore_command`, which is needed to turn a standard archive recovery into a warm standby operation. Other configuration is required as well, all of which is described in the main server manual (see *Section 25.2* - Vol.II).

pg_standby features include:

- Written in C, so very portable and easy to install
- Easy-to-modify source code, with specifically designated sections to modify for your own needs
- Already tested on Linux and Windows

F.28.1. Usage

To configure a standby server to use pg_standby, put this into its `recovery.conf` configuration file:

```
restore_command = 'pg_standby archiveDir %f %p %r'
```

where *`archiveDir`* is the directory from which WAL segment files should be restored.

The full syntax of pg_standby's command line is

```
pg_standby [ option ... ] archivelocation nextwalfile xlogfilepath
                                                    [ restartwalfile ]
```

When used within `restore_command`, the `%f` and `%p` macros should be specified for *`nextwalfile`* and *`xlogfilepath`* respectively, to provide the actual file and path required for the restore.

If *`restartwalfile`* is specified, normally by using the `%r` macro, then all WAL files logically preceding this file will be removed from *`archivelocation`*. This minimizes the number of files that need to be retained, while preserving crash-restart capability. Use of this parameter is appropriate if the *`archivelocation`* is a transient staging area for this particular standby server, but *not* when the *`archivelocation`* is intended as a long-term WAL archive area.

pg_standby assumes that *`archivelocation`* is a directory readable by the server-owning user. If *`restartwalfile`* (or `-k`) is specified, the *`archivelocation`* directory must be writable too.

There are two ways to fail over to a "warm standby" database server when the master server fails:

Smart Failover

> In smart failover, the server is brought up after applying all WAL files available in the archive. This results in zero data loss, even if the standby server has fallen behind, but if there is a lot of unapplied WAL it can be a long time before the standby server becomes ready. To trigger a smart failover, create a trigger file containing the word `smart`, or just create it and leave it empty.

Fast Failover

In fast failover, the server is brought up immediately. Any WAL files in the archive that have not yet been applied will be ignored, and all transactions in those files are lost. To trigger a fast failover, create a trigger file and write the word `fast` into it. pg_standby can also be configured to execute a fast failover automatically if no new WAL file appears within a defined interval.

F.28.2. pg_standby Options

pg_standby accepts the following command-line arguments:

`-c`

Use `cp` or `copy` command to restore WAL files from archive. This is the only supported behavior so this option is useless.

`-d`

Print lots of debug logging output on `stderr`.

`-k`

Remove files from *`archivelocation`* so that no more than this many WAL files before the current one are kept in the archive. Zero (the default) means not to remove any files from *`archivelocation`*. This parameter will be silently ignored if *`restartwalfile`* is specified, since that specification method is more accurate in determining the correct archive cut-off point. Use of this parameter is *deprecated* as of PostgreSQL 8.3; it is safer and more efficient to specify a *`restartwalfile`* parameter. A too small setting could result in removal of files that are still needed for a restart of the standby server, while a too large setting wastes archive space.

`-r` *`maxretries`*

Set the maximum number of times to retry the copy command if it fails (default 3). After each failure, we wait for *`sleeptime`* * *`num_retries`* so that the wait time increases progressively. So by default, we will wait 5 secs, 10 secs, then 15 secs before reporting the failure back to the standby server. This will be interpreted as end of recovery and the standby will come up fully as a result.

`-s` *`sleeptime`*

Set the number of seconds (up to 60, default 5) to sleep between tests to see if the WAL file to be restored is available in the archive yet. The default setting is not necessarily recommended; consult *Section 25.2* (Vol.II) for discussion.

`-t` *`triggerfile`*

Specify a trigger file whose presence should cause failover. It is recommended that you use a structured file name to avoid confusion as to which server is being triggered when multiple servers exist on the same system; for example `/tmp/pgsql.trigger.5432`.

`-w` *`maxwaittime`*

Set the maximum number of seconds to wait for the next WAL file, after which a fast failover will be performed. A setting of zero (the default) means wait forever. The default setting is not necessarily recommended; consult *Section 25.2* (Vol.II) for discussion.

F.28.3. Examples

On Linux or Unix systems, you might use:

```
archive_command = 'cp %p .../archive/%f'

restore_command = 'pg_standby -d -s 2 -t /tmp/pgsql.trigger.5442 .../archive %f %p
                                                                      %r 2>>standby.log'

recovery_end_command = 'rm -f /tmp/pgsql.trigger.5442'
```

where the archive directory is physically located on the standby server, so that the `archive_command` is accessing it across NFS, but the files are local to the standby (enabling use of `ln`). This will:

- produce debugging output in `standby.log`
- sleep for 2 seconds between checks for next WAL file availability
- stop waiting only when a trigger file called `/tmp/pgsql.trigger.5442` appears, and perform failover according to its content
- remove the trigger file when recovery ends
- remove no-longer-needed files from the archive directory

On Windows, you might use:

```
archive_command = 'copy %p ...\\archive\\%f'

restore_command = 'pg_standby -d -s 5 -t C:\pgsql.trigger.5442 ...\archive %f %p %r
                                                                          2>>standby.log'

recovery_end_command = 'del C:\pgsql.trigger.5442'
```

Note that backslashes need to be doubled in the `archive_command`, but *not* in the `restore_command` or `recovery_end_command`. This will:

- use the `copy` command to restore WAL files from archive
- produce debugging output in `standby.log`
- sleep for 5 seconds between checks for next WAL file availability
- stop waiting only when a trigger file called `C:\pgsql.trigger.5442` appears, and perform failover according to its content

- remove the trigger file when recovery ends
- remove no-longer-needed files from the archive directory

The `copy` command on Windows sets the final file size before the file is completely copied, which would ordinarily confuse pg_standby. Therefore pg_standby waits `sleeptime` seconds once it sees the proper file size. GNUWin32's `cp` sets the file size only after the file copy is complete.

Since the Windows example uses `copy` at both ends, either or both servers might be accessing the archive directory across the network.

F.28.4. Supported server versions

pg_standby is designed to work with PostgreSQL 8.2 and later.

PostgreSQL 8.3 provides the `%r` macro, which is designed to let pg_standby know the last file it needs to keep. With PostgreSQL 8.2, the `-k` option must be used if archive cleanup is required. This option remains available in 8.3, but its use is deprecated.

PostgreSQL 9.0 provides the `recovery_end_command` option. Without this option a leftover trigger file can be hazardous.

F.28.5. Author

Simon Riggs <*simon@2ndquadrant.com*>

F.29. pg_stat_statements

The `pg_stat_statements` module provides a means for tracking execution statistics of all SQL statements executed by a server.

The module must be loaded by adding `pg_stat_statements` to `shared_preload_libraries` (Vol.II) in `postgresql.conf`, because it requires additional shared memory. This means that a server restart is needed to add or remove the module.

F.29.1. The `pg_stat_statements` view

The statistics gathered by the module are made available via a system view named `pg_stat_statements`. This view contains one row for each distinct query text, database ID, and user ID (up to the maximum number of distinct statements that the module can track). The columns of the view are shown in *Table F-20* (see below).

Name	Type	References	Description
`userid`	`oid`	`pg_authid.oid`	OID of user who executed the statement
`dbid`	`oid`	`pg_database.oid`	OID of database in which the statement was executed

Name	Type	References	Description
query	text		Text of the statement (up to *track_activity_query_size* (Vol.II) bytes)
calls	bigint		Number of times executed
total_time	double precision		Total time spent in the statement, in seconds
rows	bigint		Total number of rows retrieved or affected by the statement
shared_blks_hit	bigint		Total number of shared blocks hits by the statement
shared_blks_read	bigint		Total number of shared blocks reads by the statement
shared_blks_written	bigint		Total number of shared blocks writes by the statement
local_blks_hit	bigint		Total number of local blocks hits by the statement
local_blks_read	bigint		Total number of local blocks reads by the statement
local_blks_written	bigint		Total number of local blocks writes by the statement
temp_blks_read	bigint		Total number of temp blocks reads by the statement
temp_blks_written	bigint		Total number of temp blocks writes by the statement

Table F-20. `pg_stat_statements` **columns**

This view, and the function `pg_stat_statements_reset`, are available only in databases they have been specifically installed into by running the `pg_stat_statements.sql` install script. However, statistics are tracked across all databases of the server whenever the `pg_stat_statements` module is loaded into the server, regardless of presence of the view.

For security reasons, non-superusers are not allowed to see the text of queries executed by other users. They can see the statistics, however, if the view has been installed in their database.

Note that statements are considered the same if they have the same text, regardless of the values of any out-of-line parameters used in the statement. Using out-of-line parameters will help to group statements together and may make the statistics more useful.

F.29.2. Functions

`pg_stat_statements_reset() returns void`

`pg_stat_statements_reset` discards all statistics gathered so far by `pg_stat_statements`. By default, this function can only be executed by superusers.

F.29.3. Configuration parameters

`pg_stat_statements.max (integer)`

`pg_stat_statements.max` is the maximum number of statements tracked by the module (i.e., the maximum number of rows in the `pg_stat_statements` view). If more distinct statements than that are observed, information about the least-executed statements is discarded. The default value is 1000. This parameter can only be set at server start.

`pg_stat_statements.track (enum)`

`pg_stat_statements.track` controls which statements are counted by the module. Specify `top` to track top-level statements (those issued directly by clients), `all` to also track nested statements (such as statements invoked within functions), or `none` to disable. The default value is `top`. Only superusers can change this setting.

`pg_stat_statements.track_utility (boolean)`

`pg_stat_statements.track_utility` controls whether utility commands are tracked by the module. Utility commands are all those other than `SELECT`, `INSERT`, `UPDATE` and `DELETE`. The default value is `on`. Only superusers can change this setting.

`pg_stat_statements.save (boolean)`

`pg_stat_statements.save` specifies whether to save statement statistics across server shutdowns. If it is `off` then statistics are not saved at shutdown nor reloaded at server start. The default value is `on`. This parameter can only be set in the `postgresql.conf` file or on the server command line.

The module requires additional shared memory amounting to about `pg_stat_statements.max * track_activity_query_size` (Vol.II) bytes. Note that this memory is consumed whenever the module is loaded, even if `pg_stat_statements.track` is set to `none`.

In order to set any of these parameters in your `postgresql.conf` file, you will need to add `pg_stat_statements` to `custom_variable_classes` (Vol.II). Typical usage might be:

```
# postgresql.conf
shared_preload_libraries = 'pg_stat_statements'

custom_variable_classes = 'pg_stat_statements'
pg_stat_statements.max = 10000
pg_stat_statements.track = all
```

F.29.4. Sample output

```
bench=# SELECT pg_stat_statements_reset();

$ pgbench -i bench
$ pgbench -c10 -t300 -M prepared bench

bench=# \x
bench=# SELECT query, calls, total_time, rows, 100.0 * shared_blks_hit /
               nullif(shared_blks_hit + shared_blks_read, 0) AS hit_percent
          FROM pg_stat_statements ORDER BY total_time DESC LIMIT 5;
-[ RECORD 1 ]---------------------------------------------------------------------
query       | UPDATE pgbench_branches SET bbalance = bbalance + $1 WHERE bid = $2;
calls       | 3000
total_time  | 9.60900100000002
rows        | 2836
hit_percent | 99.9778970000200936
-[ RECORD 2 ]---------------------------------------------------------------------
query       | UPDATE pgbench_tellers SET tbalance = tbalance + $1 WHERE tid = $2;
calls       | 3000
total_time  | 8.015156
rows        | 2990
hit_percent | 99.9731126579631345
-[ RECORD 3 ]---------------------------------------------------------------------
query       | copy pgbench_accounts from stdin
calls       | 1
total_time  | 0.310624
rows        | 100000
hit_percent | 0.30395136778115501520
-[ RECORD 4 ]---------------------------------------------------------------------
query       | UPDATE pgbench_accounts SET abalance = abalance + $1 WHERE aid = $2;
calls       | 3000
total_time  | 0.271741999999997
rows        | 3000
hit_percent | 93.7968855088209426
-[ RECORD 5 ]---------------------------------------------------------------------
query       | alter table pgbench_accounts add primary key (aid)
calls       | 1
total_time  | 0.08142
rows        | 0
hit_percent | 34.4947735191637631
```

F.29.5. Author

Takahiro Itagaki <*itagaki.takahiro@oss.ntt.co.jp*>

F.30. pgstattuple

The `pgstattuple` module provides various functions to obtain tuple-level statistics.

F.30.1. Functions

`pgstattuple(text) returns record`

`pgstattuple` returns a relation's physical length, percentage of "dead" tuples, and other info. This may help users to determine whether vacuum is necessary or not. The argument is the target relation's name (optionally schema-qualified). For example:

```
test=> SELECT * FROM pgstattuple('pg_catalog.pg_proc');
-[ RECORD 1 ]------+-------
table_len          | 458752
tuple_count        | 1470
tuple_len          | 438896
tuple_percent      | 95.67
dead_tuple_count   | 11
dead_tuple_len     | 3157
dead_tuple_percent | 0.69
free_space         | 8932
free_percent       | 1.95
```

The output columns are described in *Table F-21* (see below).

Column	Type	Description
table_len	bigint	Physical relation length in bytes
tuple_count	bigint	Number of live tuples
tuple_len	bigint	Total length of live tuples in bytes
tuple_percent	float8	Percentage of live tuples
dead_tuple_count	bigint	Number of dead tuples
dead_tuple_len	bigint	Total length of dead tuples in bytes
dead_tuple_percent	float8	Percentage of dead tuples
free_space	bigint	Total free space in bytes
free_percent	float8	Percentage of free space

Table F-21. `pgstattuple` **output columns**

`pgstattuple` acquires only a read lock on the relation. So the results do not reflect an instantaneous snapshot; concurrent updates will affect them.

`pgstattuple` judges a tuple is "dead" if `HeapTupleSatisfiesNow` returns false.

`pgstattuple(oid) returns record`

This is the same as `pgstattuple(text)`, except that the target relation is specified by OID.

`pgstatindex(text) returns record`

`pgstatindex` returns a record showing information about a B-tree index. For example:

```
test=> SELECT * FROM pgstatindex('pg_cast_oid_index');
-[ RECORD 1 ]------+------
version            | 2
tree_level         | 0
index_size         | 8192
root_block_no      | 1
internal_pages     | 0
leaf_pages         | 1
empty_pages        | 0
deleted_pages      | 0
avg_leaf_density   | 50.27
leaf_fragmentation | 0
```

The output columns are:

Column	Type	Description
`version`	`integer`	B-tree version number
`tree_level`	`integer`	Tree level of the root page
`index_size`	`bigint`	Total number of pages in index
`root_block_no`	`bigint`	Location of root block
`internal_pages`	`bigint`	Number of "internal" (upper-level) pages
`leaf_pages`	`bigint`	Number of leaf pages
`empty_pages`	`bigint`	Number of empty pages
`deleted_pages`	`bigint`	Number of deleted pages
`avg_leaf_density`	`float8`	Average density of leaf pages
`leaf_fragmentation`	`float8`	Leaf page fragmentation

As with `pgstattuple`, the results are accumulated page-by-page, and should not be expected to represent an instantaneous snapshot of the whole index.

`pg_relpages(text) returns bigint`

`pg_relpages` returns the number of pages in the relation.

F.30.2. Authors

Tatsuo Ishii and Satoshi Nagayasu

F.31. pg_trgm

The `pg_trgm` module provides functions and operators for determining the similarity of text based on trigram matching, as well as index operator classes that support fast searching for similar strings.

F.31.1. Trigram (or Trigraph) Concepts

A trigram is a group of three consecutive characters taken from a string. We can measure the similarity of two strings by counting the number of trigrams they share. This simple idea turns out to be very effective for measuring the similarity of words in many natural languages.

Note

A string is considered to have two spaces prefixed and one space suffixed when determining the set of trigrams contained in the string. For example, the set of trigrams in the string "`cat`" is "` c`", "` ca`", "`cat`", and "`at `".

F.31.2. Functions and Operators

Function	Returns	Description
`similarity(text, text)`	`real`	Returns a number that indicates how similar the two arguments are. The range of the result is zero (indicating that the two strings are completely dissimilar) to one (indicating that the two strings are identical).
`show_trgm(text)`	`text[]`	Returns an array of all the trigrams in the given string. (In practice this is seldom useful except for debugging.)
`show_limit()`	`real`	Returns the current similarity threshold used by the `%` operator. This sets the minimum similarity between two words for them to be consi-dered similar enough to be misspellings of each other, for example.
`set_limit(real)`	`real`	Sets the current similarity threshold that is used by the `%` operator. The threshold must be between 0 and 1 (default is 0.3). Returns the same value passed in.

Table F-22. `pg_trgm` **functions**

Operator	Returns	Description
`text % text`	`boolean`	Returns `true` if its arguments have a similarity that is greater than the current similarity threshold set by `set_limit`.

Table F-23. `pg_trgm` **operators**

F.31.3. Index Support

The `pg_trgm` module provides GiST and GIN index operator classes that allow you to create an index over a text column for the purpose of very fast similarity searches. These index types support the `%` similarity operator (and no other operators, so you may want a regular B-tree index too).

Example:

```
CREATE TABLE test_trgm (t text);
CREATE INDEX trgm_idx ON test_trgm USING gist (t gist_trgm_ops);
```

or

```
CREATE INDEX trgm_idx ON test_trgm USING gin (t gin_trgm_ops);
```

At this point, you will have an index on the `t` column that you can use for similarity searching. A typical query is

```
SELECT t, similarity(t, 'word') AS sml
  FROM test_trgm
  WHERE t % 'word'
  ORDER BY sml DESC, t;
```

This will return all values in the text column that are sufficiently similar to *word*, sorted from best match to worst. The index will be used to make this a fast operation even over very large data sets.

The choice between GiST and GIN indexing depends on the relative performance characteristics of GiST and GIN, which are discussed elsewhere. As a rule of thumb, a GIN index is faster to search than a GiST index, but slower to build or update; so GIN is better suited for static data and GiST for often-updated data.

F.31.4. Text Search Integration

Trigram matching is a very useful tool when used in conjunction with a full text index. In particular it can help to recognize misspelled input words that will not be matched directly by the full text search mechanism.

The first step is to generate an auxiliary table containing all the unique words in the documents:

```
CREATE TABLE words AS SELECT word FROM
        ts_stat('SELECT to_tsvector(''simple'', bodytext) FROM documents');
```

where `documents` is a table that has a text field `bodytext` that we wish to search. The reason for using the `simple` configuration with the `to_tsvector` function, instead of using a language-specific configuration, is that we want a list of the original (unstemmed) words.

Next, create a trigram index on the word column:

```
CREATE INDEX words_idx ON words USING gin(word gin_trgm_ops);
```

Now, a `SELECT` query similar to the previous example can be used to suggest spellings for misspelled words in user search terms. A useful extra test is to require that the selected words are also of similar length to the misspelled word.

> **Note**
>
> Since the `words` table has been generated as a separate, static table, it will need to be periodically regenerated so that it remains reasonably up-to-date with the document collection. Keeping it exactly current is usually unnecessary.

F.31.5. References

GiST Development Site *http://www.sai.msu.su/~megera/postgres/gist/*

Tsearch2 Development Site *http://www.sai.msu.su/~megera/postgres/gist/tsearch/V2/*

F.31.6. Authors

Oleg Bartunov <*oleg@sai.msu.su*>, Moscow, Moscow University, Russia

Teodor Sigaev <*teodor@sigaev.ru*>, Moscow, Delta-Soft Ltd.,Russia

Documentation: Christopher Kings-Lynne

This module is sponsored by Delta-Soft Ltd., Moscow, Russia.

F.32. pg_upgrade

pg_upgrade (formerly called pg_migrator) allows data stored in PostgreSQL data files to be migrated to a later PostgreSQL major version without the data dump/reload typically required for major version upgrades, e.g. from 8.4.7 to the current major release of PostgreSQL. It is not required for minor version upgrades, e.g. from 9.0.1 to 9.0.4.

pg_upgrade works because, though new features are regularly added to PostgreSQL major releases, the internal data storage format rarely changes. pg_upgrade does its best to make sure the old and new clusters are binary-compatible, e.g. by checking for compatible compile-time settings, including 32/64-bit binaries. It is important that any external modules are also binary compatible, though this cannot be checked by pg_upgrade.

F.32.1. Supported Versions

pg_upgrade supports upgrades from 8.3.X and later to the current major release of PostgreSQL, including snapshot and alpha releases.

F.32.2. pg_upgrade Options

pg_upgrade accepts the following command-line arguments:

`-b` *`old_bindir`*
`--old-bindir` *`OLDBINDIR`*

specify the old cluster executable directory

`-B` *`new_bindir`*
`--new-bindir` *`NEWBINDIR`*

specify the new cluster executable directory

`-c`
`--check`

check clusters only, don't change any data

`-d` *`old_datadir`*
`--old-datadir` *`OLDDATADIR`*

specify the old cluster data directory

`-D` *`new_datadir`*
`--new-datadir` *`NEWDATADIR`*

specify the new cluster data directory

`-g`
`--debug`

enable debugging

`-G` *`debug_filename`*
`--debugfile` *`DEBUGFILENAME`*

output debugging activity to file

`-k`
`--link`

link instead of copying files to new cluster

`-l` *`log_filename`*
`--logfile` *`LOGFILENAME`*

log session activity to file

`-p` *`old_portnum`*
`--old-port` *`portnum`*

specify the old cluster port number

`-P` *`new_portnum`*
`--new-port` *`portnum`*

specify the new cluster port number

`-u` *`username`*
`--user` *`username`*

clusters superuser

`-v`
`--verbose`

enable verbose output

`-V`
`--version`

display version information, then exit

`-?`
`-h`
`--help`

show help, then exit

F.32.3. Upgrade Steps

1. **Optionally move the old cluster**

   If you are using a version-specific installation directory, e.g. `/opt/PostgreSQL/8.4`, you do not need to move the old cluster. The one-click installers all use version-specific installation directories.

   If your installation directory is not version-specific, e.g. `/usr/local/pgsql`, it is necessary to move the current PostgreSQL install directory so it does not interfere with the new PostgreSQL installation. Once the current PostgreSQL server is shut down, it is safe to rename the PostgreSQL installation directory; assuming the old directory is `/usr/local/pgsql`, you can do:

   ```
   mv /usr/local/pgsql /usr/local/pgsql.old
   ```

   to rename the directory.

2. **For source installs, build the new version**

   Build the new PostgreSQL source with `configure` flags that are compatible with the old cluster. pg_upgrade will check `pg_controldata` to make sure all settings are compatible before starting the upgrade.

3. **Install the new PostgreSQL binaries**

   Install the new server's binaries and support files. You can use the same port numbers for both clusters, typically 5432, because the old and new clusters will not be running at the same time.

For source installs, if you wish to install the new server in a custom location, use the `prefix` variable:

```
gmake prefix=/usr/local/pgsql.new install
```

4. **Install pg_upgrade and pg_upgrade_support**

   Install `pg_upgrade` and `pg_upgrade_support` in the new PostgreSQL cluster

5. **Initialize the new PostgreSQL cluster**

   Initialize the new cluster using `initdb`. Again, use compatible `initdb` flags that match the old cluster. Many prebuilt installers do this step automatically. There is no need to start the new cluster.

6. **Install custom shared object files**

   Install any custom shared object files (or DLLs) used by the old cluster into the new cluster, e.g. `pgcrypto.so`, whether they are from `contrib` or some other source. Do not install the schema definitions, e.g. `pgcrypto.sql`, because these will be migrated from the old cluster.

7. **Adjust authentication**

   `pg_upgrade` will connect to the old and new servers several times, so you might want to set authentication to `trust` in `pg_hba.conf`, or if using `md5` authentication, use a `~/.pgpass` file (see *Section 31.14* – Vol.IV) to avoid being prompted repeatedly for a password.

8. **Stop both servers**

   Make sure both database servers are stopped using, on Unix, e.g.:

   ```
   pg_ctl -D /opt/PostgreSQL/8.4 stop
   pg_ctl -D /opt/PostgreSQL/9.0 stop
   ```

   or on Windows, using the proper service names:

   ```
   NET STOP postgresql-8.4
   NET STOP postgresql-9.0
   ```

   or

   ```
   NET STOP pgsql-8.3  (PostgreSQL 8.3 and older used a different service name)
   ```

9. **Run pg_upgrade**

   Always run the pg_upgrade binary of the new server, not the old one. pg_upgrade requires the specification of the old and new cluster's data and executable (`bin`) directories. You can also specify separate user and port values, and whether you want the data linked instead of copied (the default). If you use linking, the migration will be much faster (no data copying), but you will no longer be able to access your old cluster once you start the new cluster after the upgrade. See `pg_upgrade --help` for a full list of options.

For Windows users, you must be logged into an administrative account, and then start a shell as the postgres user and set the proper path:

```
RUNAS /USER:postgres "CMD.EXE"
SET PATH=%PATH%;C:\Program Files\PostgreSQL\9.0\bin;
```

and then run pg_upgrade with quoted directories, e.g.:

```
pg_upgrade.exe
        --old-datadir "C:/Program Files/PostgreSQL/8.4/data"
        --new-datadir "C:/Program Files/PostgreSQL/9.0/data"
        --old-bindir "C:/Program Files/PostgreSQL/8.4/bin"
        --new-bindir "C:/Program Files/PostgreSQL/9.0/bin"
```

Once started, `pg_upgrade` will verify the two clusters are compatible and then do the migration. You can use `pg_upgrade --check` to perform only the checks, even if the old server is still running. `pg_upgrade --check` will also outline any manual adjustments you will need to make after the migration. `pg_upgrade` requires write permission in the current directory.

Obviously, no one should be accessing the clusters during the migration.

If an error occurs while restoring the database schema, `pg_upgrade` will exit and you will have to revert to the old cluster as outlined in *Step 14* below. To try `pg_upgrade` again, you will need to modify the old cluster so the pg_upgrade schema restore succeeds. If the problem is a contrib module, you might need to uninstall the contrib module from the old cluster and install it in the new cluster after the migration, assuming the module is not being used to store user data.

10. **Restore `pg_hba.conf`**

    If you modified `pg_hba.conf` to use `trust`, restore its original authentication settings.

11. **Post-migration processing**

    If any post-migration processing is required, pg_upgrade will issue warnings as it completes. It will also generate script files that must be run by the administrator. The script files will connect to each database that needs post-migration processing. Each script should be run using:

    ```
    psql --username postgres --file script.sql postgres
    ```

    The scripts can be run in any order and can be deleted once they have been run.

Caution

In general it is unsafe to access tables referenced in rebuild scripts until the rebuild scripts have run to completion; doing so could yield incorrect results or poor performance. Tables not referenced in rebuild scripts can be accessed immediately.

12. **Statistics**

    Because optimizer statistics are not transferred by `pg_upgrade`, you will be instructed to run a command to regenerate that information at the end of the migration.

13. **Delete old cluster**

    Once you are satisfied with the upgrade, you can delete the old cluster's data directories by running the script mentioned when `pg_upgrade` completes. You can also delete the old installation directories (e.g. `bin`, `share`).

14. **Reverting to old cluster**

    If, after running `pg_upgrade`, you wish to revert to the old cluster, there are several options:

    - If you ran `pg_upgrade` with `--check`, no modifications were made to the old cluster and you can re-use it anytime.
    - If you ran `pg_upgrade` with `--link`, the data files are shared between the old and new cluster. If you started the new cluster, the new server has written to those shared files and it is unsafe to use the old cluster.
    - If you ran `pg_upgrade` *without* `--link` or did not start the new server, the old cluster was not modified except that an `.old` suffix was appended to `$PGDATA/global/pg_control` and perhaps tablespace directories. To reuse the old cluster, remove the `.old` suffix from `$PGDATA/global/pg_control`. and, if migrating to 8.4 or earlier, remove the tablespace directories created by the migration and remove the `.old` suffix from the tablespace directory names; then you can restart the old cluster.

F.32.4. Limitations in Migrating from PostgreSQL 8.3

Upgrading from PostgreSQL 8.3 has additional restrictions not present when upgrading from later PostgreSQL releases. For example, pg_upgrade will not work for a migration from 8.3 if a user column is defined as:

- a `tsquery` data type
- data type `name` and is not the first column

You must drop any such columns and migrate them manually.

pg_upgrade will require a table rebuild if:

- a user column is of data type `tsvector`

pg_upgrade will require a reindex if:

- an index is of type hash or GIN
- an index uses `bpchar_pattern_ops`

Also, the default datetime storage format changed to integer after PostgreSQL 8.3. pg_upgrade will check that the datetime storage format used by the old and new clusters match. Make sure your new cluster is built with the configure flag `--disable-integer-datetimes`.

For Windows users, note that due to different integer datetimes settings used by the one-click installer and the MSI installer, it is only possible to upgrade from version 8.3 of the one-click distribution to version 8.4 or later of the one-click distribution. It is not possible to upgrade from the MSI installer to the one-click installer.

F.32.5. Notes

pg_upgrade does not support migration of databases containing these `reg*` OID-referencing system data types: `regproc`, `regprocedure`, `regoper`, `regoperator`, `regclass`, `regconfig`, and `regdictionary`. (`regtype` can be migrated.)

All failure, rebuild, and reindex cases will be reported by pg_upgrade if they affect your installation; post-migration scripts to rebuild tables and indexes will be generated automatically.

For deployment testing, create a schema-only copy of the old cluster, insert dummy data, and migrate that.

If you want to use link mode and you don't want your old cluster to be modified when the new cluster is started, make a copy of the old cluster and migrate that with link mode. To make a valid copy of the old cluster, use `rsync` to create a dirty copy of the old cluster while the server is running, then shut down the old server and run `rsync` again to update the copy with any changes to make it consistent.

F.33. seg

This module implements a data type `seg` for representing line segments, or floating point intervals. `seg` can represent uncertainty in the interval endpoints, making it especially useful for representing laboratory measurements.

F.33.1. Rationale

The geometry of measurements is usually more complex than that of a point in a numeric continuum. A measurement is usually a segment of that continuum with somewhat fuzzy limits. The measurements come out as intervals because of uncertainty and randomness, as well as because the value being measured may naturally be an interval indicating some condition, such as the temperature range of stability of a protein.

Using just common sense, it appears more convenient to store such data as intervals, rather than pairs of numbers. In practice, it even turns out more efficient in most applications.

Further along the line of common sense, the fuzziness of the limits suggests that the use of traditional numeric data types leads to a certain loss of information. Consider this: your instrument reads 6.50, and you input this reading into the database. What do you get when you fetch it? Watch:

```
test=> select 6.50 :: float8 as "pH";
 pH
---
6.5
(1 row)
```

In the world of measurements, 6.50 is not the same as 6.5. It may sometimes be critically different. The experimenters usually write down (and publish) the digits they trust. 6.50 is actually a fuzzy interval contained within a bigger and even fuzzier interval, 6.5, with their center points being (probably) the only common feature they share. We definitely do not want such different data items to appear the same.

Conclusion? It is nice to have a special data type that can record the limits of an interval with arbitrarily variable precision. Variable in the sense that each data element records its own precision.

Check this out:

```
test=> select '6.25 .. 6.50'::seg as "pH";
          pH
------------
6.25 .. 6.50
(1 row)
```

F.33.2. Syntax

The external representation of an interval is formed using one or two floating point numbers joined by the range operator (`..` or `...`). Alternatively, it can be specified as a center point plus or minus a deviation. Optional certainty indicators (<, > and ~) can be stored as well. (Certainty indicators are ignored by all the built-in operators, however.) *Table F-24* (see below) gives on overview over the allowed representations; *Table F-25* (see below) shows some examples.

In *Table F-24* (see below), *x*, *y*, and `delta` denote floating-point numbers. *x* and *y*, but not `delta`, can be preceded by a certainty indicator.

x	Single value (zero-length interval)
`x .. y`	Interval from x to y
`x (+-) delta`	Interval from x - delta to x + delta

x	Single value (zero-length interval)
`x ..`	Open interval with lower bound x
`.. x`	Open interval with upper bound x

Table F-24. seg external representations

`5.0`	Creates a zero-length segment (a point, if you will)
`~5.0`	Creates a zero-length segment and records ~ in the data. ~ is ignored by seg operations, but is preserved as a comment.
`<5.0`	Creates a point at 5.0. < is ignored but is preserved as a comment.
`>5.0`	Creates a point at 5.0. > is ignored but is preserved as a comment.
`5(+-)0.3`	Creates an interval `4.7 .. 5.3`. Note that the `(+-)` notation isn't preserved.
`50 ..`	Everything that is greater than or equal to 50
`.. 0`	Everything that is less than or equal to 0
`1.5e-2 .. 2E-2`	Creates an interval `0.015 .. 0.02`
`1 ... 2`	The same as `1...2`, or `1 .. 2`, or `1..2` (spaces around the range operator are ignored)

Table F-25. Examples of valid seg input

Because `...` is widely used in data sources, it is allowed as an alternative spelling of `...`. Unfortunately, this creates a parsing ambiguity: it is not clear whether the upper bound in `0...23` is meant to be `23` or `0.23`. This is resolved by requiring at least one digit before the decimal point in all numbers in `seg` input.

As a sanity check, `seg` rejects intervals with the lower bound greater than the upper, for example `5 .. 2`.

F.33.3. Precision

`seg` values are stored internally as pairs of 32-bit floating point numbers. This means that numbers with more than 7 significant digits will be truncated.

Numbers with 7 or fewer significant digits retain their original precision. That is, if your query returns 0.00, you will be sure that the trailing zeroes are not the artifacts of formatting: they reflect the precision of the original data. The number of leading zeroes does not affect precision: the value 0.0067 is considered to have just 2 significant digits.

F.33.4. Usage

The `seg` module includes a GiST index operator class for `seg` values. The operators supported by the GiST operator class are shown in *Table F-26* (see below).

Operator	Description
`[a, b] << [c, d]`	[a, b] is entirely to the left of [c, d]. That is, [a, b] << [c, d] is true if b < c and false otherwise.
`[a, b] >> [c, d]`	[a, b] is entirely to the right of [c, d]. That is, [a, b] >> [c, d] is true if a > d and false otherwise.
`[a, b] &< [c, d]`	Overlaps or is left of — This might be better read as "does not extend to right of". It is true when b <= d.
`[a, b] &> [c, d]`	Overlaps or is right of — This might be better read as "does not extend to left of". It is true when a >= c.
`[a, b] = [c, d]`	Same as — The segments [a, b] and [c, d] are identical, that is, a = c and b = d.
`[a, b] && [c, d]`	The segments [a, b] and [c, d] overlap.
`[a, b] @> [c, d]`	The segment [a, b] contains the segment [c, d], that is, a <= c and b >= d.
`[a, b] <@ [c, d]`	The segment [a, b] is contained in [c, d], that is, a >= c and b <= d.

Table F-26. Seg GiST operators

(Before PostgreSQL 8.2, the containment operators `@>` and `<@` were respectively called `@` and `~`. These names are still available, but are deprecated and will eventually be retired. Notice that the old names are reversed from the convention formerly followed by the core geometric data types!)

The standard B-tree operators are also provided, for example

Operator	Description
`[a, b] < [c, d]`	Less than
`[a, b] > [c, d]`	Greater than

These operators do not make a lot of sense for any practical purpose but sorting. These operators first compare (a) to (c), and if these are equal, compare (b) to (d). That results in reasonably good sorting in most cases, which is useful if you want to use ORDER BY with this type.

F.33.5. Notes

For examples of usage, see the regression test `sql/seg.sql`.

The mechanism that converts `(+-)` to regular ranges isn't completely accurate in determining the number of significant digits for the boundaries. For example, it adds an extra digit to the lower boundary if the resulting interval includes a power of ten:

```
postgres=> select '10(+-)1'::seg as seg;
      seg
---------
9.0 .. 11             -- should be: 9 .. 11
```

The performance of an R-tree index can largely depend on the initial order of input values. It may be very helpful to sort the input table on the `seg` column; see the script `sort-segments.pl` for an example.

F.33.6. Credits

Original author: Gene Selkov, Jr. *<selkovjr@mcs.anl.gov>*, Mathematics and Computer Science Division, Argonne National Laboratory.

My thanks are primarily to Prof. Joe Hellerstein (*http://db.cs.berkeley.edu/jmh/*) for elucidating the gist of the GiST (*http://gist.cs.berkeley.edu/*). I am also grateful to all Postgres developers, present and past, for enabling myself to create my own world and live undisturbed in it. And I would like to acknowledge my gratitude to Argonne Lab and to the U.S. Department of Energy for the years of faithful support of my database research.

F.34. spi

The `contrib/spi` module provides several workable examples of using SPI and triggers. While these functions are of some value in their own right, they are even more useful as examples to modify for your own purposes. The functions are general enough to be used with any table, but you have to specify table and field names (as described below) while creating a trigger.

F.34.1. refint.c - functions for implementing referential integrity

`check_primary_key()` and `check_foreign_key()` are used to check foreign key constraints. (This functionality is long since superseded by the built-in foreign key mechanism, of course, but the module is still useful as an example.)

`check_primary_key()` checks the referencing table. To use, create a `BEFORE INSERT OR UPDATE` trigger using this function on a table referencing another table. Specify as the trigger arguments: the referencing table's column name(s) which form the foreign key, the referenced table name, and the column names in the referenced table which form the primary/unique key. To handle multiple foreign keys, create a trigger for each reference.

`check_foreign_key()` checks the referenced table. To use, create a `BEFORE DELETE OR UPDATE` trigger using this function on a table referenced by other table(s). Specify as the trigger arguments: the number of referencing tables for which the function has to perform checking, the action if a referencing key is found (`cascade` - to delete the referencing row, `restrict` - to abort transaction if referencing keys exist, `setnull` - to set referencing key fields to null), the triggered table's column names which form the primary/unique key, then the referencing table name and column names (repeated for as many referencing tables as were specified by first argument). Note that the primary/unique key columns should be marked NOT NULL and should have a unique index.

There are examples in `refint.example`.

F.34.2. timetravel.c - functions for implementing time travel

Long ago, PostgreSQL had a built-in time travel feature that kept the insert and delete times for each tuple. This can be emulated using these functions. To use these functions, you must add to a table two columns of `abstime` type to store the date when a tuple was inserted (start_date) and changed/deleted (stop_date):

```
CREATE TABLE mytab (
        ...             ...
        start_date      abstime,
        stop_date       abstime
        ...             ...
);
```

The columns can be named whatever you like, but in this discussion we'll call them start_date and stop_date.

When a new row is inserted, start_date should normally be set to current time, and stop_date to `infinity`. The trigger will automatically substitute these values if the inserted data contains nulls in these columns. Generally, inserting explicit non-null data in these columns should only be done when re-loading dumped data.

Tuples with stop_date equal to `infinity` are "valid now", and can be modified. Tuples with a finite stop_date cannot be modified anymore - the trigger will prevent it. (If you need to do that, you can turn off time travel as shown below.)

For a modifiable row, on update only the stop_date in the tuple being updated will be changed (to current time) and a new tuple with the modified data will be inserted. Start_date in this new tuple will be set to current time and stop_date to `infinity`.

A delete does not actually remove the tuple but only sets its stop_date to current time.

To query for tuples "valid now", include `stop_date = 'infinity'` in the query's WHERE condition. (You might wish to incorporate that in a view.) Similarly, you can query for tuples valid at any past time with suitable conditions on start_date and stop_date.

`timetravel()` is the general trigger function that supports this behavior. Create a `BEFORE INSERT OR UPDATE OR DELETE` trigger using this function on each time-traveled table. Specify two trigger arguments: the actual names of the start_date and stop_date columns. Optionally, you can specify one to three more arguments, which must refer to columns of type `text`. The trigger will store the name of the current user into the first of these columns during INSERT, the second column during UPDATE, and the third during DELETE.

`set_timetravel()` allows you to turn time-travel on or off for a table.
`set_timetravel('mytab', 1)` will turn TT ON for table mytab.
`set_timetravel('mytab', 0)` will turn TT OFF for table mytab. In both cases the old status is reported. While TT is off, you can modify the start_date and stop_date columns freely. Note that the on/off status is local to the current database session - fresh sessions will always start out with TT ON for all tables.

`get_timetravel()` returns the TT state for a table without changing it.

There is an example in `timetravel.example`.

F.34.3. autoinc.c - functions for autoincrementing fields

`autoinc()` is a trigger that stores the next value of a sequence into an integer field. This has some overlap with the built-in "serial column" feature, but it is not the same: `autoinc()` will override attempts to substitute a different field value during inserts, and optionally it can be used to increment the field during updates, too.

To use, create a `BEFORE INSERT` (or optionally `BEFORE INSERT OR UPDATE`) trigger using this function. Specify two trigger arguments: the name of the integer column to be modified, and the name of the sequence object that will supply values. (Actually, you can specify any number of pairs of such names, if you'd like to update more than one autoincrementing column.)

There is an example in `autoinc.example`.

F.34.4. insert_username.c - functions for tracking who changed a table

`insert_username()` is a trigger that stores the current user's name into a text field. This can be useful for tracking who last modified a particular row within a table.

To use, create a `BEFORE INSERT` and/or `UPDATE` trigger using this function. Specify a single trigger argument: the name of the text column to be modified.

There is an example in `insert_username.example`.

F.34.5. moddatetime.c - functions for tracking last modification time

`moddatetime()` is a trigger that stores the current time into a `timestamp` field. This can be useful for tracking the last modification time of a particular row within a table.

To use, create a `BEFORE UPDATE` trigger using this function. Specify a single trigger argument: the name of the `timestamp` column to be modified.

There is an example in `moddatetime.example`.

F.35. sslinfo

The `sslinfo` module provides information about the SSL certificate that the current client provided when connecting to PostgreSQL. The module is useless (most functions will return NULL) if the current connection does not use SSL.

This extension won't build at all unless the installation was configured with `--with-openssl`.

F.35.1. Functions Provided

`ssl_is_used() returns boolean`

Returns TRUE if current connection to server uses SSL, and FALSE otherwise.

`ssl_client_cert_present() returns boolean`

Returns TRUE if current client has presented a valid SSL client certificate to the server, and FALSE otherwise. (The server might or might not be configured to require a client certificate.)

`ssl_client_serial() returns numeric`

Returns serial number of current client certificate. The combination of certificate serial number and certificate issuer is guaranteed to uniquely identify a certificate (but not its owner - the owner ought to regularly change his keys, and get new certificates from the issuer).

So, if you run your own CA and allow only certificates from this CA to be accepted by the server, the serial number is the most reliable (albeit not very mnemonic) means to identify a user.

`ssl_client_dn() returns text`

Returns the full subject of the current client certificate, converting character data into the current database encoding. It is assumed that if you use non-ASCII characters in the certificate names, your database is able to represent these characters, too. If your database uses the SQL_ASCII encoding, non-ASCII characters in the name will be represented as UTF-8 sequences.

The result looks like `/CN=Somebody /C=Some country/O=Some organization`.

`ssl_issuer_dn() returns text`

Returns the full issuer name of the current client certificate, converting character data into the current database encoding. Encoding conversions are handled the same as for `ssl_client_dn`.

The combination of the return value of this function with the certificate serial number uniquely identifies the certificate.

This function is really useful only if you have more than one trusted CA certificate in your server's `root.crt` file, or if this CA has issued some intermediate certificate authority certificates.

`ssl_client_dn_field(fieldname text) returns text`

This function returns the value of the specified field in the certificate subject, or NULL if the field is not present. Field names are string constants that are converted into ASN1 object identifiers using the OpenSSL object database. The following values are acceptable:

```
commonName (alias CN)
surname (alias SN)
name
givenName (alias GN)
countryName (alias C)
localityName (alias L)
stateOrProvinceName (alias ST)
organizationName (alias O)
organizationUnitName (alias OU)
title
description
initials
postalCode
streetAddress
generationQualifier
description
dnQualifier
x500UniqueIdentifier
pseudonym
role
emailAddress
```

All of these fields are optional, except `commonName`. It depends entirely on your CA's policy which of them would be included and which wouldn't. The meaning of these fields, however, is strictly defined by the X.500 and X.509 standards, so you cannot just assign arbitrary meaning to them.

`ssl_issuer_field(fieldname text) returns text`

Same as `ssl_client_dn_field`, but for the certificate issuer rather than the certificate subject.

F.35.2. Author

Victor Wagner <*vitus@cryptocom.ru*>, Cryptocom LTD

E-Mail of Cryptocom OpenSSL development group: <*openssl@cryptocom.ru*>

F.36. tablefunc

The `tablefunc` module includes various functions that return tables (that is, multiple rows). These functions are useful both in their own right and as examples of how to write C functions that return multiple rows.

F.36.1. Functions Provided

Table F-27 (see below) shows the functions provided by the `tablefunc` module.

Function	Returns	Description
`normal_rand(int numvals, float8 mean, float8 stddev)`	`setof float8`	Produces a set of normally distributed random values
`crosstab(text sql)`	`setof record`	Produces a "pivot table" containing row names plus *N* value columns, where *N* is determined by the rowtype specified in the calling query
`crosstabN (text sql)`	`setof table_crosstab_ N`	Produces a "pivot table" containing row names plus *N* value columns. `crosstab2`, `crosstab3`, and `crosstab4` are predefined, but you can create additional `crosstabN` functions as described below
`crosstab(text source_sql, text category_sql)`	`setof record`	Produces a "pivot table" with the value columns specified by a second query
`crosstab(text sql, int N)`	`setof record`	Obsolete version of `crosstab(text)`. The parameter *N* is now ignored, since the number of value columns is always determined by the calling query
`connectby(text relname, text keyid_fld, text parent_keyid_fld [, text orderby_fld ], text start_with, int max_depth [, text branch_delim ])`	`setof record`	Produces a representation of a hierarchical tree structure

Table F-27. `tablefunc` **functions**

F.36.1.1. `normal_rand`

```
normal_rand(int numvals, float8 mean, float8 stddev) returns setof float8
```

`normal_rand` produces a set of normally distributed random values (Gaussian distribution).

`numvals` is the number of values to be returned from the function. `mean` is the mean of the normal distribution of values and `stddev` is the standard deviation of the normal distribution of values.

For example, this call requests 1000 values with a mean of 5 and a standard deviation of 3:

```
test=# SELECT * FROM normal_rand(1000, 5, 3);
     normal_rand
----------------------
     1.56556322244898
     9.10040991424657
     5.36957140345079
   -0.369151492880995
    0.283600703686639
```

```
        .
        .
        .
     4.82992125404908
     9.71308014517282
     2.49639286969028
(1000 rows)
```

F.36.1.2. crosstab(text)

```
crosstab(text sql)
crosstab(text sql, int N)
```

The `crosstab` function is used to produce "pivot" displays, wherein data is listed across the page rather than down. For example, we might have data like

```
row1    val11
row1    val12
row1    val13
...
row2    val21
row2    val22
row2    val23
...
```

which we wish to display like

```
row1    val11   val12   val13   ...
row2    val21   val22   val23   ...
...
```

The `crosstab` function takes a text parameter that is a SQL query producing raw data formatted in the first way, and produces a table formatted in the second way.

The `sql` parameter is a SQL statement that produces the source set of data. This statement must return one `row_name` column, one `category` column, and one `value` column. `N` is an obsolete parameter, ignored if supplied (formerly this had to match the number of output value columns, but now that is determined by the calling query).

For example, the provided query might produce a set something like:

```
 row_name    cat    value
----------+-------+-------
  row1      cat1    val1
  row1      cat2    val2
  row1      cat3    val3
  row1      cat4    val4
  row2      cat1    val5
  row2      cat2    val6
  row2      cat3    val7
  row2      cat4    val8
```

The `crosstab` function is declared to return `setof record`, so the actual names and types of the output columns must be defined in the `FROM` clause of the calling `SELECT` statement, for example:

```
SELECT * FROM crosstab('...') AS ct(row_name text, category_1 text, category_2 text);
```

This example produces a set something like:

```
            <== value  columns  ==>
row_name    category_1   category_2
 ---------+------------+------------
   row1        val1         val2
   row2        val5         val6
```

The `FROM` clause must define the output as one `row_name` column (of the same datatype as the first result column of the SQL query) followed by N `value` columns (all of the same datatype as the third result column of the SQL query). You can set up as many output value columns as you wish. The names of the output columns are up to you.

The `crosstab` function produces one output row for each consecutive group of input rows with the same `row_name` value. It fills the output `value` columns, left to right, with the `value` fields from these rows. If there are fewer rows in a group than there are output `value` columns, the extra output columns are filled with nulls; if there are more rows, the extra input rows are skipped.

In practice the SQL query should always specify `ORDER BY 1,2` to ensure that the input rows are properly ordered, that is, values with the same `row_name` are brought together and correctly ordered within the row. Notice that `crosstab` itself does not pay any attention to the second column of the query result; it's just there to be ordered by, to control the order in which the third-column values appear across the page.

Here is a complete example:

```
CREATE TABLE ct(id SERIAL, rowid TEXT, attribute TEXT, value TEXT);
INSERT INTO ct(rowid, attribute, value) VALUES('test1','att1','val1');
INSERT INTO ct(rowid, attribute, value) VALUES('test1','att2','val2');
INSERT INTO ct(rowid, attribute, value) VALUES('test1','att3','val3');
INSERT INTO ct(rowid, attribute, value) VALUES('test1','att4','val4');
INSERT INTO ct(rowid, attribute, value) VALUES('test2','att1','val5');
INSERT INTO ct(rowid, attribute, value) VALUES('test2','att2','val6');
INSERT INTO ct(rowid, attribute, value) VALUES('test2','att3','val7');
INSERT INTO ct(rowid, attribute, value) VALUES('test2','att4','val8');

SELECT *
FROM crosstab(
  'select rowid, attribute, value
   from ct
   where attribute = ''att2'' or attribute = ''att3''
   order by 1,2')
AS ct(row_name text, category_1 text, category_2 text, category_3 text);
```

```
 row_name | category_1 | category_2 | category_3
----------+------------+------------+------------
 test1    | val2       | val3       |
 test2    | val6       | val7       |
(2 rows)
```

You can avoid always having to write out a `FROM` clause to define the output columns, by setting up a custom crosstab function that has the desired output row type wired into its definition. This is described in the next section. Another possibility is to embed the required `FROM` clause in a view definition.

F.36.1.3. crosstab*N*(text)

```
crosstabN(text sql)
```

The `crosstabN` functions are examples of how to set up custom wrappers for the general `crosstab` function, so that you need not write out column names and types in the calling `SELECT` query. The `tablefunc` module includes `crosstab2`, `crosstab3`, and `crosstab4`, whose output rowtypes are defined as

```
CREATE TYPE tablefunc_crosstab_N AS (
    row_name TEXT,
    category_1 TEXT,
    category_2 TEXT,
        .
        .
        .
    category_N TEXT
);
```

Thus, these functions can be used directly when the input query produces `row_name` and `value` columns of type `text`, and you want 2, 3, or 4 output values columns. In all other ways they behave exactly as described above for the general `crosstab` function.

For instance, the example given in the previous section would also work as

```
SELECT *
FROM crosstab3(
  'select rowid, attribute, value
   from ct
   where attribute = ''att2'' or attribute = ''att3''
   order by 1,2');
```

These functions are provided mostly for illustration purposes. You can create your own return types and functions based on the underlying `crosstab()` function. There are two ways to do it:

- Create a composite type describing the desired output columns, similar to the examples in the installation script. Then define a unique function name accepting one `text` parameter and returning `setof your_type_name`, but linking to the same underlying `crosstab` C function. For example, if your source data produces row names that are `text`, and values that are `float8` , and you want 5 value columns:

```
CREATE TYPE my_crosstab_float8_5_cols AS (
    my_row_name text,
    my_category_1 float8,
    my_category_2 float8,
    my_category_3 float8,
    my_category_4 float8,
    my_category_5 float8
);

CREATE OR REPLACE FUNCTION crosstab_float8_5_cols(text)
  RETURNS setof my_crosstab_float8_5_cols
  AS '$libdir/tablefunc','crosstab' LANGUAGE C STABLE STRICT;
```

- Use `OUT` parameters to define the return type implicitly. The same example could also be done this way:

```
CREATE OR REPLACE FUNCTION crosstab_float8_5_cols(IN text,
    OUT my_row_name text,
    OUT my_category_1 float8,
    OUT my_category_2 float8,
    OUT my_category_3 float8,
    OUT my_category_4 float8,
    OUT my_category_5 float8)
  RETURNS setof record
  AS '$libdir/tablefunc','crosstab' LANGUAGE C STABLE STRICT;
```

F.36.1.4. `crosstab(text, text)`

`crosstab(text source_sql, text category_sql)`

The main limitation of the single-parameter form of `crosstab` is that it treats all values in a group alike, inserting each value into the first available column. If you want the value columns to correspond to specific categories of data, and some groups might not have data for some of the categories, that doesn't work well. The two-parameter form of `crosstab` handles this case by providing an explicit list of the categories corresponding to the output columns.

`source_sql` is a SQL statement that produces the source set of data. This statement must return one `row_name` column, one `category` column, and one `value` column. It may also have one or more "extra" columns. The `row_name` column must be first. The `category` and `value` columns must be the last two columns, in that order. Any columns between `row_name` and `category` are treated as "extra". The "extra" columns are expected to be the same for all rows with the same `row_name` value.

For example, `source_sql` might produce a set something like:

```
SELECT row_name, extra_col, cat, value FROM foo ORDER BY 1;
```

```
 row_name    extra_col   cat    value
----------+------------+-----+---------
  row1         extra1    cat1    val1
  row1         extra1    cat2    val2
  row1         extra1    cat4    val4
  row2         extra2    cat1    val5
  row2         extra2    cat2    val6
  row2         extra2    cat3    val7
  row2         extra2    cat4    val8
```

`category_sql` is a SQL statement that produces the set of categories. This statement must return only one column. It must produce at least one row, or an error will be generated. Also, it must not produce duplicate values, or an error will be generated. `category_sql` might be something like:

```
SELECT DISTINCT cat FROM foo ORDER BY 1;
    cat
  -------
    cat1
    cat2
    cat3
    cat4
```

The `crosstab` function is declared to return `setof record`, so the actual names and types of the output columns must be defined in the `FROM` clause of the calling `SELECT` statement, for example:

```
SELECT * FROM crosstab('...', '...')
  AS ct(row_name text, extra text, cat1 text, cat2 text, cat3 text, cat4 text);
```

This will produce a result something like:

```
                        <==  value  columns   ==>
 row_name   extra    cat1   cat2   cat3   cat4
---------+-------+------+------+------+------
  row1      extra1  val1   val2          val4
  row2      extra2  val5   val6   val7   val8
```

The `FROM` clause must define the proper number of output columns of the proper data types. If there are *N* columns in the `source_sql` query's result, the first *N*-2 of them must match up with the first *N*-2 output columns. The remaining output columns must have the type of the last column of the `source_sql` query's result, and there must be exactly as many of them as there are rows in the `category_sql` query's result.

The `crosstab` function produces one output row for each consecutive group of input rows with the same `row_name` value. The output `row_name` column, plus any "extra" columns, are copied from the first row of the group. The output `value` columns are filled with the `value` fields from rows having matching `category` values. If a row's `category` does not match any output of the `category_sql` query, its `value` is ignored. Output columns whose matching category is not present in any input row of the group are filled with nulls.

In practice the `source_sql` query should always specify `ORDER BY 1` to ensure that values with the same `row_name` are brought together. However, ordering of the categories within a group is not important. Also, it is essential to be sure that the order of the `category_sql` query's output matches the specified output column order.

Here are two complete examples:

```
create table sales(year int, month int, qty int);
insert into sales values(2007, 1, 1000);
insert into sales values(2007, 2, 1500);
insert into sales values(2007, 7, 500);
insert into sales values(2007, 11, 1500);
insert into sales values(2007, 12, 2000);
insert into sales values(2008, 1, 1000);

select * from crosstab(
  'select year, month, qty from sales order by 1',
  'select m from generate_series(1,12) m'
) as (
  year int,
  "Jan" int,
  "Feb" int,
  "Mar" int,
  "Apr" int,
  "May" int,
  "Jun" int,
  "Jul" int,
  "Aug" int,
  "Sep" int,
  "Oct" int,
  "Nov" int,
  "Dec" int
);
 year | Jan  | Feb  | Mar | Apr | May | Jun | Jul | Aug | Sep | Oct | Nov  | Dec
------+------+------+-----+-----+-----+-----+-----+-----+-----+-----+------+------
 2007 | 1000 | 1500 |     |     |     |     | 500 |     |     |     | 1500 | 2000
 2008 | 1000 |      |     |     |     |     |     |     |     |     |      |
(2 rows)

CREATE TABLE cth(rowid text, rowdt timestamp, attribute text, val text);
INSERT INTO cth VALUES('test1','01 March 2003','temperature','42');
INSERT INTO cth VALUES('test1','01 March 2003','test_result','PASS');
INSERT INTO cth VALUES('test1','01 March 2003','volts','2.6987');
INSERT INTO cth VALUES('test2','02 March 2003','temperature','53');
INSERT INTO cth VALUES('test2','02 March 2003','test_result','FAIL');
INSERT INTO cth VALUES('test2','02 March 2003','test_startdate','01 March 2003');
INSERT INTO cth VALUES('test2','02 March 2003','volts','3.1234');

SELECT * FROM crosstab
(
  'SELECT rowid, rowdt, attribute, val FROM cth ORDER BY 1',
  'SELECT DISTINCT attribute FROM cth ORDER BY 1'
)
```

```
AS
(
       rowid text,
       rowdt timestamp,
       temperature int4,
       test_result text,
       test_startdate timestamp,
       volts float8
);
 rowid |           rowdt          | temperature | test_result |      test_startdate      | volts
-------+--------------------------+-------------+-------------+--------------------------+--------
 test1 | Sat Mar 01 00:00:00 2003 |          42 | PASS        |                          | 2.6987
 test2 | Sun Mar 02 00:00:00 2003 |          53 | FAIL        | Sat Mar 01 00:00:00 2003 | 3.1234
(2 rows)
```

You can create predefined functions to avoid having to write out the result column names and types in each query. See the examples in the previous section. The underlying C function for this form of `crosstab` is named `crosstab_hash`.

F.36.1.5. connectby

```
connectby(text relname, text keyid_fld, text parent_keyid_fld
          [, text orderby_fld ], text start_with, int max_depth
          [, text branch_delim ])
```

The `connectby` function produces a display of hierarchical data that is stored in a table. The table must have a key field that uniquely identifies rows, and a parent-key field that references the parent (if any) of each row. `connectby` can display the sub-tree descending from any row.

Table F-28 (see below) explains the parameters.

Parameter	Description
`relname`	Name of the source relation
`keyid_fld`	Name of the key field
`parent_keyid_fld`	Name of the parent-key field
`orderby_fld`	Name of the field to order siblings by (optional)
`start_with`	Key value of the row to start at
`max_depth`	Maximum depth to descend to, or zero for unlimited depth
`branch_delim`	String to separate keys with in branch output (optional)

Table F-28. `connectby` **parameters**

The key and parent-key fields can be any data type, but they must be the same type. Note that the `start_with` value must be entered as a text string, regardless of the type of the key field.

The `connectby` function is declared to return `setof record`, so the actual names and types of the output columns must be defined in the `FROM` clause of the calling `SELECT` statement, for example:

```
SELECT * FROM connectby('connectby_tree', 'keyid', 'parent_keyid', 'pos', 'row2', 0, '~')
  AS t(keyid text, parent_keyid text, level int, branch text, pos int);
```

The first two output columns are used for the current row's key and its parent row's key; they must match the type of the table's key field. The third output column is the depth in the tree and must be of type `integer`. If a `branch_delim` parameter was given, the next output column is the branch display and must be of type `text`. Finally, if an `orderby_fld` parameter was given, the last output column is a serial number, and must be of type `integer`.

The "branch" output column shows the path of keys taken to reach the current row. The keys are separated by the specified `branch_delim` string. If no branch display is wanted, omit both the `branch_delim` parameter and the branch column in the output column list.

If the ordering of siblings of the same parent is important, include the `orderby_fld` parameter to specify which field to order siblings by. This field can be of any sortable data type. The output column list must include a final integer serial-number column, if and only if `orderby_fld` is specified.

The parameters representing table and field names are copied as-is into the SQL queries that `connectby` generates internally. Therefore, include double quotes if the names are mixed-case or contain special characters. You may also need to schema-qualify the table name.

In large tables, performance will be poor unless there is an index on the parent-key field.

It is important that the `branch_delim` string not appear in any key values, else `connectby` may incorrectly report an infinite-recursion error. Note that if `branch_delim` is not provided, a default value of ~ is used for recursion detection purposes.

Here is an example:

```
CREATE TABLE connectby_tree(keyid text, parent_keyid text, pos int);

INSERT INTO connectby_tree VALUES('row1',NULL, 0);
INSERT INTO connectby_tree VALUES('row2','row1', 0);
INSERT INTO connectby_tree VALUES('row3','row1', 0);
INSERT INTO connectby_tree VALUES('row4','row2', 1);
INSERT INTO connectby_tree VALUES('row5','row2', 0);
INSERT INTO connectby_tree VALUES('row6','row4', 0);
INSERT INTO connectby_tree VALUES('row7','row3', 0);
INSERT INTO connectby_tree VALUES('row8','row6', 0);
INSERT INTO connectby_tree VALUES('row9','row5', 0);

-- with branch, without orderby_fld (order of results is not guaranteed)
```

```
SELECT * FROM connectby('connectby_tree', 'keyid', 'parent_keyid', 'row2', 0, '~')
 AS t(keyid text, parent_keyid text, level int, branch text);
 keyid | parent_keyid | level |       branch
-------+--------------+-------+---------------------
 row2  |              |     0 | row2
 row4  | row2         |     1 | row2~row4
 row6  | row4         |     2 | row2~row4~row6
 row8  | row6         |     3 | row2~row4~row6~row8
 row5  | row2         |     1 | row2~row5
 row9  | row5         |     2 | row2~row5~row9
(6 rows)

-- without branch, without orderby_fld (order of results is not guaranteed)
SELECT * FROM connectby('connectby_tree', 'keyid', 'parent_keyid', 'row2', 0)
 AS t(keyid text, parent_keyid text, level int);
 keyid | parent_keyid | level
-------+--------------+-------
 row2  |              |     0
 row4  | row2         |     1
 row6  | row4         |     2
 row8  | row6         |     3
 row5  | row2         |     1
 row9  | row5         |     2
(6 rows)

-- with branch, with orderby_fld (notice that row5 comes before row4)
SELECT * FROM connectby('connectby_tree','keyid','parent_keyid','pos','row2',0,'~')
 AS t(keyid text, parent_keyid text, level int, branch text, pos int);
 keyid | parent_keyid | level |       branch        | pos
-------+--------------+-------+---------------------+-----
 row2  |              |     0 | row2                |   1
 row5  | row2         |     1 | row2~row5           |   2
 row9  | row5         |     2 | row2~row5~row9      |   3
 row4  | row2         |     1 | row2~row4           |   4
 row6  | row4         |     2 | row2~row4~row6      |   5
 row8  | row6         |     3 | row2~row4~row6~row8 |   6
(6 rows)

-- without branch, with orderby_fld (notice that row5 comes before row4)
SELECT * FROM connectby('connectby_tree', 'keyid', 'parent_keyid', 'pos', 'row2',0)
 AS t(keyid text, parent_keyid text, level int, pos int);
 keyid | parent_keyid | level | pos
-------+--------------+-------+-----
 row2  |              |     0 |   1
 row5  | row2         |     1 |   2
 row9  | row5         |     2 |   3
 row4  | row2         |     1 |   4
 row6  | row4         |     2 |   5
 row8  | row6         |     3 |   6
(6 rows)
```

F.36.2. Author

Joe Conway

F.37. test_parser

`test_parser` is an example of a custom parser for full-text search. It doesn't do anything especially useful, but can serve as a starting point for developing your own parser.

`test_parser` recognizes words separated by white space, and returns just two token types:

```
mydb=# SELECT * FROM ts_token_type('testparser');
 tokid | alias |  description
-------+-------+---------------
     3 | word  | Word
    12 | blank | Space symbols
(2 rows)
```

These token numbers have been chosen to be compatible with the default parser's numbering. This allows us to use its `headline()` function, thus keeping the example simple.

F.37.1. Usage

Running the installation script creates a text search parser `testparser`. It has no user-configurable parameters.

You can test the parser with, for example,

```
mydb=# SELECT * FROM ts_parse('testparser', 'That''s my first own parser');
 tokid | token
-------+--------
     3 | That's
    12 |
     3 | my
    12 |
     3 | first
    12 |
     3 | own
    12 |
     3 | parser
```

Real-world use requires setting up a text search configuration that uses the parser. For example,

```
mydb=# CREATE TEXT SEARCH CONFIGURATION testcfg (PARSER = testparser );
CREATE TEXT SEARCH CONFIGURATION

mydb=# ALTER TEXT SEARCH CONFIGURATION testcfg
mydb-#   ADD MAPPING FOR word WITH english_stem;
ALTER TEXT SEARCH CONFIGURATION

mydb=#  SELECT to_tsvector('testcfg', 'That''s my first own parser');
          to_tsvector
-------------------------------
 'that':1 'first':3 'parser':5
(1 row)
```

```
mydb=# SELECT ts_headline('testcfg', 'Supernovae stars are the brightest
                                                          phenomena in galaxies',
mydb(#                    to_tsquery('testcfg', 'star'));
                           ts_headline
-----------------------------------------------------------------
 Supernovae <b>stars</b> are the brightest phenomena in galaxies
(1 row)
```

F.38. tsearch2

The `tsearch2` module provides backwards-compatible text search functionality for applications that used `contrib/tsearch2` before text searching was integrated into core PostgreSQL in release 8.3.

F.38.1. Portability Issues

Although the built-in text search features were based on `contrib/tsearch2` and are largely similar to it, there are numerous small differences that will create portability issues for existing applications:

- Some functions' names were changed, for example `rank` to `ts_rank`. The replacement `tsearch2` module provides aliases having the old names.
- The built-in text search data types and functions all exist within the system schema `pg_catalog`. In an installation using `contrib/tsearch2`, these objects would usually have been in the `public` schema, though some users chose to place them in a separate schema of their own. Explicitly schema-qualified references to the objects will therefore fail in either case. The replacement `tsearch2` module provides alias objects that are stored in `public` (or another schema if necessary) so that such references will still work.
- There is no concept of a "current parser" or "current dictionary" in the built-in text search features, only of a current search configuration (set by the `default_text_search_config` parameter). While the current parser and current dictionary were used only by functions intended for debugging, this might still pose a porting obstacle in some cases. The replacement `tsearch2` module emulates these additional state variables and provides backwards-compatible functions for setting and retrieving them.

There are some issues that are not addressed by the replacement `tsearch2` module, and will therefore require application code changes in any case:

- The old `tsearch2` trigger function allowed items in its argument list to be names of functions to be invoked on the text data before it was converted to `tsvector` format. This was removed as being a security hole, since it was not possible to guarantee that the function invoked was the one intended. The recommended approach if the data must be massaged before being indexed is to write a custom trigger that does the work for itself.

- Text search configuration information has been moved into core system catalogs that are noticeably different from the tables used by `contrib/tsearch2`. Any applications that examined or modified those tables will need adjustment.
- If an application used any custom text search configurations, those will need to be set up in the core catalogs using the new text search configuration SQL commands. The replacement `tsearch2` module offers a little bit of support for this by making it possible to load an old set of `contrib/tsearch2` configuration tables into PostgreSQL 8.3. (Without the module, it is not possible to load the configuration data because values in the `regprocedure` columns cannot be resolved to functions.) While those configuration tables won't actually *do* anything, at least their contents will be available to be consulted while setting up an equivalent custom configuration in 8.3.
- The old `reset_tsearch()` and `get_covers()` functions are not supported.
- The replacement `tsearch2` module does not define any alias operators, relying entirely on the built-in ones. This would only pose an issue if an application used explicitly schema-qualified operator names, which is very uncommon.

F.38.2. Converting a pre-8.3 Installation

The recommended way to update a pre-8.3 installation that uses `contrib/tsearch2` is:

1. Make a dump from the old installation in the usual way, but be sure not to use `-c` (`--clean`) option of pg_dump or pg_dumpall.
2. In the new installation, create empty database(s) and install the replacement `tsearch2` module into each database that will use text search. This must be done *before* loading the dump data! If your old installation had the `contrib/tsearch2` objects in a schema other than `public`, be sure to adjust the `tsearch2` installation script so that the replacement objects are created in that same schema.
3. Load the dump data. There will be quite a few errors reported due to failure to recreate the original `contrib/tsearch2` objects. These errors can be ignored, but this means you cannot restore the dump in a single transaction (eg, you cannot use pg_restore's `-1` switch).
4. Examine the contents of the restored `contrib/tsearch2` configuration tables (`pg_ts_cfg` and so on), and create equivalent built-in text search configurations as needed. You may drop the old configuration tables once you've extracted all the useful information from them.
5. Test your application.

At a later time you may wish to rename application references to the alias text search objects, so that you can eventually uninstall the replacement `tsearch2` module.

References

Tsearch2 Development Site *http://www.sai.msu.su/~megera/postgres/gist/tsearch/V2/*

F.39. unaccent

`unaccent` is a text search dictionary that removes accents (diacritic signs) from lexemes. It's a filtering dictionary, which means its output is always passed to the next dictionary (if any), unlike the normal behavior of dictionaries. This allows accent-insensitive processing for full text search.

The current implementation of `unaccent` cannot be used as a normalizing dictionary for the `thesaurus` dictionary.

F.39.1. Configuration

An `unaccent` dictionary accepts the following options:

- `RULES` is the base name of the file containing the list of translation rules. This file must be stored in `$SHAREDIR/tsearch_data/` (where `$SHAREDIR` means the PostgreSQL installation's shared-data directory). Its name must end in `.rules` (which is not to be included in the `RULES` parameter).

The rules file has the following format:

- Each line represents a pair, consisting of a character with accent followed by a character without accent. The first is translated into the second. For example,

```
À        A
Á        A
Â        A
Ã        A
Ä        A
Å        A
Æ        A
```

A more complete example, which is directly useful for most European languages, can be found in `unaccent.rules`, which is installed in `$SHAREDIR/tsearch_data/` when the `unaccent` module is installed.

F.39.2. Usage

Running the installation script `unaccent.sql` creates a text search template `unaccent` and a dictionary `unaccent` based on it. The `unaccent` dictionary has the default parameter setting `RULES='unaccent'`, which makes it immediately usable with the standard `unaccent.rules` file. If you wish, you can alter the parameter, for example

```
mydb=# ALTER TEXT SEARCH DICTIONARY unaccent (RULES='my_rules');
```

or create new dictionaries based on the template.

To test the dictionary, you can try:

```
mydb=# select ts_lexize('unaccent','Hôtel');
 ts_lexize
-----------
 {Hotel}
(1 row)
```

Here is an example showing how to insert the `unaccent` dictionary into a text search configuration:

```
mydb=# CREATE TEXT SEARCH CONFIGURATION fr ( COPY = french );
mydb=# ALTER TEXT SEARCH CONFIGURATION fr
        ALTER MAPPING FOR hword, hword_part, word
        WITH unaccent, french_stem;
mydb=# select to_tsvector('fr','Hôtels de la Mer');
    to_tsvector
-------------------
 'hotel':1 'mer':4
(1 row)

mydb=# select to_tsvector('fr','Hôtel de la Mer') @@ to_tsquery('fr','Hotels');
 ?column?
----------
 t
(1 row)

mydb=# select ts_headline('fr','Hôtel de la Mer',to_tsquery('fr','Hotels'));
      ts_headline
------------------------
 <b>Hôtel</b> de la Mer
(1 row)
```

F.39.3. Functions

The `unaccent()` function removes accents (diacritic signs) from a given string. Basically, it's a wrapper around the `unaccent` dictionary, but it can be used outside normal text search contexts.

`unaccent([`*`dictionary`*`, ]` *`string`*`) returns text`

For example:

```
SELECT unaccent('unaccent', 'Hôtel');
SELECT unaccent('Hôtel');
```

F.40. uuid-ossp

The `uuid-ossp` module provides functions to generate universally unique identifiers (UUIDs) using one of several standard algorithms. There are also functions to produce certain special UUID constants.

This module depends on the OSSP UUID library, which can be found at *http://www.ossp.org/pkg/lib/uuid/*.

F.40.1. `uuid-ossp` Functions

Table F-29 (see below) shows the functions available to generate UUIDs. The relevant standards ITU-T Rec. X.667, ISO/IEC 9834-8:2005, and RFC 4122 specify four algorithms for generating UUIDs, identified by the version numbers 1, 3, 4, and 5. (There is no version 2 algorithm.) Each of these algorithms could be suitable for a different set of applications.

Function	Description
`uuid_generate_v1()`	This function generates a version 1 UUID. This involves the MAC address of the computer and a time stamp. Note that UUIDs of this kind reveal the identity of the computer that created the identifier and the time at which it did so, which might make it unsuitable for certain security-sensitive applications.
`uuid_generate_v1mc()`	This function generates a version 1 UUID but uses a random multicast MAC address instead of the real MAC address of the computer.
`uuid_generate_v3(namespace uuid, name text)`	This function generates a version 3 UUID in the given namespace using the specified input name. The namespace should be one of the special constants produced by the `uuid_ns_*()` functions shown in *Table F-30* (see below). (It could be any UUID in theory.) The name is an identifier in the selected namespace. For example: `SELECT uuid_generate_v3(uuid_ns_url(), 'http://www.postgresql.org');` The name parameter will be MD5-hashed, so the cleartext cannot be derived from the generated UUID. The generation of UUIDs by this method has no random or environment-dependent element and is therefore reproducible.
`uuid_generate_v4()`	This function generates a version 4 UUID, which is derived entirely from random numbers.
`uuid_generate_v5(namespace uuid, name text)`	This function generates a version 5 UUID, which works like a version 3 UUID except that SHA-1 is used as a hashing method. Version 5 should be preferred over version 3 because SHA-1 is thought to be more secure than MD5.

Table F-29. Functions for UUID Generation

`uuid_nil()`	A "nil" UUID constant, which does not occur as a real UUID.
`uuid_ns_dns()`	Constant designating the DNS namespace for UUIDs.
`uuid_ns_url()`	Constant designating the URL namespace for UUIDs.
`uuid_ns_oid()`	Constant designating the ISO object identifier (OID) namespace for UUIDs. (This pertains to ASN.1 OIDs, which are unrelated to the OIDs used in PostgreSQL.)
`uuid_ns_x500()`	Constant designating the X.500 distinguished name (DN) namespace for UUIDs.

Table F-30. Functions Returning UUID Constants

F.40.2. Author

Peter Eisentraut <*peter_e@gmx.net*>

F.41. vacuumlo

vacuumlo is a simple utility program that will remove any "orphaned" large objects from a PostgreSQL database. An orphaned large object (LO) is considered to be any LO whose OID does not appear in any `oid` or `lo` data column of the database.

If you use this, you may also be interested in the `lo_manage` trigger in `contrib/lo` (see *Section F.17* - page 351). `lo_manage` is useful to try to avoid creating orphaned LOs in the first place.

F.41.1. Usage

```
vacuumlo [options] database [database2 ... databaseN]
```

All databases named on the command line are processed. Available options include:

`-v`

Write a lot of progress messages.

`-n`

Don't remove anything, just show what would be done.

`-U` *`username`*

Username to connect as.

`-w`
`--no-password`

Never issue a password prompt. If the server requires password authentication and a password is not available by other means such as a `.pgpass` file, the connection attempt will fail. This option can be useful in batch jobs and scripts where no user is present to enter a password.

`-W`

Force vacuumlo to prompt for a password before connecting to a database.

This option is never essential, since vacuumlo will automatically prompt for a password if the server demands password authentication. However, vacuumlo will waste a connection attempt finding out that the server wants a password. In some cases it is worth typing `-W` to avoid the extra connection attempt.

`-h` *`hostname`*

Database server's host.

`-p` *`port`*

Database server's port.

F.41.2. Method

First, it builds a temporary table which contains all of the OIDs of the large objects in that database.

It then scans through all columns in the database that are of type `oid` or `lo`, and removes matching entries from the temporary table.

The remaining entries in the temp table identify orphaned LOs. These are removed.

F.41.3. Author

Peter Mount *<peter@retep.org.uk>*

F.42. xml2

The `xml2` module provides XPath querying and XSLT functionality.

F.42.1. Deprecation notice

From PostgreSQL 8.3 on, there is XML-related functionality based on the SQL/XML standard in the core server. That functionality covers XML syntax checking and XPath queries, which is what this module does, and more, but the API is not at all compatible. It is planned that this module will be removed in PostgreSQL 9.0 in favor of the newer standard API, so you are encouraged to try converting your applications. If you find that some of the functionality of this module is not available in an adequate form with the newer API, please explain your issue to pgsql-hackers@postgresql.org so that the deficiency can be addressed.

F.42.2. Description of functions

Table F-31 (see below) shows the functions provided by this module. These functions provide straightforward XML parsing and XPath queries. All arguments are of type `text`, so for brevity that is not shown.

Function	Returns	Description
`xml_is_well_formed(document)`	`bool`	This parses the document text in its parameter and returns true if the document is well-formed XML. (Note: before PostgreSQL 8.2, this function was called `xml_valid()`. That is the wrong name since validity and well-formedness have different meanings in XML. The old name is still available, but is deprecated.)
`xpath_string(document, query)`	`text`	

Function	Returns	Description
`xpath_number(document, query)`	`float4`	These functions evaluate the XPath query on the supplied document, and cast the result to the specified type.
`xpath_bool(document, query)`	`bool`	

`xpath_nodeset(document, query, toptag, itemtag)`	`text`	This evaluates query on document and wraps the result in XML tags. If the result is multivalued, the output will look like:
		`<toptag>`
		`<itemtag>Value 1 which could be an XML fragment</itemtag>`
		`<itemtag>Value 2....</itemtag>`
		`</toptag>`
		If either `toptag` or `itemtag` is an empty string, the relevant tag is omitted.

`xpath_nodeset(document, query)`	`text`	Like `xpath_nodeset(document, query, toptag, itemtag)` but result omits both tags.
`xpath_nodeset(document, query, itemtag)`	`text`	Like `xpath_nodeset(document, query, toptag, itemtag)` but result omits toptag.
`xpath_list(document, query, separator)`	`text`	This function returns multiple values separated by the specified separator, for example `Value 1,Value 2,Value 3` if separator is `,`.
`xpath_list(document, query)`	`text`	This is a wrapper for the above function that uses `,` as the separator.

Table F-31. xml2 Functions

F.42.3. `xpath_table`

```
xpath_table(text key, text document, text relation, text xpaths, text criteria)
                                                          returns setof record
```

`xpath_table` is a table function that evaluates a set of XPath queries on each of a set of documents and returns the results as a table. The primary key field from the original document table is returned as the first column of the result so that the result set can readily be used in joins. The parameters are described in *Table F-32* (see below).

Parameter	Description
key	the name of the "key" field - this is just a field to be used as the first column of the output table, i.e., it identifies the record from which each output row came (see note below about multiple values)
document	the name of the field containing the XML document
relation	the name of the table or view containing the documents
xpaths	one or more XPath expressions, separated by `|`
criteria	the contents of the WHERE clause. This cannot be omitted, so use `true` or `1=1` if you want to process all the rows in the relation

Table F-32. `xpath_table` Parameters

These parameters (except the XPath strings) are just substituted into a plain SQL SELECT statement, so you have some flexibility - the statement is

```
SELECT <key>, <document> FROM <relation> WHERE <criteria>
```

so those parameters can be *anything* valid in those particular locations. The result from this SELECT needs to return exactly two columns (which it will unless you try to list multiple fields for key or document). Beware that this simplistic approach requires that you validate any user-supplied values to avoid SQL injection attacks.

The function has to be used in a `FROM` expression, with an `AS` clause to specify the output columns; for example

```
SELECT * FROM
xpath_table('article_id',
            'article_xml',
            'articles',
            '/article/author|/article/pages|/article/title',
            'date_entered > ''2003-01-01'' ')
AS t(article_id integer, author text, page_count integer, title text);
```

The `AS` clause defines the names and types of the columns in the output table. The first is the "key" field and the rest correspond to the XPath queries. If there are more XPath queries than result columns, the extra queries will be ignored. If there are more result columns than XPath queries, the extra columns will be NULL.

Notice that this example defines the `page_count` result column as an integer. The function deals internally with string representations, so when you say you want an integer in the output, it will take the string representation of the XPath result and use PostgreSQL input functions to transform it into an integer (or whatever type the `AS` clause requests). An error will result if it can't do this - for example if the result is empty - so you may wish to just stick to `text` as the column type if you think your data has any problems.

The calling `SELECT` statement doesn't necessarily have be be just `SELECT *` - it can reference the output columns by name or join them to other tables. The function produces a virtual table with which you can perform any operation you wish (e.g. aggregation, joining, sorting etc). So we could also have:

```
SELECT t.title, p.fullname, p.email
FROM xpath_table('article_id', 'article_xml', 'articles',
                 '/article/title|/article/author/@id',
                 'xpath_string(article_xml,''/article/@date'') > ''2003-03-20'' ')
        AS t(article_id integer, title text, author_id integer),
      tblPeopleInfo AS p
WHERE t.author_id = p.person_id;
```

as a more complicated example. Of course, you could wrap all of this in a view for convenience.

F.42.3.1. Multivalued results

The `xpath_table` function assumes that the results of each XPath query might be multi-valued, so the number of rows returned by the function may not be the same as the number of input documents. The first row returned contains the first result from each query, the second row the second result from each query. If one of the queries has fewer values than the others, null values will be returned instead.

In some cases, a user will know that a given XPath query will return only a single result (perhaps a unique document identifier) - if used alongside an XPath query returning multiple results, the single-valued result will appear only on the first row of the result. The solution to this is to use the key field as part of a join against a simpler XPath query. As an example:

```
CREATE TABLE test (
    id int PRIMARY KEY,
    xml text
);

INSERT INTO test VALUES (1, '<doc num="C1">
<line num="L1"><a>1</a><b>2</b><c>3</c></line>
<line num="L2"><a>11</a><b>22</b><c>33</c></line>
</doc>');

INSERT INTO test VALUES (2, '<doc num="C2">
<line num="L1"><a>111</a><b>222</b><c>333</c></line>
<line num="L2"><a>111</a><b>222</b><c>333</c></line>
</doc>');

SELECT * FROM
  xpath_table('id','xml','test',
              '/doc/@num|/doc/line/@num|/doc/line/a|/doc/line/b|/doc/line/c',
              'true')
  AS t(id int, doc_num varchar(10), line_num varchar(10), val1 int, val2 int,
                                                                       val3 int)
WHERE id = 1 ORDER BY doc_num, line_num

 id | doc_num | line_num | val1 | val2 | val3
----+---------+----------+------+------+------
  1 | C1      | L1       |    1 |    2 |    3
  1 |         | L2       |   11 |   22 |   33
```

To get doc_num on every line, the solution is to use two invocations of xpath_table and join the results:

```
SELECT t.*,i.doc_num FROM
  xpath_table('id', 'xml', 'test',
              '/doc/line/@num|/doc/line/a|/doc/line/b|/doc/line/c',
              'true')
    AS t(id int, line_num varchar(10), val1 int, val2 int, val3 int),
  xpath_table('id', 'xml', 'test', '/doc/@num', 'true')
```

```
    AS i(id int, doc_num varchar(10))
WHERE i.id=t.id AND i.id=1
ORDER BY doc_num, line_num;

 id | line_num | val1 | val2 | val3 | doc_num
----+----------+------+------+------+---------
  1 | L1       |    1 |    2 |    3 | C1
  1 | L2       |   11 |   22 |   33 | C1
(2 rows)
```

F.42.4. XSLT functions

The following functions are available if libxslt is installed:

F.42.4.1. xslt_process

```
xslt_process(text document, text stylesheet, text paramlist) returns text
```

This function applies the XSL stylesheet to the document and returns the transformed result. The paramlist is a list of parameter assignments to be used in the transformation, specified in the form `a=1,b=2`. Note that the parameter parsing is very simple-minded: parameter values cannot contain commas!

Also note that if either the document or stylesheet values do not begin with a < then they will be treated as URLs and libxslt will fetch them. It follows that you can use `xslt_process` as a means to fetch the contents of URLs - you should be aware of the security implications of this.

There is also a two-parameter version of `xslt_process` which does not pass any parameters to the transformation.

F.42.5. Author

John Gray *<jgray@azuli.co.uk>*

Development of this module was sponsored by Torchbox Ltd. (*www.torchbox.com*). It has the same BSD licence as PostgreSQL.

Appendix G. External Projects

PostgreSQL is a complex software project, and managing the project is difficult. We have found that many enhancements to PostgreSQL can be more efficiently developed separately from the core project.

To help our community with the development of their external projects, we have created *PgFoundry*[1], a website that provides hosting for PostgreSQL-related projects that are maintained outside the core PostgreSQL distribution. PgFoundry is built using the GForge software project and is similar to *SourceForge.net*[2] in its feature set, providing mailing lists, forums, bug tracking, SCM, and web hosting. If you have a PostgreSQL-related open source project that you would like to have hosted at PgFoundy, please feel free to create a new project.

G.1. Client Interfaces

There are only two client interfaces included in the base PostgreSQL distribution:

- *libpq* (Vol.II) is included because it is the primary C language interface, and because many other client interfaces are built on top of it.
- *ECPG* (Vol.II) is included because it depends on the server-side SQL grammar, and is therefore sensitive to changes in PostgreSQL itself.

All other language interfaces are external projects and are distributed separately. *Table G-1* (see below) includes a list of some of these projects. Note that some of these packages might not be released under the same license as PostgreSQL. For more information on each language interface, including licensing terms, refer to its website and documentation.

Name	Language	Comments	Website
DBD::Pg	Perl	Perl DBI driver	*http://search.cpan.org/dist/DBD-Pg/*
JDBC	JDBC	Type 4 JDBC driver	*http://jdbc.postgresql.org/*

[1] *http://www.pgfoundry.org/*
[2] *http://sourceforge.net/*

Name	Language	Comments	Website
libpqxx	C++	New-style C++ interface	*http://pqxx.org/*
Npgsql	.NET	.NET data provider	*http://npgsql.projects.postgresql.org/*
ODBCng	ODBC	An alternative ODBC driver	*http://projects.commandprompt.com/public/odbcng/*
pgtclng	Tcl		*http://pgfoundry.org/projects/pgtclng/*
psqlODBC	ODBC	The most commonly-used ODBC driver	*http://psqlodbc.projects.postgresql.org/*
psycopg	Python	DB API 2.0-compliant	*http://www.initd.org/*

Table G-1. Externally Maintained Client Interfaces

G.2. Procedural Languages

PostgreSQL includes several procedural languages with the base distribution: *PL/PgSQL* (Vol.III), *PL/Tcl* (Vol.III), *PL/Perl* (Vol.III), and *PL/Python* (Vol.III).

In addition, there are a number of procedural languages that are developed and maintained outside the core PostgreSQL distribution. *Table G-2* (see below) lists some of these packages. Note that some of these projects might not be released under the same license as PostgreSQL. For more information on each procedural language, including licensing information, refer to its website and documentation.

Name	Language	Website
PL/Java	Java	*http://pljava.projects.postgresql.org/*
PL/PHP	PHP	*http://www.commandprompt.com/community/plphp/*
PL/Py	Python	*http://python.projects.postgresql.org/*
PL/R	R	*http://www.joeconway.com/plr/*
PL/Ruby	Ruby	*http://raa.ruby-lang.org/project/pl-ruby/*
PL/Scheme	Scheme	*http://plscheme.projects.postgresql.org/*
PL/sh	Unix shell	*http://plsh.projects.postgresql.org/*

Table G-2. Externally Maintained Procedural Languages

G.3. Extensions

PostgreSQL is designed to be easily extensible. For this reason, extensions loaded into the database can function just like features that are packaged with the database. The `contrib/` directory shipped with the source code contains a large number of extensions. The `README` file in that directory contains a summary. They include conversion tools, full-text indexing, XML tools, and additional data types and indexing methods. Other extensions are developed independently, like *PostGIS*[3]. Even PostgreSQL replication solutions are developed externally. For example, *Slony-I*[4] is a popular master/standby replication solution that is developed independently from the core project.

There are several administration tools available for PostgreSQL. The most popular is *pgAdmin III*[5], and there are several commercially available ones as well.

[3] *http://www.postgis.org/*
[4] *http://www.slony.info/*
[5] *http://www.pgadmin.org/*

Appendix H. The Source Code Repository

The PostgreSQL source code is stored and managed using the Git version control system. A public mirror of the master repository is available; it is updated within a minute of any change to the master repository.

Our wiki, *http://wiki.postgresql.org/wiki/Working_with_Git*, has some discussion on working with Git.

Note that building PostgreSQL from the source repository requires reasonably up-to-date versions of bison, flex, and Perl. These tools are not needed to build from a distribution tarball since the files they are used to build are included in the tarball. Other tool requirements are the same as shown in *Chapter 15* (Vol.II).

H.1. Getting The Source Via Git

With Git you will make a copy of the entire code repository on your local machine, so you will have access to all history and branches offline. This is the fastest and most flexible way to develop or test patches.

Git

1. You will need an installed version of Git, which you can get from *http://git-scm.com*. Many systems already have a recent version of Git installed by default, or available in their package distribution system.
2. To begin using the Git repository, make a clone of the official mirror:

   ```
   git clone git://git.postgresql.org/git/postgresql.git
   ```

   This will copy the full repository to your local machine, so it may take a while to complete, especially if you have a slow Internet connection. The files will be placed in a new subdirectory `postgresql` of your current directory.

   The Git mirror can also be reached via the HTTP protocol, if for example a firewall is blocking access to the Git protocol. Just change the URL prefix to `http`, as in:

   ```
   git clone http://git.postgresql.org/git/postgresql.git
   ```

   The HTTP protocol is less efficient than the Git protocol, so it will be slower to use.

3. Whenever you want to get the latest updates in the system, `cd` into the repository, and run:

   ```
   git fetch
   ```

Git can do a lot more things than just fetch the source. For more information, consult the Git man pages, or see the website at *http://git-scm.com*.

Appendix I. Documentation

PostgreSQL has four primary documentation formats:

- Plain text, for pre-installation information
- HTML, for on-line browsing and reference
- PDF or PostScript, for printing
- man pages, for quick reference.

Additionally, a number of plain-text `README` files can be found throughout the PostgreSQL source tree, documenting various implementation issues.

HTML documentation and man pages are part of a standard distribution and are installed by default. PDF and PostScript format documentation is available separately for download.

I.1. DocBook

The documentation sources are written in *DocBook*, which is a markup language superficially similar to HTML. Both of these languages are applications of the *Standard Generalized Markup Language*, SGML, which is essentially a language for describing other languages. In what follows, the terms DocBook and SGML are both used, but technically they are not interchangeable.

DocBook allows an author to specify the structure and content of a technical document without worrying about presentation details. A document style defines how that content is rendered into one of several final forms. DocBook is maintained by the *OASIS group*[1]. The *official DocBook site*[2] has good introductory and reference documentation and a complete O'Reilly book for your online reading pleasure. The *NewbieDoc Docbook Guide*[3] is very helpful for beginners. The *FreeBSD Documentation Project*[4] also uses DocBook and has some good information, including a number of style guidelines that might be worth considering.

---

1 *http://www.oasis-open.org/*
2 *http://www.oasis-open.org/docbook*
3 *http://newbiedoc.sourceforge.net/metadoc/docbook-guide.html*
4 *http://www.freebsd.org/docproj/docproj.html*

I.2. Tool Sets

The following tools are used to process the documentation. Some might be optional, as noted.

DocBook DTD[5]

: This is the definition of DocBook itself. We currently use version 4.2; you cannot use later or earlier versions. You need the SGML variant of the DocBook DTD, but to build man pages you also need the XML variant of the same version.

ISO 8879 character entities[6]

: These are required by DocBook but are distributed separately because they are maintained by ISO.

DocBook DSSSL Stylesheets[7]

: These contain the processing instructions for converting the DocBook sources to other formats, such as HTML.

DocBook XSL Stylesheets[8]

: This is another stylesheet for converting DocBook to other formats. We currently use this to produce man pages and optionally HTMLHelp. You can also use this toolchain to produce HTML or PDF output, but official PostgreSQL releases use the DSSSL stylesheets for that.

OpenJade[9]

: This is the base package of SGML processing. It contains an SGML parser, a DSSSL processor (that is, a program to convert SGML to other formats using DSSSL stylesheets), as well as a number of related tools. Jade is now being maintained by the OpenJade group, no longer by James Clark.

Libxslt[10] for `xsltproc`

: This is the processing tool to use with the XSLT stylesheets (like `jade` is the processing tool for DSSSL stylesheets).

---

5 *http://www.oasis-open.org/docbook/sgml/*
6 *http://www.oasis-open.org/cover/ISOEnts.zip*
7 *http://wiki.docbook.org/topic/DocBookDssslStylesheets*
8 *http://wiki.docbook.org/topic/DocBookXslStylesheets*
9 *http://openjade.sourceforge.net/*
10 *http://xmlsoft.org/XSLT/*

JadeTeX[11]

> If you want to, you can also install JadeTeX to use TeX as a formatting backend for Jade. JadeTeX can create PostScript or PDF files (the latter with bookmarks).
>
> However, the output from JadeTeX is inferior to what you get from the RTF backend. Particular problem areas are tables and various artifacts of vertical and horizontal spacing. Also, there is no opportunity to manually polish the results.

We have documented experience with several installation methods for the various tools that are needed to process the documentation. These will be described below. There might be some other packaged distributions for these tools. Please report package status to the documentation mailing list, and we will include that information here.

I.2.1. Linux RPM Installation

Most vendors provide a complete RPM set for DocBook processing in their distribution. Look for an "SGML" option while installing, or the following packages: `sgml-common`, `docbook`, `stylesheets`, `openjade` (or `jade`). Possibly `sgml-tools` will be needed as well. If your distributor does not provide these then you should be able to make use of the packages from some other, reasonably compatible vendor.

I.2.2. FreeBSD Installation

The FreeBSD Documentation Project is itself a heavy user of DocBook, so it comes as no surprise that there is a full set of "ports" of the documentation tools available on FreeBSD. The following ports need to be installed to build the documentation on FreeBSD.

- `textproc/sp`
- `textproc/openjade`
- `textproc/iso8879`
- `textproc/dsssl-docbook-modular`
- `textproc/docbook-420`

A number of things from `/usr/ports/print` (`tex`, `jadetex`) might also be of interest.

It's possible that the ports do not update the main catalog file in `/usr/local/share/sgml/catalog.ports` or order isn't proper . Be sure to have the following lines in beginning of file:

```
CATALOG "openjade/catalog"
CATALOG "iso8879/catalog"
CATALOG "docbook/dsssl/modular/catalog"
CATALOG "docbook/4.2/catalog"
```

---

11 *http://jadetex.sourceforge.net/*

If you do not want to edit the file you can also set the environment variable `SGML_CATALOG_FILES` to a colon-separated list of catalog files (such as the one above).

More information about the FreeBSD documentation tools can be found in the *FreeBSD Documentation Project's instructions*[12].

I.2.3. Debian Packages

There is a full set of packages of the documentation tools available for Debian GNU/Linux. To install, simply use:

```
apt-get install docbook docbook-dsssl docbook-xsl openjade xsltproc
```

I.2.4. Manual Installation from Source

The manual installation process of the DocBook tools is somewhat complex, so if you have pre-built packages available, use them. We describe here only a standard setup, with reasonably standard installation paths, and no "fancy" features. For details, you should study the documentation of the respective package, and read SGML introductory material.

I.2.4.1. Installing OpenJade

1. The installation of OpenJade offers a GNU-style `./configure; make; make install` build process. Details can be found in the OpenJade source distribution. In a nutshell:

   ```
   ./configure --enable-default-catalog=/usr/local/share/sgml/catalog
   make
   make install
   ```

   Be sure to remember where you put the "default catalog"; you will need it below. You can also leave it off, but then you will have to set the environment variable `SGML_CATALOG_FILES` to point to the file whenever you use jade later on. (This method is also an option if OpenJade is already installed and you want to install the rest of the tool chain locally.)

2. Additionally, you should install the files `dsssl.dtd`, `fot.dtd`, `style-sheet.dtd`, and `catalog` from the `dsssl` directory somewhere, perhaps into `/usr/local/share/sgml/dsssl`. It's probably easiest to copy the entire directory:

   ```
   cp -R dsssl /usr/local/share/sgml
   ```

3. Finally, create the file `/usr/local/share/sgml/catalog` and add this line to it:

   ```
   CATALOG "dsssl/catalog"
   ```

12 *http://www.freebsd.org/doc/en_US.ISO8859-1/books/fdp-primer/tools.html*

(This is a relative path reference to the file installed in *step 2*. Be sure to adjust it if you chose your installation layout differently.)

I.2.4.2. Installing the DocBook DTD Kit

1. Obtain the DocBook V4.2 distribution[13].
2. Create the directory `/usr/local/share/sgml/docbook-4.2` and change to it. (The exact location is irrelevant, but this one is reasonable within the layout we are following here.)

   ```
   $ mkdir /usr/local/share/sgml/docbook-4.2
   $ cd /usr/local/share/sgml/docbook-4.2
   ```

3. Unpack the archive:

   ```
   $ unzip -a ...../docbook-4.2.zip
   ```

   (The archive will unpack its files into the current directory.)
4. Edit the file `/usr/local/share/sgml/catalog` (or whatever you told jade during installation) and put a line like this into it:

   ```
   CATALOG "docbook-4.2/docbook.cat"
   ```

5. Download the *ISO 8879 character entities archive*[14], unpack it, and put the files in the same directory you put the DocBook files in:

   ```
   $ cd /usr/local/share/sgml/docbook-4.2
   $ unzip ...../ISOEnts.zip
   ```

6. Run the following command in the directory with the DocBook and ISO files:

   ```
   perl -pi -e 's/iso-(.*).gml/ISO\1/g' docbook.cat
   ```

   (This fixes a mixup between the names used in the DocBook catalog file and the actual names of the ISO character entity files.)

I.2.4.3. Installing the DocBook DSSSL Style Sheets

To install the style sheets, unzip and untar the distribution and move it to a suitable place, for example `/usr/local/share/sgml`. (The archive will automatically create a subdirectory.)

```
$ gunzip docbook-dsssl-1.xx.tar.gz
$ tar -C /usr/local/share/sgml -xf docbook-dsssl-1.xx.tar
```

The usual catalog entry in `/usr/local/share/sgml/catalog` can also be made:

```
CATALOG "docbook-dsssl-1.xx/catalog"
```

---

[13] *http://www.docbook.org/sgml/4.2/docbook-4.2.zip*
[14] *http://www.oasis-open.org/cover/ISOEnts.zip*

Because stylesheets change rather often, and it's sometimes beneficial to try out alternative versions, PostgreSQL doesn't use this catalog entry. See *Section I.2.5* (page 449) for information about how to select the stylesheets instead.

I.2.4.4. Installing JadeTeX

To install and use JadeTeX, you will need a working installation of TeX and LaTeX2e, including the supported tools and graphics packages, Babel, AMS fonts and AMS-LaTeX, the PSNFSS extension and companion kit of "the 35 fonts", the dvips program for generating PostScript, the macro packages fancyhdr, hyperref, minitoc, url and ot2enc. All of these can be found on your friendly neighborhood *CTAN site*[15]. The installation of the TeX base system is far beyond the scope of this introduction. Binary packages should be available for any system that can run TeX.

Before you can use JadeTeX with the PostgreSQL documentation sources, you will need to increase the size of TeX's internal data structures. Details on this can be found in the JadeTeX installation instructions.

Once that is finished you can install JadeTeX:

```
$ gunzip jadetex-xxx.tar.gz
$ tar xf jadetex-xxx.tar
$ cd jadetex
$ make install
$ mktexlsr
```

The last two need to be done as root.

I.2.5. Detection by `configure`

Before you can build the documentation you need to run the `configure` script as you would when building the PostgreSQL programs themselves. Check the output near the end of the run, it should look something like this:

```
checking for onsgmls... onsgmls
checking for openjade... openjade
checking for DocBook V4.2... yes
checking for DocBook stylesheets...
/usr/share/sgml/docbook/stylesheet/dsssl/modular
checking for collateindex.pl... /usr/bin/collateindex.pl
checking for xsltproc... xsltproc
checking for osx... osx
```

If neither `onsgmls` nor `nsgmls` were found then some of the following tests will be skipped. `nsgmls` is part of the Jade package. You can pass the environment variables `JADE` and

[15] *http://www.ctan.org/*

NSGMLS to configure to point to the programs if they are not found automatically. If "DocBook V4.2" was not found then you did not install the DocBook DTD kit in a place where Jade can find it, or you have not set up the catalog files correctly. See the installation hints above. The DocBook stylesheets are looked for in a number of relatively standard places, but if you have them some other place then you should set the environment variable DOCBOOKSTYLE to the location and rerun `configure` afterwards.

I.3. Building The Documentation

Once you have everything set up, change to the directory `doc/src/sgml` and run one of the commands described in the following subsections to build the documentation. (Remember to use GNU make.)

I.3.1. HTML

To build the HTML version of the documentation:

```
doc/src/sgml$ gmake html
```

This is also the default target. The output appears in the subdirectory `html`.

To create a proper index, the build might process several identical stages. If you do not care about the index, and just want to proof-read the output, use `draft`:

```
doc/src/sgml$ gmake draft
```

To build the documentation as a single HTML page, use:

```
doc/src/sgml$ gmake postgres.html
```

I.3.2. Manpages

We use the DocBook XSL stylesheets to convert DocBook `refentry` pages to *roff output suitable for man pages. The man pages are also distributed as a tar archive, similar to the HTML version. To create the man pages, use the commands:

```
cd doc/src/sgml
gmake man
```

I.3.3. Print Output via JadeTeX

If you want to use JadeTex to produce a printable rendition of the documentation, you can use one of the following commands:

- To generate PostScript via DVI in A4 format:

  ```
  doc/src/sgml$ gmake postgres-A4.ps
  ```

  In U.S. letter format:

  ```
  doc/src/sgml$ gmake postgres-US.ps
  ```

- To make a PDF:

  ```
  doc/src/sgml$ gmake postgres-A4.pdf
  ```

  or:

  ```
  doc/src/sgml$ gmake postgres-US.pdf
  ```

  (Of course you can also make a PDF version from the PostScript, but if you generate PDF directly, it will have hyperlinks and other enhanced features.)

When using JadeTeX to build the PostgreSQL documentation, you will probably need to increase some of TeX's internal parameters. These can be set in the file `texmf.cnf`. The following settings worked at the time of this writing:

```
hash_extra.jadetex  = 200000
hash_extra.pdfjadetex  = 200000
pool_size.jadetex = 2000000
pool_size.pdfjadetex = 2000000
string_vacancies.jadetex = 150000
string_vacancies.pdfjadetex = 150000
max_strings.jadetex = 300000
max_strings.pdfjadetex = 300000
save_size.jadetex = 15000
save_size.pdfjadetex = 15000
```

I.3.4. Overflow Text

Occasionally text is too wide for the printed margins, and in extreme cases, too wide for the printed page, e.g. non-wrapped text, wide tables. Overly wide text generates "Overfull hbox" messages in the TeX log output file, e.g. `postgres-US.log` or `postgres-A4.log`. There are 72 points in an inch so anything reported as over 72 points too wide will probably not fit on the printed page (assuming one inch margins). To find the SGML text causing the overflow, find the first page number mentioned above the overflow message, e.g. `[50 ###]` (page 50), and look at the page after that (e.g. page 51) in the PDF file to see the overflow text and adjust the SGML accordingly.

I.3.5. Print Output via RTF

You can also create a printable version of the PostgreSQL documentation by converting it to RTF and applying minor formatting corrections using an office suite. Depending on the capabilities of the particular office suite, you can then convert the documentation to PostScript of PDF. The procedure below illustrates this process using Applixware.

Note

It appears that current versions of the PostgreSQL documentation trigger some bug in or exceed the size limit of OpenJade. If the build process of the RTF version hangs for a long time and the output file still has size 0, then you might have hit that problem. (But keep in mind that a normal build takes 5 to 10 minutes, so don't abort too soon.)

Applixware RTF Cleanup

OpenJade omits specifying a default style for body text. In the past, this undiagnosed problem led to a long process of table of contents generation. However, with great help from the Applixware folks the symptom was diagnosed and a workaround is available.

1. Generate the RTF version by typing:

   ```
   doc/src/sgml$ gmake postgres.rtf
   ```

2. Repair the RTF file to correctly specify all styles, in particular the default style. If the document contains `refentry` sections, one must also replace formatting hints which tie a preceding paragraph to the current paragraph, and instead tie the current paragraph to the following one. A utility, `fixrtf`, is available in `doc/src/sgml` to accomplish these repairs:

   ```
   doc/src/sgml$ ./fixrtf --refentry postgres.rtf
   ```

   The script adds `{\s0 Normal;}` as the zeroth style in the document. According to Applixware, the RTF standard would prohibit adding an implicit zeroth style, though Microsoft Word happens to handle this case. For repairing `refentry` sections, the script replaces `\keepn` tags with `\keep`.

3. Open a new document in Applixware Words and then import the RTF file.

4. Generate a new table of contents (ToC) using Applixware.

   - Select the existing ToC lines, from the beginning of the first character on the first line to the last character of the last line.
   - Build a new ToC using Tools-> Book Building-> Create Table of Contents. Select the first three levels of headers for inclusion in the ToC. This will replace the existing lines imported in the RTF with a native Applixware ToC.
   - Adjust the ToC formatting by using Format-> Style, selecting each of the three ToC styles, and adjusting the indents for `First` and `Left`. Use the following values:

Style	First Indent (inches)	Left Indent (inches)
`TOC-Heading 1`	`0.4`	`0.4`
`TOC-Heading 2`	`0.8`	`0.8`
`TOC-Heading 3`	`1.2`	`1.2`

5. Work through the document to:
   - Adjust page breaks.
   - Adjust table column widths.
6. Replace the right-justified page numbers in the Examples and Figures portions of the ToC with correct values. This only takes a few minutes.
7. Delete the index section from the document if it is empty.
8. Regenerate and adjust the table of contents.
   - Select the ToC field.
   - Select Tools-> Book Building-> Create Table of Contents.
   - Unbind the ToC by selecting Tools-> Field Editing-> Unprotect.
   - Delete the first line in the ToC, which is an entry for the ToC itself.
9. Save the document as native Applixware Words format to allow easier last minute editing later.
10. "Print" the document to a file in PostScript format.

I.3.6. Plain Text Files

Several files are distributed as plain text, for reading during the installation process. The `INSTALL` file corresponds to *Chapter 15* (Vol.II), with some minor changes to account for the different context. To recreate the file, change to the directory `doc/src/sgml` and enter `gmake INSTALL`. This will create a file `INSTALL.html` that can be saved as text with Netscape Navigator and put into the place of the existing file. Netscape seems to offer the best quality for HTML to text conversions (over lynx and w3m).

The file `HISTORY` can be created similarly, using the command `gmake HISTORY`. For the file `src/test/regress/README` the command is `gmake regress_README`.

I.3.7. Syntax Check

Building the documentation can take very long. But there is a method to just check the correct syntax of the documentation files, which only takes a few seconds:

```
doc/src/sgml$ gmake check
```

I.4. Documentation Authoring

SGML and DocBook do not suffer from an oversupply of open-source authoring tools. The most common tool set is the Emacs/XEmacs editor with appropriate editing mode. On some systems these tools are provided in a typical full installation.

I.4.1. Emacs/PSGML

PSGML is the most common and most powerful mode for editing SGML documents. When properly configured, it will allow you to use Emacs to insert tags and check markup consistency. You could use it for HTML as well. Check the *PSGML web site*[16] for downloads, installation instructions, and detailed documentation.

There is one important thing to note with PSGML: its author assumed that your main SGML DTD directory would be `/usr/local/lib/sgml`. If, as in the examples in this chapter, you use `/usr/local/share/sgml`, you have to compensate for this, either by setting `SGML_CATALOG_FILES` environment variable, or you can customize your PSGML installation (its manual tells you how).

Put the following in your `~/.emacs` environment file (adjusting the path names to be appropriate for your system):

```
; ********** for SGML mode (psgml)

(setq sgml-omittag t)
(setq sgml-shorttag t)
(setq sgml-minimize-attributes nil)
(setq sgml-always-quote-attributes t)
(setq sgml-indent-step 1)
(setq sgml-indent-data t)
(setq sgml-parent-document nil)
(setq sgml-default-dtd-file "./reference.ced")
(setq sgml-exposed-tags nil)
(setq sgml-catalog-files '("/usr/local/share/sgml/catalog"))
(setq sgml-ecat-files nil)

(autoload 'sgml-mode "psgml" "Major mode to edit SGML files." t )
```

and in the same file add an entry for SGML into the (existing) definition for `auto-mode-alist`:

```
(setq
  auto-mode-alist
  '(("\\.sgml$" . sgml-mode)
   ))
```

The PostgreSQL distribution includes a parsed DTD definitions file `reference.ced`. You might find that when using PSGML, a comfortable way of working with these separate files of book parts is to insert a proper `DOCTYPE` declaration while you're editing them. If you are working on this source, for instance, it is an appendix chapter, so you would specify the document as an "appendix" instance of a DocBook document by making the first line look like this:

```
<!DOCTYPE appendix PUBLIC "-//OASIS//DTD DocBook V4.2//EN">
```

---

[16] *http://www.lysator.liu.se/projects/about_psgml.html*

This means that anything and everything that reads SGML will get it right, and I can verify the document with `nsgmls -s docguide.sgml`. (But you need to take out that line before building the entire documentation set.)

I.4.2. Other Emacs modes

GNU Emacs ships with a different SGML mode, which is not quite as powerful as PSGML, but it's less confusing and lighter weight. Also, it offers syntax highlighting (font lock), which can be very helpful.

Norm Walsh offers a *major mode*[17] specifically for DocBook which also has font-lock and a number of features to reduce typing.

I.5. Style Guide

I.5.1. Reference Pages

Reference pages should follow a standard layout. This allows users to find the desired information more quickly, and it also encourages writers to document all relevant aspects of a command. Consistency is not only desired among PostgreSQL reference pages, but also with reference pages provided by the operating system and other packages. Hence the following guidelines have been developed. They are for the most part consistent with similar guidelines established by various operating systems.

Reference pages that describe executable commands should contain the following sections, in this order. Sections that do not apply can be omitted. Additional top-level sections should only be used in special circumstances; often that information belongs in the "Usage" section.

Name

> This section is generated automatically. It contains the command name and a half-sentence summary of its functionality.

Synopsis

> This section contains the syntax diagram of the command. The synopsis should normally not list each command-line option; that is done below. Instead, list the major components of the command line, such as where input and output files go.

Description

> Several paragraphs explaining what the command does.

17 *http://nwalsh.com/emacs/docbookide/index.html*

Options

A list describing each command-line option. If there are a lot of options, subsections can be used.

Exit Status

If the program uses 0 for success and non-zero for failure, then you do not need to document it. If there is a meaning behind the different non-zero exit codes, list them here.

Usage

Describe any sublanguage or run-time interface of the program. If the program is not interactive, this section can usually be omitted. Otherwise, this section is a catch-all for describing run-time features. Use subsections if appropriate.

Environment

List all environment variables that the program might use. Try to be complete; even seemingly trivial variables like `SHELL` might be of interest to the user.

Files

List any files that the program might access implicitly. That is, do not list input and output files that were specified on the command line, but list configuration files, etc.

Diagnostics

Explain any unusual output that the program might create. Refrain from listing every possible error message. This is a lot of work and has little use in practice. But if, say, the error messages have a standard format that the user can parse, this would be the place to explain it.

Notes

Anything that doesn't fit elsewhere, but in particular bugs, implementation flaws, security considerations, compatibility issues.

Examples

Examples

History

If there were some major milestones in the history of the program, they might be listed here. Usually, this section can be omitted.

See Also

Cross-references, listed in the following order: other PostgreSQL command reference pages, PostgreSQL SQL command reference pages, citation of PostgreSQL manuals, other reference pages (e.g., operating system, other packages), other documentation. Items in the same group are listed alphabetically.

Reference pages describing SQL commands should contain the following sections: Name, Synopsis, Description, Parameters, Outputs, Notes, Examples, Compatibility, History, See Also. The Parameters section is like the Options section, but there is more freedom about which clauses of the command can be listed. The Outputs section is only needed if the command returns something other than a default command-completion tag. The Compatibility section should explain to what extent this command conforms to the SQL standard(s), or to which other database system it is compatible. The See Also section of SQL commands should list SQL commands before cross-references to programs.

Appendix J. Acronyms

This is a list of acronyms commonly used in the PostgreSQL documentation and in discussions about PostgreSQL.

ANSI

American National Standards Institute
(*http://en.wikipedia.org/wiki/American_National_Standards_Institute*)

API

Application Programming Interface
(*http://en.wikipedia.org/wiki/API*)

ASCII

American Standard Code for Information Interchange
(*http://en.wikipedia.org/wiki/Ascii*)

BKI

Backend Interface
(page 180)

CA

Certificate Authority
(*http://en.wikipedia.org/wiki/Certificate_authority*)

CIDR

Classless Inter-Domain Routing
(*http://en.wikipedia.org/wiki/Classless_Inter-Domain_Routing*)

CPAN

Comprehensive Perl Archive Network
(*http://www.cpan.org/*)

CRL

Certificate Revocation List
(*http://en.wikipedia.org/wiki/Certificate_revocation_list*)

CSV

Comma Separated Values
(*http://en.wikipedia.org/wiki/Comma-separated_values*)

CTE

Common Table Expression
(*http://www.postgresql.org/docs/9.0/static/queries-with.html*)

CVE

Common Vulnerabilities and Exposures
(*http://cve.mitre.org/*)

DBA

Database Administrator
(*http://en.wikipedia.org/wiki/Database_administrator*)

DBI

Database Interface (Perl)
(*http://dbi.perl.org/*)

DBMS

Database Management System
(*http://en.wikipedia.org/wiki/Dbms*)

DDL

Data Definition Language
(*http://en.wikipedia.org/wiki/Data_Definition_Language*),
SQL commands such as `CREATE TABLE`, `ALTER USER`

DML

Data Manipulation Language
(*http://en.wikipedia.org/wiki/Data_Manipulation_Language*),
SQL commands such as `INSERT`, `UPDATE`, `DELETE`

DST

Daylight Saving Time
(*http://en.wikipedia.org/wiki/Daylight_saving_time*)

ECPG

Embedded C for PostgreSQL
(Vol.II)

ESQL

Embedded SQL
(*http://en.wikipedia.org/wiki/Embedded_SQL*)

FAQ

Frequently Asked Questions
(*http://en.wikipedia.org/wiki/FAQ*)

FSM

Free Space Map
(page 175)

GEQO

Genetic Query Optimizer
(page 137)

GIN

Generalized Inverted Index
(page 165)

GiST

Generalized Search Tree
(page 155)

Git

Git
(*http://en.wikipedia.org/wiki/Git_%28software%29*)

GMT

Greenwich Mean Time
(*http://en.wikipedia.org/wiki/GMT*)

GSSAPI

Generic Security Services Application Programming Interface
(*http://en.wikipedia.org/wiki/Generic_Security_Services_Application_Program_Interface*)

GUC

Grand Unified Configuration
(Vol.II), the PostgreSQL subsystem that handles server configuration

HBA

Host-Based Authentication
(Vol.II)

HOT

Heap-Only Tuples
(*http://anoncvs.postgresql.org/cvsweb.cgi/pgsql/src/backend/access/heap/README.HOT*)

IEC

International Electrotechnical Commission
(*http://en.wikipedia.org/wiki/International_Electrotechnical_Commission*)

IEEE

Institute of Electrical and Electronics Engineers
(*http://standards.ieee.org/*)

IPC

Inter-Process Communication
(*http://en.wikipedia.org/wiki/Inter-process_communication*)

ISO

International Organization for Standardization
(*http://www.iso.org/iso/home.htm*)

ISSN

International Standard Serial Number
(*http://en.wikipedia.org/wiki/Issn*)

JDBC

Java Database Connectivity
(*http://en.wikipedia.org/wiki/Java_Database_Connectivity*)

LDAP

Lightweight Directory Access Protocol
(*http://en.wikipedia.org/wiki/Lightweight_Directory_Access_Protocol*)

MSVC

Microsoft Visual C
(*http://en.wikipedia.org/wiki/Visual_C++*)

MVCC

Multi-Version Concurrency Control
(Vol.I)

NLS

National Language Support
(*http://en.wikipedia.org/wiki/Internationalization_and_localization*)

ODBC

Open Database Connectivity
(*http://en.wikipedia.org/wiki/Open_Database_Connectivity*)

OID

Object Identifier
(Vol.I)

OLAP

Online Analytical Processing
(*http://en.wikipedia.org/wiki/Olap*)

OLTP

Online Transaction Processing
(*http://en.wikipedia.org/wiki/OLTP*)

ORDBMS

Object-Relational Database Management System
(*http://en.wikipedia.org/wiki/ORDBMS*)

PAM

Pluggable Authentication Modules
(*http://en.wikipedia.org/wiki/Pluggable_Authentication_Modules*)

PGSQL

PostgreSQL
(Vol.I)

PGXS

PostgreSQL Extension System
(Vol.III)

PID

Process Identifier
(*http://en.wikipedia.org/wiki/Process_identifier*)

PITR

Point-In-Time Recovery
(Vol.II)
(Continuous Archiving)

PL

Programming Languages (server-side)
(Vol.III)

POSIX

Portable Operating System Interface
(*http://en.wikipedia.org/wiki/POSIX*)

RDBMS

Relational Database Management System
(*http://en.wikipedia.org/wiki/Relational_database_management_system*)

RFC

Request For Comments
(*http://en.wikipedia.org/wiki/Request_for_Comments*)

SGML

Standard Generalized Markup Language
(*http://en.wikipedia.org/wiki/SGML*)

SPI

Server Programming Interface
(Vol.III)

SQL

Structured Query Language
(*http://en.wikipedia.org/wiki/SQL*)

SRF

Set-Returning Function
(Vol.III)

SSH

Secure Shell
(*http://en.wikipedia.org/wiki/Secure_Shell*)

SSL

Secure Sockets Layer
(*http://en.wikipedia.org/wiki/Secure_Sockets_Layer*)

SSPI

Security Support Provider Interface
(*http://msdn2.microsoft.com/en-us/library/aa380493.aspx*)

SYSV

Unix System V
(*http://en.wikipedia.org/wiki/System_V*)

TCP/IP

Transmission Control Protocol (TCP) / Internet Protocol (IP)
(*http://en.wikipedia.org/wiki/Transmission_Control_Protocol*)

TID

Tuple Identifier
(Vol.I)

TOAST

The Oversized-Attribute Storage Technique
(page 173)

TPC

Transaction Processing Performance Council
(*http://www.tpc.org/*)

URL

Uniform Resource Locator
(*http://en.wikipedia.org/wiki/URL*)

UTC

Coordinated Universal Time
(*http://en.wikipedia.org/wiki/Coordinated_Universal_Time*)

UTF

Unicode Transformation Format
(*http://www.unicode.org/*)

UTF8

Eight-Bit Unicode Transformation Format
(*http://en.wikipedia.org/wiki/Utf8*)

UUID

Universally Unique Identifier
(Vol.I)

WAL

Write-Ahead Log
(Vol.II)

XID

Transaction Identifier
(Vol.I)

XML

Extensible Markup Language
(*http://en.wikipedia.org/wiki/XML*)

Bibliography

Selected references and readings for SQL and PostgreSQL.

Some white papers and technical reports from the original POSTGRES development team are available at the University of California, Berkeley, Computer Science Department *web site*[1].

SQL Reference Books

Judith Bowman, Sandra Emerson, and Marcy Darnovsky, *The Practical SQL Handbook: Using SQL Variants*, Fourth Edition, Addison-Wesley Professional, ISBN 0-201-70309-2, 2001.

C. J. Date and Hugh Darwen, *A Guide to the SQL Standard: A user's guide to the standard database language SQL*, Fourth Edition, Addison-Wesley, ISBN 0-201-96426-0, 1997.

C. J. Date, *An Introduction to Database Systems*, Eighth Edition, Addison-Wesley, ISBN 0-321-19784-4, 2003.

Ramez Elmasri and Shamkant Navathe, *Fundamentals of Database Systems*, Fourth Edition, Addison-Wesley, ISBN 0-321-12226-7, 2003.

Jim Melton and Alan R. Simon, *Understanding the New SQL: A complete guide*, Morgan Kaufmann, ISBN 1-55860-245-3, 1993.

Jeffrey D. Ullman, *Principles of Database and Knowledge: Base Systems*, Volume 1, Computer Science Press, 1988.

PostgreSQL-Specific Documentation

Stefan Simkovics, *Enhancement of the ANSI SQL Implementation of PostgreSQL*, Department of Information Systems, Vienna University of Technology, November 29, 1998.

Discusses SQL history and syntax, and describes the addition of `INTERSECT` and `EXCEPT` constructs into PostgreSQL. Prepared as a Master's Thesis with the support of O. Univ. Prof. Dr. Georg Gottlob and Univ. Ass. Mag. Katrin Seyr at Vienna University of Technology.

A. Yu and J. Chen, The POSTGRES Group, *The Postgres95 User Manual*, University of California, Sept. 5, 1995.

[1] *http://s2k-ftp.cs.berkeley.edu:8000/postgres/papers/*

Zelaine Fong, The design and implementation of the POSTGRES query optimizer[2], University of California, Berkeley, Computer Science Department.

Proceedings and Articles

Nels Olson, *Partial indexing in POSTGRES: research project*, University of California, UCB Engin T7.49.1993 O676, 1993.

L. Ong and J. Goh, "A Unified Framework for Version Modeling Using Production Rules in a Database System", *ERL Technical Memorandum M90/33*, University of California, Apr, 1990.

L. Rowe and M. Stonebraker, "*The POSTGRES data model*"[3], Proc. VLDB Conference, Sept. 1987.

P. Seshadri and A. Swami, "Generalized Partial Indexes *(cached version*[4]*)*", Proc. Eleventh International Conference on Data Engineering, 6-10 March 1995, IEEE Computer Society Press, Cat. No.95CH35724, 1995, 420-7.

M. Stonebraker and L. Rowe, "*The design of POSTGRES*"[5], Proc. ACM-SIGMOD Conference on Management of Data, May 1986.

M. Stonebraker, E. Hanson, and C. H. Hong, "The design of the POSTGRES rules system", Proc. IEEE Conference on Data Engineering, Feb. 1987.

M. Stonebraker, "*The design of the POSTGRES storage system*"[6], Proc. VLDB Conference, Sept. 1987.

M. Stonebraker, M. Hearst, and S. Potamianos, "*A commentary on the POSTGRES rules system*"[7], *SIGMOD Record 18(3)*, Sept. 1989.

M. Stonebraker, "*The case for partial indexes*"[8], *SIGMOD Record 18(4)*, Dec. 1989, 4-11.

M. Stonebraker, L. A. Rowe, and M. Hirohama, "*The implementation of POSTGRES*"[9], *Transactions on Knowledge and Data Engineering 2(1)* , IEEE, March 1990.

M. Stonebraker, A. Jhingran, J. Goh, and S. Potamianos, "*On Rules, Procedures, Caching and Views in Database Systems*"[10], Proc. ACM-SIGMOD Conference on Management of Data, June 1990.

---

[2] *http://s2k-ftp.cs.berkeley.edu:8000/postgres/papers/UCB-MS-zfong.pdf*
[3] *http://s2k-ftp.cs.berkeley.edu:8000/postgres/papers/ERL-M87-13.pdf*
[4] *http://citeseer.ist.psu.edu/seshadri95generalized.html*
[5] *http://s2k-ftp.cs.berkeley.edu:8000/postgres/papers/ERL-M85-95.pdf*
[6] *http://s2k-ftp.cs.berkeley.edu:8000/postgres/papers/ERL-M87-06.pdf*
[7] *http://s2k-ftp.cs.berkeley.edu:8000/postgres/papers/ERL-M89-82.pdf*
[8] *http://s2k-ftp.cs.berkeley.edu:8000/postgres/papers/ERL-M89-17.pdf*
[9] *http://s2k-ftp.cs.berkeley.edu:8000/postgres/papers/ERL-M90-34.pdf*
[10] *http://s2k-ftp.cs.berkeley.edu:8000/postgres/papers/ERL-M90-36.pdf*

List of Volumes

Volume I.

Volume II.

Volume V.

Index

Milton Keynes UK
Ingram Content Group UK Ltd.
UKHW020624190324
439723UK00009B/1058

9 781596 822504